The Labors of Resurrection

Black Women, Necromancy, and Morrisonian Democracy

SHATEMA THREADCRAFT

OXFORD
UNIVERSITY PRESS

OXFORD
UNIVERSITY PRESS

Oxford University Press is a department of the University of Oxford.
It furthers the University's objective of excellence in research, scholarship,
and education by publishing worldwide. Oxford is a registered trade mark of
Oxford University Press in the UK and in certain other countries.

Published in the United States of America by Oxford University Press 198
Madison Avenue, New York, NY 10016, United States of America.

CIP data is on file at the Library of Congress.

ISBN 9780197758588

ISBN 9780197758571 (hbk.)

DOI: 10.1093/9780197758618.001.0001

Paperback printed by Integrated Books International, United States of America

Hardback printed by Lightning Source, Inc., United States of America

The manufacturer's authorized representative in the EU for product safety
is Oxford University Press España S.A., Parque Empresarial San Fernando de Henares,
Avenida de Castilla, 2 – 28830 Madrid (www.oup.es/en or product.safety@oup.com).
OUP España S.A. also acts as importer into Spain of products made by the manufacturer.

This book is dedicated to Black women, both those here and those passed on.

We're keeping everyone alive and making a place for the dead too.

—Deva Woodly

Contents

List of Illustrations

Acknowledgments

There are so many people without whom I could not have written this book. What I want to make clear in these acknowledgments is that this book exists because I have brilliant friends who talked with me. They talked to me about their work and things they were thinking about, they talked to me about my work. Their imprint, as I hope to make clear below, is all over this book. In fact, that was one of the charmed things about the process of writing this book: I spent so much time talking with women as they thought through the contributions of other women. So much so that I am embarrassed to be listed as the sole author some days. I am so lucky to have them all.

Juliet Hooker. I tell you all the time that I am so lucky to have you as a friend and mentor. From organizing the workshop where I first presented ideas on the Movement for Black Lives and Black Femicide, coediting the special issue where those ideas were first published, bringing together the Black/Politics/Theory/History workshop, writing with me on Zoom to keep our sanity during the pandemic, writing, revising, and talking through our books together, reading chapters and passages, offering suggestions, to talking to me almost every day while I was writing and editing, it is absolutely no exaggeration to say that this book would not exist without you. Words cannot express, so truly truly truly thank you, dear friend.

Deva Woodly, beloved witch. Thank you for talking with me about this project monthly and at times weekly. Thanks for reading passages when I got in a mood. Thank you for saying, "You're not talking about necropolitics in this project. You're talking about necromancy." Witch. Now I look completely crazy. But you were absolutely right. Thank you for believing in democracy so fervently in the moments when the rest of us wanted to give up on it. Thank you for your elan among my cast of snarky cynics. Thank you for reading chapters and just for being you, that is, the best blend of empirical rigor and whimsy!

Melynda Price. Thank you for talking with me about Clementine Barfield's work all these years and for showing me how important she remains. It was through her that I first began to see the tradition that I highlight in these pages. Reading your work on Barfield as I read Juli Grigsby's work on Margaret Prescod and talked with Juliet about her work on Ida B. Wells made things come together. And thank you for your brilliant work and for introducing me to Prescod, Juli!

Brittney Cooper. My problem child whom I will continue to troll. But, in all seriousness, in a car one day, at the height of the early phase of the Movement for Black Lives, you quoted a statistic about lethal violence against Black women that started me on this path. Thank you for your friendship and the trolling. May it ever continue.

And Melanye Price, thanks for being my friend. I'm funnier than you, even though people refuse to admit this. My time at Rutgers with you and Brittney was without question the happiest of my professional life. I miss you all and am so glad we got to hang out in central Jersey one more time in the fall of 2024. Let's do it again soon!

Brandon Terry, thank you for joking with me about all facets of Black culture, the highs and the lows. Everyone knows you are brilliant, so I won't rehearse that part, but I know that it was your jokes that got me through. You remain elusive—continue to lean into that—but when we had a chance to talk it was always utterly raucous, and I was fortified for the months to come.

All the people above are members of a group, the Black Politics/Theory/History workshop, that means the world to me. The group has been invaluable to me as I've worked on this project. It has been an honor to think with some of the best minds in Black Politics and Black History. People talk about how hard it is to find people to read your work after your first project, and because I have been so fortunate to have this group, I have not had that problem. They've read chapters and given excellent comments, nerded out on Black esoterica, and provided scholarly comradery in Evanston, Illinois; Austin, Texas; Bourdeaux and Clérac, France; and Cartagena and Palenque, Colombia. Minkah Makalani, first thanks for being a great friend since our Rutgers days, for your comments on my work, for your considerable emotional labor in the spring of 2025, and thanks for co-organizing France with me. And thanks for eventually finding Sherwin (or did he wander back?) after you lost him in Saint-Émilion. How you managed to lose Sherwin in a medieval French village, I will never know. Deva, thanks for co-organizing Colombia. Glad you got your family back after most of them fell into the hedges at that castle. I'd also like to thank the other workshop members Sherwin Bryant, Barnor Hesse, Megan Ming Francis, Robbie Shililam, Maboula Soumahoro, Jasmine Syedullah, Tianna Paschel, and Millery Polonyé.

Sophie Smith, who invited me to Oxford (and then hustled to pay for it by organizing a mini speaking tour that included the London School of Economics and Cambridge while I was there!) and then said, "I'd love to host a manuscript workshop for you at Oxford!" And how did I respond to this incredible generosity? In the only way that I could. "Girl, I don't have a manuscript. I just have this talk." But when, years later, I did get a manuscript and called her to say, "Hey, is the offer still good?" she said "of course" and organized an incredible time for me and my guests. And at that manuscript workshop, Sophie said one thing that changed a great deal for me: "I really think you need to consider including Barbara Smith. She is absolutely a part of this tradition." Randomly (and in keeping with the way things have worked out as I've worked on this book), I'd read Terrion Williamson's "Why Did They Die? On Combahee and the Serialization of Black Death" the morning before the workshop and was able to say, "Honestly, I just read a piece about her, and I think you're absolutely right." The rest, as they say, is history. It was an excellent suggestion, and I want to thank you for it and for our friendship. Here's to so much more scheming in the decades to come.

I'd also like to thank the participants in the manuscript workshop—Juliet and Deva (again, evidence that they have helped me at every turn with this project), Lawrie Balfour (whom I also want to thank for first seeing Morrison's democracies), Bonnie Honig, Brooke Ackerly, and Lois McNay. I had a full draft of the manuscript and a year's leave to get it together. Everyone read generously and gave me excellent feedback. I had so much wrong back then. Lawrie's insistence that Ida hold her own against Du Bois in the text led me to reconceive so much. One chapter on Black female activism became five and, again, here we are. The book is so much better for your generous gifts of your time. Thank you, thank you, thank you.

Naa Oyo Kwate. Thank you so much for your friendship throughout this process, for talking through my argument with me, for reading and giving feedback on parts of the manuscript, and, most of all, for having the courage to be free!

Robert Gooding-Williams, for first introducing me to Du Bois's Black Jesus, and for reading and giving comments on a portion of chapters 3 and 8.

Adom Getachew. Thank you for responding to random texts from me when clearly you had more important things to do. We are all lucky to have you on our side.

Linda Zerilli. Thank you for your comments on early presentations of the Du Bois and Morrison chapters at the Britain and Ireland Association for Political Thought and at the Second Biennial Graduate Conference in Political Theory at the University of Chicago for helping me survive that trip to Oxford and for trailblazing both at Rutgers and in the discipline. And thanks to Silvia Fedi for the Chicago keynote invite. It was a clutch invitation at a key point in the project and I got incredibly helpful feedback and encouragement.

I would also like to thank: Walter Johnson, Brandon Terry, Kirsten Weld, and my cohort of Faculty Fellows and postdocs, especially Kendra Field, at the Charles Warren Center for Studies in American History at Harvard University. Some of my best friends are historians, and it is always an absolute pleasure to learn from them. Didier Fassin, Joan Scott, and my cohort of members at the Institute for Advanced Study in Princeton. Melissa Lane, my cohort of Laurance V. Rockefeller faculty fellows and postdocs at the University Center for Human Values at Princeton University, with special thanks to Anna Stilz for giving extremely helpful comments on a portion of chapter 8 at the workshop.

To my Princeton crew (key players in the final stages of this very long slog). Reena Goldthree: thanks for helping me to organize the Friday co-writing sessions in the Department of African American Studies. It was the best blend of productivity, gossip, and fellowship! Catherine Clune-Taylor, thanks for writing with me in the mornings, and Reena, thanks for writing with me in the afternoon. I had one of the most productive writing years of my life thanks to you two! Kushanava Choudhury, thanks for writing with me on Wednesdays. It was great to relive the grad school days, to talk about our work—complete with the absolutely necessary long digressions on the multicultural folkways of absolutely everywhere—and for Aiya and Ruya to become friends. Molly Crocket: thanks so much for your friendship and support during my time at UCHV.

Ruth Homrighaus, thank you so much for your incredible editing skills and, most important, for working with me on each step of this project since the book proposal—indeed, from looking at a collection of things I'd written and telling me whether or not there was a book there—to the final missing citation. When you emailed me to tell me that you'd discovered that Lorraine

Toussaint played Tamara in the original cast of *Dreaming Emmett*, it really brought home how much you had invested in the project! Thank you, thank you, thank you.

Ruth Boatman, thank you so much for your help with the *Dreaming Emmett* manuscript and with the Toni Morrison estate.

Jenerva and Tommy Threadcraft, thanks for being amazing parents and, in particular, for the support you've given Aiya and me while I worked on this book. Shaleia, Sheryl, Tommy Jr., and Timothy thanks for being great siblings and for your support during this project. Aiya thanks for being a great daughter and for so graciously sharing your mom with this at times all-consuming project. You've been so patient and mature about it all. Sifiso, thanks for being a great partner, and thanks for all the relocating. Niyanna, thank you for being a great niece and the good one. Kayson, Chase, Jayce and Jaidir thanks for being great nephews and excellent nemeses. And for often questioning my ability to write a book without any expertise at all. Well here it is. Kayson, you once asked of my first book "well, is it any good?" Please do let me know what you think of this one. Journee thanks for being you. Jay thanks you for being a great brother-in-law. Thanks to cousins Ruby (Vonn), for your help with Aiya during my Dartmouth days), to Kirste for all your encouragement and to Jordan for being the supreme bot. And celestial thanks to Johnese Threadcraft and Mary Catherine Toney, my beloved auntie and aunt who passed on during the final months of my completing this manuscript. You both supported me so much in life. The women in these pages remind me that, thankfully, this does not have to be the end of our time together. So much love to you all.

The author would also like to acknowledge that portions of chapters 3 and 8 were published as "Anti-Black Violence and Toni Morrison's Democratic Storytelling" in the *American Political Science Review*. (First View February 19, 2025).

Introduction

Beginning in the 1970s, serial killers and serial murders targeted and terrorized Black women in American cities—in Atlanta, Boston, Detroit, Los Angeles, Newark, Pittsburgh, Pensacola, Portland, Oakland, San Diego, Seattle, Rochester, Washington, DC, and more—while largely escaping the notice of the wider public.[1] The Atlanta murders are a particularly interesting case. While the city was in a panic about the serial killing of twenty-six Black mostly male children, teens and young adults, that is the Black cultural touchstone that would become known as the "Atlanta child murders," police also discovered the bodies of thirty-four Black women and girls (as well as the bodies of four white women and girls).[2] The latter deaths received nowhere near the level of community, police, and media attention devoted to the former cases. But while the larger community may not have registered Black women and girls' deaths as acutely, the murders of this era spawned coast-to-coast Black feminist mobilization. Two years after the Combahee River Collective released its iconic Black feminist statement, for example, members of the collective mobilized in response to the murders of six Black women in Boston in 1979.

Founding Combahee member Barbara Smith would later provide an account of the context for this mobilization:

> The first story about the murders appeared on the page of the *Boston Globe* where the racing results were. In other words, buried in the back of the newspaper. People in the black community in Boston were up in arms. You have to remember we had gone through the horrors of the school desegregation crisis in 1974. And in the mid-1970s, we were also constantly dealing with police brutality. There were all kinds of things that were going on, outright racial hate activity. There was a high school football player who was shot on the football field in Charlestown, just for playing football while Black. Permanently paralyzed. There was a young man, Ted Landsmark, who was beaten at Government Center. Using what? An American flag. A big heavy flag with a heavy pole. So, we had been through a lot in Boston. I lived at that time in Roxbury, an almost entirely Black community near the Jamaica Plain border. When I used to go to the subway, the Egleston station, I saw KKK graffiti on walls. It was serious. It was completely and

The Labors of Resurrection. Shatema Threadcraft, Oxford University Press. © Oxford University Press (2025).
DOI: 10.1093/9780197758618.003.0001

> utterly serious. So, when the murders of Black women started to happen a few years later, they were immediately understood as racial crimes. But it was only Black women who were being murdered.[3]

Smith characterized the media and police response to these killings as "typically racist." Not only did the *Boston Globe* allot the murdered Black women column space adjacent to the horse racing results, but other members of the press thought they did not rate even this level of attention. A white male journalist from the *New York Times* declined to attend a press conference after a subsequent death, Smith remembered, because it was "not news": he told her that "he could call any city in the country and get that statistic." The journalist was completely comfortable, perhaps even emboldened, in making this claim in the midst of an all-out media frenzy surrounding the serial stranger rapes of white women in Boston's Allston-Brighton neighborhood.[4] The Boston Police Department, for its part, pushed back against the idea of a serial killer, arguing that unlike the white Allston-Brighton victims, the Black women victims were being terrorized individually, not serially, by members of their own community. And apparently that was just fine. One of the lead detectives on the case claimed there was nothing to be done unless the women "wanted to ostracize [themselves] from [their] family and friends." This framing helped to deflect criticism from the decision of the department, like the media, to devote more resources to the Allston-Brighton case.[5]

Combahee River Collective members attended an April 1 rally held by CRISIS, a Black female–led grassroots organization that mobilized in response to the murders.[6] (See Figure I.1.) On that day, a crowd of fifteen hundred "took to the streets to mourn the loss of their sisters, daughters, mothers and friends." The march began at the Harriet Tubman House in Boston's South End and passed by the Wellington Street apartment of victim Daryal Ann Hargett, "who was found strangled on the floor of her bedroom." Hargett's aunt, Sara Small, addressed the crowd and, as Jaime Grant has noted, asked a question for the ages—but one that was heard differently depending on the hearer's subject position: "Who is killing us?"[7]

Later in the march, as Smith stood in a field next to the Stride Rite factory—significant because the remains of two of the victims had been found wrapped in Stride Rite bags—she listened to the march's primarily male speakers advise "completely unrealistic stuff": "They were saying things like, 'We need to protect our women; women need to stay inside the house.' Nothing about sexual politics or sexual violence. It was all about

Figure I.1 Ellen Shub, Barbara Smith with megaphone protesting the murder of 9 women of color since January 4.28.79, Boston MA, 1979.

racial crimes. Well, why was it all women being murdered, if the only reason they were being murdered was because of race?"[8] Their analysis infuriated her. "I went home after this rally, and I was just *steaming*," Smith remembers. "How the crimes were being defined was not accurate, nor were the solutions useful for everybody. We didn't want to be under house arrest, nor did every single Black woman have access to a Black male bodyguard, essentially."[9] Terrion Williamson notes that the male speakers at the rally "had no substantive language for addressing the specific vulnerabilities of poor and working-class black women or the sociopolitical conditions of the violence being systematically committed against them."[10] It was Smith who would provide that language. "I started writing, that night, the draft of what became 'Six Black Women: Why Did They Die?'" she recalled in a later interview. "I called a few members of the Combahee River Collective and I literally read what I had written to them over the phone and asked, 'What do you think about it?' And they said, 'Fine, great. Go with it.'"[11]

In the pamphlet, Smith explicitly made the connections the male speakers at the rally had missed or ignored, linking the Boston women's deaths to pervasive violence against women—sexual assault, sexual harassment, and intimate partner violence. "What has happened in Boston's Black community," she wrote, "is a thread in the fabric of violence against women."

Its purpose? To instill fear, powerlessness, and to cause women to internalize their second-class status in society. Smith explicitly rejected the notion that it was men's duty to protect women from other men. While acknowledging the racism of the police and media, she celebrated the unflappable resolve of grieving Black women to maneuver around this racism via organizing and mutual aid: "In the face of police indifference and media lies and despite our grief and anger, we have begun to organize ourselves in order to figure out ways to protect ourselves and our sisters, to make the streets safe for women." Smith rejected the assumption that women required men's protection, with its embedded belief that Black women were "weak, helpless, and dependent" victims. Black women, she insisted, had to learn to protect themselves. "There are many ways to do this," she wrote, including "learning and following common sense safety measures, learning self-defense, setting up phone chains and neighborhood safety houses, [and] joining and working in groups that are organizing against violence against women." Smith also suggested that Black women stop accepting rides from strangers, choose varied routes on well-lit main streets, let others know their travel plans, travel in pairs or groups, and get to know their neighbors. "Keep an eye out for each other," Smith exhorted. "Make an effort."

Smith's pamphlet was a blockbuster success. The collective originally printed two thousand copies, but demand was so great that they eventually distributed thirty thousand copies of successive iterations of the pamphlet, including a Spanish translation. At the time of the murders, the collective wasn't well known or accepted, Smith recalls, "because we were out lesbians and feminists," but the pamphlet "drew an overwhelmingly positive community response," establishing Combahee "as a vital organization in the eyes of both black and feminist groups that were formulating resistance to violence." Smith remembers: "People really loved the pamphlet. It gave them a little ray of hope. It had information. It had analysis. Somebody was saying black women were important, and we care. And then a whole lot of organizing began to evolve."[12]

Love. Hope. Information. Analysis. Care. Organizing.

The pamphlet also became, according to Williamson, a visualization of "the ongoing nature of the crisis . . . a material artifact of the escalating terror to which black women were being subjected." This was the case because with each successive murder, instead of changing the number of Black women murdered in the pamphlet's title, Smith simply struck the old number out

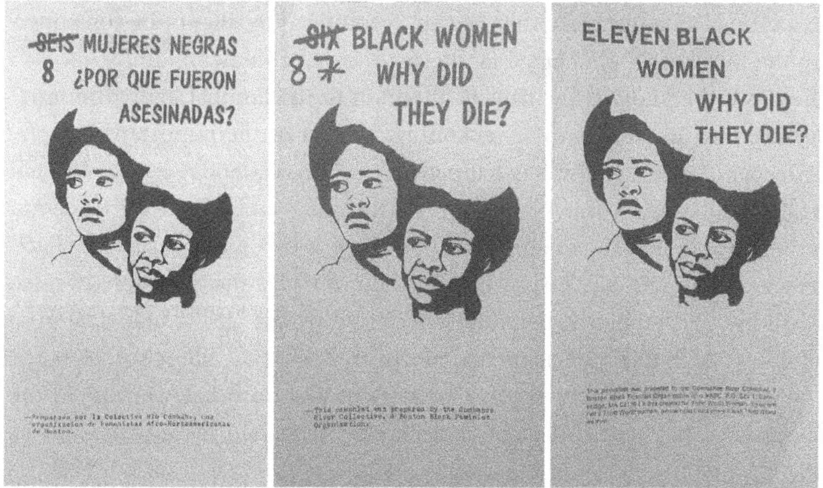

Figure I.2 Barbara Smith, *8 Black Women, Why Did They Die?*

and added a new one. Thus, the pamphlet, in its successive printings, came to be titled "Six, no Seven, no Eight, no Eleven Black Women: Why Did They Die?" Smith intended this. "At the time, they were killing a black woman almost every week. Almost every time we took it to the printers, it was a different number and instead of whiting it out, y'know, making it all nice and shit, I said . . . we should just mark this out so that people can see the progression, 6-7-8-9."[13]

Scratching out the numbers was an important part of delivering on Smith's resolve to *count*—a resolve that made her, as Catherine D'Ignazio has argued, a pioneering feminist "counterdata scientist," *and* one who was determined, as Williamson might counter, to "count it all out differently." D'Ignazio runs the Data + Feminism Lab at the Massachusetts Institute of Technology. She admits that "it is not a given that counterdata production will lead to desirable social change (or any change at all)." Yet, she says, "What is a given is that more than 150 grassroots individuals and groups across the Americas are taking action to produce counterdata—resistant records" that attempt to track fatal gender-related violence. Williamson, a scholar of serialized Black female death, has reflected at length on found bodies and lost names, on counting, on body counts, and, critically, on how body counts—and not the lives lost—often become *the* story, on refusing to count. "What, then, can be the resolution?" she asks. "Is there any possible virtue in rendering the depravity of black death visible, or are we resigned to a vicious dichotomy—either neglect counting altogether or be consumed by the numbers?" She suggests alternate ways of knowing and what else there is to be known. She directs attention to the familial and communal life-keeping, as well as their reckoning, as part of the important but oft-unrecognized "what else has happened here" that attends serialized Black death. Williamson draws attention to the long-suffering, long-laboring, unheralded familial and communal life-keepers who attend serialized Black female death, and she gives voice to their work in the assertion "*we* are what else has happened here." She is riveted by the "epistemological possibilities" of Smith's decision to effectively split the difference between counting and not counting and what it means for what we now know about what happened *and* about what else happened there in Boston in 1979.[14]

D'Ignazio and Wiliamson's work—and indeed their ambivalence about the relationship between counting and making women's lives count—has been invaluable to me. In this book, I profile women who have done the necessary work of counting but I follow Williamson most closely and highlight the political life-keeping that also often attends Black death. As with Smith, however, women sometimes fall into both categories.

Here is what I see happening in Smith's pamphlet and in the activism surrounding it: Smith brought the dead women together. I will argue that she placed the women in a line—a series, as Williamson notes—and then, crucially, placed them in a wholly different relationship and orientation to one another, to herself, and to her audience—that is, in a circle, a public. First, Smith counted, and in doing so she asserted a connection among the women that the police and other officials denied—and a significant one at that, no matter what members of the media thought. But Smith did not simply count, she claimed community with the dead. Who is killing *us*? Her radical method of enumeration was, in fact, an act of caregiving for a new collective she was calling into being, an act of caregiving for *both the living and the dead* within this new collective. By both counting and then refusing to continue counting without encouraging those to whom her numbers would circulate to reflect on each loss, on the series of those lost, before registering new loss in a document that also offered analysis and instructions for collective ameliorative aid to the living, she was able to count each of the lost women *and* to count those so moved to reckon with and reflect on each and every loss—and on the conditions that produced this serial loss—as one of an emerging "us." She called into being a public composed of women both here on earth and those who had passed on, that is, a supernatural public, and asserted its politics—vigilant, careful self- and collective defense—while acting on its behalf. She called forth a communal reckoning for those lost, and she claimed the slain women as part of a community-in-progress, members of that new number to be cared for, looked after, within a newly politically active community of righteous reckoning and loving collective care that would itself now and forever be a part of the record she was in the process of constructing. This, I argue, is the "we," that was "what else has happened here." It is that elusive yet highly sought-after we, similar though radically different from the we of "we the people" fame, a we that gives us a glimpse of Morrisonian democracy.[15]

Equally important, Smith wrote: "We've got to understand that violence against us as women cuts across all racial, ethnic and class lines. This doesn't mean that violence against Third World women does not have a racial as well as sexual cause. Both race and sex lead to violence against us." She stated the matter plainly: "It's true that the victims were all black and that Black people have always been targets of racist violence in this society, but they were also *all* women. Our sisters died because they were women just as surely as they died because they were black." Smith, then, identified the murders as *Black femicide.*

"Black femicide" is the misogynoiristic killing of Black women because they are Black women, as well as the misogynistic killing of Black women facilitated by gendered racial capitalism, gendered racialized housing discrimination, residential segregation and housing insecurity, medical racism, including obstetric racism, easy access to guns in insecure and under-resourced social contexts, gendered racially discriminatory policing, and intersections of all of the above with ableism, homophobia, transphobia, femmephobia, and whorephobia. According to a UN model, Black femicide can be understood to occur in both "active" and "passive" forms.[16]

The conditions that brought Smith to the Harriet Tubman House, to the apartment on Wellington Street, to the Stride Rite factory, and ultimately to the printing press again and again and again remain. The ensuing decades have been marked by "a long and continuous line of serial murder cases in which black women have been the sole or primary targets." With this, Williamson writes, "black female life has taken a heavy, though rarely acknowledged, toll." A minimum of five hundred Black girls and women have fallen victim to serial murder since the early 1970s, and more than fifty perpetrators—most of them Black men—have gone to prison for these killings.[17] And serial murder, though admittedly terrifying, makes up only a small part of the femicidal threat to Black women in the United States. Alarmingly, Black women constitute only 10 percent of the US female population, yet they are 59 percent of all women murdered. From 1999 to 2020, Black women aged twenty-five to forty-four were six times more likely to be murdered than their white counterparts.[18] Most of those deaths were instances of intimate partner violence, and thus should also be categorized as Black femicide.

Pregnancy and the postpartum period are particularly vulnerable times for women generally, and for Black women in particular. Indeed, researchers have suggested that pregnancy-related murders may drive most of the racial disparities in murder observed between Black and white women.[19] Murder is the leading cause of death for all pregnant women in the United States, a statistic that reveals the undeniable yet under-recognized link between comprehensive reproductive health access and public safety *and* reveals the brutal way in which some men have exercised *their* right to choose. The overall situation is dire and yet is still worse for Black women, as pregnant Black women are three times more likely to be murdered than their pregnant white and Latinx peers and eight times more likely to be murdered than their non-pregnant Black peers—indeed, Black women account for 44.6 percent of all pregnancy-related fatal intimate partner violence in the United States.[20] And should they manage to escape this fate, they are by no means out of the woods, as pregnancy-related death—considered a form of "passive" femicide—affects Black women in the United States more than any other group. US Black women are at least three times more likely to die of pregnancy-related complications and/or childbirth than white women.[21] Collectively, these deaths represent a significant yet chronically under-recognized subset of the specter of premature death that haunts all Black life.

In the pages that follow I argue that Barbara Smith is not only a pioneering feminist counterdata scientist but also a significant innovator in the less well-known and less well-received Black femicide–focused strain of a long tradition of Black women's democratic "death labor," indeed of their democratic necromancy. And despite Smith's tremendous analytic and democratic contributions, contemporary activists still struggle, as Smith did, to call attention to the deaths of Black women. This struggle and the tradition in which it is situated demand further study, particularly when considered in light of contemporary racialized necropolitics.

Democracy and (Spectacular) Black Death

Western democracies are haunted. Michael Hanchard suggests the specter of race is what haunts our democracies, but it may be more accurate to suggest that Western democracies are haunted by their own racialized death machines—by racialized premature death. That is to say, much of contemporary US racial politics are necropolitics, the politics of death. These politics include the state's use of the threat of violent death as a tool of racialized governance, state officials' efforts to convince citizens that the Black dead are the "right kind" of dead—rapists in years past and thugs today—and activists' efforts to resist and rewrite dominant narratives regarding both the dead and the state itself. The politics of lynching, for example, involved state-sanctioned attempts to deem all lynched Blacks as rapists who deserved death, and whose deaths were necessary to uphold the moral order of the nation, as well as the efforts of activists like Ida B. Wells and W. E. B. Du Bois to reject and counter these narratives. But even Du Bois, whose lynching-as-crucifixion stories represent an important attempt to reckon with death in democracy, did not adequately attend to the haunting.[22]

If that which haunts Western democracies is not adequately attended to, democracies cannot fulfill their function. That is to say, if democracy's *death worlds* are allowed to function without intervention, the *life worlds* of democracy will fail. Democratic theory has not attended adequately to the haunting, to these premature deaths, the worlds they produce, and what democracies require in their wake.

What's more, in this haunted democracy Black women confront a further complication, as not all Black deaths are created equal. If Juliet Hooker is correct in her observation that Black grief and white grievance are the two driving forces of contemporary racial politics, in this haunted democracy—in this context of pervasive premature Black death—it is essential to notice that collective Black grief has most often been reserved for those killed in ways that are *spectacular*. The focus on some of the Black dead and not others, both within Black communities and in Black politics, has had important gendered effects. Fatal violence directed against Black women is most often femicidal violence. In keeping with femicide trends the world over, Black women suffer a deficit of spectacular death when compared to Black men. They are unlikely to be killed in public, in ways that are on view and, thus, able to call spontaneous antiracist publics into being, as was the case with Mike Brown and George Floyd. As well, death as a driving force in racial politics is not a new phenomenon; the politics of spectacular death, in particular, are long-standing and have transformed Black publics and the Black people. In the context of a Black counterpublic sphere forged in and through death spectacles, and thus within a public most primed to take notice of, critically discuss, and mobilize around spectacular death, Black women's spectacular death deficit is a significant obstacle—and potentially an insurmountable obstacle, when one considers the place of spectacular death in the creation of Blacks as a political people.[23]

Black feminists have noted that not all Black deaths are created equal. Kimberlé Crenshaw has called for a redistribution of "narrative capital" in Black communities to combat the relative lack of mobilization in response to violence, including fatal violence, against Black women. She sees the mobilization asymmetry as being rooted partly in Black women's lack of narrative capital in their communities. Blacks have stock stories, she says—narratives from which to draw and to which political demands can be attached. These stories stand as a kind of fund, an important political resource. Stories matter, Crenshaw says; they have material and psychic effects. Through her organization, the African American Policy Forum, Crenshaw's #SayHerName campaign provides a platform for Black women to share their stories of violence and for the family members of those who have not survived to share stories of their Black female dead. Her call for families, for mothers, to "share their stories" attempts to address the narrative capital maldistribution around Black female death, so that the stories of Black women's deaths may circulate and move more people to action.[24]

Crenshaw is correct: all Black deaths are worthy of equal concern. Black women ought to possess more narrative capital, if "capital" is indeed the right term for what she describes. Stories indeed have material and psychic effects. Stories *do* things, including one extremely important thing: they help to build political people. There are, however, specific kinds of stories that have historically been most successfully employed in Black people-making, and in the subsequent political mobilizations such people-making has engendered, and these are stories of spectacular violence. Therefore, if Crenshaw would ask women to use stories in service of collectivizing and mobilizing Blacks in greater numbers, it may not be enough simply to direct Black women to share their stories of violence. Given the ubiquity of spectacular racist violence in the Black popular imagination, the complications of

Crenshaw's project are closely linked to Black women's lack of death spectacles, as well as to the surrounding intimate contexts in which Black women's *unspectacular* deaths occur.

At the very least, we must consider and reflect on how Black political leaders like Du Bois have written spectacular violence, and specifically death spectacles, into the story of who Blacks are and why we are here. Leaders used such violence to create Blacks as a political people, and they put these stories into the service of political mobilization. And because Black men were most likely to be subject to this form of violence, Black men have thus far held a more significant place within that people. If the aim is to bring about greater political mobilization, then the questions for Crenshaw (and indeed for us all), are these: Can Black women share stories of their experiences of violence that connect as successfully with compelling accounts of who Blacks are and why we are here? If not, might the story of who we are and why we are here have to be wholly rewritten in order to balance this mobilization asymmetry?

In our current storytelling environment, I argue, it is nearly impossible to share stories of Black women's deaths that connect as successfully with the dominant Black people-building narrative as the stories of Black men. Therefore, the story of Black peoplehood would, indeed, require rewriting for this asymmetry to be rebalanced—a complex and perhaps impossible project. Yet, as you might suspect, I do not believe that all hope is lost.

Here it is worth noting that Black women's spectacular death deficit has not stopped women like Barbara Smith, Ida B. Wells, Mamie Till-Bradley, Clementine Barfield, Margaret Prescod, and Toni Morrison, among others, from making paradigm-shifting contributions to Black publics—and to the practice of democracy itself—regarding death, by undertaking "death work," indeed, by undertaking *democratic necromancy*. Those practices may well hold the solution to the mobilization imbalance. Ironically, though the violence and death that Black women themselves experience is often hidden from view, Black women's writing, visual rhetoric, and activism have often helped Black communities truly "see" death; their efforts have occasioned profound, Black counterpublic-sphere-altering transformations in the meanings of Black death within Black communities. What is more, these exemplary democrats have developed democratic practices to address the hauntings. And, as I will demonstrate, unlike Du Bois, they have not turned away from the dead themselves in the democratic life worlds they build in the wake of death, in their "life-after-death" world-making.

The Work of Resurrection and Its Labors

Lynching remains the most powerful symbol of American racial oppression. The phenomenon has proven an unparalleled mobilizing and organizing juggernaut, and its unique hold on Black collective memory, its place within the story of Black peoplehood, ensures that a focus on spectacular death in Black politics is likely to maintain its place. We see evidence of its enduring symbolic power in the fact that many contemporary observers view the phenomenon of police violence through the lens of lynching. Yet a politics that centers bodies killed in spectacular ways functions to exclude Black female death, and the Black female living suffer the effects of this exclusion. It is therefore crucial for those concerned with the status of Black women in society to reckon with the origins of our hegemonic politics of Black death to formulate an adequate response.

Du Bois perhaps did the most to construct the dominant story of Black peoplehood. He did so by connecting lynching to the biblical crucifixion. Theologian James Cone proclaims that "Black religion comes out of suffering, and no one has engaged the question of theodicy in the black experience more profoundly than Du Bois."[25] Cone also says, "The lynching tree is the most potent symbol of the trouble nobody knows that blacks have seen."[26] Cone writes: "From Henry Smith's lynching in Paris, Texas (1893) to Emmett Till's in Money, Mississippi (1955) and beyond, black artists and writers have made the lynching theme a dominant part of their work and most have linked black victims with the crucified Christ as a way to find meaning in the repeated atrocities in African American communities. . . . No one did this with more literary passion and creative theological insight than W. E. B. Du Bois of the NAACP." Cone holds that Du Bois was the best among a group of writers and artists whose efforts helped to tie these symbols—the lynching tree and the cross—together through storytelling and imagery.

Du Bois and others, then, made lynching central to Black collective identity, to Black peoplehood, through a theologically inflected form of storytelling. It is this story—the lynching as crucifixion story, a story that has had an enormous impact on Blacks' sense of self-worth and purpose—that Kimberlé Crenshaw's storytelling efforts must contest, must challenge. This will be no easy task.

Du Bois wrote five stories in which he brought a Black or Colored Jesus to the Jim Crow South. Like others who participated in the lynching-as-crucifixion genre in his fiction and in the stories he published as editor of *The Crisis*, Du Bois preferred stories that did not simply link lynching and crucifixion but rather directly compared the lynching of African Americans to the crucifixion of Christ. In the stories the Black Jesus is crucified/lynched because of his association with Blacks and for espousing principles of racial equality consistent with his virtues. Yet the coming salvation his presence represented would not involve the supernatural.[27]

Du Bois killed his Black Jesus again and again, but he rarely resurrected him, straying from this theme only once in "The Gospel of Mary Brown," and there it brought the opposite of salvation as when Mary, the mother of Jesus, encounters her risen son she lays down and dies.[28] Edward Blum says that the thinker de-emphasized the supernatural aspects of Christ's sacrifice in order to convey that no one was coming to save Black people; they would have to save themselves. He left it to Blacks here on earth, then, to do the work of resurrection.

Du Bois, we know, came to see an important part of the work of Black resurrection as the abolition democracy, where all have the economic, social, and political capital in the form of land, schools, and the franchise—to live as equal members. The work of resurrection is the end of racial injustice, the end of the Jim Crow order via the creation of the institutions and culture necessary for the abolition democracy. In Du Bois's account, however, this is not the work of Christ, it is work that Blacks themselves must do. Du Bois turned decisively from the supernatural, from the dead, from lynched Blacks themselves even as he worked to associate them with Jesus, from resurrection, in his democratic storytelling and, instead, put his faith in the living. He insisted that Blacks not look to someone passed on for their salvation but instead follow Christ's teachings, his sacrifice, his example.

Additionally, like many democratic theorists before him Du Bois thought functionally, never expansively, about the kind of homes—and the kinds of restrained women, mothers, and children—democracies required. He celebrated and exhorted Blacks' efforts to create a "home" for abolition democracy, while studiously ignoring Black women's efforts to create such a home; in his mind they had other, more important work to do.[29] Du Bois not only tended to ignore the democratic contributions of women—he references Black women's contributions only twice in the entirety of *Black Reconstruction*—he fixated on normative sexuality and family relations in ways that severely compromised his ability to recognize the depths and multiplicity of their agency.[30] As they stood, for Du Bois, Black homes were spaces of badness, sin, evil, and much of that related to sex and sexuality. In *The Philadelphia Negro* he would write, "There can be no doubt but (t)hat sexual looseness is to-day the prevailing sin of the mass of the Negro population, and that its prevalence can be traced to a bad home life in most cases. Children are allowed on the street night and day unattended; loose talk is often indulged in; the sin is seldom if ever denounced in churches." In case there was any doubt of who and what were responsible for the "bad home life" that ultimately led to the "sin" of "sexual looseness," he outlined a taxonomy of Black households, with the highest grade given to families in which "the wife stays at home and the children at school." The second grade went to families in which "the wife in some cases helps as breadwinner." The third grade went to "those who have suffered accident and misfortune; the maimed and defective classes and the sick; many widows and orphans and deserted wives." His fourth and final grade went to homes wherein "many of these are cases of permanent cohabitation and the women for the most part are or were prostitutes."[31] His contempt for these "lower homes" could hardly be clearer.

The Black Female Necromantics and Our Haunted Democracy

The centrality of spectacular death has functioned to marginalize Black women in the stories of Black peoplehood and has ensured that they are not the main beneficiaries of large-scale Black political mobilization—but this has in no way stopped Black women's democratic work nor stopped them from attending to that which haunts our democracy. And, notably, it is *unruly* women who have best performed the work of resurrection: loud-mouthed ungovernable women, single mothers, welfare mothers, lesbians, and sex workers, as well as those who explicitly cast their lot with such women. These are not the women so long trapped in democracy's household, but those marginal to it, expelled from it, yet still constrained by its gendered "heterosexual work discipline."[32]

The loud-mouthed, ungovernable woman to whom I refer most directly is, of course, the pioneering antilynching activist and newspaperwoman Ida B. Wells. The single mothers are Emmett Till's mother, Mamie Till-Bradley; Clementine Barfield of the Detroit-based anti-youth violence organization Save Our Sons and Daughters (S.O.S.A.D.); and one Toni Morrison. The lesbians, welfare mothers, and sex workers and those who explicitly made common cause with them include the Combahee River Collective's Barbara Smith and Margaret Prescod of the Los Angeles–based Coalition Fighting Back Serial Killers. It is they who have done best the work of resurrection and they have done so via resurrection, via the labors of resurrection. In so doing they have helped to revive and expand the demographic, geographic and discursive spaces of US democracy.

Moreover, it is not simply abolition democracy toward which the women have worked, but something more. Their work has involved experimentation with novel democratic forms, and we should think about that work—both their methods and the substance of their contributions—within the framework of what I am calling "Morrisonian truant democracy."[33] This has implications for Crenshaw, as Morrisonian truant democracy does not require mass movements; indeed it hardly requires that the rest of the *demos* notice it.

The women I profile below undertook the work of resurrection Du Bois outlined. They made Black public sphere transformative, democracy expansive interventions, and, significantly, they effected these transformations not by turning away from the dead, as Du Bois would do, but via conjuring, by *resurrecting* the dead—in image, in speech, in act—and by caring for the dead, communing with the dead, and embracing the supernatural in the service of democracy, by inviting us to commune with our dead as they engaged in democratic maintenance and revival. They did the work of resurrection, then, via the labor of resurrection. Indeed, they saw that the work of resurrection was not possible without the labors of resurrection, without care and concern for the dead. The work of resurrection required "death work," death labor, it required necromancy and care, and the Black women I profile understood that.

Hooker has written of the civic capacities, including that of sacrifice, that Blacks have had to develop and cultivate in our racially inegalitarian world.[34] I am adding to this list a capacity to be in political community with the dead. This claim is not as far-fetched as it may seem and aligns with important scholarship in psychology and anthropology.[35] Ronald K. Barrett's work on race, death, and dying, for example, argues that Blacks hold a cosmological worldview that would allow them to be in such a community and they would have had considerable opportunity to hone such a capacity within conditions of pervasive racialized premature death. He writes: "The term 'transition' is traditionally used by blacks to refer to dying. Only rarely would people say 'the person died.' Saying 'the person transitioned,' means he or she has 'gone to the next life' and implies that the person has not left us, but simply changed form. They are no longer physically present, and they're spiritually 'passed' into the afterlife. The term 'passed' also is frequently used to express this transition." Having said all that, I think that in general, blacks may be characterized as having a holistic view of death and dying, in that birth and death are understood to be part of a cycle or continuum. . . . I contrast the cyclical view of life and death with the European/Western view, which is a much more linear model. In the European/Western view, you are born and eventually you die. In the traditional black cultural experience, you are born, you die, and then you continue to exist in other realms."[36]

Additionally, I use the term "labors of resurrection" in explicit contrast with Du Bois's "work of resurrection," and with gendered implications that are intentional. The book, then, is also an implicit critique—though in this section alone I will make that critique explicit—of Hannah Arendt's hierarchy of human activities. In *The Human Condition* Arendt proposed to designate "three fundamental human activities"—"labor," "work," and "action."[37] Her attempt to establish these three discrete categories of activity are the aspects of her work that has been most criticized. "Of course, behind this distinction," Seyla Benhabib notes, "lies Arendt's continuing struggle with Karl Marx's ideas."[38] *The Human Condition* is, in part, a continuing argument with Marx's thought. Arendt argues that Marx conflates two activities into his concept of labor, activities that she names labor and work. Man labors, she held, to satisfy the unyielding demands of the biological life process. "Labor is the activity which corresponds to the biological process of the human body whose spontaneous growth, metabolism, and eventual decay are bound to the vital necessities produced and fed into the life process by labor." In "labor" man tended to the needs of his body, to all things necessary for the continuation of the species and the maintenance of biological life itself. Throughout the history of Western political thought, Arendt argued, labor represented the most animal and least human activity, the individual as most enslaved to the demands of biological necessity and least free to exercise the free range of action available in other activities. Unsurprisingly, when possible, man foisted these activities onto others, namely women and servants. Indeed, this was not the form of labor Marx held to be the expression of man's inner self.[39]

She called the object-producing labor that is central to Marx's thought "work," the second capacity she outlined. "Work provides an 'artificial' world of things, distinctly different from all natural surroundings." Work's products were the durable objects man made to make a home out of nature. While Arendt held this activity in higher esteem than labor engaged in the maintenance of biological life, she believed that man's efforts to fashion objects from nature could never completely represent all of what man was. The highest honor she reserved for her final capacity, "action." By action Arendt meant man's capacity to participate with others in projects, realizable by man alone, with the goal of shaping the way human beings lived. This, for Arendt, was the uniquely human activity, the capacity for collective self-government engaged in creating human culture. Like Aristotle, she believed that man was "a creature that will reach its highest natural capacities only in polis citizenship."[40] I beg to differ.

Black female death laborers and indeed life-after-death world makers have done the practical *and* magical work necessary for democratic maintenance, for democratic revivification within our necropolitical order. Collectively, the women I profile have performed a repertoire of resurrection. The *Oxford English Dictionary* defines "resurrection" first as follows: "to restore (a dead person) to life; to raise the dead from the grave." Yet it also defines it as "to revive or revitalize (something which has fallen into inactivity, disuse, or obscurity)." Hooker writes of Wells's social scientific and fact-filled yet emotive work to "reanimate" the dead. Mamie Till-Bradley brought forth the first of what Christopher Metress has called the many "reincarnations" of her son Emmett Till when she staged and diffused the lynching-as-crucifixion story as a spellbinding, body-gripping and thus embodied, participatory Emmett Till reincarnating scenario that transformed Black political subjectivity. Clementine Barfield engaged in a secular, democratic practice of what Rebecca Louise Carter calls "restorative kinship" and repeatedly resurrected her murdered son Derick to convey the life he would have lived as part of her work to revitalize the city of Detroit in a context of pervasive youth violence and the violent War on Drugs. Margaret Prescod salvaged democratic space that had fallen into disuse and disrepair through what Juli Grigsby has named her "roving counterpublics," even as she worked to represent, to bring forward the voices and stories of the most marginal of the Black female dead within this reclaimed democratic space, the dimly lit streets of Los Angeles. Smith's revolutionary enumeration technique—one with important antecedents in the enumeration practices of Wells—not only did democratic revival work but called the dead into her new democratic collective. And what can be said of Toni Morrison?

Morrison, like Du Bois, engaged in a project of storytelling in the service of a vision of democracy. To answer the question of what can be said of Morrison's necromancy, we should begin by turning once more to Crenshaw's diagnosis and proposed solution and ask: what if the solutions to the problem of mobilization asymmetry lie, not in the number of people who are moved, but in who is moved and how? The deceased women and their families as well as Black female violence survivors are not owed movement after all, they are owed justice. Crenshaw bemoans the lack of mass response to violence against Black women, but it is to the richness and complexity of small and often unnoticed responses that we must attend. As I puzzled over the problem of mass movements, Bonnie Honig encouraged me to think about what would happen if we thought not about amplifying nondominant people-building stories in order to make "the Black people" more inclusive, so that women and other non-normative others might be thought of as truly part of that people and therefore of a people more likely to form mass movements and mass reckonings around murdered Black women and others, but saw ourselves instead as freed by Black women's incomplete inclusion and eschew, not the project of storytelling or reckoning, but the project of constituting a large stable "we." What if we thought instead about peopled moments, momentary coming together to come apart to come together again at another necessary moment? It is a productive question for me and something, it turns out, that many Black women had already put into practice. Williamson, for example, points out that there have been and continue to be gatherings around Black women's deaths that otherwise go unnoticed—gatherings that echo the grief-filled yet resolutely mutually ameliorative "we" Smith called into being. Such gatherings, she says, make the claim that someone who is valuable has died, and that this loss must be reckoned with, or "we" are all lost. But they *also* make the claim that "*we* are what else that has happened here." This "we" is often invisible to all but itself, yet this "we" reckons, as I will explain, good and well. Morrison held that such collectives had tremendous potential to enact transformative justice, and we see such collectives post- and prefigured throughout the thinker's work. This "we" is the very thing that Honig suggests as a better way forward. In other words, it is essential to notice that such gatherings of Black women and those who mourn, stand up for, and represent them appropriately, small, unnoticed, and fleeting as they may be, constitute an ideally inclusive, ephemeral, yet nonetheless world-building "we." In this death labot, Black women have *already* been building the "we" (and the world) that we (and the world) need.

But, hard as these collectives may be for outsiders to discern, there is also always more to this "we" than can ever meet the eye. For Morrison these are collectives in which the dead can and must take part. In the book I contrast Du Bois's lynching and peoplehood work, his democratic storytelling, with Morrison's stories of private and intimate violence, her ephemeral collectives composed of the living and the dead and her democratic storytelling as well as with Black women's under-recognized "death work," their democratic necromancy, *and* the democratic work of their dead. Wells, I will argue, inaugurated not only a new era of protest politics, but also a new way of *being with the dead* in politics, in our democracy, that other women, including Smith, Till-Bradley, Barfield, Prescod, and Morrison, would continue. This new way of being in democratic community with the dead is another critical part of the so often unrecognized "we" that is "what else that has happened here."

As this book charts a course from Black women who work primarily on behalf of slain men and boys to women who labor on behalf of Black women who are killed *because* they are women, that is, women who labor on behalf of victims of Black femicide, Toni Morrison's work is particularly instructive, in both its form and its object. Morrison's stories are peopled with nonnormative and unruly women and their unnoticed and under-recognized justice-seeking, feminine subjectivity-transforming ephemeral collectives. She concerns herself with intimate injustice, and with death in the wake of intimate injustice. And her work itself—and as I will argue her *democracy*—is a house, like *Beloved*'s Sethe's 124, "peopled with the living activity of the dead." Morrison takes privacy, intimacy, anonymity, and secrecy—the very things that complicate publicity and mass mobilization for Black femicide victims—as opportunities to reflect on and build complex narratives around women's deaths, their violence-filled lives, and the deaths they keep. Notably, Morrison explicitly does not tell stories for or about mass movements—but she tells stories about collectively enacted, often intimate, justice just the same.

Morrison not only advanced the resurrective concept of rememory; she did the work to recover, to write down, what was always there, unseen. Her work was the work, as Paul Taylor says, to "unforget disremembered worlds and people" and to do so beautifully. She postfigured a world of feminine activity with striking similarities to the innovative democratic practices of the women above, and in and through this she presented her own vision of democracy—Morrisonian truant democracy—inhabited by the living and the dead. Indeed, in each of the innovative democratic practices of the women above we find elements of what Morrison brings together in her vision, key elements of Morrisonian truant democracy—the resolve to record, to correct a malign and inadequate record, a concern with embodiment, with Arendtian labor, with care for the living and the dead. We see a concern with intimacy, with women who are killed or left to die because they have sex, with women who are killed or left to die because they are women, with the morally transgressive feminine dead, with the flesh. In Morrison, too, we see tremendous faith in the transformative power of the ephemeral collective, and, always, the centering of the voices, the concerns, the stories of the dead. Succinctly, like Wells, Morrison resolved to correct the record, and Morrisonian democracy contains Till-Bradley's attention to embodiment, Barfield's care-filled restorative kinship, Smith and Prescod's concern with femicide, and Prescod's ephemeral publics expressly concerned with the well-being of outlaw women and others so sexually profiled.

Black women receive ample, if largely symbolic, recognition for keeping Black communities (and, lately, US democracy) alive, but they have not received the recognition they are due for how well they have kept the Black dead; thus they have not received the recognition they are due for helping to build, to maintain—and when needed to *resurrect*—the very *people* from which they are so often excluded, both in life and in death. This volume corrects the omission as it attends to their ongoing exclusion. *The Labors of Resurrection* engages with Achille Mbembe's concept of necropolitics and Melissa Wright's insights into the gendered politics of death to interrogate contemporary US racial politics. Drawing on insights from history, anthropology, literature, philosophy, and feminist political theory, it considers how state officials, Black activists, and others past and present assign meaning to the bodies of the dead, and it describes and analyzes the challenge contemporary Black feminist activists face, as well as their significant and under-recognized democratic innovations in their endeavors to drive concern toward the more private deaths of Black women. In this sense, my work here reflects on what Black women have done with death, whether spectacular or hidden from view, because Black female death work holds crucial lessons for our politics and for thinking about effective political formations in the wake of ongoing disproportionate unspectacular death and violence.

The Black female necromantic democrats I profile in this volume sought to interrupt our democratic death worlds via the labors of resurrection, expressly working to bring the dead back into the life world and to acknowledge and honor the presence of the dead in this world. Their work confronts the reality of the multifaceted death machine haunting democracy, and thereby brings a view of democracy to the fore to which democratic theorists must attend. As we shall see, haunted necropolitical orders require practices of democratic necromancy, however truant. The dead *must* be represented in a haunted democracy; their voices and concerns must be placed into democratic dialogue and deliberation to address the causes of their premature death; and their imagined futures must figure into our collective planning as well. Black female democrats, the necromantics, through their labors of resurrection, have created space and given voice to those who are no longer physically present but who are surely with us still. They have taken resurrection—the necromantic phenomenon at the center of the Christian worldview—and claimed it as central to the practices of democracy. In so doing, Black women death laborers and life-after-death world makers have performed the practical *and* magical work necessary not simply for democratic maintenance, for democratic repair, as they are now so often given credit for, but for democratic revival.

1

Necropolitics and Vision

Black women in the United States have been subject, and continue to be subject, to a host of biopolitical practices that, in their effect, often have more in common with Achille Mbembe's concept of necropower than with Michel Foucault's account of biopower and normalization but are nonetheless not identical to the genderless phenomenon Mbembe describes. Their experiences with ostensibly life-extending institutions, practices, and prohibitions like shelter obstetric care, and even the legal prohibition of intimate partner violence, when coupled with an understanding of the necrotizing impact of stress and its tendency to "weather," or prematurely age, the body, for example, appear more necropolitical than biopolitical in effect. This is not to say that Black women are *not* subject to textbook forms of Foucauldian normalization, or the dispersed gendered disciplinary power that functions to produce "properly embodied femininity" that Foucauldian feminists like Sandra Bartky have proposed. Nor is it to suggest that Black women have not been subject to aspects of Mbembe's formulation of necropower. It is to highlight, rather, the *intersectionality* of power, the fact that neither biopower nor necropower intersects with the Black female body in the same ways that it does for Black men and white women. In this chapter I demonstrate how Black femicide, both in its active manifestations including intimate partner violence and intimate partner violence–related police killings and in its passive manifestations including maternal deaths and botched and denied abortions, first, is the most significant threat of premature death Black women face, and second, is facilitated by a surrounding racialized necropolitical context while, finally, keeping in view the fact that this context is always both productive as well as destructive of the Black female body.

The operation of necropower in the United States is a racialized phenomenon; it is also gendered and, therefore, intersectional. As well, it should be noted that in modernity, both the threat of death *and* the threat of

The Labors of Resurrection. Shatema Threadcraft, Oxford University Press. © Oxford University Press (2025).
DOI: 10.1093/9780197758618.003.0002

sexual assault emerged as tools of racialized governance; Angela Davis, as we know, argued that rape was used as a Black female–directed counterinsurgency tactic on plantations. Upon examination, the latter phenomenon reveals the inadequacy of our understandings of both necropower and biopower. Given the above, when theorizing modern and contemporary gendered biopower formations it is necessary to trace not only the transformation of gendered power formations that aim to train the body as an object of the male gaze but also the transformations of power formations that functioned to produce rape as, to borrow from Saidiya Hartman, the normative mode of sexual relations for Black women—this power produced, then, not simply an objectified body, but an assaulted, distressed, and weathered Black female body. Stress, as we now know, is itself necrotizing; therefore, institutionalized sexual assault is best understood as the intertwining of biopower and necropower, at once productive and destructive.[1]

This chapter draws attention to the fact that Black women are subject to distinct forms of gendered *and* gendering necropower, which include state-produced disproportionate exposure to fatal intimate partner violence as well as other forms of Black femicide, including the so-called passive Black femicides of pregnancy and abortion-related deaths as well as state-facilitated and state-perpetuated sexual assault. I consider the complex contours of this power as a starting point for understanding, in later chapters, some of the ongoing obstacles to organized efforts to resist it.

The threat of death takes different forms for Black women than it does for Black men. Therefore, the always contested sovereign production of meaning regarding the bodies of the dead as techniques of governance—and by extension the threat of death and the struggle around the meanings given to corpses as a site of organized political resistance—also functions differently for Black women and Black men. The gendered public/private divide plays a role in the operation of intersectional necropower *and* in the interpretation and subsequent legitimation and delegitimation of Black women's deaths. Men confront the threat of violent-death-as-a-technique-of-governance as a straightforwardly public phenomenon, while for women that threat is at once less straightforward, most often intimately enacted, and almost wholly private.

The privacy of the threat women face creates significant problems regarding the literal and symbolic visibility of their deaths, and thus for the subsequent contested meaning-making. Quite apart from the fact that the deaths do not happen in a place where they can be witnessed and filmed, calling spontaneous anti-racist counterpublics into being, as was the case for Michael Brown and George Floyd, the necropolitics themselves are complicated, with perhaps the most significant complication being that the deaths are often not carried out by something outside and apart—by an agent of an othered racist state—but by those with whom the women are intimate. Even when state agents carry out the fatal violence against Black women, it is within, and quite often concerns, the domain of intimacy. The above complicates the interpretation and contestation of their deaths.

US activists and large-scale mobilizations have been most concerned with straightforward public manifestations of necropower, with spectacular lethal police violence (and to a lesser extent vigilante violence), and thus primarily with the deaths of Black men. The connection between spectacle and mobilization can be seen in the relative lack of attention given to police murders of Black women, which often occur in private.[2] Black women's "spectacular death deficit" is not a new phenomenon. Crystal Feimster writes that of the four thousand plus Blacks lynched between 1880 and 1930, fewer than two hundred were women.[3] And Amy Helene Kirschke notes that "Many female lynching victims were never suspected of a crime." Rather, "they died in place of a male target, such as a husband, father, or brother."[4] That is, their deaths stemmed from their intimate relationships. Today, Sam Singyangwe of Mapping Police Violence reports that only about one in twenty Blacks killed by police are women.[5] Many of these women, again, are killed because of their connections to male partners and relatives and because of intimacy.[6] Again when Black women are killed by police, they are rarely killed in public. Black women suffer a spectacular death deficit in a broader social and historical context in which Blacks are most primed to and equipped to mobilize around spectacular death. I turn to this considerable obstacle in subsequent chapters.

Black women are dying *and* those who are not are making their lives within life-after-death worlds. This chapter considers the phenomenon of Black femicide as part of the intersectional operation of modern power with reference to racialized patterns of employment, housing, and policing, and the production of "properly embodied Black femininity," first situating this form of US intersectional necropolitics alongside —and juxtaposing them to—the work of Michel Foucault, Achille Mbembe, and Melissa Wright.

Death and Living Death: Modern Power, Black Femicide, and the Production of Properly Embodied Black Femininity

Michel Foucault distinguishes between an older sovereign power and modern "biopower" as the difference between "the right to take life and let live" and "the right to make live and let die." "Biopolitics," he says, "will derive its knowledge from and define its power's field of intervention in terms of the birth rate, the mortality rate, various biological disabilities and the effects of the environment." Biopower is about regularization: "The mortality rate has to be modified or lowered; life expectancy has to be increased; the birth rate has to be stimulated."[7]

Achille Mbembe finds Foucault's concept of biopower insufficient to account for modern power formations in which the death project overtakes the life project. "Is the notion of biopower sufficient," he asks, "to account for the contemporary ways in which the political, under the guise of war, of resistance, or of the fight against terror, makes the murder of the enemy its primary or absolute objective?" Mbembe continues: "My concern is those figures of sovereignty whose central project is not the struggle for autonomy but the generalized instrumentalization of human existence and the material destruction of human bodies and populations." He holds that multiple sovereignties emerged in modernity, and to comprehend them we must examine the "repressed topographies of cruelty," with the plantation and the colony important among these.[8] Melissa Wright puts Mbembe's innovation here in succinct terms: "While using Foucault's argument as a point of departure, Mbembe argues that biopolitics is not sufficient for explaining how the threat of violent death continues to prevail as a technique of governance in contemporary settings, and he challenges Foucault's reliance on Western European examples to develop his theory of the kinship binding the production of states to the reproduction of their subjects."[9]

Mbembe forwards the concept of "necropower" to account for the various ways in which, in our contemporary world, "weapons are deployed in the interest of maximum destruction of persons and the creation of death-worlds, new and unique forms of social existence in which populations are subjected to conditions of life conferring upon them the status of the living dead."[10] Yet Mbembe does not turn away from Foucault completely; rather, he takes Foucault as his point of departure for thinking about the significance of the body in politics. "Mbembe employs Foucault's analysis," according to Wright, "to turn attention to how the meaning of death in necropolitics, like the meaning of life in biopolitics, emerges through interpretations of embodiment—of corpses, of who kills and who is targeted for death." Indeed, Mbembe asks readers to consider the place given to "life, death and the human body," especially the "wounded or slain body," and how these are "inscribed in the order of power."[11]

Mbembe asks two important questions. First, "Is the notion of biopower sufficient?" That is to say, there are many instances in which sovereign power appears to be oriented *more* toward the death of the other than the life of its own. The US military budget and the general rollback of welfare services attest to this, as does the stunning recent decline in white male lifespan. In Mbembe's account, death is where the action is in contemporary power formations. This leads to Mbembe's second interesting question: "But under what practical condition is the right to kill, to allow to live or to expose to death exercised? Who is the subject of this right?" He answers that we see it in the camp, yes, but also much earlier in the plantation and the colony, in starkly racialized spaces. Here, Mbembe, like others in the tradition of Afro-Modern thought, is highlighting the "dark side" of the twin faces of modern power and specifying its technoscience and its geography.[12]

Mbembe's critique is powerful, yet he proceeds as though necropower operates on genderless bodies. Melissa Wright does much to correct this omission. She takes Mbembe's question regarding dead bodies, their inscription in the order of power, and, importantly, the subsequent interpretations of their meanings seriously and goes on to assert that the politics of death and the politics of gender go hand in hand in successful deployments of necropower. In making this assertion, Wright gives particular attention to the significance of the gendered public-private divide—the fact that we understand public space as male space and private space as feminine space. In addition, Wright draws out and expands on Mbembe's point regarding the struggles over of the *meaning* of death, and thus of life, through interpretations of embodiment. Wright argues that any examination of necropower must attend to the often decisive role that state power plays in assigning meaning to the bodies of the dead. One important terrain of power concerns the sovereign's ability to make definitive pronouncements regarding who the dead were in life, and therefore to determine what their deaths mean to the body politic—particularly whether or not the body politic is better off now that they are dead. The sovereign must control both the power of death *and* its meaning.

The meaning-making power of sovereignty can be contested, and Wright draws illuminating attention to those contestations through consideration of Mexican antifemicide activists' work to counter the assignment of meaning to female dead bodies.[13] Between 1994 and 2001, the murder rate increased 600 percent for women in Ciudad Juárez.[14] The rise in deaths occurred during a period of rapid social change in the city, and many women were engaging in public/paid labor in the maquiladors that sprung up after the North American Free Trade Agreement (NAFTA). Activists concerned about the female dead challenged the state's claims that all dead women were sex workers, but in this they confronted the very strong association between working women and "working women"—that is, between women who worked outside the home in public space and sex workers. Because of the tendency to see a woman in public as a "public woman," state officials could readily explain all women's deaths as a kind of public cleansing that rid the body politic of contamination, helping to restore the moral and political balance of society. Possessing a dead body indicted any female subject as a sex worker; death was all the proof one needed of her transgressions into public space and sex work. Such a death should not trouble women who were not sex workers, who did not transgress and were properly private women. Officials also asserted that keeping women at home—and presumably out of all paid labor—would keep them safe, thereby ceding any role for the state itself in protecting the women, since women were, by definition, safe at home. Their deaths certainly did not suggest a weak or failing state, unable to protect all of its citizens. The activists countered that the subjects, the women, were not sex workers but good daughters, working in factories to support their families, and therefore that lethal violence against them was evidence of a severely weakened state, if not a failed one.[15]

Blacks in the United States have not only been either wholly excluded or insufficiently included within the life extension and regularization projects that comprise Foucault's biopolitics, they have also endured subjection to what Mbembe calls "death-worlds."[16] In the period of enslavement, during Jim Crow, and within contemporary militarized policing regimes, the threat of death has been and continues to be used as a technique of racialized governance. This is, however, not to suggest that Black communities have been and are *solely* death worlds. Black contributions to US culture attest to these communities as sites of significant *life world* creation. In truth, though they are spaces of significant, unjust, and unnecessary premature death, they are more accurately described as life-after-death worlds.[17] They remain important spaces of liveliness.

In the US context, similarly, the #BlackLivesMatter/Movement 4 Black Lives campaign has gained considerable ground in the meaning-making contests Wright highlights within a long-standing necropolitical struggle: not in stopping the production of dead bodies, as that continues apace and may yet increase, but in the extremely important contest over the meaning of the bodies of the Black dead. Today, because of the campaign, a growing number of people now ask, "Is the proper body for the subject who finds himself at odds with the criminal justice system, in the grip of state power, a deceased one?"

Because of the #BLM/M4BLcampaign, a Black man killed by the police can no longer simply be written off as a thug who deserved his death and whose death helps to restore the moral order of the nation, as this claim has become highly contested. The movement has also convinced many who once opposed it to make at least verbal concessions to the Black Lives Matter/M4BL cause. It has been able to do this in part due to technological innovations, such as smartphones and social media, especially "Black Twitter," that have allowed Blacks both to broadcast death spectacles so that disproportionate state violence could not be denied and to bring rhetorical strategies honed in Black counterpublics to bear on a global superpublic and challenge those who have long controlled the instruments of mass communication as never before.[18]

Yet, in a context in which activist-state necropolitical meaning-making contests have taken center stage, Black feminist activists have been far less successful in drawing attention to the bodies of the Black female dead due to the complicated intersectional necropolitics that Black women face. Black women are rarely killed in public, and rarely killed by the police. They do not leave behind discrete, embodied, individual racist targets for antiracist protests. They are primarily victims of Black femicide, a phenomenon in which biased police and policing, alongside employment discrimination, racialized housing insecurity, and other social inequities, nonetheless play a significant contributing role. A survey of the causes of Black femicide will reveal its status as a complex but ultimately state-produced and state-facilitated phenomenon.

Black Femicide—An Overview

As noted in the Introduction, Black women make up 10 percent of the US female population, yet they represent 59 percent of women murdered.[19] In the United States, as in the world generally, men are more likely to be killed than women overall, but Black women in the United States are more likely to be killed than white men.[20] A survey of mortality data from thirty states found that from 1999 to 2020, Black women aged twenty-five to forty-four were six times more likely to be murdered than their white counterparts.[21] The rate of death is not only utterly sobering, it is also on the rise. Black femicide activist Rosa Page points out that the rate of death went from one Black woman killed by an intimate partner every nineteen hours in 2015 to one every six hours in 2022.[22] Black women were twenty times more likely to be murdered than white women in Wisconsin in 2019–2020, up substantially from their six times greater likelihood from 1999 to 2003. Most of those deaths were the result of intimate partner violence.[23] These deaths, then, are a form of femicide.

The intimate partner violence Black women experience is made more deadly by a surrounding context of workplace discrimination and related resource deprivation, by housing insecurity, medical neglect, and inadequate public safety provision. Policymaking, including gun control policy, actively contributes to this disproportionate premature death; 72 percent of murdered Black women killed are killed by guns. Societal hierarchies are another factor, as homophobia, transphobia, femmephobia, and stereotypes and profound misrecognitions that normalize violence against women who defy gender norms (including sex workers, single mothers, trans women, and, indeed, at some level all Black women) all expose Black women to disproportionate violence and premature death.[24]

Black femicide is the misogynoiristic killing of Black women *because* they are Black women, as well as the misogynistic killing of Black women facilitated by racist stereotypes, gendered racial capitalism, race-based housing discrimination, residential segregation, housing insecurity, and medical racism.[25] Diana E. H. Russell has done essential work in defining femicide, a term she first heard as early as 1974. Russell offered a definition of "femicide" at the First International Tribunal of Crimes against Women in 1976 as the hate killing of women by men. In her testimony, she stated, "From the burning of witches in the past, to the more recent widespread custom of female infanticide in many societies, to the killing of women for so-called honor, we realize that femicide has been going on a long time."[26] Here it is worth pausing to note, as Russell makes women being burned at the stake a foundational example regarding femicides past, that Black femicide has a very long history in this country as Kali Gross has found that from 1608 to 1805, 87 percent, that is, "the overwhelming majority," of women burned at the stake in the United States were Black.[27] In Russell's book with Jill Radford, they would define femicide as "the misogynistic killing of women by men."[28] Femicide is a distinct form of murder. Catherine D'Ignazio points out that femicide is a crime motivated by a woman's gender that takes different forms from the murder of men: "Men are not frequently violated and killed in their homes, for example, and men's bodies are not typically desecrated in brutal and sexualized ways."[29]

Soon after the publication of Russell and Radford's book, activists began to call attention to the abovementioned 600 percent increase in the murder of women in Ciudad Juárez, Mexico. The anthropologist Marcela Lagarde y de los Rios would expand our understanding of femicide considerably by drawing attention to the surrounding contexts in which the murders take place, to "neoliberal economic policy, the rise of the maquiladoras and the feminization of their labor force, the migration of rural women, the on-going presence of intimate partner violence (still accounting for at least 30 percent of murders in Juárez between 1993 and 2007), as well as the predominating culture of machismo and subordination." Lagarde y de los Rios made the deaths an issue when she ran for the legislature and after her election undertook one of the most thorough state-sponsored studies of femicide to date. In translating the term "femicide" into Spanish, she chose the term "feminicidio" and, in so doing, made a significant theoretical shift meant to signal gender-related killing and "to link these killings and disappearances to human rights violations and to the climate of impunity created by state inaction." Femicide, she held, was a crime of the *state*, whereby the state fails to ensure the right to life for half of its citizens.[30]

D'Ignazio argues that Lagarde y de los Rios's formulation laid the groundwork for more intersectional elaborations of the concept of femicide in other contexts. The Colombian Group Red Feminista Antimilitarista, for example, developed the concept of "neoliberal feminicide," defined as "the extreme violence of capital on women who find themselves impoverished, stripped of power and significance in the modern capitalistic and patriarchal coloniality." According to their view, femicides targeted women for being women, yes, but especially women "from specific social classes, impoverished women, women street vendors, trans women, women who practiced prostitution." D'Ignazio's genealogy of the organizing and conceptual labor regarding femicide acknowledges earlier and concurrent organizing around Black women's deaths initiated by Barbara Smith and the women of the Combahee River Collective, as well as around indigenous women's deaths "in the unceded territories of the xwməθkwəy̓əm (Musqueam), Sḵwx̱wú7mesh (Squamish), and Selílwitulh (Tsleil-Waututh) Nations" in Downtown Eastside Vancouver, Canada. On February 14, 1991, mother Linda Ann Joe and family members memorialized the life of Cheryl Ann Joe, a twenty-six-year-old Coast Salish woman who was sexually assaulted and murdered. Others joined what became the Women's Memorial March, which then helped to lay the groundwork for the Missing and Murdered Indigenous Women/Missing and Murdered Women, Girls, and Two Spirit (#MMIW/#MMIWG2) and the Missing and Murdered Indigenous Persons (#MMIP) Movement.[31]

In 2014, the United Nations published technical guidance regarding femicide, the "Latin American Model Protocol for the Investigation of Gender-Related Killings of Women (Femicide/Feminicide)." The document elaborated two categories of femicide: "active femicide," which included intimate partner violence, honor killings, female infanticide, and the like, and, notably for Black women in the United States, "passive femicide," whose forms include unsafe abortions, maternal mortality, and deaths linked to organized crime. Passive femicide is an important category. Sex workers, for example, are at higher risk of murder than women who do not participate in the sex trade; a 2004 US study found them eighteen times more likely to be murdered than women not involved in the sex trade.[32] Yet a study in the *Lancet* found that, in an analysis of 2,112 sex worker deaths, 12.5 percent had been murdered, while 35.5 percent died of abortion-related complications and another 16.6 percent died of "other maternal causes."[33]

Intimate partner violence is a significant factor in the disproportionate violence and death to which Black women in the United States are subject, as it is for women around the world.[34] Yet the intimate partner violence they experience is a phenomenon made more deadly by its surrounding context. For example, economic vulnerability increases women's exposure to violence and makes any violence they experience more consequential. A lack of resources makes leaving the relationships in which one is embedded—intimate, familial, communal, economic—much more difficult. Women who decide to leave such relationships need significant cash on hand to change their living arrangements and find suitable shelter, access to childcare in an emergency, and networks to find new employment. Yet, for women, leaving a violent relationship is not always the safest option, as they are often far more likely to be killed if they leave. Women with fewer resources often have family and communities with less to offer after a violent event—a spare room, a space at a women's shelter—thereby making what one might call "relationship truancy," or getting away for a bit, a less viable option.[35]

In a groundbreaking investigation, Catherine Squires and her colleagues on Minnesota's Missing and Murdered African American Women Task Force drew attention to housing insecurity and race-based vulnerability to human trafficking as significant factors in the disproportionate murder and disappearance of Black women and girls. Housing insecurity significantly increases women's exposure to violence. Housing is a huge problem in Black female life generally. Black women's relative housing insecurity is in part a consequence of decades of unaddressed housing crimes and discrimination and the contemporary failure to enforce fair housing laws.[36] George Lipsitz notes that housing crimes committed against Black women by landlords, real estate agents, bankers, and municipal officials who violate fair housing laws go unpunished, leaving less-resourced women with few options besides highly surveilled public housing, which then increases their risk of police contact and subsequent incarceration—both risk factors for gender-related violence. Thus Kimberlé Crenshaw argues that these unpunished crimes lead to Black women being overpoliced, and these crimes are therefore an under-recognized driver of the phenomenon of mass incarceration.[37] These housing crimes must be understood as a major contributing factor in femicidal violence against Black women.

Black women experience rates of eviction higher than those of both white women and Black men, which, given their role as primary caregivers, has broad communal impact. One in five Black women reported that they had been evicted, compared to one in fifteen white women.[38] Not only is eviction "associated with higher risk of high blood pressure, sexually transmitted diseases, depression, anxiety, exposure to violence and higher mortality rates" for women specifically, it's also linked to "physical and sexual assault, drug use, mental illness and future housing precarity."[39]

Sex trafficking is another factor in disproportionate Black femicide. Women involved in the sex trade are eighteen times more likely to be murdered than women who are not.[40] Though the public's perception of the trafficking victim is white, Black women are 40 percent of sex trafficking victims. According to Cheryl Nelson Butler, "the modern-day commercial sex industry perpetuates a long and bitter history of sexual exploitation and racial subordination of people of color. This is especially true when it comes to the sexual exploitation of minors." Butler argues that "racial ideologies formulated during slavery and colonization were perpetuated in order to justify targeting people of color for sexual exploitation in America's modern-day commercial sex industry. Racial fetishes drive the supply of, and demand for, commercial sex with people of color. Structural racism also coerces people of color to engage in prostitution."[41] Squires and her colleagues point out that several factors heighten Black women and girls' vulnerability to trafficking, including "a history of sexual and physical abuse, homelessness, unstable housing, low social economic status" and "system involvement." Because Black women and girls are overrepresented in these "systems"—they are 5 times more likely than white women to be incarcerated, 1.2 times more likely to be detained, 2.7 times more likely to be referred to juvenile justice, and 3 times more likely to be removed from their homes and placed in foster care than white girls, such that 23 percent of youth in foster care (or what Dorothy Roberts refers to as an apartheid system of family policing) are Black—it means that they are particularly at risk of trafficking. But the public and law enforcement rarely view Black women and girls as victims because of stereotypes that see Black women and girls as "less innocent and more sexually aware."[42] The stereotypes emerged, of course, to justify a particular phase of racial capitalism and the brutal gendered forms of exploitation Black women endured within the system of slavery. It is unsurprising that stereotypes that emerged to prop up the older system of human trafficking endure in human trafficking today.

Relatedly, recent studies suggest that much of the disproportionate violence to which trans persons are subject is, in fact, a form of Black femicidal violence. Alexis Dinno found that while "overall in the United States during 2010 to 2014, transgender residents may have been at lower risk for homicide than were cisgender residents . . . transfeminine residents aged 15 to 34 years who were Black or Latina were almost certainly more likely to be murdered than were their cisfeminine comparators." Indeed, "a large majority of transgender homicide risk is borne by young Black and Latina transfeminine individuals."[43] Part of the disproportionate risk of violence for transfemmes of color is rooted in familiar, though intensified, racist stereotypes held by their cis male romantic partners. "Cisgender straight men reduced participants to their body parts, assuming that they were substance users or sex workers, and viewing them as less than human and hypersexual. These perspectives that transgender women of color face when seeking romantic partners are complex and highlight how intersectional stigma may contribute to gender-based violence."[44] These stereotypes are obviously not only racist, but sexist, classist, and whorephobic, and therefore consistent with Lori Saffin's claim that we must understand the disproportionate violence to which trans women of color are subject as an intersectional problem. Saffin points out that what we commonly understand as racial violence often involves policing gender and sexual boundaries and therefore racialized people who are also gender expansive are more vulnerable to hate-based violence.

Employment and housing insecurity as well as system involvement are also factors in disproportionate fatal violence against Black transfemmes. Saffin's conception of violence against transfemmes of color directs attention to the same structural forces that intensify violence against cisBlack women, that is, racism's impact on secure employment and housing as well as its impact on foster care, or as Roberts refers to it, the racist system of "family policing," juvenile justice, and overall carceral system involvement and how these phenomena intersect with classism, as gender expression has a profound impact on one's class status, including one's ability to train for and secure formal employment, as well as femmephobia and, I would add, whorephobia to increase the risk of violence. This is not to suggest that the risks are the same, as research is clear that, among Black women, transfemmes are at greater risk of violence than their cisgender counterparts. I have drawn attention to the fragility of formal and informal support systems in under-resourced communities, yet trans women of color have limited access to even these fragile systems. They are often kicked out of families, ostracized, marginalized, and forced out of schools and foster care homes before they are able to acquire resource-related skills. With little social support, they have limited access to formal employment and face discrimination when they are able to gain qualifying employment skills. They are therefore concentrated in marginal, dangerous, criminalized informal work, which in turn puts them at high risk of both interpersonal and police violence.[45]

Part of what police are policing *is* gender normativity; they are looking for "gender outlaws." This claim is borne out by the fact that 40 percent of girls in the juvenile justice system identify as lesbian, bisexual, transgender, or gender-nonconforming.[46] Eric A. Stanley argues that the "domain of gender" is "among the most volatile points of contact between state violence and one's body."[47] The events preceding the uprising of June 28, 1969, at the Stonewall Inn are just the most well-known example of police expressly policing gender expression. Police and policing, then, help to compel normative—that is, binary—gender expression. Gender normativity, or the imposition of a gender binary onto bodies, is, according to Stanley, "a product of and a producer" of the prison-industrial complex.[48] This is why Saffin, Stanley, and others hold that there can be no true gender self-determination *without* the abolition of the prison industrial complex. Dean Spade agrees with this position and argues that, therefore, contemporary trans activism should not follow mainstream lesbian and gay rights organizations, with their focus on hate crimes and antidiscrimination laws, as this will not do enough to increase the life chances of most trans people. Spade's book on critical trans politics and administrative violence suggests the "administrative realm" of the law "may be the place to look for how law structures and reproduces vulnerability for trans populations." Spade's view is consistent with those of Richie, Crenshaw, Squires, and others who indict systems, including ostensibly biopolitical systems, for producing disproportionate Black feminine death. Spade says:

> In order to properly understand power and transphobic harm, we need to shift our focus from the individual rights framing of discrimination and "hate violence" and think more broadly about how gender categories are enforced on all people in ways that have particularly dangerous outcomes for transpeople. Such a shift requires us to examine how administrative norms or regularities create structured insecurity and (mal)distribute life chances across populations. This attention to the distribution of life chances acknowledges that even when laws are changed to say different things about a targeted group, that group may still experience disproportionate poverty as well as a lack of access to healthcare, housing, and education. Those laws will do nothing to prevent violences like criminalization and immigration enforcement.

Hate crime laws, Spade explains, above all give more resources to the people who so often abuse trans, gender nonconforming, and queer people.[49]

Black women, then, are under significant threat from what has been defined as "active" femicide. Yet they are also at risk of what is known as "passive" femicide.

Passive Black Femicide

Abortion bans kill. It is important that I state this plainly before I begin. What we do not know and have been forced to forget about women's bodies, and specifically Black women's bodies, is a crime; arguably, it borders on a crime against humanity. Yet what we do know is this: abortion care has been fully integrated into reproductive care, it is a crucial part of miscarriage care, and, therefore, it is often a part of a woman's overall reproductive journey. Women without abortion access have been left to die or to suffer life altering illness or disability. Because of demographic distribution wherein Blacks are concentrated in the South, 57 percent of Black women now live under abortion bans or severely restrictive abortion laws.[50] Threats to contraception not only threaten women's lives and—though this is something that is often dismissed in doctors' offices and in the halls of power—the quality of their lives, but broader gynecological, immunological, dermatological, and mental health care.[51] Those who deny women access to abortion, like those who disseminate vaccine skepticism or work to increase access to guns, quite frankly, counterproductively seek to unsolve problems we have mastered in a world with no shortage of looming threats. They represent, therefore, not government, but its opposite.

Human pregnancy is a dangerous miracle that social conditions can either ameliorate or make even more perilous. Despite tremendous advances in obstetric care, if pregnancy were a job, it would be one of the ten most dangerous jobs in America. And gestation and parturition are even more dangerous for Black women, for whom it can rank, as it did in 2021, as high as the second most dangerous job, after loggers and above that of roofers and deep-sea fishermen. What's more, when one considers Black women's acute risk of fatal intimate partner violence during pregnancy and the postpartum year, it may well be the most dangerous job in America.[52]

The Black maternal mortality crisis, which has received considerable attention in recent years, is a textbook case of passive Black femicide as it is defined by the United Nations. Black women are three to four times more likely to die of pregnancy-related complications or in childbirth than white women. Black infants die at about twice the rate of white infants and have done "since the first national comparative statistics appeared in the late 19th century."[53] Annie Menzel argues that the long twentieth century was marked by a growing concern for the health of white babies at the same time that Black babies emerged as a site for the punitive control of Black mothers and Black birth practitioners. Tellingly, in a culture steeped in misogyny and misogynoir, while Black infant mortality has long been an object of punitive concern, the persistent disparities in the Black maternal death rate only emerged as an object of discussion in the 1980s.[54]

The disproportionate Black maternal and infant death rates are, in part, a consequence of "obstetric racism," a subset of the broader phenomenon of medical racism. Dana-Ain Davis originally defined obstetric racism as "critical lapses in diagnosis; being neglectful, dismissive, or disrespectful; causing pain; and engaging in medical abuse through coercion to perform procedures or performing procedures without consent."[55] She would go on to expand the definition to include "ceremonies of degradation, which represents the ways that Black women experience feeling or being degraded; medical abuse, which involves thinking or feeling that one was used for purposes of experimentation; and what I call 'racial reconnaissance,' which describes the Herculean effort that Black women make to avoid or mitigate the racist encounters they presume they will encounter at IVF clinics."[56]

But this maternal morality disparity and Black women's ongoing experience of obstetric racism is also a consequence of what Menzel refers to as an "agnotological project"—that is, the deliberate production of ignorance—waged against Black midwives by white male obstetricians and white female nurse managers. This project entailed forced deskilling and forced forgetting imposed on Black midwives (who Menzel argues accepted in-kind payments for care and often understood their work as a kind of calling, not through the logic of the market) under threat of violence and incarceration, in a context in which the emerging capitalist hospital birthing regime was not required to serve Black patients and instead conformed to the dictates of the Jim Crow racial order. Davis sees the denigration of Black midwives, and indeed the targeted attack of them, as a form of racialized reproductive abuse.[57]

My home state of Georgia offers an important case in point. In Georgia, in the 1950s—during the time in which my grandmothers were birthing and losing children—the majority of Black births were attended by midwives. But Wangui Muigai points out that "beginning at the turn of the 20th century the practice was increasingly attacked by physicians who viewed midwives as a 'problem,' as they were 'untrained, dirty and even criminal.'" Tightened regulations, increased surveillance, and officials' expressed goal of diminishing their ranks succeeded in driving down the number of midwives. Georgia's nearly 3,000 registered midwives in 1930 dropped to 1,322 by 1950. With the decline in midwives, Black women began to use public clinics, but these remained inaccessible or inequitably accessible. The clinic in Dougherty County, Georgia, for example—the largest population center close to my grandmothers—was only open to Black women on Friday mornings.[58] Though federal money, and thus Black tax dollars, went into constructing hospitals in the South, medical centers like this clinic remained deeply segregated and inaccessible to Southern Black women. Menzel points out that state-imposed restrictions on midwives led not to improvements in Black birth outcomes but simply to a decline in midwives. As doctors were no more willing to serve poor Black women and were not required to, the reforms "deprived many women of experienced birth attendants without providing them with access to medical and nursing services."[59]

Today, researchers point to several factors in the persistent maternal and infant mortality disparities among Black women, including disproportionate racialized stress and its connections to the phenomenon of "weathering," as well as epigenetic changes in Black birthing bodies. There has long been an overemphasis on individual behavior in Black pregnancy outcomes, including in recent research into the impact of stress on gestating bodies, with insufficient attention to structural factors. Menzel notes that Leith Mullings and Alaka Wali's Harlem Birth Right Project, "an ethnographic participatory action research project," is a significant departure from this line of inquiry as it challenged this behaviorialist framing and provided "a more complete picture of both what 'stress' entailed as well as highlighting the crucial supports that Black women themselves forged and sustained."[60] Mullings and Wali's study was an inquiry into the "broad social context of gender roles and pregnancy outcomes" among Black women. "How women in Harlem perceive and experience pregnancy," they wrote, "reflects complex conditions and relationships, which, at first glance, may appear to be individual histories and behaviors. Although individual risk factors are important, what appear to be personal risk factors and individual lifestyle choices are best understood in the context of a larger structure of constraints and social choices conditioned by race, class, and gender."[61]

Mullings and Wali's study examined housing, environmental factors, work and economics, and social support, as well as health care access. What they found were both sources of stress *and* of resilience, as Black women created and maintained community-building collective sources of support to deal with housing insecurity, workplace insecurity, environmental toxicity, and inequitable and inadequate access to health care through gestation and beyond. These "practices of resilience," according to Menzel, "helped to foster collective life in the face of the many sources of strain undercutting Black maternal well-being." Thus, they argued, to be effective, public health interventions "'must confront . . . the ways in which gender inequity, racial discrimination and class inequity impose limitations on access to health care and perhaps more importantly, on secure jobs, adequate housing, good nutrition, adequate childcare, a safe and healthy environment, and necessary social service,' as well as building on already existing and effective 'individual and collective coping strategies around housing, family and community.'"[62]

Mullings and Wali coined the term "Sojourner Syndrome" to help them conceptualize the "multiplicative effects of race, class and gender on health." Sojourner Truth's life and legend, they explain, "embodies . . . the assumption of economic, household, and community responsibilities, which express themselves in family headship, working outside the home (like a man), and the constant need to address community empowerment—often carried out in conditions made difficult by discrimination and scarce resources." Sojourner Truth also "speaks to the contradictions between ideal models of gender and the lives of black women: exclusions from the protections of private patriarchy offered to white women by concepts of womanhood, motherhood, and femininity; the experience of being silenced; and, not least, the loss of children. Exploration of the consequences of these intersecting responsibilities that exist for African American women across class may give us insight into the way race, class, and gender structure constraints and choices, and therefore risk, for black women."[63] Notably, Mullings and Wali demonstrate that the very same factors that expose Black women to "active" Black femicide factor in their experiences of "passive" Black femicide.

Yet the threat, quite literally, goes deeper. Arline Geronimus, we might say, effectively identified the significant embodied consequences of "Sojourner Syndrome." Geronimus proposed the concept of "weathering" to account for the bodily impact of racism. Allostatic load scores are a measure of stress-associated body chemicals and their cumulative effect on the body's systems. "Poor and nonpoor black women," Geronimus says, "had the highest and second highest probability of high allostatic load scores respectively and the highest excess scores compared with their male counterparts. Racial/ethnic differences in chronic morbidity and excess mortality are pronounced by middle age. Evidence of early health deterioration among Blacks and racial differences in health are evident at all socioeconomic levels." Geronimus posits that Blacks experience early health deterioration as a consequence of the cumulative impact of repeated experience with social or economic adversity and political marginalization: "On a physiological level, persistent, high-effort coping with acute and chronic stressors can have a profound effect on health. The stress inherent in living in a race-conscious society that stigmatizes and disadvantages Blacks may cause disproportionate physiological deterioration, such that a Black individual may show the morbidity and mortality typical of a White individual who is significantly older. Not only do Blacks experience poor health at earlier ages than do Whites, but this deterioration in health accumulates, producing ever-greater racial inequality in health with age through middle adulthood."[64]

Menzel explains that public health experts understand weathering as a partial explanation for "the gaping inequities in the Black-White infant and maternal survival, life expectancy and overall health": "The body's allostatic load—chemical elements like adrenaline and cortisol that respond to crisis conditions—becomes an allostatic overload when crisis conditions are constant, triggering inflammatory processes and the abovementioned cellular ageing. The 'crisis ordinary' of gendered anti-Blackness, as psychological, emotional, ecological, and physical aggressions and deprivations target Black women's existence in the United States over the lifetime, issues in a persistently elevated allostatic load, predisposing Black women to myriad chronic and life-shortening health conditions."[65]

What's more, Menzel points out that this is also an intergenerational problem. Advances in the field of epigenetics, which have led to the overturning of the dominant "genetic determinism" of the twentieth century, have also helped to shed light on the impact of stress across multiple generations. Epigenetics "tracks the ways that experiences, environments and exposures alter gene expression in ways that can be intergenerationally heritable, without changing the genetic code." Menzel writes:

> The assaults of gendered anti-Blackness can persist over generations through changes effected in the matrilineal epigenome, even as external circumstances shift. Through processes like methylation (molecular groups attaching to genes, hindering their expression, or detaching from

> them, allowing expression) the fetus is subject not only to the outcome of the gestating body's stress (ie born too early or too small) but to alterations in its own chemical determinants of gene expression, or epigenetic markers, potentially from several generations back. . . . While weathering impacts two generations—the gestating body directly, the fetal body indirectly—epigenetic inheritance can endure over multiple generations. The same elevated stress hormones thought to cause inflammation in the uterus, for instance, also impact the epigenetic markers relevant to the fetus's own physiological stress response. High levels of cortisol in the gestating body overtax the fetus's HPA (Hippocampus-Pituitary-Adrenal) Axis, also known as the "stress axis," predisposing it to higher than average levels of cortisol in response to stressful events over its own lifetime. If that fetus then is born and grows to gestate another fetus in turn, this stress/inflammation pattern may repeat—even if the environment undergoes significant transformation.[66]

Wary of potential ableism, as well as the new avenues epigenetics may open in ongoing efforts to pathologize Black women, Menzel endorses Michael Lu and Neal Halfon's "life course" approach to epigenetics, which extends the concept of weathering and "conceptualizes birth outcomes as the end product of not only the nine months of pregnancy but the entire life course of the gestating person before the pregnancy, including fetal life . . . positing that each pregnancy is shaped by a social context that presents harmful 'risk factors' and mitigating 'protective factors.'" Lu and Halfon judge the Black/white infant mortality gap "as reflecting the fact that the white maternal body is cushioned by far more protective factors, while fewer risk factors bear down upon it, while Black mothers face the converse situation." They point to "the limits of prevailing approaches to studying stress and maternal health, which are often limited to 'acute, individual psychological stressors that occurred immediately before or during the pregnancy' and self-reports of stress," while "it is 'chronic social stressors . . . factors in the community, social relationships, economics, discrimination, politics, housing, etc. . . . that over time cause wear and tear on the body's allostatic systems, and that underlie racial disparities in birth and other health conditions.'"[67] Again we see evidence that active and passive Black femicide share root causes.

Of course, the acute problem of passive maternal Black femicide occurs alongside the phenomenon's more "active" variants. Black expectant mothers are more likely to die from intimate partner violence than from causes related to obstetrics, and Black women are eleven times more likely to be murdered while pregnant or within a year of childbirth than their white counterparts.[68]

Black Femicide and Policing

Police are not the immediate cause of death for most Black women, but they are very much implicated in Black women's disproportionate exposure to premature death. Police aid in the project to "make die" without themselves pulling the trigger in a number of distinct ways. Due to discriminatory racist/sexist attitudes that preclude them from seeing Black women as victims of male violence, many police do less to protect Black women from this form of violence. Studies have shown that their presence in situations of intimate partner violence tends to escalate male violence while functioning to restrain Black female actions in their own defense. Further, police themselves often perpetuate violence against Black women in these and other situations and, as a consequence of their biased involvement, increase Black women's contact with institutions that bring about their disproportionate premature death, including jails and prisons. Years of investment in policing as the solution to social ills over other proven methods of safety provision like affordable housing has proven deadly for Black women.

Amber Simmons reports that officers tend to dismiss the testimony of Black female domestic violence victims, to classify these women as "the aggressor in some way," and to "refuse to help" Black women or report their abuse.[69] Police exhibit particularly problematic behavior in this regard at the intersection of intimate partner violence and the drug trade. Many Black women are in jail as a result of the War on Drugs, for example, are simply guilty by association and are very often survivors of male violence. When it comes to women involved in and associated with men in the drug trade, Crenshaw says that police, courts, and activist organizations ignore the violence and coercion that marks many women's participation in said trade.[70]

The police are not only less likely to offer aid of any kind when confronted with violence against Black women, their presence also tends to escalate all forms of male violence against these women. Mandatory arrest laws are of particular concern here. They only make some women safer. We know that, perversely and tellingly, it seems that white women have gained safety at Black women's considerable expense when it comes to these policies. Crenshaw cites a Milwaukee study that concluded that the safety mandatory arrest brings to white women comes at the direct expense of Black women who are at serious risk of police violence during intimate partner violence calls, as "mandatory arrests prevents 2504 acts of violence against primarily white women at the price of 5409 acts of violence against primarily black women."[71] Again, violence is a stressor, stress is weathering, and thus, it is also itself a necropolitical force. But it is more than this. Crenshaw also cites a Harvard study that concluded that "Intimate Partner Violence homicides increased by about 60 percent in states with mandatory arrest laws."[72] And we know that this homicide burden is not borne equally.

Black antiviolence feminist activists and organizations attribute the increased risk of death, in part, to the gendered demobilizing impact of mandatory arrest laws. Crenshaw notes that when police are called after an incident of intimate partner violence, "research suggests that women of color are more likely to be arrested themselves for behavior that may be consistent with self-defense but interpreted through the lens of stereotype as overly aggressive."[73] "Indeed," Beth Richie argues, "the victimization of some Black women seems to invoke a set of institutional reactions that lead to further vilification, rather than protection or support." She explains: "The political dynamics of a prison nation interact with racial and other stigmas in such a way that women of color are more likely to be treated as criminals than as victims when they are abused."[74] This criminalization often leads to "system involvement," which, as we know, increases their risk of premature death. Black and Latinx women are particularly vulnerable to "dual arrest," wherein both perpetrator and survivor are arrested, and to retaliatory arrest, "wherein a perpetrator has a survivor arrested by lodging a complaint at a later date."[75]

INCITE!, a women of color antiviolence organization that has been particularly critical of mandatory arrest laws, is also critical of the broader criminalization approach to gender-based violence of which mandatory arrest laws are a part, which leads to, among other things, harsh sentences given to women who kill their batterers. INCITE! holds that the true impact of mandatory arrest laws is that they have decreased the numbers of women who kill their batterers, not the number of batterers who kill women. Thus, as they point out, the mandatory arrest laws in fact protect batterers more than they protect survivors, in part by restraining and demobilizing women, diminishing their willingness to engage in armed self-defense while failing to de-escalate and decrease violence perpetuated by batterers, thereby exposing women of color and Black women in particular to a greater risk of death. INCITE! also notes that support for policing and criminalization in general takes resources away from social service programs, like housing support, that could provide women the means to leave abusive relationships.[76] In Crenshaw's view, "mandatory arrest polices appear to have done little to protect women of color against domestic violence" while heightening "the risk of serious injury and death for women of color and for Black women in particular." In INCITE's analysis, police involvement protects abusive men and (some normative) white women but increases Black women's exposure to violence and death. Crenshaw credits INCITE! with having predicted these higher fatalities—predictions that, sadly, went unheeded.[77]

The police themselves are also major perpetrators of violence against Black women, particularly those in under-resourced communities, and much of that violence is also connected to the sphere of intimate relations, and therefore should be understood as a form of Black femicidal violence. Police violence against Black women is consistent with other forms of gender-based violence in that it most often takes place on the feminine side of the gendered public/private divide. Andrea Ritchie summarizes police physical violence against Black women: "I do think that much of the police violence that black women experience also happens in private, as it did for Breonna Taylor."[78] Indeed, the circumstances of Breonna Taylor's death echo those of many other Black women whose names we are now called upon to say, including Eleanor Bumpurs, Aiayana Stanley-Jones, Rekia Boyd, Atatiana Jefferson, Katheryn Johnston, Charlena Lyles, and Pearlie Golden. That is, Black women are rarely killed by police, but when they are, it is most often in their homes.

Within the context of the War on Drugs and women associated with men in the drug trade, if and when there is subsequent state violence, it becomes an extension of intimate partner violence.[79] Ritchie points out that, as was the case for Breonna Taylor, much of the police violence Black women experience is, "in the context of the war on drugs, and sort of by association, in the way that the officers somehow thought that she was (romantically) associated with (someone and) something that she was not at all associated with." Police also often hurt and sometimes kill Black women who ask for help in their intimate relations with Black men and when they have been physically and sexually assaulted by Black men. As Ritchie says, police violence against Black women "happens in the contexts of calls for help, calls for help in a mental health crisis, calls for help for domestic violence, calls for help around sexual assault, calls for help, as in Atatiana Jefferson's case." This means that "a wellness check can wind up being a deadly intervention with police."[80]

Black female survivors of intimate partner violence are at increased risk for police sexual violence (PSV). Sexual assault, then, like the threat of death, remains a tool of governance for marginalized people. This has been true for a very long time, and it remains true even as Black women, who have historically been subject to institutionalized sexual assault, have gained formal legal protection from said assault. The power formation under which they long lived and labored, then, has simply undergone a transformation. And sexual violence is a source of stress, which in turn weathers the body and is thus a necropolitical force. Police, in both failing to prevent and in perpetuating sexual violence, then, are necropolitical even when they do not directly kill.

Sexual assault is a gendered violation to which women are disproportionately subject, but, again, this burden is not borne by all women equally. Dara Purvis and Melissa Blanco's study of police sexual violence notes this inequity: "While women generally are disproportionately impacted by rape and sexual assault, women of color run an even higher risk of rape or sexual assault as a result of their race and their gender. Although 60 percent of the population identifies as white, only 18 percent of rape victims are white women. The rate of victimization of nonwhite people is strikingly disproportionate to their numbers in the overall population."[81]

In a broader cultural context in which women in general, and Black and other women of color in particular, are presumed to have consented to any sexual act, police officers exploit the decreased credibility attributed to women and women of color in particular, the "testimonial injustice" they confront.[82] What this means in practice, according to Purvis and Blanco, is that the "victimology of PSV is deeply intersectional as police officers typically target the most vulnerable—namely women of color, transgender and gender non-conforming people, victims of domestic abuse and people suspected of engaging in criminalized activity—to reduce the risk that their conduct will be reported." Of course, Black women, who are disproportionately survivors of intimate partner violence and disproportionately suspected of criminal activity, are at particular risk. Purvis and Blanco write: "Sexual exploitation of Black women by White men in formal positions of power over them has been a shameful part of the nation's history since slavery. This exploitation is worsened by stereotypes and revisionist history that sexualizes Black women and girls, characterizing them as more likely to have consented to what was in fact a sexual assault. Given the communities that are more likely to have repeated interactions with law enforcement and the ongoing role of purported consent in PSV, it is unsurprising that Black women have been disproportionately victimized by PSV."[83]

Chagmion Antoine notes that police racial profiling "takes gender-specific forms that often lead to sexual assault."[84] Antoine cites a 2006 report by the United Nations Human Rights Commission that found "women of color experience particular impacts of current law enforcement policies and practices across the U.S.": "For instance, women are routinely profiled as drug couriers by law enforcement officers in the context of the U.S. Government's 'War on Drugs,' leading to arbitrary stops, strip searches and detentions. The long prison sentences meted out for drug-related offenses in the US also provide law enforcement officers with increased leverage for extortion schemes such as those in which officers routinely demand sexual acts in exchange for leniency."[85]

And PSV is pervasive. Police sexual misconduct is the second largest category of reported police misconduct after police brutality. It is also routinely under-reported, where identified cases are recognized as only the tip of the iceberg. Scholars agree that police sexual violence is "functionally impossible" to gauge, given the barriers to reporting. It is, then, quite possibly the largest category of police misconduct. An AP investigation revealed that between 2009 and 2014 almost a thousand US police officers lost their licenses as a result of sexual violation allegations.[86] A *Buffalo News* study found seven hundred cases of PSV from 2005 to 2015, with most of the cases involving "officers wielding their authority over motorists, crime victims, informants, students and young people in job-shadowing programs."[87]

One predictable result of the above—in particular the by turns apathetic or violent and punitive police response to male violence against women of color alongside the antiviolence movement's non-response to violence directed against criminalized Black women—is that prisons and other systems of incarceration often warehouse female violence survivors, and survivors of color in particular. An ACLU report indicates that "nearly 60 percent of people in women's prisons worldwide, and as many as 94 percent of some women's prison's populations, have a history of physical or sexual abuse before being incarcerated."[88] Indeed, as the organization Survived + Punished has argued, jails and prisons, and not women's shelters, are what our society offers marginalized survivors of male violence. Sadly, for many Black women, interpersonal and police violence and abuse is only the beginning of the violence they will experience, as the police are only one part of a criminal punishment system that includes jails, prisons, and immigration detention centers: "Once incarcerated or detained, many women and trans and gender non-conforming people experience sexual violence from guards and others." Survived + Punished insists that "for many survivors, the experience of domestic violence, rape and other forms of gender violence are bound up with systems of incarceration and police violence." The organization holds that for Black, Native, and immigrant survivors in particular, "being controlled by police, prosecutors, judges, immigration enforcement, homeland security, detention centers and prisons is often integrated with the experience of domestic violence and sexual assault."[89]

Richie points out that we live in a context in which there is mass incarceration of "women from low-income communities who break laws in order to survive abusive relationships," and where they are punished for "the so-called deviant behavior that women engage in to cope with the devastation that they face."[90] The fact that so much police violence takes place in response to calls for help sends a message that no help is coming, and perhaps violence and punishment await, particularly if a woman acts in her own defense. Black women, then, become self-policing subjects in the face of intimate physical and sexual violence—fully aware that police punish Black women when they help themselves in the face of intimate partner violence and therefore self-restrained.

Heartbreakingly, what might be called the "sexual assault to prison pipeline" is often preceded by "the sexual assault to juvenile detention pipeline." Malika Saada Saar and her colleagues in the Human Rights Project for Girls write: "The most common crimes for which girls are arrested—including running away, substance abuse, and truancy—are also the most common symptoms of abuse. Indeed, child sexual abuse experts list these behaviors as warning signs that an adolescent has been abused and needs therapeutic intervention."[91]

The police violence Black women experience does not simply take place within the private sphere; it is most often directly connected to the feminized domain of intimacy. State violence in this domain becomes an extension of—a continuation of—intimate partner violence and sexual assault. The privacy of police violence against Black women not only makes it unlikely to be viewed by unrelated and presumably impartial others, as was the case with George Floyd; it makes the violence harder to "see" in other ways as well. The association of the surrounding context, the intimate sphere, with sex, sexuality, and intimacy functions to obscure violence that is already obscured by virtue of its association with criminality. The hermeneutical impact of both the criminalization of survivors and the private circumstances of the violence and death they experience is considerable, and this aids the Black feminine body project, both the ongoing production of assaulted, stressed, and weathered bodies and the interpretation of the meaning of the bodies of the Black female assaulted and, eventually, the Black female dead.

Regarding the necropolitics at play here, as Mbembe says, the meaning of death emerges through interpretations of embodiment—of who dies, who kills, and who is targeted for death. The meaning of violence against Black women, of their deaths, emerges through interpretations of embodiment inflected through the sphere of intimate relations. The women are hurt and killed by partners or police, the latter of whom are ostensibly there to help. The injuries and deaths occur in private; they are connected to the realm of sex and sexuality, to heated, irrational, and overly emotional domestic disputes—he said, she said, so who can really say?—often in contexts of nonnormative family formation, and therefore they do not fit the standard (masculinist) conception of racist violence, even though structural racism is a significant factor. But they also do not fit the standard conception of intimate partner violence. Conservative antiviolence activists have defined the male violence victim as a middle-class and white woman, and they have hailed the police, the courts, and prisons as that woman's protectors. Exactly how ungrateful are these Black women not to ask for and accept the help of these good men coming to rescue them? Why don't they cooperate and help to prosecute these violent men when offered a chance to do so?

The often young, poor, and Black female corpses of Richie's concern are interpreted as nonnormative at best, and as criminals at worst—but always as somehow deserving of their deaths, not as victims of male violence. Tragically, before the women are ultimately killed, they confront, again, ostensibly biopolitical agencies that render them little aid and, through their inaction, also ultimately help to produce the meaning of their corpses. Police sins of omission and commission, alongside the broader lack of institutional support, produces Black feminine embodiment as assaulted and assaultable, raped and rapeable, criminal, and eliminable. The women's punishment, their criminalization, in the wake of male abuse determines the meaning and interpretation of their subsequent deaths at the hands of intimate partners. Police, then, help to produce the abused dead Black woman as abusable, as criminal, as deserving of her death.

Confronting the Lady Leviathan and Racialized Modern Power

To understand the full scope of what the above means for political theorists, I want to consider the challenge it presents to the feminist critique of modern sovereignty presented by Moira Gatens and the feminist critique of embodiment and power presented by Sandra Bartky. Here, I point to how Crenshaw, Ritchie, Kaba, and Richie's arguments, and the arguments of other intersectional and abolitionist theorists, can enrich feminist political theory.

Feminist thinkers have noted that while Thomas Hobbes was concerned about the dangers posed by and to the body in a world of rough equality, he was expressly concerned with male embodiment, and that his awareness of the threats posed by embodied desires did little to guarantee the equitable treatment of women. Moira Gatens, for example, has argued that Hobbes privileged the concerns of the male body over those of the female body and sought to create an all-powerful state to protect and enhance the power and safety of men. Indeed, Hobbes's idea of the body politic is as a work of "creative artifice" analogous to the creation of man by God; here, Hobbes explicitly uses the image of the male body. As well, feminist scholars have pointed out that the modern body politic is more than symbolically male; it is literally so. By using male bodies as models for the lives its legal and political arrangements are designed to enhance and protect, modern political systems marginalize the concerns of women. Modern states, Gatens points out, have given little attention to abortion, gender-based violence, rape, and maternal allowances, for example.[92]

Intersectional feminist thinkers have analyzed how recent feminist-led attempts to correct these sovereign omissions have played out in the lives of Black women. When, as a result of feminist movement in the United States, activist institutions, police, and the courts began to address issues such as rape and intimate partner violence, for example, they did so under the assumption that the woman to be protected was white. Crenshaw, in one of two articles in which she defined and outlined the concept of intersectionality, demonstrated how antiviolence crisis centers were not designed to meet the most pressing needs of Black survivors of male violence, who, because of housing segregation and broader societal discrimination, were more likely to have acute housing needs after an assault. Centers directed resources not to these needs but toward counseling survivors through the criminal trials of their assailants. These resources were of little help to Black survivors, whose cases were rarely prosecuted due to systemic racism.[93]

Intersectional abolitionist feminists like Richie have taken Crenshaw's original critique of the criminal justice system further. Richie argues that the dominant, conservative arm of the antiviolence movement has grown too close to the state and now performs key ideological and material work to enhance state power. This relationship bred a carceral feminist state-building project that endangers poor women, women of color, and particularly Black women. In practice, the laws and policies that supposedly protect "women" from male violence only protect certain white women from that violence, and they do so at the expense of increased state and interpersonal violence against Black women and the loss of Black female life.[94]

Abolition feminists hold that police do not provide ameliorative aid to marginalized victims of male violence and are, in fact, major sources of violence against them. Indeed, Richie argues that, given the significant role of police in violence against marginalized women, feminists must expand the conception of gender-based violence beyond the narrow framing that circulates in the media and popular culture to include police violence against Black women, and that they must confront the surrounding activist inaction in response to these forms of male violence against Black women and the broader punitive institutional context in which this violence occurs which punishes and dissuades Black female defensive action. In the account Richie presents, Black women suffer from what Kristie Dotson has named "second order epistemic oppression" and what Miranda Fricker has termed "hermeneutical injustice," as in "the prevailing analysis and dominant rhetoric . . . about violence, race, class, gender and sexuality conspire to limit the comprehension of the experience of male violence for black women."[95] Richie faults the influential—and, I argue, state-capacity-building—carceral wing of the anti-gender-based violence movement, which she says, among other things, "helped to create a simplistic and narrow understanding of violence against women, so that many black women and their experiences aren't included in the definition." She explains: "The success of the anti-violence movement... has brought with it unintended negative consequences for women whose experience of male violence does not fit within the dominant paradigm with which the anti-violence movement established its credibility." Black women's experiences of state violence offer, she says, "a way to broaden our understanding of violence against women of color and to problematize the evolution of anti-violence work in the United States."[96]

Police, in her account, are not protecting Black women from male violence; they are a part of that violence, and they and the surrounding somehow at once inactive and punitive institutional context of which they are a part—a context that she has named the "prison nation"—further endanger the lives of Black women. As Richie says, then, "there is evidence that *some* women (read: middle-class white women) are safer in 2012 than they were twenty-five years earlier because of the success of the antiviolence movement in changing policy and because of America's growing prison nation and the concurrent focus on punishment in the United States. At the same time, there is growing concern about women with less power who are in as much danger as ever, precisely because of the ideological and strategic direction the antiviolence movement has taken during the buildup of America's prison nation."[97] Richie argues, then, that feminists must attend not only to the (structurally produced) more numerous, brutal, and socially consequential physical and sexual assaults Black women experience at the hands of intimate partners and community members, but also to the violence they are subject to at the hands of state agents, including their physical and sexual exploitation by police officers and the physical and sexual violence they experience in state custody.

Elizabeth Hinton presents an account of the expansion of police authority and budgets as an executive-led project beginning with the Johnson administration that is consistent with older centralized accounts of power's emanation, of the state claiming new authority over the lives of its subjects, and through which an emerging punitive response to social problems that does not directly kill Black women might be framed (incorrectly) as simply letting Black women live while making Black men die.[98] Conservative feminists lobbied congressional lawmakers, who in turn made law. But power is not always unitary, and police are paradigmatic examples of a Foucauldian conception of power. Therefore, it is also instructive to think of the direct nonlethal force and violence, including sexual violence, to which police subject Black women not solely in relation to the destructive force of an emergent Lady Leviathan but also as the flip side of feminine Foucauldian normalization—as necropolitical, but aimed at producing not death but a specific form of Black feminine embodiment, as assaulted and assaultable, raped and rapeable, even as it facilitates and ultimately brings about Black women's disproportionate premature deaths.

Racism is very much an embodied phenomenon. The early twentieth century saw the debunking of biological conceptions of race. Yet the Covid-19 pandemic has highlighted how the structures of modernity continue to make racism an embodied, biological phenomenon. The biological impact of racialized exposure to particulate matter is one example of how racism becomes embodied.[99] We know, as well, that Black women evince the most significant embodied effects of racist misrecognition. Geronimus's concept of "weathering" is again instructive, as Geronimus argues that Blacks experience early health deterioration as a consequence of the cumulative impact of repeated experience with social or economic adversity and political marginalization.[100] Disproportionate institutional and interpersonal violence surely qualifies as "acute and chronic stressors," and self-regulation in a context in which defensive actions are punished surely qualifies as "high effort coping." Therefore, we should expect these conditions to produce the disproportionate physiological deterioration Geronimus has observed. Police, through inaction and action, "weather" the Black female body.[101]

With this in mind, we can turn to the work of feminist Foucauldians. Sandra Bartky sought to explain how a deinstitutionalized and dispersed power produced conformity to a normative feminine body type and a desire to conform. Bartky was puzzled that in a world in which women had more freedom than ever before, more access to paid work, and more sexual liberty, modern power still succeeded in producing "properly embodied femininity," "a practiced and subjected" feminine body of a certain size and configuration, trained in a repertoire of gestures, both in movement and at rest, and trained to display the surface of the body as primarily ornamental. Bartky suggests that women take up feminine bodily practices because a "panoptical male connoisseur resides in the consciousness of most women." "Woman," she says, "lives her body as seen by another, by an anonymous patriarchal other." And while Foucault's account concentrates on the power vested in disciplinary institutions, Bartky suggests women are disciplined by a deinstitutionalized and dispersed panoptical gaze. For Bartky, a woman who wears makeup and watches what she eats has much in common with the inmate of the panopticon. She is a self-policing subject. Her self-surveillance is a form of patriarchal discipline.[102]

Black women's distance from normative white femininity makes their efforts regarding the above not only more time-consuming and more expensive in a colonial marketplace not designed to serve them, but also more destined to fail—or, since all feminine projects ultimately fail, to fail more spectacularly. Yet we know from Black feminist historical accounts of Black women's experiences in the period of enslavement and the Jim Crow era that modern power's preferred forms of Black feminine embodiment and the methods used to obtain said embodiment were quite different. Black women were never understood to be primarily ornamental, for example.

Mbembe reminds us, however, that multiple power formations originated in modernity, and this should inform our account of Black women's experience of power. Black women are, indeed, no longer enslaved, no longer subjects of a separate, unequal system of law, and so, as Bartky says, have more formal freedom, including freedom from legal sexual exploitation and now formal equality. They also have formal access to all paid work, though their "productive" labor is nothing new. These changes have done little, however, to alter the production of "properly embodied Black femininity" as an assaulted and frequently terrorized body. Black women have formal freedom from sexual violence and assault and yet are among the most frequent subjects of sexual violence and assault. Because the forces that operate to produce this body are destructive as well as productive, disabling of intimacy even as they enable other forms of often criminalized intimacy, and often leading to premature death when they do not lead to immediate death, this power formation is something closer to necropower than biopolitical normalization, though still ultimately a perverse mix of the two.

The contemporary power that produces "properly embodied Black femininity" is both vested in disciplinary institutions and deinstitutionalized, and therefore vested in the wider population. This power is dispersed throughout a population authorized through relative impunity to commit frequent, brutal, and consequential violence against Black women—more violence than against any other group with the possible exception of Native women, who are themselves the objects of ongoing settler colonial violence. The institutionalized and dispersed powers are mutually reinforcing; they are often continuous. The power that can "make (men) die" enables and affirms the deinstitutionalized power—through (its continuation of male) violence and its (support for conservative antiviolence) discourse, its police action and activist inaction—thereby heightening Black women's exposure to death, even as it directly assaults and ultimately weathers them, producing properly embodied Black femininity. This heightened exposure can be traced to the failures, omissions, and externalities of white feminist state-building—the expansion of state capacities regarding regulation of the sphere of intimate relations that have come as a result of a particular kind of feminist movement and from the cooperation of conservative antiviolence activists and the state.

Bartky's account of patriarchal power is insufficient to account for the power the feminine descendants of plantation inhabitants confront today. Modernity's preferred forms of Black feminine embodiment were and are different, and so are the methods used to obtain them. Black women lived under two regimes—the slave regime and Jim Crow—in which sexual assault was the normative mode of sexual relations, and rape was used as a systematic weapon of gendered racial subordination and subjection.[103] Though Black women are no longer enslaved, their formal equality has done little to change the production of "properly embodied Black femininity." Black women inhabit a still-rapeable body, a body disproportionately subject to institutionalized and deinstitutionalized male violence. This body is also self-regulating, as every time Black women do not call for help in situations of male violence—either out of fear of what will happen to themselves or to their families—they are self-policing subjects. The body has internalized the violent regime that subjects it and creates it as the proper object of assault. This has fatal consequences.

2

Taming the Lady Leviathan, Tending the Grassroots

Black Women Confront Black Femicide

While Black femicide is a national problem, the phenomenon is particularly acute in the Midwest, which has higher rates of Black female murder than the South, West, or Northeast. In an effort to understand the scope of the problem and develop solutions, Minnesota legislators and activists established the Missing and Murdered African American Women Task Force in 2021.[1] The task force issued its final report in December 2022.[2]

The report drew attention to the specific stereotypes that distort the public perception of Black women and girls and highlighted four key areas that contributed to violence against them: work and wages, housing, health, and the criminal justice system. It recommended the establishment of the Missing and Murdered African American Women Office; the creation and funding of spaces and resources targeted at saving Black women and girls; the development of culturally appropriate antiracist training and education for "system professionals"; training and hiring that incentivized Black employment in the system; the improvement of interagency coordination to make services more accessible and responsive; and the identification and implementation of "better pathways for long-term housing."[3] This final recommendation is one on which the report's authors and the survivors they interviewed were in alignment. The women interviewed identified housing as "one of the main areas . . . contributing to their vulnerability to violence" and as a "barrier to accessing resources."[4]

Yet violence survivors interviewed for the report also called attention to another important, and often overlooked, resource in addressing the problem: Black women themselves. While the report's authors acknowledged the importance of recruiting and retaining Black women into state programs,

The Labors of Resurrection. Shatema Threadcraft, Oxford University Press. © Oxford University Press (2025).
DOI: 10.1093/9780197758618.003.0003

the survivors favored direct resource transfers to grassroots and even improvised community-based Black female–led initiatives. "They described how Black women and girls support each other in crises," the report explains, "often much better than systems do." Funding for grassroots initiatives would allow women to "organize mutual aid and secure spaces that fit their needs based on their shared experiences." In the Black community organizations they were familiar with, Black survivors were "doing the work" without the resources afforded to state agencies and nonprofits, and the women interviewed wanted the state "to direct funding to folks who are embedded in communities and trusted."[5]

In response to the report, in 2023 Representative Ruth Richardson authored HF55 to establish the Office of Missing and Murdered African American Women and Girls, the first such office in the nation. Representative Richardson's initiative is noteworthy for pioneering an official response to the problem of Black women's disproportionate death in the form of an office dedicated to studying and responding to it. Yet, when asked, the survivors themselves pointed researchers in a different direction, toward mutual aid. In so doing they highlighted an important strain in the tradition of Black women's responses to disproportionate Black death and Black femicide in particular.

Contemporary activists confronting Black femicide as well as the dearth of state and community responses to disproportionate violence against Black women have taken a variety of approaches, including advocating for police and media reform, engaging in independent media and data activism, and providing armed self-defense training services with the expressed goal of cultivating survivors' and potential survivors' capacities for self-help, as well as calling for and facilitating community accountability mechanisms in the pursuit of transformative justice alongside mutual aid. This chapter surveys these responses to highlight the vibrant, yet under-recognized organizing work, to draw attention to their connections to and departures from the Black female necromantics I discuss in later chapters and thereby place contemporary efforts within a lineage of Black female death work. The media and data activists, of course, follow a path forged by Wells into which Smith made significant innovative inroads. Wells also advocated armed self-defense and pledged to "sell her life as dearly as possible." Abolition feminist efforts to enact transformative justice via mutual aid, coupled with their critiques of the police, policing, and incarceration as drivers of violence against

Black and other marginalized women, echo the theory and practice of Smith and Prescod, respectively.

The chapter ends with a discussion of Kimberlé Crenshaw's #SayHerName campaign. Crenshaw, like Prescod and contemporary abolition feminists, sees police, policing, and incarceration as key drivers of violence against Black women, yet she has stopped short of calling for the abolition of police. The #SayHerName campaign has called on Black female survivors of violence and the families of women who have not survived to share their stories of abuse in an effort to mobilize greater numbers of Black community members to action regarding this disproportionate violence and death. Indeed, Crenshaw is not alone among contemporary activists in drawing attention to the need for storytelling. I draw attention to Crenshaw because storytelling is central to her analysis and I, too, believe that stories have an important role to play in addressing violence and indeed in our multiracial democracies haunted by the specter of premature Black death. Yet I hold that we must consider Crenshaw's call alongside the work of W. E. B. Du Bois and Toni Morrison, two thinkers who wrote powerfully and eloquently regarding Black death and democracy, the latter of whom provides a model for thinking about storytelling in the service of confronting Black femicide and, alongside Wells, Till-Bradley, Barfield, Smith, and Prescod, a model for building much needed political community with the dead. I turn to their work in the coming chapters.

The women profiled below represent a diverse collection of activists and organizations confronting what I understand as the phenomenon of Black femicide. That is, they agree that the disproportionate violence and death to which Black women are subject is a problem and have mobilized to combat it, but I am no way arguing that they are in agreement on what exactly that problem is—that it is Black femicide, for example—or its root causes. Their understandings of how racialized misogyny factors into the disproportionate murders are diverse, yet all hold that interpersonal and/or institutionalized racialized misogyny as well as how these phenomena interact with other entrenched social hierarchies play a role in the disproportionate murder of Black women. The Black and Missing Foundation, Inc., for example, is explicit about how racist-sexist stereotypes underlie police and media inaction. Rosa Page coined the term "black femicide" and understands the phenomenon much as Smith and I do. Abolitionists, by contrast, while recognizing pervasive racist, sexist, classist, homophobic, transphobic, and whorephobic disdain for Black women, would attribute much of the blame for disproportionate violence and death to police, policing, and prisons and our increasingly punitive society.

Police and Media Reform: The Black and Missing Foundation

On May 27, 2004, twenty-four-year-old Tamika Huston went missing from her home in Spartanburg, South Carolina. Derrica Wilson, who had worked in law enforcement, and her sister-in-law Natalie Wilson, a public relations expert, took an interest in the case. They noted how fiercely Huston's aunt, Rebekah Howard, worked to find Tamika, pitching the case to *America's Most Wanted*, *Dateline NBC*, and *USA Today* without success. The national media remained focused on cases like those of missing white women like Natalee Holloway and Laci Peterson. The women would go on to found the Black and Missing Foundation (BAMFI) in 2008 to ensure that "black and other people reported missing" would not "slip through the cracks." The foundation works to raise awareness of cases and to "help families navigate police and the media—two spaces that can be hostile for people of color." Specifically, it is "committed to removing barriers and eradicating the stereotypes and narratives surrounding our missing with law enforcement and the media." While the organization does public awareness campaigns and provides a forum for the loved ones of missing persons to spread "word of their disappearance, with pictures and profiles of missing individuals," it is most focused on media and police reform, and frankly, media reform in the service of police reform.[6] And while the organization works for robust investigations of all the Black missing, its founders were first mobilized by the disappearance of a Black woman. They are particularly attuned to how missing Black women and girls are characterized, to how police officers' tendency to characterize Black girls as runaways makes them vulnerable to sex trafficking.

BAMFI wants to challenge what it sees as the predominant stereotypes regarding the Black missing—"the runaway child, the thug or criminal, and the undeserving poor." It has called attention to disparities in Amber Alerts issued for Black and non-Black children, noting that Black children are more likely to be classified as runaways, with few resources devoted to their return. Wilson testified before Congress in a hearing on "The Neglected Epidemic of Missing BIPOC Women and Girls" as to how investigations into missing

Black people, particularly missing Black women and girls, are hindered by racist and racialized sexist stereotypes: "When children of color go missing, they are often stereotyped by law enforcement as runaways. From our interactions with families, we find that nine out of 10 children of color missing are classified as runaways. If you are classified as a runaway, you don't get the amber alert or any media attention at all. There is no urgency to find them. . . . We must remember that these children are minors and stop adultifying them. Even if they did run away, they are still children who need to be found. Sadly, black girls are more often victims of sex trafficking and not runaways." Wilson continued:

> With missing adults, particularly Black women and girls, they're often not viewed as victims. This stigma hampers efforts to find them because there's a mindset that their actions or deviant behavior led to their disappearance. These individuals are viewed as a burden to society and on our tax dollars, and we must not forget they are our daughters and mothers. In our nearly 14 years as an organization, we have seen firsthand how our nation has become de-sensitized to the plight of missing people of color who come from marginalized communities. The perception is when someone of color is reported missing, no one will miss them, so why dedicate the resources to finding them. Race shouldn't be a barrier to media coverage and law enforcement support[7]

Speaking to Aman Nawaz on *PBS NewsHour* after a Black woman escaped a serial killer in Kansas City—confirming what community members suspected and reported, but police dismissed—Wilson said: "Most recently, we had a case out of Fort Worth, TX, and a mother whose daughter was missing. She went to law enforcement. And the officer said, 'How do we know that your daughter is not laid up with some man?' And how disheartening and disrespectful is that?"[8]

Wilson emphasized the importance of the media in her remarks before Congress, pointing out that people of color make up 40 percent of those missing, but their stories are "rarely told" in the media, receiving only 7 percent of national coverage, while their families struggle to claim "law enforcement resources." "We can all name Gabby Petito, Natalee Holloway, Chandra Levy, and many other white women who have gone missing," Wilson said, "but can any of you name a person of color that has garnered national media coverage?" When the Black missing do receive coverage, the efforts are often successful: "Within minutes of a segment airing on The View, we received a tip that led directly to a missing child."

While BAMFI is very much concerned with the lack of media amplification of Black disappearances—and they argue that diversifying newsrooms will help mitigate disparities in media coverage—they see greater cooperation from law enforcement as the key to ensuring Black women's safety. A major organizational goal is to change the hearts and minds of law enforcement so that police direct more resources toward the Black missing. The organization understands the media as key to a robust law enforcement response. As Wilson says, "Media coverage is important because it alerts the community that someone is missing, but it also adds pressure to law enforcement to add resources to the case, which increases the chance of recovery."[9] As Wilson would go on to tell *NewsHour*, "We believe that these law enforcement officers need better training and they need sensitivity training, because these, again, are missing, valuable members of our community. . . . Are officers really conducting a thorough investigation, or are they allowing their biases to cloud the case? In some instances, officers aren't even taking a police report."[10] Still, the organization's founders remain optimistic that police can change and come to value Black (female) life.

Many of the activists and entrepreneurs profiled below share Smith's more pessimistic view of law enforcement, the media, or, in the case of Rosa Page, institutionalized data collection, and often take a more antagonistic approach to these institutions or simply ignore them.

Media Activism

There are also anti–Black femicide activists who, faced with an institution like the mainstream media—an institution that continues, as Smith said, to be "typically racist"—forgo reform in favor of institutional bypass. The work of Erica Marie Rivers offers a case in point. Rivers asks, "Why is it that, according to the National Crime Information Center of the FBI, approximately 33 percent of people reported missing are Black, but that isn't reflective of the evening news?" She points out that "The families are going to the police, we are saying hey, listen to us, we are writing to media outlets, but nobody puts us on the front page."[11] In response to this disparity, in 2018 the "journalist turned activist" began to tell the stories of missing and murdered Black women and girls, both on social media and on her website, Our

Black Girls. The site, she says, "centers on the often-untold stories of Black girls and women who have gone missing or, in some cases, were found dead under mysterious circumstances." Significantly, Our Black Girls wants not only to amplify the cases of missing Black women but to contextualize them. Rivers writes:

> The women in these stories I report are more than the highlight clip on the ten o'clock news. These *are and were* our sisters, many of whom endured deception and/or violence. We shouldn't sweep their stories under the rug and move on to the next topic. We need to remember what they went through in order to change patterns of behavior. We need to teach our children to protect themselves from predators who seek to do them harm. We need to teach each other how to avoid those who whisper sweet nothings in our ears but also use emotional or physical abuse to control us. We need to recognize that all that glitters isn't gold. We need to highlight stories of our missing Black Girls because their stories go under-reported in the media—if they're reported at all. We cannot control the actions of those who are set in their diabolical ways, but we can learn from one another's experiences.
>
> We need to bring awareness to the stories of Black girls who have been mistreated, are missing and who have been murdered because they matter. Their lives matter. They are real people, not just sensationalized news bulletins. Let's keep their stories alive. . . . This is a grassroots website that is birthed out of a heartfelt desire to make sure that these women who are underrepresented, aren't forgotten. We have to look out for one another, and this is my way of making sure my sisters' voices are heard.[12]

In this passage, Rivers presents four key themes: evil, the inherent value of Black female life alongside the instrumental value of Black female death, Black woman-facilitated self-help, and comprehensive, non-sensationalized storytelling both to keep the women present with us, to "keep their stories alive," and also as part of facilitated self-help. First, there is evil in the world. Black women live in a context of violence and deception, wherein they are mistreated and "cannot control the actions of those who are set in their diabolical ways." Second, the women who do not survive these violent, deceptive, diabolical circumstances, "they matter." Though their lives have inherent value, they also serve as a lesson to us, as "we can learn from one another's experiences," "in order to change patterns of behavior." This, then, is a call for Black women to practice self-help in their violent worlds, but also to teach young women and one another. Finally, we must "keep their stories alive," and Rivers herself created the site to ensure that these women, who are both sensationalized and under-represented in the media, are not forgotten. We must take the time to reflect on their lives and deaths and not "sweep their stories under the rug and move on to the next topic." Rivers's independent media activism, ultimately, is in the service of self-help and a somewhat disaggregated, atomized conception of mutual aid.

Black Girl Tragic, a play on the phrase "Black Girl Magic," provides another example of activist media response: "Black Girl Tragic is an online space to tell stories of girls and women of color who have had their lives cut short by violence, whether inflicted on self or by others. We aim simply to tell stories. . . . The site arose from a need to disrupt the 24/7 news cycle, which focuses on one crisis and moves to another. Our goal at Black Girl Tragic is to highlight the discrimination, abuse, mistreatment, unfairness and tragedy inflicted upon women of color throughout the diaspora."[13] Again, Black women live in a global diasporic context of discrimination, abuse, mistreatment, unfairness, and tragedy. The site tells stories in an effort to disrupt sensationalized media accounts, which present life as a decontextualized series of crises.

Data Activism

Despite what you may have heard, Black women count and there are Black women who count. Black femicide activist Rosa Page also believes in the power of stories, but her work takes a different form in its emphasis on data. Specifically, she collects what Catherine D'Ignazio refers to as "counterdata," that is, data that is not collected by formal institutions and is used to serve populations that have been objectified by such data collection historically. This is "data in the service of democratic dissent." D'Ignazio reports that "more than 150 grassroots organizations and individuals across the Americas have turned to counterdata science to document and challenge feminicide and fatal gender-related violence." She counts Rosa Page among them.[14] Page's counterdata work makes her a direct political descendant of Ida B. Wells and Barbara Smith.

Page is credited with coining the term "Black femicide."[15] Based in Arkansas, Page is the mother of four daughters and has worked as a nurse, including as an ER nurse, for over thirty years. In the course of her work, she became increasingly alarmed at the rate of death for Black women. In 2015, she encountered an FBI statistic that claimed that a woman was killed every nineteen hours. She was convinced this number was incorrect, particularly for Black women. And it wasn't only the data that concerned Page. The *Washington Post* reported, "She also couldn't understand why it wasn't easier to find clear, accessible information about the victims, the names and stories of the women and girls were scattered across news sites and often squeezed into briefs that said little about them." So Page resolved to change that by collecting her own data. She founded "Black Femicide-US" in 2015 and began "scouring police websites, media homepages and online sites that track homicides for the names and photos of Black women and girls." Page compiled this information on the Twitter account "Black Femicide—America" and the Facebook page "Black Femicide—U.S."[16] She calculated that a Black woman was killed every nine hours in 2015. The FBI would later confirm her suspicion that Black women were being killed at a much higher rate than women of other groups.[17] By 2020, she estimated that a Black woman was killed every six hours, and she started the hashtag #every6hours. Page says that she received a lot of pushback about this claim, but on September 28, 2021, the FBI corroborated the statistic. Page's work to challenge formal data, and her public call to have the record corrected, revealed what D'Ignazio refers to as "missing data" about femicide in the United States, that is, "those data that are neglected to be prioritized, collected, maintained and published despite demands." "Missing data is political," she says, as "it is missing precisely because there is a demand that it be produced."[18]

Page's work is similar to the efforts of other women around the world who become convinced that official data does not tell the whole story and take matters into their own hands. Carmen Castello, a retired social worker in Puerto Rico, is another case in point. Castello began scouring lesser-known news sources to track women's murders. She was contacted by the organization Proyecto Matria and Kilometro Cero, which was also interested in the problem. The organizations verified her data, triangulated it with official records, and determined that the Puerto Rican officials undercounted women's deaths by a third.[19]

Page has encountered widespread resistance to the term "femicide" and to an understanding of so-called relationship violence as rooted in a hatred of women. She laments the fact that we do not generally conceive of men who kill women as committing hate crimes and, relatedly, that the US government does not recognize femicide as an official cause of death. Yet men who kill women are rarely violent toward other men, she argues, but will have had violent incidents with mothers, sisters, and female coworkers. Context matters. Page holds that if researchers abandon the relationship-violence framing and simply zoom out from an incident of fatal violence within an intimate relationship to the wider context of the killer's life, the death itself begins to look much more like a hate crime.[20]

Page's research has yielded other significant insights, including a phenomenon at the intersection of intimate partner violence and mass violence that further buttresses her claims regarding the failure to name what are pervasive misogynistic hate crimes. We know that most mass violence, unlike the public mass violence events that receive the most attention, involves a current or former male partner killing a female partner or ex and others in a home. Page says that her research reveals that within these incidents, the perpetrator will frequently kill all the femme folk in the home and only injure masculine folk in non-life-threatening ways.[21]

She is vocal about misogyny in Black communities and in US society at large. (In fact, Page has gone so far as to say that Black cultural misogyny is responsible for disproportionate Black femicide, because Black communities do not value Black women as much as they value Black men—but this, of course, would not make Black communities unique.) This misogyny, Page says, is demonstrated in the fact that the deaths of women and girls count less. They are certainly *counted* less: "As Black women, we're truly not valued. Whether we're talking about within or outside of the community. We're just seen as caretakers of others. . . . Our worth is based on how much we can take, being strong, who we're taking care of. We're just seen as the workhorses of the community." In fact, Page characterizes Black America as a dystopian matriarchy—an incredible term—in which Black women are the backbone of the community and do the work, but their lives are not thought of as equally valuable relative to those of Black men. Consciously or not, Black women internalize this role and are willing to sacrifice themselves in order to avoid ending or even disrupting Black male life. They have internalized the community norm that male life is more valuable—that we can't have another Black man killed by police or another Black man in jail—at the expense of the women's own lives, safety, and security.[22]

Regarding the police and the media, Page represents something of a split case. She believes that a media landscape dominated by white men will never cover the problem of Black femicide adequately. She therefore employs a form of self-help, working to collect and contextualize the data in one place. This self-help is connected to a lobbying effort aimed at correcting the official record. Page also sees law enforcement as part of the problem, as the police, like society at large, tend to view intimate partner violence through an individualistic lens, as something that happens when a couple has problems and not the consequence of a man enacting misogynistic violence, violence that targets only the women in his life. The police often encourage couples to cool off and patch things up, she says. But despite her understanding of law enforcement's systemic issues, Page has kept her faith in the institution, as she believes that we cannot stop the phenomenon of Black femicide without the assistance of law enforcement.[23]

trina reynolds-tyler is a native of the South Side of Chicago, an abolitionist and trained restorative justice practitioner. She is a (counter)data scientist, and thus in a direct line of descent from Wells through Smith, who centers the practice of narrative justice in her research as data director at the Invisible Institute, as well as a Pulitzer Prize–winning journalist. reynolds-tyler leads the team behind "Beneath the Surface," a data science project that uses narrative justice and machine learning in an effort to better understand how marginalized communities experience police violence and "investigates the intersections of gender-based violence and policing." The "Beyond the Surface" project is undertaken by "a team of data analysts, journalists, artists, organizers and survivors in Chicago who investigate state violence against Black women and girls. Through our data science and narrative justice practices, we are working to expand the public conversation about unconstitutional policing beyond the fatal shootings of Black men." The project critiques the practice of using "primary complaint" categories in Chicago Police Department (CPD) data collection regarding police misconduct, arguing that "Basic descriptive statistics about the experiences of Black women and trans people are incomplete or missing entirely from the public discourse about police violence. When someone files a complaint, although there may have been multiple allegations reported, the complaint receives a primary complaint category determined by the person intaking the complaint. A complaint may be primarily categorized as an 'illegal search' for example, when the underlying narrative also contains an allegation of sexual violence. . . . This practice veils information about sexual violence in common analysis of police misconduct."[24]

reynolds-tyler worked with Sarah Conway of the City Bureau on the Pulitzer Prize–winning "Missing in Chicago" investigation of the CPD's handling of missing persons cases. The investigation states that "Chicago's missing person crisis is a Black issue." Two-thirds of all missing persons in Chicago are Black and, according to police data, Black women are 30 percent of missing persons despite comprising 2 percent of the city's population. They reported: "From 2000 to 2021, Chicago Police categorized 99.8 percent of missing person cases as 'not criminal in nature.' Our investigation calls this number into question. Our reports found 11 missing persons cases that the department listed as 'closed-non-criminal' even though the victim had been murdered." More broadly, they reported:

> While police officials have publicly claimed that services for families are equal and fair across race and ZIP codes, massive gaps in missing persons data make it impossible to prove, according to a two-year investigation by City Bureau and the Invisible Institute. Instead, interviews with current and former police officers, national experts, and researchers, along with dozens of anecdotes from impacted family members, reveal a pattern of neglect, incompetence, and illegal behavior from police officers in missing person cases. Under Illinois law and Chicago police policy, police officers cannot deny a missing person report for any reason. However, reporters found dozens of people who say they were told to wait, or outright denied the ability to file a report—delaying investigations during the critical early hours of missingness.
>
> Families of the missing say that police officers are dismissive of their cases, neglect their investigations, and stigmatize their loved ones—including multiple cases where police declined to investigate key leads or lost evidence, leaving families to conduct their own searches.
>
> Analyzing police data on missing person cases from 2000 to 2021, reporters found discrepancies that call into question the department's data-keeping practices. Current and former police officers say that the missing person report is one of the last remaining paper reports used by Chicago police. Police records also show that, from 2017 to 2021, a little over 45 percent of cases are missing a key data point about the time and date police arrived to investigate these cases. And reporters identified multiple cases that ended in homicide that were marked 'non-criminal' in the data—as well as four cases where detectives explicitly noted that the missing person had returned home, despite family members saying their loved ones never returned home alive.[25]

Activists like Page and reynolds-tyler do the hard and necessary work of holding official institutions accountable regarding their data collection practices.

Armed Self-Defense

In late 2022, the now defunct Instagram page "BlackFemicide US," run by Rosa Page, reposted a link advertising the "Atlanta Women's Self Defense Retreat, Part 3." The retreat was organized by My Sister's Keeper Defense and was to be held in Atlanta, September 30–October 2, 2022. The event would go on to sell out. The link, posted July 14, 2022, advertised the following: "Our 3rd all-inclusive retreat was created for women who want to learn how to thrive and survive with self-defense, mental wellness, and survival skills. Day 1 will start with our Sister Discovery Brunch, then you'll learn resilience techniques, emergency preparedness and vehicle maintenance. Day 2 will cover life skills, meditation and first aid/stop the bleed. Day 3 we'll visit the gun range to learn firearm shooting fundamentals and end with our Sister Send Off Lunch."

In January 2017, the group's founder, army veteran Marchell "Tig" Davis, received 3,000 responses to her first Facebook ad. Her first class sold out in three days, the second sold out the same day, and by February 2017 classes were selling out a month in advance. Five years later she began hosting retreats where "students learn vehicle maintenance like changing a tire and checking oil, resilience skills, candle making, yoga, first aid/stop the bleed, how to build a go-bag and firearm shooting fundamentals." Davis explains: "I'm a survivor of sexual assault and domestic violence and those experiences changed my perspective of personal safety. I realized I had to become my own savior. I started teaching other women how to defend themselves using firearms. My ultimate goal is to teach 1 million women how to defend themselves with firearms."[26] Davis is absolutely clear about her mission: "As a domestic abuse and sexual assault survivor, I think it's important that women feel like they're in control of their safety. My Sister's Keeper Defense is here to empower women and make sure that no one else becomes a victim."[27]

One of Davis's most significant contributions was her creation of the National Black Self Defense Directory, "a directory of Black owned firearm instruction companies, gun ranges and authorized firearm dealers (FFL)." *Black Gun Owners* Magazine reported that the database contained "a consistently updated list of quality instructors." It noted that "[t]he directory is categorized by women firearms instructors (red), coed firearms instruction businesses (black), FFL's and gun ranges (green) and firearms gear and accessories (grey)."[28] The directory came into being because a Black female survivor believed that Black women needed firearms training for their defense. The directory contained over 370 Black-owned self-defense companies, and, indeed highlights the eighty-two companies owned by women. Many of the female founders are veterans and retired police officers, but there are also counselors, nurses, and even a doula—which should not be surprising, given that pregnancy and postpartum are particularly dangerous periods in a Black woman's life, the times when they are most likely to die by gun violence.

The reasons women articulate for providing self-defense training deserve consideration. Every entrepreneur made reference to the context of pervasive violence in which their Black female clientele must operate. Companies owned by Black women often market themselves as expressly serving women and modeling a different kind of gun owner so that women may come to see themselves as people who are comfortable with firearms. She Loaded is one such company: "She Loaded was created to equip the everyday woman with self-defense devices for personal protection," its website states.[29] Likewise, Avery Skipalis of Skip's Tactical Solutions says, "I think it's important that not only men, but women feel like they're in control of their own safety. Sometimes it's hard to believe you can do something until you see someone who looks like you doing it."[30] These business owners are, therefore, simply addressing a market failure, providing a service that they feel women need.[31]

But many women-led companies see themselves as doing more than giving women guns. Mary E. Edwards-Fears, CEO and co-owner of Girls Getta Grip Gun Club, a retired police captain of the Saint Louis Metropolitan Police Department, sees her company as an extension of the community service work she did for women before she retired from the force: "During my police career I did safety programs for Girl Scout groups, church groups and I even facilitated range visits for certain groups on my off days. This is why we at Girls Getta Grip Gun Club have made women's safety our business. We welcome ladies from all walks of life into our Club! My team and I are extremely proud to report that we have spent the past 3 years training over 300 women on firearms safety."[32]

Perhaps most interesting, the directory includes nurses, social workers, a doula, and other healers who have come to see gun ownership and self-defense training as a part of trauma-informed women-focused community care. Oshun Defense, for example, is a Houston-based company created by Raven Lemon, who is a trauma-informed firearms instructor and doula and whose profile includes the hashtags #selfdefense and #birthworker. The company's Instagram account evinces an overall concern with gun violence as a threat to Black life—during the February 2021 power crisis in Houston, for example—but it is particularly attuned to violence against pregnant women. The name fits, as the powerful Yoruba Goddess Oshun is both creator and destroyer: Oshun is not only the goddess of love, femininity, and the creative power of fertility but is also an angry and retributive goddess who will punish the earth and its inhabitants. On February 21, 2021, Lemon posted: "The most vulnerable time in any woman's life is when she is pregnant. Every day there are cases of Black Women being murdered by their child's biological parent, going missing, robbed or anything else while pregnant. These people don't value life and they definitely don't value us. I have been working on a class for about a month dedicated to pregnancy and postpartum self-defense. We are going to cover everything you need to know prior to pregnancy or even once you are pregnant that will help keep you safe. We all know someone who needs it. One of the biggest pieces of free game that I can give is just that it can be you, so please take your safety seriously." She has vowed to spread the word to #protectourwomen.[33]

Finally, women who identify as intimate partner and sexual assault survivors are well represented among these female-led companies, and their owners articulate tragic and triumphant reasons for why they are training other women to use guns in their own defense. They run the gamut of the political spectrum, from left to right. Take the case of 3rd Eye Watching. CEO and firearms instructor Nakita Price is a wife, mother of four, and grandmother of two. She created the company because she found the firearms industry male-dominated, and many trainers had backgrounds in law enforcement and the military. She says: "I come from a different perspective (Black, disabled, female, civilian, domestic violence, and sexual assault survivor). I'm unlike most in this industry and because of that I'm able to tap into my experiences and my students find me more reliable because of it. I never saw a lot of minorities, women, disabled, elderly or LGBTQ+ folks participating, training or instructing and representation is very important to us, not only as instructors but also as participants. . . . I offer a safe space for folks to come learn and ask questions about the different defensive options they have when it comes to their self-defense needs, as well as techniques they can learn to better prevent and protect themselves from being victimized."[34]

Danniella "Danni" DuPree, owner of Defensive Unicorns, is a nurse. She is also a "Proud mother of three boys, domestic violence survivor from my past marriage and now NRA Pistol Instructor." DuPree writes: "I entered the firearms world after tragedy struck my personal life and decided to learn to protect myself and my children. I host women empowerment classes to create a safe space to heal from trauma while teaching women to become their own defenders."[35]

And then there is Antonia Okafor, director of women's outreach and national spokesperson for Gun Owners of America and the president of EMPOWERED, "a nonprofit group designed to educate, train and equip young women in the use of firearms for protection on college campuses" and to advocate for their Second Amendment rights. Okafor has served as a campus correspondent for Campus Reform. She believes that "gun rights are women's rights" and says:

> I am a sexual assault survivor myself and so a big aspect of my life has always been about trying to get that power back, empowering myself again and empowering other women, other peers of mine. It's through that realization, through actually that feminist mindset of independence, of wanting to be able to take care of myself and be proactive before anybody wanted to be able to make me a victim again. . . . I was always going towards that path of trying to empower myself and other women around me. And so, in college, it was then that I realized through the epidemic of sexual assault cases on college campuses. . . . I realized that if I truly wanted to empower myself and empower other women around me, I needed to be an advocate for the Second Amendment and I needed to be an advocate for myself and protecting myself.

Trans women are also represented among those providing self-defense training. Their organizations are unique, however, in that unlike the companies that sell defense lessons, they integrate defense training into their broader mutual aid work. I address this below. Two organizations, Thorn and Molasses, advocate for and provide self-defense training and defensive aids for trans and gender-nonconforming BIPOC. Eva Reign interviewed organizers in both groups for *Them* magazine's "In Bloom" series, which highlights "the beauties and struggles that characterize being Black and trans in America today." Thorn cofounder Wriply Bennett says Thorn came about when fellow cofounder Rachel contacted them about gathering a self-defense kit for a Black trans woman. Wriply recalls saying, "Well, shit, I need a self-defense kit." They began gathering supplies for those in need, particularly sex workers. They provide stun guns, pocketknives, pepper gel, and personal alarms to trans and gender-nonconforming BIPOC.

Molasses member Cae Monāe notes the dangers that arise for trans women from a transphobic media environment that often blames trans women and gender-nonconforming folk for their deaths. She also articulates something more than mere self-defense, advocating collective vengeance: "I'm hungry for this, I think the media conversation is absolutely disgusting and atrocious. A lot of people believe we're getting killed because we deserve it. We certainly do not. It is because of those hateful perspectives [that] all trans women should be armed, specifically Black trans women and gender non-conforming folk. You should be armed and I'm not afraid to talk about it. . . . For me, baby this is about trans vengeance. If I'm going to put my life on the line, it's going to be for my girls. Period." In the interview, Monāe also drew attention to slow death and its systemic causes: "The violence is not always as simple as being attacked on the street. What also comes into play is how our Black trans brothers and sisters and siblings are treated in terms of healthcare. I had a sister just last year who suffered an asthma attack and ended up in the hospital dead. Why is that? It makes me sick to my stomach."[36]

Armed self-defense is offered to Black women both as a product and as a form of individual and collective care in response to an environment of disproportionate violence against Black women without adequate—and often *any*—institutionalized response. Like Smith, the entrepreneurs who take up this work in response to disproportionate violence against Black women are interested in direct and practical solutions that depend on individual initiative, not on influencing the police or the media to effect change. Smith, however, combined self-defense with calls for mutual aid. In their decision to bypass the police, in particular, armed self-defense advocates have much in common with abolition feminists, yet their solutions are far more individualized and perhaps more indicative of a more atomized worldview than the communal, mutual aid–based approaches on offer from abolitionists. They also call on women to defend themselves in a context in which Black women are often harshly punished for taking such actions. But many women may have no choice but to do so. As well, unlike abolitionists, self-defense advocates do not articulate a critique of policing as a contributing factor in the violent world that these arms trainers correctly perceive.

Abolition: Mutual Aid, Community Accountability, Harm Reduction, and Transformative Justice

Contemporary prison industrial complex abolitionists, specifically the abolition feminists among them, conceive of the disproportionate fatal violence against Black women, women of color, trans and gender-nonconforming folk (particularly Black transfemmes, who bear the lion's share of violence against trans persons), and other marginalized women as an intersectional issue. As they understand it, this issue has roots in the more frequent and severe intimate partner violence to which these women are subject, as well as in the state violence to which these women are subject in under-resourced communities in the broader context of what Beth Richie calls America's "prison nation" of mass incarceration and an overall punitive approach to social problems.[37] Abolition feminists see the police as escalating the violence Black women experience at the hands of intimate partners; they see police, prisons, and the prison industrial complex as perpetrators and incubators of violence against marginalized women. More damning, groups like Survived + Punished, an abolitionist organization that works to free all criminalized survivors of gender-based violence, contend that jails and prisons, not women's shelters, represent our institutional response to violence against Black and other marginalized women, in that as many as 90 percent of the populations of some women's prisons are survivors of gender-related violence.

Broadly, PIC abolition feminists condemn the path taken by mainstream antiviolence organizations, that is, toward conceiving of and addressing gender-based violence narrowly as crime rather than as part of the broader societal problem of gender inequity. Abolition feminists advocate for mutual aid–based solutions to Black femicide, working to nurture community capacity to respond to gender-based and gender-related violence via community accountability and harm reductionist approaches as part of a broader vision of transformative justice. They endeavor to redirect resources from police to communities and support what they understand as an under-resourced but ever-present community capacity for violence prevention.

Contemporary abolition feminists are heirs of Barbara Smith. Not only do they call for mutual aid in response to disproportionate violence and death, they understand the disproportionate violence and death to which Black women are subject as an intersectional problem rooted in racism, sexism, and classism, as well as in settler colonialism, xenophobia, homophobia, femmephobia, and US militarism and imperial policy. As we shall see, their faith in community capacity for violence prevention makes them heirs of Clementine Barfield. And their understanding of police as a driving factor in the disproportionate violence and death Black women experience places them in the lineage of Margaret Prescod, who as we shall see blamed "broken windows" policing in general, and its targeting of Black sex workers particularly, for siphoning resources away from communities, away from the women who did the work to make these communities function, and toward police, who were then empowered to harass members of those same communities and criminalize the survival actions of resource-starved residents. She understood the violence police perpetuated against "street women" and sexually profiled women on the street as giving the go-ahead to violent men to help the police to "clean up the streets." Contemporary abolition feminists, in this sense, carry forward a critique Prescod began to articulate in the 1970s.[38]

The mainstream antiviolence movement emerged within a political context increasingly focused on crime. In response, Mimi Kim argues, "Gender violence as a crime became a rallying point for feminists to fight for institutional change and to attempt to gain popular support." Early demands for awareness of and accountability for gender violence gave way to expanding the criminal justice response to this violence. Antiviolence activists pushed for the addition of domestic violence to the criminal code, the enhancement of criminal penalties for gender violence, and mandatory arrest policies. They lobbied to include the Violence Against Women Act (VAWA) as part of the 1994 Crime Bill, which, according to Kim, "marked the concretization and acceleration of the collaboration between the feminist antiviolence movement and the agenda of law enforcement." This response to gender-based violence "contributed to the shift from gender violence envisioned as a broad social and political problem to one defined more narrowly as a crime." What began as a movement for broad social change "succumbed to pressures to professionalize and adopt an individualized direct service, case management model of service delivery."[39]

Yet there was pushback regarding this approach from the beginning, and the predominantly women of color feminists who were critical of the criminalization approach became increasingly frustrated with each passing year. Kimberlé Crenshaw writes: "Mandatory arrest policies and other pro-policing remedies were seen as important victories by many advocates despite the serious reservations of many women of color and other advocates. . . . For those who understood domestic violence as part of a broader system of gender subordination rather than an exclusively criminal problem the shifts to federally supported police involvement presented a serious threat to the grassroots origins of domestic violence advocacy. Some were particularly critical of this shifting emphasis as many warned that any strategy predicated on criminalization would likely result in higher fatalities and an increase in arrests for women of color."[40]

The "critique of criminalization" that emerged in the 1970s was "muted by the 1980s," according to Kim. The cases of Joan Little, Inez Garcia, and Yvonne Wanrow, which highlighted the interconnectedness of gender and state violence, received much publicity "but did not lead to an overarching analysis of race, gender and state violence with the vigor to reverse trends that effectively strengthened policing." Women of color formed the WOC Caucus as part of the National Coalition Against Domestic Violence in the early 1980s, but they focused their efforts on greater representation "and greater influence in terms of placement in positions of power."[41]

But by the turn of the century, more radical Black and other women of color antiviolence activists had given up on reforming mainstream antiviolence organizations that insisted police were key to solving the problem of violence against women.[42] They decided to strike out on their own. In 2000, the founding members of INCITE! held a conference, The Color of Violence: Violence against Women of Color. They gave themselves the goals of developing "analyses and strategies" toward ending violence toward women "that place women of color at the center"; addressing all forms of violence against women of color, "including attacks on immigrants' rights and Indian treaty rights, the proliferation of prisons, attacks on the reproductive right of women of color, medical experimentation on communities of color, homophobia/heterosexism and hate crimes against queer women of color, economic neo-colonialism, and institutional racism"; and encouraging a resurgence of political organizing in the antiviolence movement. INCITE!

formed after the conference "to continue efforts to develop strategies to end violence that addressed community and state violence simultaneously."[43]

INCITE! works to organize grassroots responses to the ways in which sexual and domestic violence connect to state violence and to call attention to the urgent (though often invisible) problem of law enforcement violence against women of color and trans people of color. The organization seeks to "build coalitions between anti-police brutality/prison, immigrant rights, LGBT, and antiviolence groups to prioritize police brutality against women of color and trans people of color." INCITE! asks people to document violence by police, immigration, customs, and military actors against women of color and trans people of color, and they call on any woman who has experienced such abuse to "share your story."[44]

In 2001, the organization produced a joint statement with the abolitionist organization Critical Resistance, the "Statement on Gender Violence and the Prison Industrial Complex, 2001," which encouraged the emerging abolitionist movement to take an intersectional, gender-informed approach to PIC abolition: "We call social justice movements to develop strategies and analysis that address both state AND interpersonal violence, particularly violence against women." This statement placed the pitfalls of the law enforcement approach to ending violence against women of color front and center in its abolitionist analysis and took direct aim at the ways in which mandatory arrest policies and an overall "tough on crime" approach led to an increase in violence against women of color. "Law enforcement approaches to violence against women MAY deter some acts of violence in the short term," it said. The statement continued: "*However, as an overall strategy for ending violence, criminalization has not worked.* In fact, the overall impact of mandatory arrests laws for domestic violence have led to decreases in the number of battered women who kill their partners in self-defense, but they have not led to a decrease in the number of batterers who kill their partners. Thus, the law protects batterers more than it protects survivors." Second: "*The criminalization approach has also brought many women into conflict with the law*, particularly women of color, poor women, lesbians, sex workers, immigrant women, women with disabilities, and other marginalized women. For instance, under mandatory arrest laws, there have been numerous incidents where police officers called to domestic incidents have arrested the woman who is being battered. Many undocumented women have reported cases of sexual and domestic violence, only to find themselves deported. A tough law and order agenda also leads to long punitive sentences for women convicted of killing their batterers. Finally, when public funding is channeled into policing and prisons, budget cuts for social programs, including women's shelters, welfare and public housing are the inevitable side effect. These cutbacks leave women less able to escape violent relationships."[45]

The joint statement pointed out that investments in policing and prisons did not stop violence against women. They simply continue the violence, as, for example, a growing number of gender-related violence survivors are now behind bars. Organized women and their allies, in their account, hold the collective power to end violence against women, and, for women of color and other marginalized women, alliances with the police not only actively work against that goal, they are simply wrongheaded. The antiviolence movement's reliance on state funding isolated it from other movements for social justice, while its reliance on the criminal justice system takes power "from women's ability to organize collectively to stop violence" and invests it in the state. The statement indicts the individualism of mainstream antiviolence's punitive approach and the ways it functions to limit the imaginations of community members. When people can only think to call the police in response to violence, focus is taken away from consideration of how "communities can collectively respond to violence." INCITE! and Critical Resistance, by contrast, would return the focus to building community capacity.[46]

Beth Richie, a founding member of INCITE!, puts the matter plainly: police, in her account, are not protecting Black women from male violence. Rather, they are a part of that violence, and the broader prison nation of which they are a part must be abolished in order to ensure Black women's safety. In her book, *Arrested Development: Black Women, Violence and America's Prison Nation*, Richie writes: "I am challenging the antiviolence movement's uncritical positioning around state policy and punitive interventions, which I argue have contributed to the ongoing escalation of male violence against Black women." Indeed, "Black women who experience male violence illustrate the perils inherent in relying on intervention strategies that emerge from conservative public policies *that focus on punishment rather than on prevention of violence and that ignore the broader need for redistribution of social power along gender and racial lines.*" Occupying a stigmatized social position makes Black women easy targets for victimization *and* all but invisible to those who claim to be there to help: "The further the women's sexuality, age, class, criminal background, and race are from hegemonic norms, the more likely it is that they will be harmed—and the more likely that their harm will not be taken seriously by their communities, by antiviolence programs, or by the general public. Black women similar to those whose stories I have recounted will be left to cope without formal institutional support. . . . And for that, they will be punished." The support of which Richie speaks is both material and ideological. The women will not have been offered material relief by community members, activists and the public and those same groups will not have constructed and circulated accounts—stories—of why women in their circumstances should be helped. Alone in the face of violence any actions they take—either in defense or in deflection—will be scorned and often, in the punitive climate of the prison nation, criminalized. Richie continues, "The punishment—the isolation, further stigmatization, or long prison sentences—is made possible by the social climate that constitutes the prison nation."[47]

The criminalization approach, then, left activists with an even greater level of violence to respond to, with much more work to do. Survived + Punished is one organization created to confront the consequences of what they call "criminalized survival," that is, the coping strategies survivors engage in in response to violence under conditions of community and institutional neglect, strategies for which Richie says that marginalized survivors are so often punished. Survived + Punished demands the immediate release of criminalized survivors of gender-based violence who are imprisoned for "survival actions," including self-defense, "failure to protect" children from abusive partners, removing children from abusers (one senses an utterly maddening "damned if you do" scenario here regarding the prior two offenses), migration offenses, acting as accomplices in criminalized activity like the drug trade due to coercion, and securing resources necessary for survival. The organization works toward prison abolition, but also toward more immediate goals, such as the commutation of survivor sentences. It calls on volunteers to write letters to criminalized survivors, combating their isolation and creating "pathways for connection, collaboration and coalition."[48] Notably, the group's video project, *No Perfect Victims*, emphasizes survivor testimony, that is, storytelling, over the image of the battered woman, complete with exaggerated depictions of the visible traces of violent assault, that is the coin of the legal realm in cases of intimate partner violence. Kelli Moore says, "*No Perfect Victims* prioritizes not the police-generated look of DV [domestic violence] victimization but the experiences of DV survivors who have been incarcerated."[49]

It is important to acknowledge that contemporary Black feminist abolitionists are part of a multiracial network of activist formations that includes significant contributions from Asian-American feminist antiviolence activists, including Mimi Kim, Hyejin Shim, Mia Mingus, and sujatha baliga. The contemporary activist nexus between Black and Asian American abolition feminists is perhaps best illustrated by the case of Survived + Punished. Members of the national Free Marissa Now Mobilization Campaign to Free Marissa Alexander and the Chicago Alliance to Free Marissa Alexander (now Love & Protect) organized a defense campaign workshop for an INCITE! Color of Violence conference. Alexander had been convicted of aggravated assault with a deadly weapon and received a twenty-year sentence for firing a warning shot after her abusive husband assaulted her and threatened her life. At the conference, Free Marissa activists met members of the Stand with Nan-Hui defense campaign and connected with members of the California Coalition for Women Prisoners, which works to free people in women's prisons. Nan-Hui Jo, a Korean intimate partner violence survivor, served time for child abduction after she attempted to flee the country to protect herself and her child from an abusive husband. Upon her release from state custody, she was taken into immigration detention. The collective of organizers from Free Marissa, Stand with Nan-Hui, and the California Coalition "exchanged stories about the promise and challenges of defense campaigns, and ideas about the intersections of criminalization and surviving domestic violence." They came together to form Survived + Punished in Chicago in March 2016.[50]

Longtime antiviolence organizer Mimi Kim is another founding member of INCITE! Her growing frustration with the limited options offered to survivors led her to ask, "Why wasn't there a space for the people closest to and most impacted by violence to envision and create ways to make it stop? Why weren't violence intervention resources offering education, skills, and support useful to everyday people wanting to stop violence among those they care about? Why did community education teach how to recognize forms of violence but not how to stop it?" Kim would endeavor to correct these considerable omissions. She looked to restorative justice initiatives for guidance.

Restorative justice practices originated in the 1980s in New Zealand to address the overrepresentation of Māori youth in the criminal justice system. Kim writes, "Restorative justice is the most long-standing and familiar concept attributed to alternative responses to violence." Restorative justice practices move from adversarial, individualistic, and binary (that is, victim/perpetrator) understandings of harm to focus on how violence impacts communities on multiple levels. It aims not at punishment, but restoration and the integration of all parties into the community, Kim says. Yet restorative justice programs are housed within law enforcement agencies. Transformative justice arose as an alternative among prison abolition–aligned social movements, building on many of the practices of restorative justice within more informal spaces:

> Rejecting the criminal justice system as primarily responsible for the violent oppression of marginalized communities, transformative justice responses to gender violence and other forms of interpersonal or community violence seek resolutions within more intimate systems of community or civil society. Following more radical political traditions, transformative justice relies upon the leadership and interests of marginalized communities. At the level of individual- or community-level acts of violence, those most impacted by violence understand best the immediate and underlying conditions in which interpersonal acts of violence are embedded. Ultimately, as community members directly impacted by violence but also sharing home and collective space with victims and perpetrators of violence, they hold the potential for greater investment in the well-being of all parties involved and the creation of conditions that could prevent future harm, including that perpetrated by the state.

Transformative justice efforts also came to be affiliated with approaches referred to as "community accountability" and "community-based responses," which "shift the focus of violence from individual actors to communities, the latter taking a role both as perpetrators and casualties of violence." Kim explains: "Communities are also sites for prevention, intervention, and transformation, spaces where interventions can be imagined, initiated, and implemented. The emphasis on the level of community is also posed as an alternative and challenge to the authority of the criminal justice system, child welfare system, or even nonprofit organizations." In contrast to "conventional anti-violence services," Kim writes, "its approach prioritizes the engagement and coordination of social networks—that is, friends, family, and community members tied to specific situations of violence."[51]

Kim founded Creative Interventions in 2004 "to shift education and resources back to communities" and "place knowledge and power among those impacted by violence." The organization strives to make "support and safety more accessible, stop violence at early stages of abuse and create possibilities for once abusing individuals and communities to evolve towards healthy change and transformation." Kim and sujatha baliga's CHAT project works to respond to the problem of intimate partner violence. One of the CHAT project's transformative justice–based principles is that it "Builds the capacity of the social network of survivors (and people who have caused harm) to provide support, safety and the prevention of future violence," drawing on the experience and leadership of baliga and Kim.[52]

Trans abolition feminists, who hold that there can be no true gender self-determination without the abolition of the prison industrial complex, have also been a part of these women of color antiviolence activist theorizations and mobilizations from the beginning. They have drawn attention to the limits of the law, and criminal law in particular, for providing ameliorative aid and flourishing for trans folk and have also helped to expound on the significance of mutual aid within social movements.[53] We know that trans identity and gender expansiveness impacts familial status, class status, access to schooling, and health care. As Lori Saffin writes, the marginalization of trans folk within all of these social systems functions to concentrate many of them in marginal, criminalized work and to subject all others to profiling, therefore exposing all to police surveillance, harassment, and violence within carceral institutions.[54]

Dean Spade has argued that the solution to the problem of premature trans death lies in turning decisively away from hate crime and antidiscrimination efforts—approaches that only punish the most violent of the myriad harms trans citizens endure (with the police prominent in that number) and feed the violent, resource-engorged transphobic monster that is the criminalization approach to social harm—and toward a focus on the life-altering biopolitical administrative systems that now also threaten and, ultimately, shorten trans life: the departments of Health, Motor Vehicles, Corrections, Child Welfare and Education, and federal agencies like the Customs and Border Protection, US Immigration and Customs Enforcement (ICE), the Bureau of Indian Affairs, the Bureau of Prisons, the Food and Drug Administration, and the Environmental Protection Agency.

Spade believes that there is a place for law reform work in trans activism, but it cannot be central and must, instead, be placed in service of social movement building and mass mobilization. Law reform can be a tool to help trans folk survive so they might be helped in the short term and subsequently recruited into organizing work. As they are vulnerable to deportation, eviction, and the criminal justice system, they will often need legal assistance, and this assistance can be a tool for organizations to support members. And "because of the enormous role of harmful administrative and legal apparatuses in trans people's lives," legal help can be the point at which people are politicized, "turning individual experiences of harm into a shared understanding of collective struggle." Law reform work can in this way provide opportunities to develop new leaders and expose contradictions in the systems of control that trans people face.[55]

Legal reform has a place in ameliorating trans life and in trans flourishing, Spade says, but it is expressly subordinate to, and indeed subservient to, social movement work. Importantly, Spade points out that "effective social movements always include elements of mutual aid," and "providing for one another through coordinated collective care is radical and generative." Spade defines mutual aid as a "form of political participation in which people take responsibility for caring for one another and changing political conditions not just through symbolic acts or putting pressure on their representatives, but by actively building new social relations that are more survivable." The Black Panther Party's "survival" programs, which included a free breakfast program, free medical clinics and ambulances, a rides-for-the-elderly program, and a school with "a liberating and rigorous curriculum," are perhaps "the most famous example on the Left." People respond to such programs, and the state often takes notice: it is no coincidence that the FBI's dismantling of the Panthers occurred alongside the government's cooptation of some of the party's programs. Spade also emphasizes that these were not simply spaces for the meeting of needs, but spaces that facilitated thought: "The Black Panthers' program mobilized people by creating spaces where they could access basic needs and build shared analysis about the conditions they were facing."[56]

Many trans POC-serving organizations have put mutual aid into practice in novel ways. The organization Molasses, for example, advocates for self-defense, but its strategy differs from those of the women advocating armed self-defense discussed above, as Molasses is not selling a service, but offering self-defense as part of its mutual aid work. This connects Molasses in significant ways to the abolitionist organizations profiled here, but also to the more individualistic women above who advocate arms training. Molasses is a Chicago-based collective of Black, trans, and gender-nonconforming artists and organizers that "aims to create both community and opportunities for black trans and gender-variant people and queer people of color through cultural work, coalition-building and linkages to (self) care." It provides a combination of self-defense training and mutual aid, including emergency monetary aid and care packages. The organization hosted a Trans Self Defense Series over three Saturdays in November 2020 and hosted defense workshops again in 2021. Onyx, one of the founders of Molasses, is explicit about the group's opposition to nonviolent defense strategies in the violent contexts in which trans and gender-variant BIPOC often find themselves: "We don't support propaganda or rhetoric surrounding a nonviolent, peaceful, or passive approach when people's lives are being threatened. We support [trans] folks fighting back and defending themselves." Molasses member Choya says that self-defense tools and skills aren't just nice to have, "they are an absolute necessity for people, particularly Black trans people." It is "equally important," Choya says, to have guidance in the use of self-defense tools: "We don't expect people just to be able to pick up a weapon and be like, 'Oh, hey!' There's obviously also going to be space for folks to talk about using these things. With Molasses, we're trying to create that space."[57]

Mia Mingus's pods and pod mapping is an example of a community accountability and mutual aid–based response in the interest of transformative justice regarding intimate and community violence. One's "pod," according to Mingus, is "the people that you would call on if violence, harm, or abuse happened to you," if you "wanted support in taking accountability for violence, harm, or abuse that you've done," or "if you witnessed violence or someone you care about was being violent or being abused." Mingus found that "asking people to organize their pod" was a more effective technique than asking them to organize their communities. In this way, the "shared language and concept" of the pod made transformative justice "more accessible": "Gone were the fantasies of a giant, magical 'community response,' filled with people we only had surface relationships with; and instead, we challenged ourselves and others to build solid pods of people *through relationship and trust.* In doing so, we are pushed to get specific about what those relationships look like and how they are built." This approach put "relationship-building" squarely "at the very center of transformative justice and community accountability work."[58]

Alongside community accountability and mutual aid-focused approaches, PIC abolition feminists are also calling for what Shira

Hassan, citing the street-based originators of the practice, has called "survivor-led collectivized liberatory harm reduction" and what Kaba calls "organized survival." Hassan writes that harm reduction "is a philosophy and set of empowerment-based practices that teach us how to accompany each other as we transform the root causes of harm in our lives." In practicing harm reduction, "We put our values into action using real life strategies to reduce the negative health, legal and social consequences that result from criminalized and stigmatized life experiences such as drug use, sex, the sex trade/sex work, surviving intimate partner violence, self-injury, eating disorders and other survival strategies deemed morally and socially unacceptable." In Hassan's view, "Liberatory Harm Reductionists support each other and our communities without judgment, stigma or coercion and we do not force others to change. We envision a world without racism, capitalism, patriarchy, misogyny, ableism, transphobia, policing, surveillance, and other systems of violence. Liberatory Harm Reduction is true self-determination and total bodily autonomy."[59] Harm reduction, Hassan argues, is a strategy that has been coopted by public health, but it was created by Black, indigenous, and Latinx sex workers; people who used IV drugs; street youth; and other marginalized folk. In practice, it involves getting people the resources they need to make relationships safer, especially considering that these relationships may not be ending anytime soon.

Hassan and Kaba, along with Deana Lewis, Rachel Caidor, Keisa Reynolds, and Ana Mercado, are founding members of Just Practice. The Just Practice website presents a simple equation: Liberatory harm reduction + abolition = Just Practice. Founded in 2014, Just Practice is "a BIPOC, survivor led, mostly queer and disability centered network of organizers who have been working to interrupt, transform and respond to violence without the use of prisons, police and most state systems for the last decade." The organization builds organizer capacity for harm reduction and transformative justice; it "is for activists, movement builders, community members, and non-profit workers who want to deepen their harm reduction skills and transformative justice practices."[60]

Just Practice advertises the "Transformative Justice Help Desk," by Interrupting Criminalization, another organization run by Kaba and staffed by Hassan. The Help Desk offers assistance to anyone working on "projects and community-wide interventions to end violence without using the police"; "Community Accountability Facilitators" currently experiencing challenges; and "Abolitionist Social Workers or Service Providers" within "larger institutions like hospitals, schools, or non-profits."[61]

Abolitionist feminists have developed a variety of approaches to the problem of intimate partner violence, as well as their expansive view of gender-related violence and, ultimately, to Black femicide. They hold that addressing the above requires collective work to build community capacities to prevent and address the complex problem of gender-related violence.

Kimberlé Crenshaw, the pioneering legal theorist who coined the term "intersectionality," credits abolitionists with anticipating the problems of the criminalization approach to intimate partner violence and, like abolitionists, understands police as major contributors to the problem of disproportionate violence against Black and other marginalized women, but she has stopped short of calling for the abolition of police. In her #SayHerName campaign's efforts to expand the public's understanding of police violence beyond the narrow frame of violence against Black men, the organization has much in common with reynolds-tyler's Beyond the Surface project. In addition to calling for crucial reforms in the institution of policing, which would place her alongside members of BAMFI, she has called, as well, for Black female survivors of violence and the family members of those who have not survived to "share their stories" in the interest of increased political mobilization in Black communities. Storytelling figures centrally in her project. Crenshaw is not unique; indeed, her call for storytelling is echoed by many of the activists featured above. As I have said, storytelling is of particular interest when thinking about democracy and disproportionate Black death. I take this up in subsequent chapters.

#SayHerName

Eleanor Bumpurs, Aiayana Stanley-Jones, Rekia Boyd, Atatiana Jefferson, Katheryn Johnston, Charlena Lyles, Pearlie Golden, Sandra Bland, Breonna Taylor: The African American Policy Forum and the Center for Intersectionality and Social Policy Studies launched the #SayHerName campaign in December 2014 to bring "awareness to the often-invisible names and stories of Black women and girls who have been victimized by racist police violence and provides support to their families." AAPF founder Crenshaw noted that "although Black women are routinely killed, raped and beaten by the police, their experiences are rarely foregrounded in popular understandings of police brutality."[62] Crenshaw facilitated an arresting demonstration of her point in a 2016 TedWomen Talk when she asked members of the audience to stand. She informed them that she would recite a list of names. She asked audience members to sit once they heard a name that they did not know. She began with Eric Garner, Mike Brown, Tamir Rice, and Freddie Gray. At this point, Crenshaw paused and asked the assembly to take note of the fact that about half of the people in the room remained standing. She continued with Michelle Cuseau, Tanisha Anderson, Aura Russer, and Megan Hockett. By the end of her recitation, only four audience members remained standing.[63]

In a report titled "Say Her Name" focused on police brutality against Black women, Crenshaw and Andrea Ritchie note that the "resurgent racial justice movement in the United States" has a "clear frame" for understanding "police killings of black men and boys," which encompasses these victims' systematic criminalization "across disparate class backgrounds and irrespective of circumstance." The situation for Black women is very different, however: "Black women who are profiled, beaten, sexually assaulted and killed by law enforcement are conspicuously absent from this frame, even when their experiences are identical. When their experiences with police violence are distinct—uniquely informed by race, gender identity and sexual orientation—black women remain invisible." In response, they explain, #SayHerName "sheds light on black women's experience of police violence in an effort to support a gender inclusive approach to racial justice that centers all black lives equally." Crenshaw and Ritchie's aim with their "Say Her Name" report was to provide "a tool for the resurgent racial justice movement to mobilize around the stories of women who have lost their lives to police."[64]

Crenshaw's #SayHerName is an important strategic response to mobilization asymmetry regarding the deaths of Black men in comparison to those of Black women. It is a significant foray into the complex world of intersectional coalition building by the thinker who first theorized the concept of intersectionality, and it is notable that #SayHerName puts stories and storytelling at the forefront of its agenda. In an act of tremendous bravery and a genuine demonstration of faith in her project, Crenshaw shared the story of her own experience with gender-based violence, as well as her community's response to that violence—an experience that was important to Crenshaw's development and elaboration of the concept of intersectionality.[65] Her organization provides a forum for Black female survivors of violence to tell their stories and, importantly, encourages the relatives of women who have not survived to share the stories of their loved ones.

The #SayHerName campaign addresses two audiences: formal institutions, on the one hand, and Black communities and Black civil society organizations, on the other. Regarding formal institutions, the campaign has not gone so far as to call for the abolition of police, but, like abolition feminists, they have called for a redirection of resources from police to mental health services, domestic violence services, shelters for the unhoused, and an investment in forms of community safety that do not rely on the police. They want police and cities held accountable for violence against women, and they call for the creation of reforms that address the home as a major site of police violence against women, including an end to no-knock warrants and the practice of sending police to perform mental health wellness checks and to respond to domestic disturbances. They also call for an end to police searches for the purpose of assigning gender, and they call for officers to respect gender identity and expression.[66]

Regarding the initiative's second audience, #SayHerName asks members of Black communities to "honor the memories and tell the stories of Black women and girls who have been killed by the police. #SayHerName."[67] The AAPF believes that saying the names of women killed by police in Black communities is a vital first step, as "knowing their names is a necessary but not a sufficient condition for lifting up their stories, which in turn provides a much clearer view of the wide-ranging circumstances that makes Black women's bodies disproportionately subject to police violence. To lift up their stories and illuminate police violence against women, we need to know who they are, how they lived and why they suffered at the hands of police."[68]

Several of the organization's recommendations are addressed to members of Black communities and Black civil society organizations. The organization asks that "at protests, demonstrations, and other actions against police violence, include the faces, names and stories of Black women alongside those of Black men." They also call on local and national organizations and social movements to "find ways to support all families who have lost a loved one to police violence and all surviving victims of state violence."[69] They have taken up the latter work themselves, as the group hosts an annual "Mothers Weekend" to learn about what the mothers of Black women killed by the police need and "provide a space where these mothers can begin to construct a community of support and a network for activism."[70]

Saying the names, storytelling, and contextualization regarding the murders is an important first step. But there is more. Notably, the AAPF wants a reckoning within Black communities, and they seek to bring this reckoning into being, in part, via the creation of spaces to address patriarchy, homophobia, and transphobia within these communities. The organization wants individuals and organizations to be held accountable for the ways they have recreated systematic oppression, and they want community members to develop "skills to talk about the multiplicity of ways in which state violence affects all Black women and girls." Such an approach aims to move stakeholders "beyond a frame that highlights only killing" and includes "all Black women—transgender, nontransgender, and gender non-conforming . . . in this reconceptualization."[71]

Crenshaw has called for a redistribution of "narrative capital" in Black communities to combat the lack of mobilization in response to violence against Black women relative to that of Black men. She sees part of the mobilization asymmetry as being rooted in Black women's lack of narrative capital in their communities. Blacks have, she says, stock stories, stock narratives from which to draw and to which political demands can be attached.[72] These stories stand as a kind of fund, an important political resource. These stories matter, Crenshaw says; they have material and psychic effects. Her call for women to "share their stories" attempts to address this narrative capital maldistribution, so that the stories may circulate and move people to action.

The allure of grassroots mobilization like that envisioned by Crenshaw is undeniable. Black women, like all members of oppressed groups, would benefit from such a social movement. Deva Woodly argues that social movements are necessary to democracy, and in particular to our multiracial democracy long characterized by group-based oppression. Social movements, Woodly says, represent democracy's Fifth Estate. She cites Jeremy Sawyer and Anup Gampa's work, which posits that social movements are the only phenomena that have been successful at changing society-wide attitudes and potentially helping members of oppressed groups overcome the forms of misrecognition under which they suffer. Not only do social movements build long-neglected political capacities among subordinate group members, they are also capable of creating new associations with the groups participating and can change observers' implicit evaluations of the group in ways that exposure to exceptional members of the group (like Barack

Obama) cannot. They help to change what a group means to others in a society.[73]

Additionally, Crenshaw is absolutely correct that Black women's experiences of violence should occasion greater response. Black women should possess more narrative capital, if "capital" is indeed the right term for what she describes. Stories have material and psychic effect. Stories do things. They do one extremely important thing: they help to build political people. Yet we must not only attend to the fact that some embodied storytellers are attributed excesses of credibility while others suffer from credibility deficits, where women and marginalized women in particular are often given less credibility. This is especially true when stories concern sex and sexuality. We must attend as well to the fact that there are specific kinds of stories that have been most successfully employed in US Black people-making historically, and in the subsequent political mobilizations they engendered, and those are stories of spectacular violence.[74] Black women—even when they are killed by the police—die unspectacularly and in ways connected to the realm of sex and sexuality in a context in which the "Black people" have been made through stories of spectacular violence. The "Black people" may very well have to be remade for women's stories of unspectacular violence to mobilize them in comparable ways. This is why, if Crenshaw would ask Black women to use stories in service of collectivizing and mobilizing Blacks, it may not be enough simply to direct Black women to share their stories of violence. That is to say, bringing about narrative capital redistribution in the interest of more intersectional political mobilization and movement building may be more complicated than simply sharing stories—and the complications are not unrelated to Black women's lack of death spectacles. Spectacular violence is a phenomenon that has been ever present to the Black eye and has been constitutive of the Black body. It has played a key role in mobilizing Black communities. I therefore hold that the long-standing significance of spectacular violence in Black communities cannot be ignored in calls for women to "share their stories."

Crenshaw and others confronting Black femicide and disproportionate Black female exposure to violence who call for storytelling, for narrative, must reflect on how Black political leaders like W. E. B. Du Bois have written spectacular violence, and specifically death spectacles, into the story of who Blacks are and why they are here. Leaders used such violence to create Blacks as a political people, and they put these stories into the service of political mobilization. And because Black men were most likely to be subject to this form of violence, they have thus far held a more significant place within that people. This is a part of why their deaths matter more. The questions for Crenshaw (and, indeed, for us all), then, are these: Can Black women share stories of their experiences of violence that connect as successfully with compelling accounts of who Blacks are and why we are here? Can this be accomplished without the crucial act of witness? Will the story of who we are and why we are here need to be wholly rewritten in order to balance this mobilization asymmetry? Is that what Black feminists should aim for with their stories? These are the challenges she confronts. They are a problem for us all.

Death Work and Life Work

In the chapters that follow, I turn to a consideration of the phenomenon of premature Black death, storytelling and democracy, the construction, cultivation, and circulation of the violent stories of Black peoplehood, the theory and practice of the Black female necromantics Ida. B. Wells, Mamie Till-Bradley, Clementine Barfield, Margaret Prescod, Barbara Smith, and Toni Morrison and consider how the work of Page, reynolds-tyler, Richie, Kaba, and Crenshaw echoes and contrasts with earlier Black women's theorizing in response to premature Black death. Page and reynolds-tyler's counterdata practices have undeniable resonances with Wells and Smith's pioneering counterdata activism, though the earlier activists advanced a more radically democratic account of the work of enumeration than that on offer from Page but were in line with the abolitionist reynolds-tyler's work. And of course, as a data-driven investigative journalist, reynolds-tyler is without question one of Wells's descendants. Ritchie and Kaba's critique of policing, as well as their faith in the capacities of Black women and Black communities, echoes the work of Prescod and Barfield, respectively. Finally, the theme of storytelling—Page's search to find "clear accessible information . . . the names and stories of the women and girls"; reynolds-tyler's commitment to narrative justice, indeed to "building the bridge between data science and narrative justice, while centering survivors' experiences"; Richie and INCITE's call for victims of police violence to "share your story"; Kaba and Survived + Punished's choice, in their film *No Perfect Victims*, to focus on survivor testimony and not the image that has long been the coin of the realm in intimate partner violence legal cases; and #SayHerName's work to provide a forum for Black female survivors and the kin of those who have not survived to tell their stories, and the organization's further demand that those stories be amplified by community members and Black organizations—figures in all of the women's responses, but in none more prominently than in the #SayHerName campaign. #SayHerName's work to provide a forum for Black female survivors and the kin of those who have not survived to tell their stories is of particular interest because Crenshaw is the most explicit about where she wants the stories shared and what work she wants the stories to do. Morrison's account of storytelling for justice can enrich Crenshaw's vision. Therefore, I place Crenshaw in conversation with Toni Morrison. But in order to adequately account for all that Morrison offers, I must situate her work—and Crenshaw's—alongside that of W. E. B. Du Bois. I turn to Du Bois in the next chapter.

First, however, I want to acknowledge that alongside this critical death work, this organizing around premature Black female death, this death laboring, there is also life labor, that is life after death labor. What follows will be an extensive meditation on Black women's practice of necromancy, of the work that they have done with and for the dead. Yet it is only right to note at the outset that Black women have also been at the forefront of Black birth work that is also a part of the necessary life-after-death work in these life-after-death worlds, and through this work they have confronted one of the key drivers of passive Black femicide, that is, the Black maternal mortality crisis. It is life work haunted by death.

It has been established that Black women's reproductive health efforts contributed to a shift from thinking about reproductive rights to thinking about a broader concept of reproductive justice. The pioneering reproductive justice activist Loretta Ross holds that "reproductive justice is based on the human right to make personal decisions about one's life and the obligations of government and society to ensure that the conditions are suitable for implementing one's decisions." Ross holds that reproductive justice "centers the human rights 1) to have a child, 2) not have a child, 3) to parent children in healthy and safe environments." She continues, "In addition, reproductive justice demands sexual autonomy and gender freedom for every human being."[75] The Birth Justice movement, as part of the broader reproductive justice movement, is one in a long line of Black female-led mutual aid formations. It aims to improve the quality and nature of access and care for marginalized birthing people. For example, Southern Birth Justice's "Birth Justice Framework" acknowledges that "People of color, immigrant peoples, and LGBTQ+ communities have survived a history of traumatic oppression around our decisions to have or not have babies. . . . Birth Justice includes access to health care during the childbearing year that is holistic, humanistic, and culturally centered. This health care is across the pregnancy spectrum, including abortion, miscarriage, prenatal, birth and postpartum care. Birth Justice includes the right to choose whether or not to carry a pregnancy, to choose when, where, how, and with whom to birth, including access to traditional and indigenous healers, such as midwives and other birth workers, and the right to breastfeeding support." Southern Birth Justice programming includes the National Black Midwives Alliance, Doula Training, Birth Justice 101 Workshops, the Mobile Midwife Clinic, which provides visits with midwives, meetings with doulas as well as "free perinatal services, classes, demonstrations, storytelling and more." The programming also includes the Circle of Mamas, which provides a childbirth preparation series that "aims to build with and inform teen mothers and parents of their rights during pregnancy, birth and postpartum as well as increase access to comprehensive health information." The program also "builds movement for Birth Justice by exposing a generation of teen parents to the midwifery model of care."[76]

The Birthing Project began as a community service project where volunteers gave support to pregnant teens and women to lower infant mortality. Tia Murray and Annie Menzel write, "Public health scholar and birth advocate Kathryn Hall-Trujillo founded The Birthing Project—which also claims the designation 'the underground railroad for new life'—in 1988 in response to high rates of Black infant mortality in her California community, and over the years it has operated in approximately a hundred sites nationwide and internationally. It entails one-on-one support for pregnant people from members of the same community, who help them navigate prenatal care, resources, postpartum wellness and the first years of motherhood." It is a Black doula, birth worker, and community advocate–led network. It is the only global Black "maternal and child health program" striving to improve Black birth outcomes through support to pregnant and postpartum women. The model, operating from an understanding that medical and obstetric racism is pervasive, has been replicated in over 100 communities in the US and thirteen countries worldwide. Its official name is, indeed, Birthing Project USA: The Underground Railroad for New Life, and "at any given time," the Birthing Project's website states the organization is "operating from homes, churches, service groups, places of employment, clinics, health departments and hospitals," as long as volunteers can "commit to being conductors on The Underground Railroad for 18 months."[77] Black women, doing underground work. Underground work. So aptly named and it is, by far, not the only underground work they do.

As Deva Woodly mused after a deep sigh when I told her about this project, "Black women. We're keeping everyone alive and making space for the dead too." On that note, let us begin.

3
The Democratic Storytelling of W. E. B. Du Bois

Lynching is an important frame that activists, academics, journalists, civil society organizations, and others have used to make sense of contemporary police violence. Historian and cultural critic Karlos K. Hill has pointed out that "at the current moment, some African Americans are using the history of white on Black lynching and particularly victimization narratives of the lynched Black body, to make sense of recent police killings," calling these frequent and callous killings "modern-day lynchings." Among the critical antiracist observers making similar comparisons are NAACP president Cornell William Brooks; Keeanga-Yamahtta Taylor, who referred to Trayvon Martin and Mike Brown as "lynching victims"; and National Book Critics Circle Award–winning journalist Isabel Wilkerson, who wrote an opinion piece entitled "Mike Brown's Shooting and Jim Crow Lynchings Have Too Much in Common: It's Time for America to Own Up." Brooks, speaking at St. Paul's Progressive Baptist Church in 2016, promised, "We will stand up and stand against police misconduct, police brutality, and we will bring this twenty-first lynching to an end." Christopher Magan, reporting for the *Pioneer Press*, noted Brooks's "stark imagery," which made a direct comparison between the "'lynching ropes and white sheets' of the last century with present-day 'guns and badges and blue uniforms.'" The practice of connecting lethal police violence to lynching extends, moreover, beyond the borders of the United States. A report of the United Nations Human Rights Council stated, "Police killings of black people in the United States are reminiscent of lynchings and the governments must do far more to protect them."[1]

Observers have also made this connection via visual and digital culture. The artist Dread Scott created a flag in 2015 in response to the murder of Walter Scott in Charleston, South Carolina, that was a remix of a flag that flew in front of the NAACP's Fifth Avenue headquarters from 1920 until 1930 anytime anyone, presumably male or female, was lynched. See Figure 3.1. Digital activists created a graphic that places Emmett Till's name

The Labors of Resurrection. Shatema Threadcraft, Oxford University Press. © Oxford University Press (2025).
DOI: 10.1093/9780197758618.003.0004

Figure 3.1 Dread Scott, "A Man Was Lynched by Police Yesterday," 2015.

alongside the names of Oscar Grant, Jordan Davis, Trayvon Martin, and Michael Brown to spell the phrase "BLACK LIVES MATTER," as well as victims of police violence from earlier eras, such as Amadou Diallo. One also created a #blacklivesmatter graphic that prominently featured a noose.

The murder of George Floyd in 2020 intensified comparisons between police killings and lynching. Floyd's brother, Phillonese Floyd, testified before the House of Representatives Judiciary Committee for its hearings on racial injustice and police brutality: "They lynched my brother. That was a modern-day lynching, in broad daylight." Lyla Smith-Abass, an independent Sexual Violence Advisor at SurvivorsUK, wrote a poem, "The Lynching of George Floyd," that began: "There was a lynching in Minneapolis. / A lynching? That's just history, news past, news old. / No, there was a lynching in Minneapolis, truth be told."[2] Cornel West affirmed this interpretation of events, telling *Democracy Now*'s Amy Goodman, "George Floyd was lynched for all the world to see." M. Lee Pelton, the president of Emerson College, opened a letter to "the Emerson community" with the following: "I didn't sleep Friday night. Instead, I spent the night, like a moth drawn to a flame, looking again and again at the video of George Floyd's murder at the hands of a Minneapolis police officer. It was a legalized lynching." Mitchel F. Crusto,

Henry F. Bonura Jr. Distinguished Professor of Law at Loyola University, New Orleans, in a law review article entitled "Black Lives Matter: Banning Police Lynchings," contended that "the police use of lethal force against African Americans constitutes 'lynching'—a State-sponsored act of terror that supported systemic racism." Brooklyn's Urban Assembly Unison School released its own "Public Statement on the Lynching of George Floyd."[3]

This linkage between police killings today and lynching, a phenomenon that was commonplace a century ago, reflects the scholarly understanding of lynching as formative for Blacks. But why and how did lynching become *formative*, in the sense that it has formed and shaped Black consciousness and the self-understanding of Blacks as a people? This chapter considers the contributions of W. E. B. Du Bois toward making this violence particularly meaningful. Through his stories in the pages of his influential journal *The Crisis*, Du Bois helped to write lynching into the story of Black peoplehood, by connecting lynching to the biblical crucifixion and forging a direct connection between Blacks' experiences of racial violence and their ethical virtue. For this reason, the ethical dimensions of the tradition of storytelling about racist violence and its formative impact on the creation of Blacks as a political people cannot be ignored. Due to Du Bois's and others' work, Black people's endurance of anti-black violence has come to represent the courageous confrontation of evil, self-sacrifice, and democratically oriented pacifism. Their endurance of violence highlights Blacks' ongoing unrequited commitment to human brotherhood against all odds—a brotherhood that, as we shall see, excludes women.

Du Bois on Lynching and the Black People

Amy Louise Wood notes that antilynching activism began in the 1880s but only acquired "cohesive political force" after 1909, when the NAACP was founded and put antilynching work "at the forefront of its agenda," devoting "a large portion of its resources to investigating and publicizing as many lynchings as it could."[4] It is worth noting that Paula Giddings might dispute this apparent dismissal of Ida B. Wells's considerable political achievements in the 1890s.[5] What is not in dispute, however, is that the chief operator in this later effort was the NAACP's W. E. B. Du Bois. Du Bois—who chose his hero, Prussian minister Otto von Bismarck, as the subject of his first college graduation oration because Bismarck had "made a nation out of bickering people"—helmed the NAACP's influential monthly news organ *The Crisis* from 1910 to 1934. In this role, he embarked on a project of Black collective memory formation, part of which involved bringing lynching to the forefront of African American discussions and giving it its central place in the African American theodicy.

In founding *The Crisis*, Du Bois joined a tradition of Black activist-journalists. The Black press itself had come into existence in the 1820s with an explicit mission of educating and organizing Blacks. Shawn Leigh Alexander writes: "Beginning with the first newspaper published by African Americans in North America in 1827, *Freedom's Journal*, and culminating with the creation of *The Crisis*, the African American press was designed specifically to educate its readership about the issues important to the race and to spark coordinated action." Indeed, "many of the prominent activists of the [post-Reconstruction] period were also journalists who used the printed page as a way to push their particular kind of reform." As Blacks were pushed out of the formal public sphere, and thus as the influence of Black elected officials waned, these activist-journalists saw their influence grow from the 1880s through the first decades of the twentieth century.[6]

The success of the NAACP and Du Bois's efforts must be understood at least in part as being due to the reach of *The Crisis*. It was "arguably the most widely read and influential periodical about race and social justice in US history."[7] Du Bois himself would call the success of *The Crisis* "phenomenal." If demand is any indication of the above, he may not have exaggerated the impact: "From the one thousand I ventured to publish first, it went up a thousand each month until by 1918 . . . we published and sold over a hundred thousand." He would note that *The Crisis* "circulated nearly a million and a half copies, net paid circulation," reaching "every state in the Union, beside Europe, Africa and the South Seas." Its readership of 100,000 in 1919 was more than that of *The New Republic* and *The Nation*, making its circulation "one of the largest in the land." And the number of people who read the journal far exceeded its subscription numbers, as "it was a magazine that passed through ten times more hands than bought it." Alexander quotes the founder of the Southern Poverty Law Center and NAACP chairman Julian Bond's father, Horace Mann Bond, as saying, "Through *The Crisis* Du Bois helped shape my inner world to a degree impossible to imagine in the world of contemporary children and the flood of various mass media to which they are exposed." Langston Hughes echoed Bond's sentiments, saying, "So many thousands of my generation were uplifted and inspired by the written and spoken words of Dr. W. E. B. Du Bois that for me to say that I was so inspired would hardly be unusual. My earliest memories of written words are those of Du Bois and the Bible." On the fortieth anniversary of the publication, George Schuyler noted that the early *Crisis* "created an intellectual revolution in the most out-of-the-way places," becoming "the bible of the militant Negro of the day and 'must' reading for the growing number of his white champions." Notably, Schuyler highlighted the role of the *Crisis* as "an inspiration of Negro rights" that "welds together the same kind of people for the same cause with the same singleness of purpose."[8]

Du Bois's overriding concern was indeed with welding together Blacks as a people. "Through the pages of *The Crisis*," Amy Helene Kirschke and Phillip Luke Sinitiere argue, "Du Bois sought to forge [for Blacks] a collective memory, a unique identity." His training as a historian, they argue, drove his concern with collective memory formation and his awareness of the role group members played in confirming one another's memories. Racism had functioned to alter Black identity and to exclude Blacks from their place in American history. Du Bois felt that Black history had to be recovered *and* reconstructed with an eye toward creating a new Black collective identity—indeed, a new people. In their essay about Du Bois as print propagandist, Kirschke and Sinitiere argue that Du Bois did not want Blacks' past to be lost, but he wanted to choose the memories they shared through the essays and artwork he published. "African Americans could develop a shared identity by identifying, exploring and agreeing on memories," they explained—a process that Du Bois fostered through selecting and interpreting memories "to serve the changing needs of African Americans."[9]

Blacks' needs were certainly changing in this period, and Du Bois would meet the moment. Yet while Kirschke and Sinitiere give the thinker due credit, Du Bois was by no means the first Black leader to concern himself with Black identity formation, with people-building or even with biblically inspired people-building narratives. Early-nineteenth-century Black political leaders used political rhetoric wherein the "national community was imagined in the character and events found in the Exodus story."[10] This story was not mobilized to evoke ties of blood or in a quest for land but to highlight Blacks' moral and civic obligations to one another to build racial solidarity. Eddie Glaude argues that so pervasive was this rhetoric that by the mid-1840s the Exodus metaphor was "the predominant political language," and the analogy "diffused into the popular consciousness of black

America," such that "Exodus became the taken-for-granted context for any discussions of slavery and freedom."[11] What Du Bois did was build upon and transform the people-building narrative work of his predecessors including David Walker, and the *Freedom's Journal*'s Samuel Cornish and John Russwurm with a new biblical story for a new era of unfreedom and racialized violence—one marked not by slave discipline and lost children wandering in a foreign desert but by disfavored sons living uneasily at home amid the horrors of the American gothic pastoral, around every corner confronting the spectacular ritualistic violence of lynching.

Du Bois, then, no matter how he himself conceived of his people-building project, did not have to construct a people from scratch; he was fortunate to be able to build upon and transform the collective identity his predecessors constructed. But he should be credited for the ways in which he marshaled his skills to respond to drastically changed circumstances. Du Bois's framing not only elevated an admirable and solidaristic sacrificial ideal of Black manhood but also offered a persuasive rejoinder to the religious, ritual, and communal work that lynching was doing for white people and white peoplehood in his era. Michael Gorup argues that mass spectacle lynchings were white supremacist people-making rituals that "played a constitutive role in affirming and circulating the notion that the sovereign people were white, and that African Americans were their social subordinates."[12] Lynchings were events at which the (white) people was made manifest, events that sought "to suture the people's (racialized) body through the ritual performance of violent expulsion."[13] In a world of newly masterless slaves—a world thus teeming with domestic enemies and a social order upended and struggling through its transformation to a new era, spectacle lynchings can be understood, as Donald Matthews holds as religious ritualistic human sacrifices or even, as Orlando Patterson persuasively argues with reference to the physiological connections between smell and taste within a culture wherein barbeque was one of the most popular cuisines, as cannibalistic blood sacrifices.[14] Such blood sacrifice "enacts and symbolically recreates a disrupted or threatened social world and resolves through the shedding of blood, a specific crisis of transition"—a rite of passage not "for the individual but for the community."[15]

Du Bois, then, operated in a wider social context in which white supremacists were using lynchings to reconstitute themselves as a racially exclusionary collective. Yet there was something of a silver lining amid the tragedy, as Kirschke and Sinitiere argue that Du Bois understood the unique role of traumatic experiences in collective memory formation; they served as unifying events. Lynching held tremendous potential for Blacks in this regard. There was just one problem. Kirschke quotes NAACP field secretary Daisy Lampkin, who said, "We were so ashamed that whites could do that to us, could lynch us, that we hardly wanted to talk about it publicly." Du Bois worked to change that. Lynching was shameful; opposing it, decidedly, was not and Du Bois grasped the transformative potential of collective antilynching efforts. "Opposition to lynching was a profoundly significant and mobilizing political force. Du Bois recognized this and used (narrative and) imagery to convert a shameful secret into a catalyst for change. Yet he went beyond merely using it as a political tool; he also used it to craft a sense of collective identity for the African American community. Lynching was an act that could unite the black community through sorrow, but it needed to be owned by the black community and used as a symbol to motivate and inspire action."[16]

Du Bois wrested ownership of lynching from its white perpetrators and helped to inspire subsequent action by rewriting the lynching story as what Rogers Smith refers to as an "ethically constitutive" story.[17] Indeed, Du Bois rewrote the lynching story as the crucifixion story, and in so doing cast Black men into the "stirring roles" that ethically constitutive stories best do, as "more than saints"—as virtuous saviors. Assessing the quality of Du Bois's theological contribution, the preeminent African American theologian James Cone writes, "Black religion comes out of suffering, and no one has engaged the question of theodicy in the Black experience more profoundly than Du Bois." "The lynching tree," Cone also argues, has become "the most potent symbol of the trouble nobody knows that Blacks have seen." In the lynching era, 1880–1940, "the lynching tree joined the cross as the most emotionally charged symbols in the African American community," representing "both death and the promise of redemption, judgment and the offer of mercy, suffering and the power of hope."[18] But it was not Black preachers who made this connection; it was artists and writers "who wrestled with the deep religious meaning of the 'strange fruit' that littered the American landscape." Cone explains: "From Henry Smith's lynching in Paris, Texas (1893) to Emmett Till's in Money, Mississippi (1955) and beyond, Black artists and writers have made the lynching theme a dominant part of their work and most have linked Black victims with the crucified Christ as a way to find meaning in the repeated atrocities in African American communities."[19]

Gwendolyn Brooks, the first Black winner of the Pulitzer Prize, is one example. In 1957, Brooks would summarize five decades of Black visual and literary work, including the likes of Countee Cullen, Langston Hughes, Aaron Douglas, Georgia Douglas Johnson, and Zell Ingram, in spare but characteristically poetic fashion, reflecting on the mob violence in response to school desegregation in her poem "The Chicago Defender Sends a Man to Little Rock." Brooks ends the poem saying, "The loveliest lynchee was our Lord."[20]

The playwright Georgia Douglas Johnson is another example in the tradition. Blum says that in her "Sunday Morning in the South," she played her audiences' physical senses against one another. While their eyes witnessed a white mob lynching an innocent Black man, the audiences' ears heard hymns from the Black church. The groans of the victim were matched by the music of "Amazing Grace" and "Alas and Did My Saviour Bleed." Aaron Douglas's "The Crucifixion" (1927) depicts Simon of Cyrene—Black Simon—bearing the cross for Jesus "up Golgotha's rugged road." See Figure 3.2. Douglas produced the piece for James Weldon Johnson's *God's Trombones: Seven Negro Sermons in Verse*, which renders sermons in the style of Black preachers as poetic verse, thus associating the Black experience with biblical stories. Langston Hughes penned the striking "Christ in Alabama" in December 1931, and it appeared in *Contempo* beneath Zell Ingram's drawing "Black Christ." See Figure 3.3. Countee Cullen's arresting poem "The Black Christ" is a "tale of a black man executed by a lynch mob but miraculously still alive," a man for whom "the air about him shaped a crown." Artistic and literary giants worked to link these phenomena in the minds of their audience. But Cone concludes that no one did it better, "with more literary passion and creative theological insight[,] than W. E. B. Du Bois of the NAACP."[21] He was the best among those whose efforts firmly tied these symbols—the lynching tree and the cross—together for Blacks through storytelling and imagery.

The lynching-as-crucifixion work that Du Bois and others did was also only part of a larger Black counterpublic sphere effort around spectacular violence. *The Crisis* itself became something of a one-stop shop for African Americans who were concerned about lynching and readers who not been concerned about it could not help but become so. Du Bois addressed an astonishing range of topics in the pages of *The Crisis*, yet lynching and mob violence were among the most common themes. In the period

Figure 3.2 Aaron Douglas, "The Crucifixion," 1927.

between 1910 and 1918 "some form of the word 'lynching' appeared on nearly two thousand pages" of the journal. Readers could give to antilynching funds, read lynching exposés, find antilynching candidates for whom to vote, or simply join the premier organization fighting against lynching.[22]

Wood points out that the NAACP was aided in its efforts to publicize lynching by the rise of the Black press, especially by newspapers like the *Richmond Planet*, *Amsterdam News*, and *Chicago Defender* that circulated nationwide. The *Defender* and the *Richmond Planet*, in particular, kept

CONTEMPO

A Review of Books and Personalities

Volume I. Number 13 — Dec. 1, 1931, Chapel Hill, N. C. — Ten Cents a Copy

Lynching by Law or by Lustful Mob North and South: Red and Black

By LINCOLN STEFFENS

The first time I heard of the now famous Scottsboro case, the narrator told how those colored boys under sentence saw it. And they saw what they saw of it from a rear car. There was some sort of a row—a scrap—or a fight going on in a car so far ahead that they could get glimpses of it only as the train bent around the curves till, by and by, the train stopped. Then they saw a lot of the fighters jump off that front car and run away. They went up forward to hear more about it.

It was later, when the train arrived at its destination, that those witnesses of the incident, were arrested as the scrappers and—rapists. They were so dazed that they never quite recovered from their frightful astonishment.

But you don't have to go by this casual alibi. Take the record of the trials, the speed of them, the ages of the convicted and the circumstances, and one can realize for himself that there was no justice in these cases. There was the opposite. There was righteousness in it.

In Alabama and some parts of the South the more respectable people are yielding to the Northern clamor against lynching. There is lynching in the North, too, but it is not against blacks. It is against the Reds. And it is not by mobs. It is by the police, the courts and juries; and therefore legal, regular, righteous. The righteous people of the South have been gradually waking up to the idea that they can save their face by taking justice out of the rude hands of the mob and putting it in the delicate hands of the lawyers, and judges and a few representatives of the better people in a jury. That is to say, they can lynch their blacks the way the superior North, West and East get their Reds.

Well, now, you can see that the Alabama righteous must feel the Scottsboro case was a perfect example of the new ideal of justice modelled on the great (anti-) Red North. They had some blacks in a jam where the whites might have wreaked their fear of the colored folk by a deeply satisfying lynching. And they did not

(Continued on page four)

Christ in Alabama

By LANGSTON HUGHES

Christ is a Nigger,
Beaten and black—
O, bare your back.

Mary is His Mother—
Mammy of the South,
Silence your mouth.

God's His Father—
White Master above,
Grant us your love.

Most holy bastard
Of the bleeding mouth:
Nigger Christ
On the cross of the South.

Notes from Nowhere

Langston Hughes, prominent poet and novelist, is soon to be the guest of the editors of CONTEMPO * * * Phillips Russell, of historical and literary biography fame, recently married Cara Mae Green, sister of Paul Green of *The House of Connelly* * * * William Faulkner while guest of CONTEMPO was surprised to learn that the University of North Carolina library cannot afford a copy of any of his novels * * * And while we are local, a John Reed Club has come, and the Carolina Playmakers are sponsoring a Theatre Guild production of *Elizabeth the Queen* * * * When the first version of Archibald Henderson's *Shaw* appeared, Max Beerbohm made cartoons and caricatures out of the illustrations and by changing words cleverly mutilated the text to create idiotic meanings. This copy of the book is now in the hands of the heirs of the late William Archer * * * Presidential prospects for 1932 are having a time at getting their new books blurbed in the various literary journals and reviews: they all seem to have memoirs or expose items * * * Barrett H. Clark will contribute a regular theatre feature to CONTEMPO * * * And now Cape and Smith part the way, but Hal Smith, maker of Cape and Smith in America, is to make a prominent Harrison Smith with such authors as William Faulkner, J. Middleton Murry, Evelyn Scott, Marcus Hindus and Claire Spencer * * * We wonder why the

(Continued on page four)

Revolts and Rackets

By LOUIS ADAMIC

In a sense *The Populist Revolt* is a timely book. Its subject is—remotely—of current interest. It deals with the expansion, overproduction, underconsumption, unemployment, misery, falling prices, agricultural and bank failures—the familiar cycle of boom, deflation, depression—which produced or accompanied the so-called Populist Movement of the 'eighties and 'nineties. It tells of its picturesque leaders from the South and West—of "Pitchfork" Ben Tillman of South Carolina, "Sockless" Jerry Simpson and Mary Elizabeth Lease ("the Patrick Henry in petticoats") of Kansas, "Bloody Bridles" Waite of Colorado, Watson of Georgia, Macune of Texas, Weaver of Iowa, Ignatius Donnelly of Minnesota, and others. Their fantastic movement for farm and labor relief left permanent marks on America's business and political organization.

But this book's timeliness lies in the fact that the

(Continued on page four)

Southern Gentlemen, White Prostitutes, Mill-Owners, and Negroes

By LANGSTON HUGHES

If the 9 Scottsboro boys die, the South ought to be ashamed of itself—but the 12 million Negroes in America ought to be more ashamed than the South. Maybe it's against the law to print the transcripts of trials from a State court. I don't know. If not, every Negro paper in this country ought to immediately publish the official records of the Scottsboro cases so that both whites and blacks might see at a glance to what absurd farces an Alabama court can descend. (Or should I say an American court?) . . . The 9 boys in Kilbee Prison are Americans. 12 million Negroes are Americans, too. (And many of them far too light in color to be called Negroes, except by liars.) The judge and the jury at Scottsboro, and the governor of Alabama, are Americans. Therefore, for the sake of American justice, (if there is any) and for the honor of Southern gentlemen, (if there ever were any) let the South rise up in press and pulpit, home and school, Senate Chambers and Rotary Clubs, and petition the freedom of the dumb young blacks—so indiscreet as to travel, unwittingly, on the same freight train with two white prostitutes . . . And, incidently, let the mill owners of Huntsville begin to pay their women decent wages so they won't need to be prostitutes. And let the sensible citizens of Alabama (if there are any) supply schools for the black populace of their state, (and for the half-black, too—the mulatto children of the Southern gentlemen. [I reckon they're gentlemen.]) so the Negroes won't be so dumb again . . . But back to the dark millions—black and half-black, brown and yellow, with a gang of white fore-parents—like me. If these 12 million Negro Americans don't raise such a howl that the doors of Kilbee Prison shake until the 9 youngsters come out, (and I don't mean a polite howl, either) then let Dixie justice (blind and syphilitic as it may be) take its course, and let Alabama's Southern gentlemen amuse themselves burning 9 young black boys till they're dead in the State's electric chair. And let the mill-owners of Huntsville continue to pay women workers too little for them to afford the price of a train ticket to Chattanooga . . . Dear Lord, I never knew until now that white ladies (the same color as Southern gentlemen) travelled in freight trains . . . Did you, world? . . . And who ever heard of raping a prostitute?

Facts About Scottsboro

By CAROL WEISS KING
(Attorney for Defense)

On March 25, 1931, two white girls, seven white boys and fifteen to eighteen colored boys were hoboing through Alabama on a freight train. As a result of that episode eight of the Negroes, all under 20, have been sentenced to death and the ninth Negro, a boy of 14, is awaiting trial—the jury in his case having disagreed as to whether he should be electrocuted or serve a life sentence.

The uninitiated might suppose that the Negroes had been guilty of some offense warranting the severe penalty which the Circuit Court of Jackson County, Alabama, has decreed. They were, how-

(Continued on page four)

Figure 3.3 *Contempo* journal, Vol. 1, issue 1, with Langston Hughes poem.

lynching and public antiblack violence ever on Black minds. Of the *Defender* Ethan Michaeli writes, "As with any other newspaper in the country there were plenty of crime stories laced with salacious details, but the articles that really built circulation were those focused on the atrocities in the South. Week after week, droves of news readers were drawn in by headlines like "100 Negroes Murdered Weekly by White Americans," "Texas Has Bloody Spree," and "Fifty Years of Frenzied Hatred." In the *Richmond Planet*, "statistical tables enumerated the loss of life every week for the entire duration of the paper's forty-five-year run." It is worth noting, as Jacqueline Goldsby has, that lynching was not front-page news within the Black activist press, as that was reserved for "black achievements, debates, contests and commerce with the larger world that affirmed Black life." But "placed inside the inner leaves of black newspapers reports of lynching took up a greater number of columns, comprising as much as two full pages of print and visual text."[23]

Du Bois's intuition regarding the collectivizing and mobilizing power of traumatic events was correct. The register at which he spoke resonated. His collective memory project—his peoplehood project—might well have been the most successful project he undertook. Robert Zangrando, for example, writes that the NAACP's broader antilynching campaign "had an urgency, a public visibility and dramatic quality that no other civil rights activity quiet matched." It gave the NAACP a stability and recognition and was the wedge issue through which the organization was able to draw attention to other issues regarding equal rights for Black Americans. The campaign drove membership and provided major opportunities to organize and fundraise. It also gave Blacks opportunities to develop their political skills—skills that Zangrando says many would go on to use in the civil rights movement. In fact, the antilynching campaign was so important to the organization, he says, that the NAACP kept its focus on the practice long after the phenomenon had waned. Lynching, indeed, made Blacks a political people.[24]

One of the greatest scholars in the history of the study of race became a propagandist and worked to make a political people from spectacular death events. What was for decades the most sophisticated antiracist political organization broadcast tales of spectacular death to Black audiences. And both scholar and organization worked within a Black counterpublic sphere wherein the Black press was eager to further amplify such death tales. This all functioned to ensure that Blacks were in constant critical conversation about this form of spectacular violence. Their efforts helped to ensure that spectacular violence played an important role in the making of Black peoplehood in this era and beyond.

Du Bois's Black Christ and Lynching-as-Crucifixion

Du Bois wrote five stories in *The Crisis* in which he brought a Black or "colored" Jesus to the Jim Crow South, and all but one, "The Son of God," appeared in the December or Christmas issue of the journal.[25] Edward J. Blum argues that these tales "were an integral part of Du Bois's challenge to racial and economic discrimination." According to Blum, Du Bois preferred stories that did not simply link lynching and crucifixion but rather directly compared the lynching of African Americans to the crucifixion of Christ. In the stories, the Black Jesus is crucified/lynched because of his association with Blacks and for espousing principles of racial equality consistent with his virtues. The struggle for racial equality, then, becomes a divine one.[26]

Du Bois lynched his Black Jesus again and again, but the lynched Black Jesus was rarely resurrected in his tales. Indeed, Du Bois resurrected his Black Jesus only once, in "The Gospel According to Mary Brown," and this act brought the opposite of salvation. When His mother encountered her risen Son, she was not saved; instead, "softly Mary laid herself down at His feet, and died."[27] Most often the lynched Black man's resurrection came about only through his association with Christian virtues; he was, through his sacrifice for racial equality, no longer fallen. He, himself, however, remained dead. Blum notes that this important point of divergence in Du Bois's version of the lynching-as-crucifixion genre was not an accident: "Unlike other African American writers . . . Du Bois tended to diminish or neglect the resurrection in his stories and instead focused heavily on the teachings of Christ." Blum continues: "The Black Christ of Du Bois's works sympathized with oppressed African Americans; he understood their sorrows and their joys; he confronted the evils of white society with love, justice, and compassion; and then he died—or rather, was murdered. And in most of Du Bois's tales, nothing happened three days later. Downplaying or erasing the resurrection, Du Bois underscored his focus on Christ's teachings, on the evil violence committed by whites, and on the heroic sacrifices of African Americans."[28] He explains: "The specific omission of the resurrection is quite telling, and it fit with his general erasure of supernatural biblical events when narrating tales of Jesus in America. The ethics of the Sermon on the Mount and the self-sacrifice of the crucifixion were the central elements of Christ's spirit, according to Du Bois. By minimizing the supernatural aspects of the biblical stories, Du Bois drew attention to his view of Christianity as an ethical system and to his insistence that African Americans rely on themselves, rather than divine intervention for their liberation. Hope in the miraculous was not a lesson Du Bois gleaned from biblical text, nor one he sought to inculcate in his readers."[29]

According to Blum, "Du Bois focused on Jesus' ethical teachings, especially those of the Sermon on the Mount, to underscore his conviction that Christianity was a religion of brotherhood and of liberation for the oppressed."[30] Indeed, Du Bois translated the Sermon on the Mount into the contemporary American idiom in "The Son of God":

> Heaven is going to be filled with people who are down-hearted and you that are mourning will get a lot of comfort some day. It's the meek folk who are lucky, and going to get everything; and you that are hungry, too. Poor people are better than rich people because they work for what they wear and eat. There won't be any rich people in Heaven. You got to be easy on guys when they do wrong. Then they'll be easy on you, when you get in bad. God's sons are those that won't quarrel. You must treat other people just like you want to be treated. Let'm call you names. Listen! They have called some of the biggest folks that ever lived, dirty names. What's the difference? Which ones do we remember? Don't work all the time. Sit down and rest and sing sometimes. Everything's all right. Give God time. And say, you know how folks use to think they must get even with their enemies? Well, I'll tell you what: you just love your enemies. And if anybody hits you, don't hit 'em back. Just let them go on beating you.[31]

In "The Gospel According to Mary Brown," the lone story in which his Christ is resurrected, a Black Mary births a Black Christ, Joshua, "where field on field of green cotton" flowers in spring. He comes to carpentry by way of plantation labor. White men do not give him his due esteem. He suffers silently but with what whites see as too much dignity: "He was oppressed, yet opened not his mouth." He preaches a gospel of social equality and, for this, is menaced by a mob that interprets his prophecy that the meek shall inherit the earth to mean Blacks will own white cotton land. The mob cannot abide the thought that if the Son of God is Black, God himself may also be. Joshua eventually calls them Pharisees and hypocrites. For this crime, they ask a judge—a man from the North who *is* in fact "The North," keen to wash its hands of the problem of lynching—to crucify him. This Pontius, too, washes his hands of the matter, saying, "I am innocent of his blood." Joshua's claim that the races are equal gets him sentenced to treason, and he is lynched by the bloodthirsty mob. He is risen, but upon seeing him back from the dead, his mother, Mary, falls at his feet and dies.

The "northern judge" takes center stage in "Pontius Pilate." Pontius Pilate is a federal judge in Mississippi. A bishop comes before him, representing a mob that wants to lynch a man, Christ. This man has broken no formal law that Pilate is aware of, but rather the most sacred unwritten one of preaching and even practicing a belief in "the equality of all men." The bishop tells the Northerner, "Remember, Sir, in Mississippi there is one Crime of Crimes, one beside which all crimes fade to innocence—Murder, Arson, Rape, Theft—nothing beside the Crime of Race Equality. Sir, this man, whom we have brought before you, not only preaches openly the equality of all men, but (and the Bishop shuddered) *practices it!* . . . He blasphemed against the White Race."[32] Mississippi federal judge Pilate finds no fault with this argument but washes his hands of the man, and the mob has its way with him. He is lynched.

In "The Second Coming," a Black Savior is born to a white woman, Lucy, in "an old black rickety stable," amid racialized political unrest in Valdosta, Georgia. Blacks are leaving the town in droves, and those who are not voting with their feet in favor of political equality are demanding the actual vote. Three men of God are called to Valdosta to witness the birth: one white, one Black, and one Japanese. The Black man who witnesses the birth says, "But He was to come the second time in clouds of glory, with the nations gathered around Him and angels," and as he says this, "a shaft of glorious light fell full upon the child, while without came the tramping of unnumbered feet and the whirring of wings." The two colored men of God understand the significance of the birth, but the white priest cannot accept a Black Savior and leaves as if nothing has happened. Even as the child enters the world, his lynching/crucifixion is foreshadowed by the white supremacist governor of Georgia, who asks the disbelieving white priest, "Did you hear anything? Do you hear that noise? The crowd is growing strangely on the streets and there seems to be a fire toward the East. I never saw so many people here—I fear violence—a mob—I fear—hark!" He sees the birth itself and the gathering surrounding it as foreshadowing a lynching.

Notably, an infamous lynching took place sixteen miles north of Valdosta. A pregnant Mary Turner was lynched and her child cut from her stomach and killed. True to the form of most women who were lynched, she was lynched in connection to her husband's lynching the previous day. Turner had complained about her husband's murder and threatened legal action.

The murder of the baby is a particularly gruesome detail, and it is very often told. I first encountered it in Angela Davis's *Women, Race and Class*. It is significant that, when referencing a place with an infamous female lynching, Du Bois still tells a male story.

Du Bois wrote "Jesus Christ in Georgia" in response to a lynching, and the story was "routinely reprinted in *The Crisis* following subsequent lynchings."[33] It tells of a stranger who visits a town as a convict escapes. All the Black characters in the story recognize the stranger as Jesus and they are forever changed by this recognition. Many of the white characters understand that the stranger is someone special, but their dawning recognition of his identity is thwarted by the realization that he is Black, a "mulatto." They thus miss out on the life-altering encounter afforded Blacks.[34] Throughout the story, the stranger inquires as to whether the other characters are upholding Christian virtues. The "farmer's wife"—who is never given her own name—is asked if she loves her neighbors as she loves herself. She responds that she tries. The stranger presses her:

> . . . and then [she] looked the way he was looking; down under the hill, where lay a little, half-ruined cabin.
> "They are niggers," she said briefly.
> He looked at her. Suddenly a confusion came over her, and she insisted she knew not why—
> "But they are niggers."

After this encounter, a mob lynches an escaped convict for attacking the racist woman, identity unknown, relationship remarked. In reality, the escapee and the racist woman run into each other as she is running away from the stranger in angry terror after realizing that he is Black. The mob also crucifies Black Jesus. We learn of this from the woman's perspective after they part ways:

> For a time, she lay still listening to the departure of the mob. Then she rose. She shuddered as she heard the creaking of the limb where the body hung. But resolutely she crawled to the window and peered out into the moonlight; she saw the dead man writhe. He stretched his arms out like a cross, looking upward. She gasped and clung to the windowsill. Behind the swaying body and down where the little half-ruined cabin lay, a single flame flashed up amid the far-off shout and cry of the mob. A fierce joy sobbed

> up through the terror in her soul and then sank abashed as she watched the flame rise. Suddenly whirling into one great crimson column it shot to the top of the sky and threw great arms athwart the gloom until above the world and behind the roped and swaying form below hung quivering and burning a great crimson cross. . . .
>
> There, heaven-tall and earth-wide, hung the stranger on the crimson cross, riven and blood-stained with thorn-crowned head and pierced hands. She stretched her arms and shrieked. He did not hear. He did not see. His calm dark eyes all sorrowful were fastened on the writhing, twisting body of the thief and a voice came out of the winds of the night, saying, "This day thou shalt be with me in Paradise!"

In the story, racism prevents the practice of Christianity: it prevents the whites from seeing Jesus among them and from upholding the Christian virtue of loving thy neighbor. Du Bois gives no indication that Blacks face similar obstacles to putting these Christian virtues into practice; he suggests the opposite, in fact. Not only does he conflate the lynch mob with those who killed Jesus, but Du Bois's Jesus casts his lot with those in the half-ruined cabin, and he sees and hears the cries of the Black thief and not those of the racist white woman. He is lynched for pressing the issue that they are neighbors and that they too be loved. They are his people.

Du Bois wrote "The Son of God" for *The Crisis* in 1933. It is told from the perspective of an abusive and skeptical Joseph—Joe—who comes to accept his wife's unwavering conviction that her child, Joshua, is the son of God. "Joshua" is "a silent, brooding but infinitely sympathetic child, whose smile was benediction." He asks "few questions," takes "no orders," and goes "his own still way." He is bitterly disliked by "the Methodist preacher, whom he had very calmly but decisively disputed in Sunday School," being unafraid to tell preachers "what was what." Joe never liked that Joshua, a carpenter, "was always out of a job and never made much money," though he was a "rather good carpenter," if slow, because he was always out about his "father's business." Joshua "kept running with curious people. Outcasts and tramps." Joe complains: "[he's] hanging around with a lot of Communists and talking on street corners, and saying things about property that white folks aren't going to stand for. The police will get after him one of these days and first thing you know he'll be in jail." Joshua even walked down Main Street with "Jackson's Babe, a strumpet." When he leaves home for the wilderness, Joe speculates that he will return rich. Of course, Mary knows, "He is despised and rejected of men. A man of sorrows and acquainted with grief." The story continues:

> Then at last it came like a flash in the sky, when the young man was in his thirties, yet seemed to them still a baby. He had been seized by a mob and they had hanged him at sunset. The charge against him wasn't clear: "Worshipping a new God." "Living with white women!" "Getting up a revolution." "Stealing or blasphemy," the neighbors muttered. Joe came home cursing and half drunk
>
> "Trying to get out of his place; that's it," he yelled. "Criticizing white folk—I told him—I warned him—"
>
> But Mary left her tub; set aside her broom and laid the thimble and scissors carefully in the machine drawer; she put on her black dress and went into the parlor and sat there in the darkness, tall and stern, with an oil lamp in the window that lit the rigid halo of her hair and threw across the yard the black shadow of a noosed and hanging rope. And Mary said;
>
> "His name shall be called Wonderful, Councilor, the Mighty God, the Ever-Lasting Father and the Prince of Peace."
>
> "You crazy fool," shrieked Joe. "You always was dippy about that idiot."
>
> But Mary talked on.
>
> "Behold the Sign of Salvation—a noosed rope" . . .
>
> He saw the shadow of the Noose across the world and heard Mary's voice looming in the night:
>
> "He is the Son of God!"
>
> And Joe buried his head in the dirt and sobbed.

In Du Bois's stories, Christ embodied virtues, including the courageous confrontation of evil, self-sacrifice for one's beliefs, loving one's neighbor, and a commitment to human brotherhood, asceticism, and pacifism. These were the same virtues Du Bois sought to encourage in Blacks. The incidents that led to lynching were already connected to the confrontation of evil. Blacks were lynched to uphold white supremacy. Generally, the proximate incident was an assertion of political or economic equality, standing up for oneself and the principle of racial equality in a labor dispute, for example. Lynchings occurred when Blacks directly confronted the evil of racial inequality, just as Jesus confronted evil, and that confrontation itself evinced the ethic of self-sacrifice, as all knew that it was dangerous to do so. Pacifism—that is, continuing to work for the peaceful resolution of disputes within the democratic process, continuing to work to repair the brotherhood of man, without begrudging all that this system had taken from Blacks materially—would complete the ethic.

And the Blacks the lynched man left behind, who gained those same Christian virtues via their racial, historical, and, importantly, *political* association with the lynched man, were not simply given them so that they might feel better about themselves and rest easy. The lynched man could, indeed, only inspire as Jesus did and does. They were left to do the real work of resurrection, to save their own bodies and souls via a self-sacrificing political struggle for Black liberation here on earth, because Black Jesus was gone, and no one was coming to save them. They had to save themselves. The lynching victim and all Blacks gained virtue via their racial, historical, and political association with the biblical Christ. Those left behind were asked to make use of that virtue, to assume his virtues, to do the political work of saving themselves and, indeed, the nation.

On "Ethically Constitutive," People-Building Stories

That Du Bois employed storytelling in his efforts to create a new Black identity is unsurprising. Rogers Smith argues that stories—and particularly ethically constitutive stories—play an important role in the creation of political peoples. Nor were Du Bois's efforts misguided, as Smith assures us that "enduring, productive political communities" are essential to human flourishing. "Humans," he says, "have never successfully pursued any of their aspirations and endeavors" without first becoming "organized into particular political peoples." Smith defines people-building stories as "persuasive historical stories that propel people to embrace valorized identities, play stirring roles and have the fulfilling experiences that political leaders strive to evoke in them." A story that embraces the ethical identity of Jesus Christ and rewrites his life and actions within a Black cultural milieu is surely what Smith has in mind. Such stories must also "inspire senses of trust and worth" in order to persuade "a critical mass of constituents while also advancing partisan and elite interests." Lynching-as-crucifixion stories were acceptable stories, trustworthy because they fit within a broader Black religious tradition—a broader tradition of storytelling, in fact—that connected violence and the sacred. They shored up Blacks' much-maligned sense of self-worth by associating them with someone they trusted, in whom they had tremendous faith, who was worthy above all others. In these stories, Black men could play the role of savior to the American nation while advancing Du Bois's interest in racial equality.[35]

It is important to note that, as Smith explains, "no political peoples are natural or primordial." Rather, "people are human creations." Humans create peoples, not spontaneously, but most often through the organizing work of "mobilizing leaders" like Du Bois, whose efforts arrange mass publics into new political communities. But leaders are not magicians; those who would create new people are required to work with the material they have, including individuals and collectives "with entrenched economic interests, political and religious beliefs."[36] The crucifixion, of course, held tremendous advantages given Du Bois's collectivizing aims. His audience, no matter what their level of literacy and exposure, would have been familiar with the story. Connecting lynching to the most theologically significant biblical story was a move with practical persuasive appeal.

But Blacks' familiarity with the biblical story alone was not enough. People can be familiar with stories that do not speak to them. Du Bois's effort to tell the lynching story as a crucifixion story worked because of its compatibility with the Black religious worldview. Lynching as crucifixion worked well within the story of Black peoplehood because it involved purifying suffering, and suffering—purifying suffering in particular—is central to Black Christianity. This is Cone's argument, affirmed by other scholars. Cornel West, for example, says that Blacks have understood their experience in America as a theodicy. Anthony Pinn, too, points to the central place of the struggle against evil in Black religion and says that historically, many, even most, Blacks have responded to the moral evil of racism by finding solace in a concept of "redemptive suffering." This, he says, is the dominant understanding of suffering in Black religious thought. Many Blacks, from the eighteenth through the twenty-first centuries, have understood racist evil as part of God's way of teaching and purifying them.[37] The narrative practice of linking lynching to crucifixion, then, worked well within a religious tradition of connecting Blacks' "experience of violence and the sacred." Yet Du Bois's reworking of the crucifixion also raised the stakes, appropriating the Bible's climatic story for political purposes, giving Blacks the opportunity to play one of history's most stirring roles, and creating a narrative association to one of the world's most valorized identities, that of Jesus Christ. Du Bois turned Black men in the throes of profane political, economic, and gendered conflict into spiritual martyrs. In so doing, he endowed purifying suffering with new political purpose.

In Smith's view, economic and political power stories, while components of people-making, are insufficient. Ethically constitutive stories proclaim community members' "culture, religion, language, race, ethnicity, ancestry, history" or similar factors to be "constitutive of worth and delineate their obligations." Ethically constitutive stories present the traits they emphasize as having tremendous—often priceless—ethical worth. In this case, those traits would be, again, the courageous confrontation of the evil of racism, self-sacrifice for one's beliefs, loving one's neighbor, and a commitment to human brotherhood, asceticism, and pacifism: "To believe oneself to be a beloved child of God"—here, *the* child of God—"or a member of a superior race or the descendent of heroic ancestors or the bearer of a brilliant culture is to have a firm basis for a sense of meaning, place, purpose and pride." Moreover, when "racialist theories" are deployed for people-building, preferred races are portrayed as "morally meritorious," "as playing primary roles in advancing the political purposes of God, nature, reason, history and often the interests of all humanity."[38]

Lynching-as-crucifixion stories became ethically constitutive stories for Blacks. Du Bois was able to depict lynching victims as morally meritorious, the lynched Blacks' deaths as advancing the purposes of both God *and* the American nation. The redemption of lynching victims did indeed redeem "the entire race" through the association of Black victims and all Blacks with Christ, but it did more than even this, as "the alleged Black sinner (and indeed all Blacks) became more than a saint." Blum explains: "He became a potential savior, not only for the oppressed but also for white perpetrators." In conflating "Blackness and the divine" through a "Black Christ," authors like Du Bois "answer the problem of evil" not just for people of color, but for all of humanity: "They accepted the reality of their historical situation, but with theological and literary skill, they endeavored to recast it as a cosmic tale."[39]

Ethically constitutive stories offer us "sturdy anchors in morally compelling identities and worth." These identities give us "a sense of belonging, a sense of place in the world, a sense of partnership in a larger, meaningful collective existence and its shared endeavors." Du Bois endeavored to create just such a partnership among Blacks; what better shared endeavor than saving the world from evil. In this way, ethically constitutive stories help us "cement and sustain the communities that sustain us." Economic and political power stories cannot compete, as neither can as capably and as satisfyingly define or ground us. Thus, it is ethically constitutive stories that are "best equipped" "to engage commitments to imagined political communities through economically and politically difficult times." Blacks, of course, would have more than their share of those. They have, Smith says (and the lynching-as-crucifixion story as well as its recent transformation into the police violence-as-lynching story demonstrates), "unparalleled capacities to sustain allegiance."[40]

Du Bois made lynched Black people martyrs to the American democratic experiment and to an aborted multiracial democracy. This gave their lives and their suffering meaning and worth, purpose and pride. It also gave the lives and suffering of those they left behind here on earth meaning and worth, purpose and pride, and inspired those others to continue the work of the departed. In Du Bois's hands, then, lynching brought Black men closer to God; it was, in fact, proof of their proximity to God, that they were indeed God's favored children. Through Du Bois, the lynched man became a saint, became the son of God, suffering as he suffered, and a potential savior of the American nation. Du Bois's highly successful efforts to write lynching into the African American theodicy answered the important questions of who Blacks were and why they were here: they were real men, true patriots, more than saints. And they were here to save a most wayward nation.

Unequal Suffering and Unstable People-Building

But not all Black suffering is created equal. Lynching-as-crucifixion, given the demographics of lynching victims, is a masculinist people-building project. Elizabeth Alexander, who has offered a brilliant analysis of the place of violence in the creation of Blacks as a people—where Blacks learn who "we" are through experiencing and witnessing public violence—has noted that "the focus in American narratives of [spectacular] violence against Blacks is usually male. The whipped slave, the lynched man, Emmett Till, Rodney King; all of these are familiar and explicit in the popular imagination." Alexander's work emphasizes the formative impact of spectacular violence—violence that is witnessed by and retold within collectives—in creating Blacks as a people, which is, again, a significant obstacle for feminists concerned with the private violence Black women experience to overcome.[41] Because, in a context in which Du Bois and others have tied together the experience of lynching—and indeed as we see the experience of spectacular violence—and the divine, and men are more likely to experience forms of spectacular violence than women, because they are more likely to be lynched than women, more likely to be shot in public than women, then men are more closely associated with Christ and His virtues. Women, then, become the stones that the people-builders rejected.

What if, however, that is not such a bad thing? Bonnie Honig has asked what would happen if we thought not about amplifying nondominant stories of Black peoplehood in order to make "the people" more inclusive, so that women and other nonnormative others might be thought of as truly a part of that people, which is, in a sense, Crenshaw's project, but rather understood ourselves to be freed by the phenomenon of incomplete inclusion and eschew the project of constituting a stable "we." We can think instead about peopled moments, momentarily coming together only to come apart and come back together again at another necessary moment.

Barbara Smith, Ida B. Wells, and Toni Morrison—with their fruitfully unstable "we's"—provide a way to think about the challenge Honig presents. They also represent significant challenges to Du Bois's thinking regarding democracy and death. Wells is the ideal place to begin as she was Du Bois's contemporary, and a woman for whom lynching was arguably more of a central preoccupation than it was for Du Bois. Wells did not choose the path of divine martyrdom. She chose radical humanization instead. Her practices of "bringing out the dead," discussed in the next chapter, are instructive as we wrestle with the limits of Du Bois's people-building. Morrison, too, chose radical humanization over martyrdom, but she also chose to celebrate the flesh, the profane, while encouraging us to deepen and sustain our connections with the morally transgressive feminine dead among us. Her democracy is concerned with repairing, not the public wrongs and spectacular breaches that most concerned Du Bois, but the intimate injustices at the core of most femicides. Balfour has described Morrison's democracy as the fugitives' democracy, but we should also attend to Morrison's endorsement of a truant democracy, especially as it is enacted by wayward women.[42]

Du Bois did not want Blacks to look to a risen Jesus for their salvation, only to his life as an ethical and political example for the coming struggle. He, thus, depended on the Blacks who had been left behind by his dearly departed Black Jesus, living Blacks, to do the work of resurrection, to enact their own salvation within the white democracy. He came to see the work of resurrection as the construction of a multiracial democracy, to include democracy in industry, to be built on an abolitionist democratic foundation, where all have the economic, social, and political capital they need, in the form of land, schools, and the franchise, to live as equal members.[43] Du Bois was also famously worried about normative family relations and sexuality.[44] He certainly did not see wayward women as playing a central role in saving Black people, much less the nation. In light of this, it is not only important to me as a Black feminist but also, I want to insist, conceptually and institutionally relevant, that unruly women—loud-mouthed, ungovernable women, single mothers, welfare mothers, lesbians, sex workers and those who explicitly cast their lot with such women—that is, not women trapped in the household but those marginal to it and expelled from it but still constrained by its gendered and what Wilmette Brown called its heterosexual work discipline, that it is they who have done some of the best work of resurrection. And they have done so via the labors of resurrection, by tending to, caring for, and communing with the dead, even the morally transgressive dead, by building political community with the dead whom they, unlike Du Bois, have seen fit to resurrect in a variety of ways.

4

Princess. Prophet. Miracle Worker

Ida B. Wells and the Empirical Miracle, or, Variations on the Black "We"

Saidiya Hartman, contemplating the "violence of the archive," asks, "Is it possible to construct a story from 'the locus of impossible speech' or resurrect lives from the ruins?" Furthermore, "Can beauty provide an antidote to dishonor and love a way to 'exhume buried cries' and reanimate the dead?" And finally, "And what do stories afford anyway? A way of living in the world in the aftermath of catastrophe and devastation? A home in the world for the mutilated and violated self? For whom—for us or for them?"[1]

Facing the violence of lynching and witnessing the construction of an archive of said violence that not only did further violence to the dead but would also bring forth more violence for the living, Black activists managed to construct a story—two, in fact—from this locus of impossible speech. They employed the tools of both God and man in their response, in their counterarchive. Michele Kuhl writes: "Over time, black activists found two effective mechanisms for decoupling lynching from the rumors of black rapists. One strategy, martyrdom discourse, grew out of black Christian theology that sacralized suffering to explain oppression. Statistics, the second strategy, flourished as social scientists increasingly looked at hard data to map the accusations that prompted lynching." Ironically, the pioneering social scientist and non-believer W. E. B. Du Bois famously lost faith in the power of social science alone to bring an end to racist violence and turned to propaganda. He presented lynching stories as Christian martyr tales alongside statistics and investigative reporting in his journal, *The Crisis.* By contrast, the radical Sunday School teacher Ida B. Wells, who innovated the social scientific approach to lynching that Du Bois and others at the NAACP would appropriate, never lost faith in this empirical approach. She never trafficked in martyrology regarding lynching victims, choosing instead to rely on the arduous labor of radical humanization via her efforts

The Labors of Resurrection. Shatema Threadcraft, Oxford University Press. © Oxford University Press (2025).
DOI: 10.1093/9780197758618.003.0005

to excavate the interiority of those lost. This was the work of "reanimation," to borrow Juliet Hooker's term—indeed, the labor of resurrection.[2]

Wells stood "in the aftermath of catastrophe and devastation," in "the ruins," again and again, and she resolved that, at least regarding lynching, the dilemma of which Hartman speaks would not be ours. She built a counterarchive. This new archive faced the violence—the dishonor—squarely. It faithfully rendered the details of what was often gruesome Black death. But it also pieced together and held the beautiful antidote. Wells focused on the quotidian with an eye toward conveying an interiority, a humanity that would otherwise have been lost to history. She marshaled the facts as an act of care. It was through her counterarchive's attention to the mundane details of Black lives before violence, and through her insistence on placing those details alongside accounts of the devastated families and communities that lynching left behind, that she managed an empirical miracle—that is, to exhume buried cries and reanimate the dead.[3]

And with this work of radical humanization, this labor of resurrection, Wells also brought a new era of Black protest politics to life. We might echo Hartman's question, here, and ask, *For whom—for us or for them?* The answer, certainly, is *for both.* Wells would linger among the things left behind in domestic space after violence to give an account of who the dead were, but also to keep us accountable to them. In so doing, she also inaugurated an ongoing effort to change the meaning of Black death—and thus Black life—via statistics, investigation, and unflinching, unflowery word and image. Today, Black counterpublics enter dialogue with the dominant public sphere regarding its ever-present death worlds—even if the dialogue does not remain in these registers—via statistics, via the image, through investigation with an eye toward interiority, contextualization, and by "saying their names" because Wells showed us the way.

Wells conceived of lynching as a secular problem in need of secular solutions. Lynching, for her, was no plot in the Black theodicy, but she was delivered a prophesy—that newswriting was the *word* that would save. It would save Black life, just as it now endangered it. As well modernity's unrivaled prophetess underwent a series of noteworthy empirical conversions, first from Victorianism complete with a belief in the God-ordained meanings of man and woman and its complement, the doctrine of racial uplift to an understanding of human meaning created through discourse and protest politics, second to an understanding of and faith in the emerging ironclad relationship between the photographic image and truth, and, finally, to the necessity of recording, counting and "saying their names"—via her encounters with the work and activism of T. Thomas Fortune, Catherine Impey, and John Mitchell Jr. respectively, along her incredible way—though, characteristically, she would innovate on each thing in which she came to believe. It is just so fitting, for both the woman and her age, to witness her tinkering with a prophesy and thereby bringing about an empirical miracle that would reshape Black political consciousness and Black politics itself. Collectively, these conversions helped her improve upon the parts of and ultimately the totality of what Leigh Raiford refers to as the "truth apparatus" of her time—statistics, photography, investigative journalism, and thus the entire genre of newswriting—parts that had gone unused or had been deliberately misused by her white counterparts. This helped her perform not one but two miracles.[4]

She expressly did not rely on any "fine spun theology," in pursuit of her miracles, indeed she remained faithful to her self-professed, if deceptively complex and epistemologically dexterous, "plain-spokenness"—yet her legacy cannot be wholly divorced from the Black religious tradition. Her Black audience would have held a worldview that allowed them to continue their bonds, including their political bonds, with deceased community members. Because of this, and alongside her "reanimation" labor, she was able to perform her miracles, not only to reanimate the dead, but to bring to life a new era of Black protest politics, which included the work of caring for and "bringing out the dead," in politics, of standing with and acting with the dead in Black politics.

The multivalent strategy she put together through faith, encounter, observation, and tinker—a concerted project of political education in enclaved Black publics and trolling in counterpublic ones, expanding the frame of the lynching photo in service of the antilynching cause, counting the dead and undertaking a rigorous accounting of their lives, their possessions, and dispossessions as mourning practice, saying their names as part of the work of "bringing out the dead"—is worthy of consideration by political theorists. For example, in our own age of national, scientific, social scientific, racial, and gendered misinformation it is important to note that Wells may well have told the truth more freely than anyone before or since, but she also understood that the truth sincerely told was not always the best response to a lie.

The Prophetic Princess and Her Calling

Known to her contemporaries as "the princess of the press," Ida B. Wells first claimed public attention in Memphis, Tennessee, where she became a co-owner of a newspaper, the *Memphis Free Speech*, as a young woman. In 1892, when Wells was thirty years old, her close friend Thomas Moss, who owned a grocery store in the part of Memphis known as "the Curve," was lynched alongside two other men by a Memphis mob. This event, Wells later wrote in her famous essay "The Lynching at the Curve," showed her "what lynching really was": "an excuse to get rid of Negroes who were acquiring wealth and property, and thus keep the race terrorized." In response, she said, "I began an investigation of every lynching I read about." Wells's investigation put her on a trajectory to become the single most famous antilynching activist in the world. Her scathing editorial for the *Free Speech* put her directly at odds with Edward Carmack, the racist editor of the *Memphis Commercial*, and led to the office of the *Free Speech* being burned to the ground by an angry mob. After relocating to Chicago, Wells researched and wrote a lecture titled "Southern Horrors: Lynch Law in All Its Phases," which she published in pamphlet form in 1892. In 1893 and again in 1894, she traveled to Great Britain to deliver a series of antilynching lectures, followed by publication in 1895 of *The Red Record*, a hundred-page pamphlet that contained fourteen pages of statistics alongside extensive, graphic accounts of lynching.

The womanist theologian Emilie Townes argues that Wells met several of Jacqueline Grant's criteria for being a prophetic voice in the Black church.[5] Townes would surely know, yet if this is true, then Wells can lay claim to being a prophet of two realms, the secular and the sacred—and within the realm of the secular, she was prophetic in two senses. Wells brought the fire of the Black Christian prophetic tradition to the cool, dispassionate secular realm as she confronted evil, exposed the oppressive nature of society, and sought to create communities of justice and unity through the tweaked lingua franca of secular truth, statistics, investigation, and photography. But she also saw the endpoint of the communication revolution through which she lived: that the realm of the sacred was waning in its power to save. Jacqueline Goldsby writes that from Wells's first published essay on lynching in 1886, she "professed her faith in the power of news writing as the scripture by which black people might save their lives." She was visionary, as Goldsby notes, because newspapers of the 1890s were "culturally positioned to do the work the Bible had once performed as the arbiter of meaning in daily life."[6] Somehow, Wells sensed this then, knew this then, six years before the events of the lynching at the Curve would compel her to begin piecing together how exactly these new scriptures would save Black lives and catalyze the final phase of her evolution from Victorian and disciple of the gospel of racial uplift to a staunch adherent of protest, to an understanding of how media and not God now made the meanings of man and woman.[7] In this sense, Wells positioned herself to become the unrivaled prophetess of Black modernity.

Wells grasped the immense cultural shift taking place around her, effectively seeing the future, though it must have helped that she herself was so at home in newswriting. It is perhaps not surprising that a woman whose earliest memories were of reading the newspaper to her politically conscious father and his "admiring" friends would find herself—"the real 'me,'" as she put it—in newswriting. It is surprising that a woman born enslaved in Mississippi would forge a groundbreaking and celebrated place for herself in such work, and rare indeed that a Black woman's preferred unflowery, "plain-spoken" mode so fit her medium, indeed her very age. Early on, she committed to direct, plain-spokenness, saying, "I wrote in a plain, commonsense way on the things which concerned our people. Knowing that their education was limited, I never used a word of two syllables where one would serve the purpose." This was unique in a time when she, too, was unique, as she was one of very few Black women in the press and the only one writing about "politics" and not simply "women's issues." Goldsby notes that whereas Wells's female peers—women like Anna Julia Cooper, Frances Ellen Watkins Harper, and Victoria Earle Matthews—wrote "intense but refined essays" and stories about "mob violence," Wells employed a writing style that was "simple, plain, and natural." This commitment to plain-spokenness alongside her radical break from a Victorian understanding of how meaning was made meant that Wells alone would speak not of "outrages" or, somewhat paradoxically, "unspeakable crimes," but—so necessarily—of rape.[8]

It was Wells who first saw lynching for what it truly was: not as a crime representing some throwback to the age of chivalry, but as a thoroughly modern one, endorsed and even called into being by newspapers, staged for publics convened by trains, making use of telephone poles when no suitable trees could be found, circulated via gruesome staged photographs, all to uphold a new racialized "industrial slavery."[9] Wells was similarly prescient—again, prophetic—regarding the solutions to lynching. As a modern crime, it had to be met with modern methods, the press central among them. She did this work alongside other press prophets T. Thomas Fortune, John Mitchell Jr., Monroe Trotter, and Josephine St. Pierre Ruffin, all of whom "waged vigorous campaigns of counterterrorism through newsprint."[10] But no one would do it quite like Wells: no one else would so skillfully recalibrate and mobilize the era's truth apparatus.

Wells found herself, her words, her calling, and our way in newswriting, yet important encounters helped her along her incredible path.

From Uplift to Protest Publicity: T. Thomas, Teaching, and Trolling for Truth

Well on her way by the late 1880s, the 1892 "lynching at the Curve" would see Wells turn fully not only from a Victorian understanding of human meaning, but also saw her turn from the Victorian aspirations of racial uplift to be fully converted to the protest gospel of T. Thomas Fortune.[11] Like Fortune, Wells came to believe the press should play a central role in the defense of Black life and to believe in Black protest, as opposed to racial uplift. Wells came to believe, however, that protest had to be preceded by a Black press–led political education project, complemented by rigorous investigative journalism—both as essential parts of the work of transforming Black political subjectivity and orienting it toward protest, and that trolling had an important role to play in Black counterpublic work.

Fortune believed that civil rights were universal, not earned; this placed him squarely at odds with the philosophy of uplift. A fellow journalist, in fact at the time "the most noted man in Afro American journalism," Fortune saw an important role for the press in protest. He founded *The Freeman* because "He felt the need of a journal to contend for the just rights of his race and thought that much good might be done through such an agency." He founded the Afro-American League to move beyond fighting words. In 1891 in *The Afro-American Press and Its Editors*, Irvine Garland Penn would report that "As editor of the *Freeman*, he was the first to suggest and further the Negro League idea to prevent mob violence and intimidation of his people in the South." Gidding says of his Afro-American League, "It was to be a nationally coordinated effort to take on multiple issues, including voting rights, lynch law, unequal distribution of school funds, discrimination in public accommodations, and the penitentiary system, and to have a proactive, militant stance in demanding the civil rights due to blacks as American citizens."[12]

By 1889, Wells believed in Fortune's Afro American League with "all her heart and soul," and though she published a "black behavior" column in the *Christian Index* she "increasingly turned her attention to racial inequities, not just racial inadequacies." She began to take her cues from the League and by 1890 the Indianapolis Freeman would mock her relationship with Fortune in a cartoon "Fortune and His Echo." But, of course, Wells was no mere echo. She was a preternaturally quick study and rapidly came into her own. She would innovate on both the forms of protest for which she called and the modes of newswriting she mobilized, both in enclaved publics and counterpublicly, in the service of protest.

After her friend Moss was lynched, she would write, "There is therefore only one thing left that we can do; save our money and leave a town which will neither protect our lives and property, nor give us a fair trial in the courts, but takes us out and murders us in cold blood when accused by white persons." Many heard and heeded her call. Immediately after the editorial's publication, thousands of Black Memphians left for Oklahoma Territory and "The nation's first antilynching movement had begun." Wells would launch a full-frontal assault on Victorianism and mark the most significant terrain on which the coming racial battles must be fought—the daily press. Giddings writes that "When Wells [in 'The Truth about Lynching'] counseled blacks that wealth and social advancement were not agents of change in themselves, she was laying the groundwork for protest movements in a post-Victorian world where conflict had its place, where progress was not inevitable without political protest and action, and where language, not natural law, defined the meaning of race."[13]

Wells and Fortune's understanding of the defensive function of the Black press was consistent with the understanding held by the institution's founders. As the pioneering newswoman came to dedicate her life to the antilynching cause, she faced many of the same problems that had led to the 1827 creation of the first Black newspaper, *Freedom's Journal*. The Black press came into existence as an act of self-and community defense, as John Brown Russwurm and Samuel Cornish established the *Journal* to confront antiblack discrimination and public denigration, from press and pulpit. Aware of the need for countervailing voices, the editors at once made known and assigned themselves the mission of defending half a million free people of color from daily slander. "We wish to plead our own case," they wrote. Wells, too, saw Blacks slandered daily, a fact made even more urgent in her era because of the growing power and status of newspapers. Not only could the newspaperman reach those that the preacher could not, but all those he reached now began to take his word as the gospel. Wells, too, wanted to use the press to help Blacks defend themselves, to help spread the good word.[14]

To undertake her own defensive press work, Wells would engage in two conversations—a counterpublic conversation and one with Blacks, a conversation within what Catherine Squires refers to as an "enclave public," in a safe space, generally hidden from the wider public view. Pushed into enclave spaces "by repressive state policies," Squires explains, Blacks "have used these enclave spaces to create discursive strategies and gather oppositional resources." Squires argues that the "enclave response" to "conditions of intense opposition" is usually followed by the emergence of counterpublics "in response to a decrease in oppression or an increase in resources." Counterpublics "project the hidden transcripts, previously spoken only in enclaves, to dominant publics."[15] Wells would bring three innovations and one incredible tactic to her dual-track public sphere work—political education, investigation alongside statistical analysis, the PR campaign, and, funnily enough, trolling.

Wells knew that it would never be enough to undertake statistically informed investigations of lynching. She needed to engage the meaning-making juggernaut that was the white press in an expressly counterpublic mode. At the time, the mainstream press was not only "an immense social institution of overwhelming capabilities" that endangered Black lives, it also "ignored Black people unless they were committing crimes or being lynched," as Otis Sandford puts it. Given the cultural force and weight of the white press and the way in which Blacks were portrayed in it, Wells knew she had to confront the beast head on. Yet the grounds on which the Black press had to engage the white press are best analogized to that of asymmetric warfare. In a context in which white papers only mentioned Blacks when they committed crimes or would be or had been lynched—and even then only to encourage, condone, or apologize for the lynching—Wells gambled that the best way to maximize the chance of counterpublicity was to innovate in her methods. So she devised a strategy that merged investigation and statistics with what we would refer to today as expert trolling and a public relations campaign to maximize her chances for genuine counterpublicity.[16]

Wells tends to be associated with reporting only the cold, hard facts, because that is how she represented herself and wanted to be seen, but she also made liberal use of irony to convey and platform Black truth. Goldsby points out that Wells understood that the conventions of white newswriting could not simply be repeated while contesting and contextualizing lynching. They had to be parodied and exposed. Wells used statistics to refute the ideology of lynching, but she also used the stunt-prone, racist editor of the *Memphis Commercial*, Edward Carmack—a vituperative, emotionally unstable foil to her dispassionate use of statistics and ideological deconstruction, and, ultimately, her patsy in her efforts to take on the white press. It was fitting revenge for the role he'd played in the destruction of her newspaper.

Wells would write: "I take the statistics of lynching and prove that according to the charges given, not one-third of the men and women lynched are charged with assaults on white women, and brand that statement a falsehood invented by the lynchers to justify acts of cruelty and outrage."[17] But she did not leave it there. She then baited and skillfully used the vitriol and arrogance of Carmack to platform her cause and analysis in the mainstream US press and to shine a light on white Southern depravity. Wells saw his intemperance as her "missing piece," and coolly exploited it to get more coverage for her cause. Carmack was known to provoke feuds and attack other newspaper editors, a practice that eventually got him killed. He may well have witnessed the lynching of Wells's friend Moss and his colleagues, as Carmack's paper detailed every step of the lynching and ran before-and-after lynching sketches of the victims.[18]

In "Southern Horrors," Wells demonstrated that the charge of rape was only mobilized to justify a third of lynchings. This enraged Carmack, who professed disdain for lynching—primarily for how it tarnished the South's bruised reputation—but supported the practice in cases of interracial rape. Lisa White writes, "By logically refuting the rape myth, Ida Wells forced Edward Carmack into a corner from which he characteristically came out fighting." Meaning that he walked right into and remained ensnared in her trap. Wells, then, parodied his Foghorn Leghorn bluster regarding Southern mores and chivalry—expressly mocking his style while telling her own story—making liberal use of irony, turning his victims into her criminals. "Memphis knew of the awful crime, knew then and knows today who the men were who committed it," Wells wrote, "and yet not the first step was ever taken to apprehend the guilty wretches who walk the streets today with the *brand of murderer upon their foreheads*, but safe from harm as the most upright citizens of the community." Here, White says, Wells reversed criminal guilt while "mimicking the white press's rhetoric about her own 'crime.'" The lynch mob was guilty. They, and not the Black men they murdered, had brands on their foreheads.[19] Wells would then send her columns to Carmack to make sure he had seen them, provoking him into their era's equivalent of rage tweeting.

Wells, in fact, expressly goaded Carmack into the fight she wanted, got her cause into his and other white papers, and kept him in a frenzied cycle of rage that caused him to go on a misogynoirist rant that went beyond even the period's extremely permissive pale in this regard. White tells the story: "Acting on the adage that any publicity is good publicity, Wells regularly sent copies of articles she wrote in exile back to Carmack, who would respond belligerently, then forward copies of his wrath to Wells and other editors. In response to her constant barrage of embarrassing publicity for Memphis and the South, especially when she traveled to Great Britain on anti-lynching lecture tours, in 1893 and 1894, Edward Carmack published a series of tirades trying to discredit her." Members of the British press were utterly scandalized by his words and his "coarse tone," considering his columns about Wells to be altogether unpublishable.[20] "In the May 26, 1894 issue of the Memphis Commercial, Carmack called Wells a series of derogatory names, including, 'notorious negro courtesan, disreputable colored woman, half-cultured hater of all things Southern, saddle-colored Sapphira, intriguing adventuress, strumpet, malicious wonton paramour to both J. L. Fleming and Taylor Nightingale, unimportant adventuress, and infamous slanderer and traducer.'" He sent this to her, and she, in turn, sent it to other editors, and, importantly without comment but clearly with a delightful "wow, why is he so obsessed with me? It's weird right?" subtext. Those editors would then condemn his outrageous attacks while Wells's hands remained clean.

White writes: "Undoubtedly, Ida Wells, as an African American and, equally contemptuously, as a woman, did not even register on Carmack's scale of worthy opponents. However, her endless prodding and repetitious attacks, which mimicked his own rhetorical tactics, left him no option other than to defend his own honor as well as that of other southern white men. . . . In the process, he unintentionally granted her access to the venue for protest that she so desperately needed, the white press, and to his dismay, fostered more embarrassment than respect for Southern culture."[21] And Wells, the saddle-colored Sapphira, intriguing adventuress, the infamous slanderer and traducer, never directly attacked him—indeed if she were ever accused of imitating, of mocking his writing style, she could ask, quite credulously, if the man himself was doing something other than simply reporting the facts, after all. She could thusly remain a cool observer of his utterly unhinged name-calling while enticing others to look on in horror—she herself seeming to have never entered the fray.

Wells also went to Great Britain to maximize her chances for genuine counterpublicity. She traveled to England with the aim of rekindling the British antislavery tradition in progressive and reform circles there, of reviving the abolitionist spirit among its reform set to fight the "new" South's "industrial slavery" and the new labor discipline—lynching—that accompanied it. Her tour was in fact a public relations campaign that helped change the terms of her debate with the dominant public sphere. In Britain she gained access to a venue with considerable power and influence relative to the mainstream US press. What's more, it was so much more powerful that she, a Black woman of considerable epistemic deficits, now had white British men ventriloquize her words. And, as icing on the cake, the bad press abroad aided in her campaign to drive Carmack over the edge.

Taking stock of her British tour, Wells wrote of her success in turning the tide against lynching:

> From one end of the United States to the other press and pulpit were stung by the criticism of press and pulpit abroad and began to turn the searchlight on lynching as never before. As a result, the lynching record of 1893 began steadily to decline and has never since been so high. Nor have there been the reckless statements by prominent persons in defense or condonation of lynching there were before this crusade began. The universally accepted statement that lynching was necessary because of criminal assaults of black men on white women has almost entirely ceased to be believed. This was because of the power of truth which the British people afforded me opportunity to present. They gave a press and a platform from which to tell the Negro's side of the gruesome story. Of lynching, and to appeal to Christian and moral force for help in the demand that every accused person be given a fair trial by law and not by the mob.[22]

Not only did the mainstream press in the United States begin to engage Wells and her arguments, but, as Paula Giddings states, because of this tour the fight against lynching became a national campaign. It became a part of the Republican platform.[23]

But Wells did not envision using the refashioned parts of her era's truth apparatus solely to persuade whites regarding lynching. She also—and perhaps primarily—wanted the Black press to educate Blacks to bring about a change in their political consciousness, one that would orient them toward protest. The Black press had to undertake this work because it was best positioned to do so in her era, as "the people must know before they can act, and there is no educator to compare with the press."[24] Wells held that the Black press had an important role to play in the moral, financial, and, most importantly, political education of Blacks, that the future of the Black race so depended on the actions of the Black press that "a fearlessly edited press is one of the crying necessities of the hour." She wrote: "This is the greatest need of all among the masses of the South—the need of the press as an educator. Children of a larger growth, the masses of our people have never been taught the first rudiments of an education, much less the science of civil government. The vast army who makes the industrial wealth of the South today have had neither the experience of slavery nor the training of the schoolroom, to teach them some valuable lessons, yet they are citizens in name, making history every day for the race."[25]

The need was dire. Wells would insist that press missionaries never let violence drive them permanently from their work, "So great is the race need for instruction along the lines of education, of money-saving and character-making; of learning trades, cultivating self-dependence; of building good foundations upon which their citizenship is to stand; so imperative the necessity for leading the race up to the clear heights of thought, then down into the valley of action, that if persecuted and driven from one place, we must set up the printing press in another and continue the great work."[26]

But the press did not only have to educate Blacks regarding the "foundations" of citizenship; it had a duty to educate Blacks about political action. Wells held that the press must educate Blacks about the power of collective action, specifically of the power of organized labor and of boycotts as the instruments of what she repeatedly referred to as a "bloodless revolution," that is, of the collective economic power that Blacks could wield to bring an end lynching and all racial subordination. Her writings reveal her beliefs about the role of money in politics and the power of money—its far greater power than that of moral suasion, in particular—to transform politics. For

Wells, things were quite simple: "The white man's dollar is his god, and to stop this will be to stop outrages in many localities." White men may have had new bibles, but they remained faithful to the country's old religion. Wells held that Blacks, in fact, had unrealized power, as laborers and as consumers, in the economic organization of the South and could use that power to change the existing political hierarchy. Quite simply: "To Northern capital and Afro-American labor, the South owes its rehabilitation. If labor is withdrawn capital will not remain. The Afro-American is thus the backbone of the South. A thorough knowledge and judicious exercise of this power in lynching localities could many times effect a bloodless revolution." It was the job of the press to help Black people understand this.

Regarding the power of organized labor, Wells said: "The Afro-American needs to be taught the power of union, to realize his own strength; how to utilize that strength to secure to himself his inherent rights as did the plebians of Rome. He makes the money of the South but has never been taught that a husbanding of resources will cease to enrich gigantic corporations at his own expense. Intelligently directed, by exercise of this power alone, the race can do much to bring about a change in race condition. The sudden withdrawal of the labor force of any one community, paralyzes the industry of that community."[27]

When it came to Blacks as consumers, consistent with her belief that money held the true power to transform politics, Wells saw boycotts as superior to lawsuits: "The Afro-American must be taught that there is one potent, never-failing method of dealing with prejudice; when you touch a white man's pocket, you touch his heart, and his prejudices all melt away. Before the almighty dollar he worships as to no other deity, and through this weakness, a taking away of this idol, the Afro-American can affect a bloodless revolution." But, again, Blacks had to be presented with this information: "He must be taught his power." Prophetic indeed. And who best to teach Blacks these important truths with the immediacy necessary to confront a problem so urgent? Neither the teacher nor the preacher, who faced significant limitations in her era, but the presswoman.[28] For Wells, the press could both speak to *and* shape nations. The press must provide education in the service of political transformation to orient Blacks toward their own defense in the fight for their rights. The press must do its education for defense work until Blacks, so transformed by the press's efforts, could do it for themselves, that is "till the evils we suffer are removed or the people better prepared to fight their own battles."[29]

Wells saw the press as the institution through which to bring about the political transformation of Blacks. The investigations she envisioned taking place within the Black press would play an important role in that transformation. Lynching investigations served her goal of education toward Black political self-defense, as they not only often brought about the character rehabilitation of the Black dead and dispelled any lingering beliefs within the Black community that the lynching victims may have deserved to die but also revealed the fallacy of uplift, as they often demonstrated that it was Black economic success and monetary and capital accumulation that so often produced the racial conflicts that led to lynching, and therefore investigations helped to prove protest was the only option for Black safety and equality. Investigations also functioned to expose the structural inequalities that allowed the white press to produce and disseminate false meanings of Black life. Finally, she envisioned the process of collectively organizing investigations as a political capacity and influence building exercise, one that could strengthen the capacity of the Black press to shape Black public opinion, as a national effort complete with an organizational structure nimble enough to operate within a system of pervasive white violence, as she wanted these investigations to be both funded and undertaken by members of the Black press throughout the nation. They were much smaller, had less reach, and were undercapitalized relative to the white press, but collectively they could build the capacity to coordinate among themselves to investigate lynching across the nation and disseminate the real story to their Black audiences.

The political education project had to challenge how Blacks saw themselves and make apparent the structural conditions that created such negative self-conceptions. Wells saw that when faced with a barrage of lies and character assassinations from the white press, Blacks often accepted what they read about themselves as gospel. Wells challenged Bishop Tanner, who held that it was a "ray of light" that only "men of disreputable character suffered" at the hands of lynchers. Wells put the matter plainly: "I will simply ask the bishop and those who believe him, to remember who sits in judgment on the 'supposed' character of the lynched.... Who supposes the victims of lynch law are bad characters? Those who supposed they are justified in murdering them and must have some excuse for their crimes?"[30] Wells would go on to outline the conditions that led to whites' meaning-making advantage regarding the dead: "The press agents, telegraph wires and newspapers belong to the Southern whites—the colored man has no facilities if he has the courage to tell his side of the story. To accept the Southern white man's report that all lynched are disreputable or supposed disreputable characters is to believe the race so criminal, ignorant and bestial it must be hunted with dogs and killed like wild beasts."[31] She wrote: "To read the white papers the Afro-American is a savage that is getting away from the restraint of the inherent fear of the white man which controlled his passions, and from whom women and children now flee as from a wild beast. This impression has gained ground from the white papers and has blasted the race's reputation in many quarters."[32] But significantly, Wells did not think that it was up to Tanner and others to simply "snap out of it." The Black press had a duty to counteract this, to inoculate Blacks against the falsehoods of the mainstream press. Blacks received asymmetrical information. The cure was the whole truth, which necessarily included Blacks' side of the story.

Wells would present her inoculation plans to members of the National Press Association. Undercapitalized as they were, she said flatly, "The Afro American papers are the only ones which will print the truth." Her remedy was simple: "Every single report which is published be investigated by detectives and let the negro witness ask that his statements be published side by side with that of the lynchers."[33] Thorough investigation, that included Black perspectives, was the method by which the Black press should respond to the slander. She pointed out that her own paper presented the facts of the "lynching at the curve" and provided character statements to counteract the libel against the victims, whom the white press had characterized as "three negroes who kept a low dive." The "low dive" in question was a grocery store. Wells wondered pointedly, "How many such have gone down to a violent death without anything to chronicle the true facts in their cases will never be known."

But the Southern Black press had a violence problem. If they told the truth freely, as she had done, they would be run out of town, as she had been. She told members of the National Press Association, that, therefore, the time had come for them to stop sitting idly by: "The Afro-American journal has not troubled itself to counteract [the opinion that Afro-Americans are wild beasts]—those of the South because they dare not in many cases, and those of other sections seeming to care not. But not only the reputation of individuals but that of the race is involved. The clearing of this odium attached to the race name is not only the duty of one section but belongs to all, and the National Press Association should no longer sit idly waiting for the garbled accounts of the Associated Press, which it in turn gives the world."[34] She charged the association with the duty of coordinating a national lynching investigative operation whose findings could be distributed to the nation's Black press: "So frequent and serious has the grave charge of rape become, there should be full investigation of every such accusation which is considered sufficient excuse for the most diabolical outrage and torture. Afro-American Southern journalism cannot do it and hope to continue existence; but this united body as an association, can do something toward changing public opinion and molding public sentiment in our favor. This is *the* work of the association. . . . The time for *action* has come. Let the association tax itself to hire a detective, who shall go to the scene of each lynching, get the facts *as they exist* in each case of outrage—especially where the charge of rape is made—furnish them to the different papers of the association and those so situated shall publish them to the world. Money should be placed in the treasury at this session for that purpose, and a tax assessed by which it shall be kept up. It will pay from every point of view. You are thus in the position, despite the connivance of press agents, telegraph operators, and civil authorities to secure correct information, and vindicate the race from the charge of bestiality which stands before the world to-day practically unchallenged."[35] She reminded the association, "A correspondent of *The Age* did it in Paris, Texas, in the month of September, and uncovered a tale of cruelty, outrage and murder against the race which would make sick the hearts of a savage. Our race papers since have used that account extensively. This could be done in every case, and for every garbled and slanderous dispatch sent out by the Associated Press, this association would be in position to match with the true account of these race disturbances and lynchings."[36] Of course, what she proposed would not be cheap, and in addition to taxing itself to fund investigation, the cost of the coordinating the national investigative apparatus presented an opportunity to collectivize, to build political capacity, as she held, "The race must rally a mighty host to the support of their journals, and thus enable them to do much in the way of investigation."[37]

Wells had a significant test case regarding the role of the Black press in changing Black political consciousness in her own life. In fact, Wells and Fortune's commitment to protest had already begun to change the way Black communities responded to racial violence. Not only had Wells's March 1892 editorial in the *Free Speech* prompted thousands of Blacks to leave Memphis for the Oklahoma Territories, Giddings writes, "The response of the black press to the Memphis events, which began to appear in late March, was unprecedented. No other event in recent years, including Carrollton, evoked such comment—or fury. The circumstances of the lynching, the rising militance, the consciousness raised by [Fortune's] Afro-American League and the palpable protest led by Wells with her wide readership and unadulterated race-first position made the Memphis murders reverberate through both religious and secular black publications as no others had before it." One thousand Blacks at Bethel AME would refuse to sing "America" and instead sang "John Brown's Body." Giddings explains: "In the same month Barnett and Fortune among others attended a mass antilynching meeting in New York City. Two thousand Blacks, including Fortune, met in Cooper Union in lower Manhattan regarding events in Memphis in what the New York Times called 'the largest assemblage of blacks ever held in that city to date.'"[38] Wells, as we now well know, was on to something.

Widening the Frame, Reanimating the Dead: Anti-Lynching Photography as Family Portrait

If the lynching at the Curve completed Wells's conversion to protest, it was Catherine Impey's actions, and those of other English reformers, that helped to convince Wells of the power of the photographic image in the fight against lynching, her second significant conversion. Wells did not pioneer the use of lynching photos in antiracist work—that distinction belongs to the beleaguered Impey—but she would once again innovate and set the standard for how such photos were used. Wells saw clearly how best to frame and contextualize such photos.

Lynching photos were initially a symbol of white supremacy, recruiting devices for that cause previously used to terrorize Black people and their allies. The outspoken antilynching judge Albion Tourgee received a postcard of Ray Porter's lynching in 1891, accompanied by "an incendiary message." He was not the only person on these macabre mailing lists.[39] Tourgee sent the postcard to Impey, who published it in the January 1893 issue of her anti-imperialist, antiracist journal *Anti-Caste*. Impey endured a great deal of criticism for her decision to print the photo, which critics believed was "an embellished drawing." When they came to understand "it was indeed a photograph of an event," however, they "were moved from skepticism to zealous antilynching advocacy." The Reverend C. K. Aked would use Porter's photo to publicize Wells's lecture tour. And at one of her lectures on the tour, delivered to sixteen members of Parliament, attendees passed around a lynching photo.[40]

The Brits may have shown her a new way of using such photos, but Wells never thought that a photo could "speak for itself." Even as she witnessed English activists deploying the photograph in novel ways, she knew that any image must be accompanied with framing words. Of her British tour, she wrote: "British people took with incredulity my statements that colored men were roasted or lynched in broad daylight, very frequently with the sanction of officers of the law, and looked askance at statements that half-grown boys shot bullets into hanging bodies, and, after cutting off toes and fingers of the dead or dying, carried them about as trophies. . . . But when I showed them photographs of such scenes, the newspaper reports and the reports of searching investigations on the subject, they accepted the evidence of their own senses against their wills."[41] Wells published Porter's photo with her July 1893 essay "Lynch Law" and included it in her July 1893 front-page, six-column *Inter-Ocean* article on C. J. Miller's lynching, "The Brutal Truth." Wells's strategy "would be adopted and repeated into and across the twentieth century." When the NAACP's Walter White endeavored to publish as many lynching photos as he could, for example, he followed a "path broken by Ida B. Wells."[42]

Wells would also transform the lynching photo itself, another of her significant innovations. She not only believed that images only spoke the right way when presented alongside contextualizing reporting and investigation, she also stretched the bounds of the lynching photo itself, as she would do with investigative reporting on lynching, toward interiority and contextualization. Wells, for example, did not simply run Porter's photo with her exposé of the Miller lynching. She had posed as Miller's widow to go undercover, investigate the circumstances of his death, and record some of his last words for her piece and for history. After Moss's lynching, Wells commissioned a portrait of herself with his family. See Figure 4.1. Leigh Raiford reads this portrait, too, as a lynching photo, what she names the "political portrait," and typical of Wells's ability to stretch interpretive boundaries.[43] It was a move that compelled Wells's audience, then and now, to expand their understanding of lynching photographs as "not simply the icon of the black man hanging from a tree but as a family left behind."[44]

The family portrait emerged as a trope at the invention of the daguerreotype, functioning to document family history and convey private sentiment.

Figure 4.1 Ida B. Wells (standing, left) with Maurine Moss, widow of Tom Moss, with Betty and Tom Moss Jr.

The portrait of Wells with Thomas Moss's widow, Betty; his daughter, Maurine; and his son, Thomas Jr., according to Raiford, participates in this trope while also insisting its audience "acknowledge the tragedy of a family lineage cut short by the cruel lynching of the patriarch."[45] Notably, Wells stands in the photo, stepping into the masculine role of protector that would have been occupied by the Thomas Moss if he had not been murdered. "Here," Raiford explains, "lynching is not solely represented by the abject and desecrated black male body but also by the family the children left behind, and importantly by the women who survive and take up the political struggle." With the photo, Wells telegraphs a new form of Black, and here feminine, political subjectivity—one that stretched the bounds of protest beyond the boycotts and collective labor action Wells expressly called for, emphasizing mourning, too, as a political act, as protest.[46]

But what Wells is doing with the photograph and its explicit reference to life outside of and before tragic violence is more than political mourning: it is also a political resurrection and a new way of being with the dead in politics. Raiford suggests that in the portrait Wells and Betty Moss initiate something akin to the political practice of contemporary families who refuse to mourn passively and instead circulate postmortem photos of Black male homicide victims. She quotes Deborah McDowell, who says the families "choose to exhibit the body not as still life, but as living still in memory."[47] Moss is "living still," still with us, in the context of the newly inaugurated political subjectivity that Wells is calling into being. As well, Wells's efforts to convey mundane yet important aspects of C. J. Miller and Moss's inner lives before the violence, these "small, needful facts"—their words, their intimate and familial relationships—are part of what Hooker calls her reanimation work. Wells, then, performs resurrective labor as a part of this new politics she is in the process of inaugurating.

Measured Magic and the Ephemeral Remains of the Dead: Record, Requiem and Resurrection

Wells's work to expand the boundaries of the lynching photo is in keeping with her most significant conversion of all, to the practice of "saying their names." Two years after her first published writing on lynching in which she expressed tremendous faith in the power of newswriting to save Black lives, a report by John Mitchell Jr. on "Southern Outrages" would forever change Wells's views. She wrote of the report's impact on her: "My eyes filled with tears and my heart with un-speakable pity, as I thought of *The Richmond Planet's* list of unfortunates who had met such a fearful fate. No requiem, save the night wind, had been sung over their dead bodies; no memorial services to bemoan their sad and horrible fate had before been in their memory, and no record of the time and place of their taking off, save this, is extant; and like many a brave Union soldier their bodies lie in many an unknown and unhonored spot."[48]

It is worth pausing to note both Mitchell himself and the fact that he had more than a passing interest in memorializing Black death. Mitchell, the "fighting editor," was the radical editor of the *Richmond Planet*, former Richmond correspondent for the *New York Freeman*, president of the Afro-American Press Association, and then vice president of the National Press Association. The *New York World* referred to him as "One of the most daring and vigorous negro editors."[49] Shelby Pumphrey writes that "The *Planet* regularly published the details of national lynchings. Dedicated readers could expect an updated annual count of the total numbers of persons lynched to be included in the weekly." Indeed, the *Planet* ran statistical tables enumerating "the loss of life (to lynching) every week for the entire duration of the paper's forty-five-year run (1884–1929)." And in the 1890s the paper ran those tables with gun ads on the facing page. The *Planet* also reported on mob violence, pogroms, and recovery efforts.[50] Pumphrey continues, "While many of the victims were Virginians, there were also reports from outside the state and even the region. This information was typically listed alongside of Mitchell's detailed political cartoons. As head of the nation's leading black journalists' association, Mitchell encouraged his colleagues to fearlessly engage in similar discourse through their individual periodicals. . . . Mitchell led a fiercely fought campaign that included both raising awareness about lynching victims and their families via *The Planet* and also working on behalf of African Americans that were unfairly treated by the criminal justice system."[51]

Wells was deeply moved by Mitchell's lists of "unfortunates," that his dead passed without record or requiem. Mitchell insisted that the Black press should provide a record; she made the record requiem. She would record. She would provide a "litany of loss"—but she would also excavate quotidian details of their lives before the violence to, as Hooker says, "reanimate" the dead. Her lament for those without record and requiem became, through her seemingly dispassionate, fact-filled reconstructions, a lamentation.

Wells was not given to displays of emotion, but she cried when she heard of these murdered Blacks, their names before unknown to us, their deaths unheralded, lying in unmarked graves. This emotional response, this mourning, underpinned her subsequent empirical work. Mitchell's report convinced Wells of the need to "say their names."[52] Sometimes the work of saying their names was quite literal. Because of the strength of her conviction and her investigative work to make it so, we know that Sam Hose, whose lynching would lead Du Bois away from Atlanta and to his own antilynching work in *The Crisis*, was not Sam Hose at all. "His true name as Samuel Wilkes," Wells reported. In her recovery work, Wells labored to convey Wilkes's biography, his challenges, his inner life. We know that he taught himself to read and write and "was considered a bright, capable man," and "the mainstay of the family." We know that Wilkes supported a disabled mother and brother. The results of Wells's investigation do much to communicate the kind of man he was.

Wells would say their names both as a call to mourn and to "bring out the dead," to ward against the dead being "unknown and unhonored." Hooker's work reflecting on how Wells used fact for affect and Terrion Williamson on "bringing out the dead" is instructive here. As she would do with lynching photos, Wells expanded the practice of saying their names toward interiority and contextualization. Because of Wells's efforts, for example, we know not just about a New Orleans mob but also a great deal about mob victim Robert Charles's inner life—his work with the Colonization Society, his study of racial oppression, his correspondence with Bishop Henry McNeal Turner, his work with Turner's organization, and the search for meaning, purpose, and self-respect that surely led him to defy the indignity of the New Orleans Police officer, leading to his death. Wells wrote: "The reporters of the New Orleans papers, who were in the best position to trace the record of this man's life, made every possible effort to find evidence to prove he was a villain unhung. . . . For this reason, as a matter of duty to the race and the simple justice to the memory of Charles, an investigation has been made of the life and character of Charles before the fatal affray that led to his death." We can surmise how Turner would have advised him; Wells invites us to do so. Wells even wrote to the president of the organization regarding Charles's character and printed the character letter for all to see. "Robert Charles was not an educated man," Wells told the world. She continued:

> He was a student who faithfully investigated all the phases of oppression from which his race has suffered. . . . He knew that he was a student of a problem which required all the intelligence that a man could command, and he was burning his midnight oil gathering knowledge that he might better be able to come to an intelligent solution. To his aid in the study of this problem he sought the aid of a Christian newspaper, *The Voice of Missions*, the organ of the AME Church. He was in communication with its editor, who is a bishop, and is known all over this country as a man of learning, a lover of justice and the defender of law and order. Charles

> could receive from Bishop Turner not a word of encouragement to be other than an earnest, tireless and God-fearing student of the complex problems which affected the race.

In her report on the hate strike, riot, and massacre in East Saint Louis, Illinois, Wells never shied away from gruesome facts. She reported on horrific lynchings, replete with white barbarism, including what she dubbed "the most sickening sight of the evening," a lyncher "literally bathing his hand" in the victim's blood. She stated that a woman's tongue was shot off. And, demonstrating the plain-spoken fearlessness that would get her into trouble with Blacks and whites alike, she foregrounded white feminine agency, detailing considerable violence and theft perpetrated by individual white women and roving white female mobs. Yet Wells also took pains to juxtapose this barbarism with humanizing portrayals of the massacre's Black victims and survivors. She used quotidian details about Black life and Black interiors to highly emotional effect, to make present—to resurrect—Black interiority. She reported not only on shattered skulls, but shattered lives:

> I went . . . inside a dozen of their three and four room houses and saw the mob's work of destruction. In every case, the houses had been fired from the rear and as soon as the occupants came out, they were then shot at or beaten. In most of the homes in which I went, the inmates had gone before the mob got there. When these cottages were found to be empty, the mob went into them, threw the mattresses, quilts, blankets and wearing apparel that was not new, on the floor and then cut, tore and trampled these things under foot and set fire to them. Pictures, bric-a-brac, everything that they could destroy, they did. . . . Most of these houses had brass or iron bedsteads, and the mattresses were good, worth $4.00 or $5.00 a piece. In two of those homes, I saw a piano. In one of them the woman found a few of her records, but her victrola and most of the records had been taken away. The windows were broken, and doors had been split open, evidently with an ax. One woman found her pictures and some of her wearing apparel in a white neighbor's house, and when she accused the woman of taking them, this woman said that all the others were taking things and she did so too.

We see Wells counting up the losses, but also taking account of what the losses mean:

> Mrs. Flake is a widow with three children, 11, 8 and 6 years old. She is a laundress who came to East St. Louis four years ago from Jackson, Tenn. She took care of her little family by taking in washing, and she worked from Monday morning until Saturday night at the ironing board. She too had three rooms full of nice furniture. Both of the two front rooms having nice rugs on the floor, a brass bedstead and other furniture to correspond. She had about a hundred dollars worth of furniture ruined, fifty dollars worth of clothing and about fifty dollars more of bedding, mattresses, etc. The mob had taken a phonograph for which she had paid $15.00 and twenty-five records for which she had paid 75 cents and $1.00 each. She got away with her children before the mob reached her house and she too came back that morning to get some clothes for herself and children. The mob hadn't left much, but out of the debris, she was able to pack one trunk with some clothing and quilts for herself and children. It was in this house that I picked up one child's new shoe and although we looked the house over, we couldn't find the other. In its spasm of wanton destruction, the mob had doubtless carried it away. Mrs. Flake also had life insurance policies for herself and children, but she couldn't find any of the books.[53]

Wells reports that the widow Flake had already made arrangements to leave, as she was "too anxious to get away from the town where such awful things were transpiring, and where not even widows and children were safe from the fury of the mob bent on killing everything with black skins."[54]

In her pamphlet *The East St. Louis Massacre: The Greatest Outrage of the Century* (1907), Wells built, Hooker says, "a litany of loss with each successive chapter on an individual victim." The chapters are named for victims, with titles like "Mrs. Ballard's Story," "Mrs. Lulu Thomas' Story," "Clarissa Lockett's Story," "Story of William Gold," and "Story of James Taylor." Wells lamented the lives lost to violence that went "unhonored and unknown," and, in her deceptively unsentimental way, she turned her lament into a lamentation, a heartfelt expression of sorrow, of mourning. But her litany was also the labor of resurrection: through this painstaking work to render the quotidian details of Black lives before violence she was able to, as Hooker says, "reanimate Black lives lost to violence."[55]

Wells would say their names as she excavated the ephemeral remains of their shattered lives—the correspondence, the ledger books, the life insurance policies, broken records, strewn quilts, broken windows, photos left behind, "one child's new shoe and although we looked the house over, we couldn't find the other"—effectively communicating both the monetary value of the ephemera and (for those who were capable of understanding) the sentimental value to convey Black interiority, the lost hopes and dreams. Hooker sees this as a part of Wells's humanizing *and* politicizing grief work. To Hooker, Wells exemplifies "a strand of African American political thought on loss that does not forego grievance but makes a space for a more capacious approach to Black grief." In her work, she says, Wells was not simply trying to call a public into being that could face the fact of white violence, she was reckoning with loss in a capacious way. We think of Wells in the way that she presented herself, as unsentimental, as reporting the facts. But in Wells's writings, Hooker writes, "we find a mix of sentimental and unsentimental elements in service of documenting myriad iterations of black loss." Wells's work always encouraged reflection on loss and provided ample space to grieve. Wells's multivalent accounting of Black loss spoke to an audience with variable civic capacity. Hooker outlines how Wells enumerated in the service of empathy, how she counted to care. "For most of her white readers, who were unaccustomed to extending the same care and concern to Black people, the detailed list of material goods lost could read as mere statement of facts, to be sure. But for those who had developed the civic capacity to care about the losses of racialized others, and for Black audiences [who presumably possessed these civic capacities to care], these inventories of dispossession were profoundly affective." Hooker says that through this work Wells reanimated the dead. Wells marshaled empirics bringing to life the Black interior, and thereby raise the dead.

Wells's Supernatural Publics: Bringing the Dead into Political Community

Many have commented on Wells's self-professed commitment to render the "cold hard facts" about lynching, and she did indeed write, as Goldsby has said, in a realist style about the minutiae of what violent racists did to the Black body—she took summary of what bullet holes did to flesh. Her approach was appropriate. "Faced with such horrific brutality, Wells would write in kind," Goldsby puts it. But for all Wells's facts and frankness, eschewing the sentimental style of her Black female contemporaries, Hooker reminds us that Wells was also attentive to affect in Black life, to love, care, and sentiment. Hooker argues that Wells used mundane accounts and accountings of disordered—shattered—Black interiors to communicate, to foreground Black interiority. Wells, she says, would use fact *and* affect in her pioneering death work: "Wells combines profuse statistical data (fact) with quotidian details (affect)." The facts indeed evoked the affect, as Hooker says that Wells's work was "heartrending because of abundant quotidian details of Black life."[56]

I see this as evidence that Wells inaugurated not only a new politics but a new way of *being with the dead* in politics. Her work forever altered the Black public sphere and helped to initiate its fully realized post-emancipation counterpublic, beginning a profound Black political transformation, that is, Du Bois's work of resurrection, but it did so as an act of care for both *the living and the dead.* Wells's work of resurrection, then, proceeded via the labors of resurrection, through care for the dead. As Williamson would say of Barbara Smith's death work decades later, Wells used statistics, but her work was so much more than counting; hers was a care-filled method of being accountable to the lives lost, of "bringing out the dead." The careful reconstruction of interiority alongside her pioneering statistical analysis was Wells's version of Smith's scratching out the numbers while retaining them, it was her labor of resurrection, and enabled Wells to carry the voices of the dead with her into the new public she was bringing into being as she called for protest, resistance, and the world they deserved. Wells began the "work of resurrection" in earnest—saving Blacks by inspiring them, persuading them, and providing the blueprint for the coming political struggle for racial equality—but she understood that it required the labor of resurrection, required the reanimation of, care for, and accountability to the dead, and that the political work must be done with and for the dead.

Williamson is interested in Black women's practices—in the face of government and media inaction in response to Black femicide—of "bringing out the dead." She quotes Grace Kyungwon Hong as saying, "to bring out your dead is not a memorial, but a challenge, not an act of grief, but of defiance, not a register of mortality and decline, but of the possibility of struggle and survival."[57] This, too, is a part of what Wells did. The women Williamson considers, and Smith of the Combahee River Collective, specifically, are, in an important sense, Wells's political daughters. As we have seen, Smith's pamphlet, "Six Black Women: Why Did They Die?," became a visualization of "the ongoing nature of the crisis . . . a material artifact of the escalating terror to which black women were being subjected." Williamson argues that the Combahee River Collective and those who joined their action in response to Black women's deaths in Boston "expanded the archive, essentially becoming an archive in and of themselves." Furthermore: "When the local community activist Sara Small cried out 'Who is killing us?' to the crowd of people gathered for the memorial march in Boston in April 1979, she was not just asking a question in need of an answer, she was staking a claim for the collective. In that single utterance, wherein the terms of death were made deliberately communal, Small scratched out the numbers. She, in accordance with and alongside the CRC, interdicted the bare tabulation of death, counted it all out differently, and said that *we* are what else has happened here."[58] She expressly rendered the dead as part of that emerging we. Bringing out the dead. Counting it all out differently. *We* are what else has happened here. Creating an archive, a counterarchive but also becoming an archive in and of themselves. This is the legacy of Wells.

But Wells also refused Hong's binary between memorial or challenge, grief or defiance. Wells reckoned with our loss—she openly mourned—*and* brought out our dead. Each tear-filled memorial was always a challenge. She practiced defiant grief. She suggested protest politics as *the* possibility for struggle and survival via her register of mortality and loss, her litany, her lamentation reanimated the dead as it called a new "we" into being around them. Wells demanded that we reckon with the dead, with their humanity. That we be accountable to them. That we, first, sit with each of the lost and then stand up for them. Each name she called came with a story that brought forward the voices, the interiority of the lost. Each small, needful fact part of a care-filled memorial for a Black life lost was also always a challenge to the political order that produced that loss. Wells counted each death and then counted it all out differently. She enumerated—but as Hooker tells us, for those adept enough to recognize it, even this was not mere tabulation—but lamentation. She did the necessary work of recording the numbers and then went on, like Smith, to scratch them out by telling the story of each life before loss and with that story calling a collective into being around the lost and now-reanimated life. Williamson sees this counting, and subsequent refusal of mere tabulation, as both fighting an official record system that was deliberately lax regarding the deaths of Black women and as an act of claiming the dead as a part of "us," the "we"-in-progress, the supernatural "we" that is "what else has happened here." Wells claimed political community with the dead, calling into being the "we" that would be what else would happen here as a collective of the living and the reanimated dead. This, then, would be the archive, the new record.

She would provide the blueprint for both counting and being politically accountable to the dead. She would give both record and requiem, thereby refusing mere tabulation. She would affirm the value of their lives by undertaking the painstaking, careful, and care-filled work of transcribing the humanity of those who had been killed, and notably doing this not via appeals to the sacred but via the mundane, via empirics, telling their quotidian stories, excavating their hopes and dreams in the process. Therefore, her method expressly renders this new "we" she is calling forth not as a unity—a collective united in divine sameness—but as a multiplicity. Giddings applauds the work Wells did to counter the stereotype and caricature on display in the white press, to make white women, Black men, and Black women most of all "more than mere abstractions" in her writing. Indeed, and though she labored to honor the tremendous losses and inner lives of survivors, most of all Wells would give those who did not survive, victims, flesh and blood in black and white, resurrecting them for Black politics. She would resurrect the lost within our democracy by recording their deaths, but most pointedly by recording their lives, by reconstructing and disseminating their interiority, counting them, yes, but going on to count it all out differently, by providing an accounting of their lives as an act of mourning, by being politically accountable to them by calling others into the struggle for them as they mourned them, thus keeping the dead within the bounds of our democracy. The archive she created claimed those lost as part of (the now politically mobilized) us—"who is killing us"—and by reanimating them claimed them as with us still in the fight to struggle and survive. That is, though she had an explicit program for persuading others to stand with her, it is important to note that her initial collective, the collective that brought her so uncharacteristically to tears and those with whom she first resolved to stand on March 5, 1888, that day that Mitchell spoke to her and through her changed all our lives, were the dead themselves that she would go on to do the work of reanimating, resurrecting.

Mitchell showed Wells the importance of "saying their names." Her innovations concerned what beyond their names she would say, how she would make the record requiem, how she would, via wholly secular methods, reanimate—resurrect—the dead, and thus perform her empirical miracle, and in so doing, inaugurate not only a new Black protest politics, but a new way of being and acting with the dead in politics. Her counting and reanimation became not only a way of bringing the dead into a public she was calling into being but a method of accountability to the dead. Wells memorialized the dead but, more than this, she expressly cared for them—and with and through the dead, she cared for us, for democracy.

Regarding the "we are what else has happened here," in thinking about death work and democracy, there are notable contrasts between Wells and Du Bois that I would like to highlight in closing. Wells, as I said, inaugurated not only a new politics, but a new way of being with the dead in politics, caring for the dead, keeping the dead in politics, that other women, including Mamie Till-Mobley, Clementine Barfield, Barbara Smith, and Margaret Prescod, would continue. Bonnie Honig has encouraged me to think not about amplifying nondominant stories of peoplehood to make "the people" more inclusive so that women and other nonnormative folk might be thought of as truly part of that people, but instead to be liberated by this incomplete inclusion. When we abandon the project of constituting a stable "we," we can instead look for peopled moments, episodes where people come together briefly to come together again at another moment. The small dispersed wes perhaps provide a way to dethrone the dominant story of peoplehood by a thousand cuts, or better yet a way around it to create democratic subject transforming Morrisonian truant democracy in its clearings. Williamson directs us to exactly this kind of "we." These gatherings around the women's deaths that are ignored by police, by the media, by mainstream Black civil society organizations, by the wider Black community, and the life keeping their members perform make the claim not only that someone who was valuable has died and that this loss must be reckoned with or we are all lost, that the lost are a part of us, but also that "we"—our new collective and its struggles in response to these deaths—"are what else has happened here." For Black femicide activists and all those who struggle on behalf of Blacks who are not cis, straight, and male, Wells with her collectives of the living and the reanimated, her individuated and disunified collectives begins this work in the service of a more usable we.

Finally, Williamson is interested in the "epistemological possibilities" of Smith's decision to scratch out and retain the numbers. And there is, indeed, so much to think about regarding how Wells worked to know differently and how she worked to level the epistemic playing field, through trolling as part of an effort to expose the deficiencies of the white truth apparatus, through statistically inflected conjure. The above also makes clear that the political possibilities called forth by this alternate epistemology and in Smith's and Wells' ephemeral "we" are unfathomably rich. It makes clear that these collectives can change not only the make up of the Demos but what we can know about ourselves and the world. But it is indeed worth reflecting on what more can be known and what we can know differently from scratching it out, retaining it, and counting it all out differently, from trolling for truth. This suggests that these wes can also be sites of necessary knowledge production. Aimi Hamraie's work on disability justice, specifically their work on how crip technoscience and disability justice workers' epistemic activism—that is, activism around how we know things and come to know things—changed the sites of knowledge production and who produces it, is instructive for thinking about these collectives, and thinking of them as engaged in forms of democratic *and* epistemic tinkering. Hamraie sees knowledge as a kind of design and therefore that all meaning-making is also always world-making. These two ways of thinking about what is happening here, the way I am outlining in these pages and Hamraie's, seem the correct approaches to reflecting on the projects in which the women I profile are engaged. I address their epistemic activist/design possibilities in the Conclusion.

5

Emmett Till Is with Us Still

Mamie Till-Bradley, Reincarnation, and the Lynching-as-Crucifixion Scenario

Emmett Till is with us still. According to Christopher Metress, author of the book *The Lynching of Emmett Till* and editor of a documentary of the same name, "Till's murder has woven itself intimately into the fabric of American poetry, drama, fiction and memoir" thanks to writers like Langston Hughes, Gwendolyn Brooks, and many others, while "Till's image has emerged as one of the most powerful and haunting reminders of racial injustice in America." Metress focuses his analysis on Till's "many various incarnations," one of the most recurrent of which is Till as a figure of disruption, embodied in the slogan, "No Justice, No Peace!": "When the system fails, so the logic goes, those whom the system fails must seek to generate unease, disturbance, and disruption. When the system failed African Americans in 1955, they took to the streets and agitated for justice, but it was justice they never received. Since then, many African American writers have retold the Emmett Till story as a means of continuing that agitation, imagining Till as a figure of disturbance and disruption who unsettles the peace of those who victimized him and then refused to grant him justice." By "refusing to let Till's story die and resurrecting him as an agitator of the peace," those who invoke him "are passing their own judgement on the injustices of the past."[1] Till-as-disruptor is an incarnation that took time to develop, however. The earliest—and still quite prevalent—incarnation of Till, Metress holds, was that of "sacrificial lamb." For this incarnation, he gives ambivalent credit to Till's mother, Mamie Till-Bradley, saying that she "may have been the genesis of this configuration."[2]

Here, Metress far undersells the value of Till-Bradley's resurrective labor. In truth, the recurrent incarnation of Till in Black cultural production as a disruptor—indeed all subsequent incarnations—would not have come into being without Till-Bradley's creation and dissemination of that first

The Labors of Resurrection. Shatema Threadcraft, Oxford University Press. © Oxford University Press (2025).
DOI: 10.1093/9780197758618.003.0006

sacrificial incarnation of her son as a Black Christ child among the wider public. Till-Bradley's staging of her son's death tapped into both the by then long-standing lynching-as-crucifixion story *and* an ongoing practice of Black re-enactment of antiblack violence among themselves, which itself led to a wave of young people psychically changing places with Till—as Elizabeth Alexander says "feeling their fate as interchangeable with Till's"—and thus in an important sense being reincarnated as him.[3] It was not simply that Till was reincarnated but that young Blacks were reincarnated as Till. In order to understand the significance of Mamie Till-Bradley's democratic necromantic contribution I turn to Elizabeth Alexander's seminal essay, "Can You Be BLACK and Look at This? Reading the Rodney King Video(s)," and Erica Edward's writing on the role of "scenario"—that is, a mode of theater in which players follow an outline with much room for improvisation—in Black politics. Till-Bradley's resurrective labor disseminated a more participatory version of the lynching-as-crucifixion story, complete with a resurrection into political struggle in which audience members were invited to and did take part.

Again, I argue that unruly women, loud-mouthed ungovernable women, single mothers, lesbians, sex workers, and those who have made common cause with these nonnormative women, it is they who have best done Du Bois's work of resurrection and more. Till-Bradley, as we know, was a single mother. She was also a survivor of male violence who obtained a restraining order against Till's father, Louis Till, from whom she separated after his infidelity and who, during that separation choked her until she was almost unconscious. She responded by throwing scalding water on him. She had two other brief marriages before she and her son relocated to Chicago's South Side.[4] As well, in keeping with the theme of the exemplary democratic contributions of unruly, ungovernable woman, her decision to publish the photos of Till's mutilated body, while lionized today, was at the time considered quite scandalous.

Till-Bradley, like Wells, performed resurrective labor for her son and for us all. Till-Bradley did not take Wells's secular route in her own resurrective labor, and among the women I profile, she is alone in foregrounding the biblical crucifixion. Like Du Bois, she took inspiration from the biblical crucifixion; the crucifixion expressly guided her understanding of her and her son's place in history. Yet her immersive version of events shifted Blacks' experience of the lynching-as-crucifixion story from association to identification.

Setting the Stage

The funeral of Emmett Till stands as the most effective political use of a dead body in the twentieth century. Abducted, beaten, mutilated, and shot in the head, the fourteen-year-old's body spent three days in the Tallahatchie River before it was recovered in August 1955 and returned to Chicago at the insistence of his mother. When the body arrived home from the Mississippi Delta, where Emmett had been on summer vacation, Mamie Till-Bradley famously demanded that the world see it too, pressing for an open-casket funeral that would be attended by thousands. Staged photographs of Till's lynched body were published alongside images of Till in life and his grieving mother in *Jet* magazine and the *Chicago Defender*, where they sparked a national controversy and made an indelible impression on Black Americans—often credited as a turning point in the Civil Rights Movement.

Much has been made, and rightly so, of Mamie Till-Bradley's decision to "let the world see" what had happened to her boy. "I knew that I could talk for the rest of my life about what had happened to my baby," she said.

> I could explain it in great detail. I could describe what I saw laid out there on that slab at AA Rayner's, one piece, one inch, one body part at a time. I could do all of that and people still would not get the full impact. They would not be able to visualize what had happened, unless they were allowed to see the results of what had happened. They had to see what I had seen. The whole nation had to bear witness to this. . . . So, I wanted to make it as real and as visible to people as I could possibly make it. I knew if they walked by the casket, if people opened the pages of *Jet* magazine and the *Chicago Defender*, if people got to see it with their own eyes, then together we might find a way to express what we had seen.[5]

In pushing for the publication of photographs of her son's body, Till-Bradley bucked the trend of the Black press of her time, whose preferred depictions of lynchings were political cartoons. Like Ida B. Wells before her, she embraced the power of the photographic image, and she included prior photos of Till, some with her, alongside what have become iconic photos of his mutilated body. Till-Bradley employed the techniques of antiracist Black lynching photographers, who themselves followed Wells's pioneering nineteenth century presentation, by placing photos of lynched

Blacks alongside photos of the victim alive, well-dressed, and surrounded by family.

Yet hers was an explicitly Christlike display: "We gave Mr. Rayner the clothes to be used to dress Emmett. The black suit I had bought him for Christmas. The last Christmas. The best ever. I also gave him three photographs from that holiday. The shot of Emmett in his fine clothes, the shirt and tie and the hat we had given him. The picture of Emmett leaning on his television set. And, of course, the ones of Emmett and me together. Our mother-and-son portrait. I wanted the photographs displayed inside the open casket. People needed to see those, too. People needed to see what was taken away from me, what was taken from us all." Till-Bradley's inclusion in her evocative triptych of scenes of Christmas—the holiday celebrating the birth of Christ—is significant; she also evoked the birth of Christ at the funeral by burying Till as Christ in his last Christmas clothes. With the pictures above him, his lynched/crucified body became the final scene in this Black passion play. Till-Bradley also placed herself within the frame, in the photograph of the two of them and in the candids that would be taken that day, so that the entire scene recalled the birth and death of Christ, complete with an evocation of *La Pietà*. Thus, her visual rhetoric was far more complex than simply allowing others to see. Convinced that words were insufficient to convey the enormity of what had happened, she professed her faith in the power of the visual and chose to communicate via thoughtfully staged Christ-inflected images of her son and her own grieving Mary-inspired actions.

Till-Bradley was explicit about the fact that the biblical crucifixion guided her understanding of events and her role in history. It provided her script, the outline from which she could improvise. She understood herself as having been chosen to play the role of Mary, mother of Jesus, but improvised a recognizably Black maternal performance of grief. Till-Bradley did not invent the lynching-as-crucifixion story she staged, and she certainly did not choose the role, but once she understood the role to have been divinely chosen for her, she stepped into it wholeheartedly. What's more, she staged her own immersive, transformative presentation of the lynching-as-crucifixion story within a wider Black cultural milieu replete with storytelling regarding antiblack violence. The above only makes her resurrective accomplishments—the fact that Till's lynching is *the* lynching in Black collective memory and the ubiquity of his reincarnation in Black politics—that much more impressive.

Till-Bradley's understanding of her son was not simply, as Metress says, that of sacrificial lamb, but as the Black Jesus Christ. Mattie Smith Colin, who covered Till's death and trial for the *Chicago Defender*, reported the following from the scene in which Till-Bradley greeted her son's body at the train station: "'Oh, God, Oh God. My only boy.' Mrs. Mamie Bradley wailed. . . . Limp with grief and seated in a wheelchair among a huge throng of spectators, 'Lord you gave your Son to remedy a condition, but who knows but what the death of my son might bring an end to lynching!!!'" Colin also reported that Till-Bradley cried out, "Lord take my soul, show me what you want me to do and make me able to do it."[6] The *Defender* went on to publish an eight-part account of "Mamie Bradley's Untold Story" as told to Ethel Payne, in the final installment of which Till-Bradley revealed that her Central Station prayer was answered by a "presence" one night:

> The presence said to me, "Mamie, it was ordained from the beginning of time that Emmett Louis Till would die a violent death. You should be grateful to be the mother of a boy who died blamelessly like Christ. Bo Till will never be forgotten. There is a job for you to do now." "What shall I do?" I asked. The voice replied, "Have courage and faith that in the end there will be redemption for the suffering of your people, and you are the instrument of this purpose. Work unceasingly to tell the story so that the truth will arouse men's consciences and right can at last prevail." The voice died away and the presence left the room. I lay down and slept peacefully.[7]

Blacks would be redeemed, saved from lynching, through Till's death. It was her job as his mother to work unceasingly to tell the story to bring about that salvation. This she would well do.

Till-Bradley's understanding of her son as Christ was in keeping with the connection developed by artists and writers in the lynching era, 1880–1940, between the Cross and the lynching tree. James Cone writes: "From Henry Smith's lynching in Paris, Texas (1893) to Emmett Till's in Money, Mississippi (1955) and beyond, Black artists and writers have made the lynching theme a dominant part of their work and most have linked Black victims with the crucified Christ as a way to find meaning in the repeated atrocities in African American communities."[8] To this now all-too-familiar lynching-as-crucifixion plot, Till-Bradley added attention to embodiment—to her son's body and her own—as well as attention to staging, to dramaturgy, and to an embodied performance *in which her audience could participate.* In

Du Bois's account, Blacks could identify with Christ via ethical and political association. In Till-Bradley's they could, as Till, *become* him. Du Bois told it as a story; she staged it as an immersive play, and members of the "Till Generation" essentially testify to having joined her in the production.

The funeral of Emmett Till was an impressive affair. A loudspeaker broadcast the service outside the church. While there is some dispute regarding how many viewed Till's body—estimates vary from an amazing 10,000 to an unreal 600,000—Ruth Feldstein says there is "little dispute that the memorial service for young Till had mobilized Chicago's Negro community as it had not been over any similar action in recent history." In the media, reports from the days and weeks that followed supported this view. As well, the photos of the funeral inspired sermons throughout the nation. The *Cleveland Call and Post* surveyed Black radio preachers and found that after the photos, five out of six of them devoted their sermons to Till. But of course it was the photos of the funeral that became iconic. Congressman Charles Diggs, one of only three Black congresspeople at the time and the only one to attend the Till murder trial, called the *Jet* photographs "probably one of the greatest media products in the last 40 or 50 years." He explained that the pictures "stimulated a lot of anger on the part of blacks all over the country."[9] Diggs credited his attendance at the funeral as an inspiration for his later voting, civil rights work, and racial justice advocacy. Metress notes that the photos of Till's funeral "had this transformative effect" on "countless blacks," "altering the way they felt about themselves and their vulnerabilities, and the dangers they would be facing in the civil rights movement."[10] Joyce Ladner offers herself as an example: "More than any other single atrocity, the *Jet* magazine photographs of Emmett Till's grotesque body left an indelible impression on many young Southern blacks who, like my sister and I, became the vanguard of the Southern student movement."[11]

But the impact Till had on a generation—in truth on generations—cannot be limited to what the world saw in his casket that day. Till's was not the only body over which Till-Bradley had control; she had her own to maneuver, as well, and the lasting impact of Till's lynching owes as much to Till-Bradley's own performance and her staging of herself as mourning mother, both before and after the funeral, as it does to her masterful staging of her son's body. Feldstein notes, for instance, the flurry of headlines about the weakness of Mamie Till-Bradley's body, her repeated collapses. The weakness of Till-Bradley's body had political value, Feldstein points out, becoming "an important resource in the mobilizations the trial generated—even as the emphasis on her body's limits suggested that, somehow, she was not part of the active political community around her seeking [legitimate] power." No: she was simply "limp with grief."

Till-Bradley's performance of grief was often contrasted with men who displayed no emotion. A photo from an article entitled "Nation Shocked, Vow Action in Lynching of Chicago Youth" appeared with the caption: "Near collapse from shock and grief, Mrs. Bradley sobs hysterically as the body of her son, 14-year-old Emmett Till, is taken from train at Chicago's Illinois Central Station. Mrs. Bradley's condition made it necessary for her to use wheelchair during this ordeal. Offering comfort in photo are Crosby Smith of Mississippi, an uncle of the lynched boy; and Mrs. Lillian Smith of Chicago, aunt of Mrs. Bradley." The accompanying article states: "A morbid silence engulfed the station. Veteran newspaper men and photographers, whose daily schedules included murders and fatal accidents, were grim-faced as they watched the procedure and then went about their work." A *Chicago Defender* article written at the time of Till's murder trial is entitled "Till's Mother, Reed Collapse; Send Both to Hospital for Rest." Till-Bradley is here pictured in a wheelchair, flanked by male medical staff. Her presentation and its contrast to the men who surround her suggest that there was a female-gendered locus for grief and a male-gendered locus for action.[12]

Till-Bradley continued to perform her part as the Black Mary in the crucifixion/resurrection scenario after Till's funeral in political and religious collectives. For months after Till's death, Black political and religious leaders held "Emmett Till" protests rallies across the country, attracting thousands in New York, Chicago, Baltimore, St. Louis, Detroit, and Los Angeles, and "the mother of the slain boy, Mamie Till Bradley joined forces with the NAACP and toured the nation, telling her story to packed auditoriums and churches, helping to generate the most successful fundraising and membership campaign in NAACP history."[13] And for those who did not attend the rallies, the media accepted and disseminated her understanding of events. Metress notes that the *Pittsburgh Courier*, for example, printed the following short poem, T. R. Skelton's "Ode to Mississippi," as a letter to the editor:

> Bow thy head O state of Mississippi
> Let tears of shame course down thy cheek
> Ravished the standard of humanity
> A boy's body floats in a creek.
> God so loved the world, He gave His Son

> To teach the Brotherhood of Man,
> What now, unrelenting state, will be done
> To wash the body's blood from your hand?[14]

An NAACP flyer also echoed her understanding of events, speaking of what might have been responsible for the changes in the attitudes and political leanings of Black Mississippi residents: "Or is it as Mrs. Bradley hysterically shouted about the untimely death of little Emmett, "Darling you have not died in vain—Your life has been sacrificed to something!"

Feldstein's analysis of Till-Bradley's feminine grieving, as well as the masculine behavior with which it was often contrasted in the press, is illuminating. So, too, is the absent action. The repetition, the repeated staging and circulation of this performance of overwhelming maternal grief in the wake of young masculine death, framed by the silent, older masculine resolve, invited younger audience members and readers into the scene—and we know from memoir and testimony that they took this invitation. The lynching was front-page news, the biggest story of the year. Each staging called forth a performance. And in testimony and recollection we observe storytelling sessions, re-enactments catalyzed by and a continuation of Till-Bradley's lynching-as-crucifixion/resurrection scenario. People were grabbed by the story she told, she enacted, grabbed by Till, communing with him, their bodies possessed by him. Her staging brought an inevitability, an interchangeability, an as yet unseen level of identification to a relentless cycle of antiblack violence and re-enactment within Black life. Alexander says that through the story of Till a generation came to understand "the ways in which their fate was interchangeable with Till's." Indeed, members of this generation and beyond changed places with him—often speaking of feeling what he felt, of their efforts to feel what he felt—and through this experience, this reincarnation as Till, they speak of being transformed. This new interchangeability is the product of Till-Bradley's resurrective labor. This outcome owes much to Till-Bradley's styling of her own body, what she said, the sounds she released, and how she moved—as well as to her implicit suggestion that her son's death was something to be immersed in, moved through, acted out. It was her visual rhetoric, her sonic rhetoric, the moans she uttered, and the way in which she styled both Till's body and her own that ensured Till's undying impact. Till-Bradley's immersive staging, during the funeral but also before it at the train station and after it at rallies around the country, stagings echoed in press coverage, invited young Blacks to commune with her dead son, bringing his experience forever into their bodies and thereby sparking the transformation of which so many of them speak—and, with it, intense identification, collectivization, and mobilization.

So, What's the Scenario?

The generation of young people who witnessed Till's death through pictures—encountering him in what Hunter-Gault called "black America's weekly Bible," *Jet* magazine—felt what happened to him and were forever changed; they gained a new understanding of who they were, as vulnerable Black bodies. Alexander says the experience became "the basis for a rite of passage that indoctrinated these young people into understanding the vulnerability of their own black bodies, coming of age and the way their fate was interchangeable with Till's," as well as "a consolidation of their understanding of themselves as black in America."[15] They have been called the "Emmett Till generation." They inhabited Till as a rite of passage, experienced reincarnation as Till as part of a ceremonial ritual, and afterwards they were reborn. After the experience, they became someone new. Till-Bradley's intervention in this process was one that interrupted and transformed the ongoing experience of witnessing, re-enacting, and reliving antiblack violence and death that Alexander argues is an ever-present part of the cycle of Black life. Till-Bradley reoriented that cycle of reenactment toward Till-as-Christ in her staging of what was at that point a decades old lynching-as-crucifixion story, transforming it into a lynching-as-crucifixion "scenario" in the sense that Erica Edwards understands it, and inviting those who witnessed Till's death to themselves *become reincarnations of Till.*

Alexander provides insight into the process through which Till—and the Till generation—was reincarnated and why. As we have seen, Alexander argues that antiblack violence—and specifically spectacular violence *and* its attendant dramatic storytelling—created Blacks as a people. The experience of collectively witnessing violence, either in real time or through storytelling, creates us, shapes us, not only as a political people but as people, full stop. Notably, Alexander's understanding of the creation of Blacks as a people is at once more democratic and participatory than Rogers Smith's version, as ordinary people and not elites drive the circulation of stories. They do not share said stories for political purposes but because how could they not?

Their experiences of the violence they witness are so immediate, so visceral. Alexander's understanding is also more embodied and less liberal than that of Smith, as the stories do not come to fully formed people. Individual Blacks are profoundly shaped by, changed by—and after Till *reborn through*—the stories they re-enact and circulate. Indeed, because the violent stories help to make us, the constant generation and circulation of these stories are a part of a continual act of Black formation through antiblack violence. This matters in analysis of the uptake of Till-Bradley's transformative staging of what was in the 1950s already an old story. Before Till, it was an associative story—Blum emphasizes that it was the racial and political association with the lynched man as Christ that did the political work—though an association that nonetheless had a formative impact on the teller and witness; as Alexander demonstrates with Till, this association became absolute identification. By changing the ever-present cycle of telling stories about death to a process of viscerally reliving the death of Christ (through Till) and the resurrection, Till-Bradley could place new emphasis on the formative aspect of—the rebirth inherent in—this tragic cycle, as well as that for which Blacks had been reborn – the salvation of racial equality - making it a meaningful transformative experience, giving clearer and more immediate political and spiritual meaning to an ongoing cycle of transformation through death.

The title of Alexander's article, "Can You Be BLACK and Look at This?," is taken from a line that appears in a work of visual art by Pat Ward Williams. The piece is a meditation on a lynching photograph. Williams asks, "Who took this picture?" and then "Can you be BLACK and look at this?" Alexander's essay is a potent rejoinder: not only have you, as a Black person, long looked at exactly this, but "looking at this" *made* you Black in an important sense. Writing during the 1990s, an extraordinary decade in which the pained and violated Black body was constantly on display, Alexander goes on to present a "traumatic archive" of cases held in the minds *and bodies* of Black people in order to "articulate the ways in which a practical memory exists and crucially informs African Americans about the lived realities of violence and how its potential informs our understanding of ourselves as a larger group."[16] The violence depicted in slave narratives and lynching—*specifically the lynching of Emmett Till*—are the most important in this formative archive of violence, she says.

The traumatic archive of which Alexander speaks would be terrifying enough if it were housed in some forgotten, remote library. But it is not. The archive is held in the minds and the very bodies of Black people, "in the flesh as forms of memory." It is never forgotten and, what's more, it is "reactivated and articulated at moments of collective spectatorship."[17] Each new spectacle of violence calls forth all the old ones to be experienced, spoken of, acted out, and relived anew. And because the archive is in the body, the body is implicated in these reactivations. It acts them out as it remembers and that process always sparks change, transformation in the body.

Alexander points out that one of the most frequent experiences Blacks have within the dominant public sphere is that of witnessing white-perpetrated, or at least white-staged, violence against Black bodies. While white men are the "primary stagers and consumers" of such historical spectacles, she says, "black people have also been looking . . . forging a traumatized collective memory which is reinvoked at contemporary sites of conflict."[18] Till-Bradley was able to at once interrupt *and* accelerate this process by restaging her son's violated, deceased Black body, placing it in an antiracist display in order to initiate a significant change in what had been an ongoing process of violent mass transformation.

"We" have learned who "we" are, Alexander says, through our experiences of, witnessing of, and storytelling about public violence against "us." In her account, it is not only the experience of violence nor the constant threat of violence that forms Black collective memory and thereby makes Blacks into a "we," but also the act of collectively witnessing violence, sharing stories of the violence, re-enacting the violence—which provides the opportunity for the stories' audiences to become "witnesses once removed"—and finally the resulting traumatic archive of violence stored in the minds *and bodies* of Blacks that, together, does this "we"-making work.[19] This collective memory, this archive, is visceral; it lives in skin. It is reinvoked, reactivated—relived—at each new antiblack violence event. Violence, the constant threat of violence, witness, storytelling, dramatization, circulation, reinvocation, and reactivation not only create Black people as a collective body but comes to reconstruct the bodies of individual Blacks.

Alexander does not focus on the ethical content of the stories, as Smith does, though that content is implied: antiblack violence is wrong. In Alexander's account, we must attend not only to the content of the stories themselves, but when and how they are told and, crucially, retold, and where these stories are kept in us. Still, the violence related in the stories is key for her, as Blacks' relationships to themselves and to one another—their understanding of themselves as a part of a larger collective—is "crucially forged by incidents of physical and psychic violence."[20] In practical terms,

Blacks' relationships to one another, their bonds with unrelated others, are forged through the acts of experiencing and witnessing violence and through subsequent dramatic storytelling about the violence witnessed. Stories are important as vehicles both for the circulation of the facts and the dramatic impact of witnessed violence, for the opportunity they provide for more extensive collective witness of violence, and for their ability to bring violence that has been witnessed into the bodies of Blacks, to reanimate scenes of violence within individual Black bodies. The violent storytelling, the storytelling about violence, provides important moments of connection to other Black people. They help to "make" Black people, and therefore this process helps to make Black people "the same" in important ways. Stories transmit knowledge, yes, but they also irrevocably shape *and* bind us.

How does storytelling about violence reconstruct us as individuals and not simply as a political collective? The storytelling and dramatization Alexander describes is, in fact, people taking part in—and being changed by—violent antiblack scenarios. And after Till-Bradley's master staging, all would come to understand all other antiblack violence events and themselves—as Till-Bradley's staging introduce a profound sense of interchangeability – this move from association to identification - that had not been a part of the story and re-enactment before—with reference to Till-Bradley's presentation of the Emmett Till lynching-as-crucifixion "scenario."

Erica Edwards argues that the "scenario"—that is, a mode of theater in which players follow an outline with much room for improvisation—has been important in Black politics. She sees the "charismatic scenario," for example, as the "aesthetic vehicle through which common sense Black nationalism was staged through repetition."[21] Edwards writes, "The scenario as a mode of formal theater emerged in the mid-16th century Italian genre of commedia dell'arte, in which players followed not a script, but rather an outline." Significantly, Edwards points out that "a scenario is not only a sketch, but also a mode of thinking, a way of transporting historical knowledge through [embodied] ritual." She quotes Diane Taylor as saying, "People learn, experience and come to terms with past and future behaviors by physical doing them, trying them on, acting them through and acting them out." A scenario, Edwards says, "grabs the body while leaving it 'space to maneuver,'" making scenarios well equipped to get history into the Black body and not simply into the Black body politic: "A scenario is thus a malleable historical container, a loosely scripted series of directions that served as the basis for reenactment, ritual role-playing and other forms of performance that transmit and transport history and historical knowledge." Improvisation was key to the genre, as the room to improvise "allowed for variations and surprises." For example, "Contemporary events"—say, an unceasing litany of antiblack violence and death—"could be easily folded into the loosely structured plot, allowing actors to adapt to audience responses, which in turn helped shape the drama."[22] Edwards argues that the charismatic scenario enjoyed wide circulation—in religious services and political collectives—and it was reproduced in print culture, in pamphlets and novels. This was also the case for Till-Bradley's lynching-as-crucifixion scenario. Till-Bradley's transformation of the lynching-as-crucifixion story, as well as the cycle of antiblack violence re-enactment, came complete with the resurrection Du Bois spurned, and thereby added an emphasis on, and consciousness of, rebirth to the "traumatic" cycle Alexander outlines, in the process giving the cycle of antiblack violence re-enactment itself both sacred and secular, divine and political, meaning, and thus giving that story—and not simply others through it—new, and arguably transcendent, life.

Storytelling, dramatization, and re-enactment (ritual role-play, as Edwards would say) are crucial to the formation of collective memory in Alexander's account, to this violence-inflected process of people formation, as ultimately they help to place the violent archive into the body as well as the body politic. Alexander demonstrates the importance of the above in quotes she includes from Shelby Steele and Muhammad Ali regarding Till. Steele refers to his and his peers' repeated storytelling sessions about the Till lynching. "Oh, how we probed his story," he says. Later in life he would come to be critical of the sessions, but he accurately identifies them as "a ritual of group identification." Steele says, "By telling his story and others like it, we came to *feel* the immutability of our victimization, its utter indigenousness."[23] Alexander quotes Ali as saying, "I felt a deep kinship to him when I learned he was born on the same year and day that I was. My father and I talked about it at night and dramatized the crime. I couldn't get Emmett out of my mind until one evening I thought of a way to get back at white people for his death." Here, Ali acted out a scenario and improvised his own ending. Alexander's analysis draws attention to how immersed the storytellers are in the events they relate, how identified they are, about how telling is always, essentially, re-enacting, how they are in the process of reliving the events as they share them. But this is the case because of the incredibly high stakes involved. The Emmett Till narratives, those of Ali and Steele, she says, illustrate how, paradoxically, in order to survive Black people had to "witness *their own* murder and defilement and then pass along the epic tale of violation."[24] They are telling a story not about Till, but about themselves. They *become* him. They are the actors in the stories they tell. They are, then, never simply telling a tale. They are performing a scenario regarding death wherein their very lives are at stake. This did not end with Till. Black viewers of the Rodney King tape, the occasion for Alexander's essay, speak of feeling his pain, of hurting as he hurt. Alexander quotes a man who told the *Revolutionary Worker*, "By the time they was done I needed 28 stitches in my head. When I saw the Rodney King video, I thought of myself laying on the ground and getting beat. I felt the same way all our people felt when we blew up."[25] But Till's remains the master scenario.

Forever Till

There is a reason that Till's is the "single story that stood atop the pinnacle of racial victimization."[26] The unique resurrective labor of his mother, Mamie Till-Bradley, is that reason. Till-Bradley, like Du Bois, disseminated a lynching-as-crucifixion story, but unlike Du Bois she attended to embodiment, to the embodied resurrection, via her staging of the Till-as-Christ scenario. She transformed Du Bois's lynching-as-crucifixion story into the body-gripping lynching-as-crucifixion/resurrection scenario that it became for those of the Till generation and beyond. Du Bois may well have written the best texts to turn lynching into crucifixion, but Mamie Till-Bradley staged the best version of the story, sparking an interactive, body-gripping, individual (and thus public) body-transforming lynching/crucifixion/resurrection scenario, a scenario performed on stages large and small, churches, political rallies, barbershops, and houses, circulated in newspapers and on radio waves throughout the nation, ensuring Till's singular transformative—resurrective—effect on generations of young people.[27]

The invitation Till-Bradley extended to take part in the crucifixion scenario started the life-saving work, the paradoxical work, as Alexander says, where in order to survive, Black people had to "witness their own murder and defilement and then pass on the epic tale of violation." It resolved the paradox through its emphasis on rebirth, resurrection. They died but they were born again into the work of Du Bois's resurrection, to the work of Black political equality. Till-Bradley's scenario ensured the mass preservation of the Till body archive and its transformative effect on Black political subjectivity. It most effectively sparked the people-building chain of events Alexander describes, that is, the process of Blacks witnessing antiblack violence and death, experiencing that violence and death as their own, storing the experience within their bodies, and finally being reborn to tell the tale and into the fight for racial justice. The ubiquity of the Till body archive, as an archive referenced in all subsequent (and even now in prior) antiblack violence and that initial archive's ongoing resurrective effect, can be credited to the labors of Till-Bradley.

Yet there are significant limitations to Till-Bradley's labors of resurrection. Martyrdom and redemptive suffering require blamelessness, an association with Christ. There are also gendered limitations. And while the Till-Bradley initiated reincarnations are participatory and a form of reincarnation for democratic struggle, they are not the outcome of a democratic process. For Clementine Barfield and her organization SOSAD, as we shall see, the democratic work itself is necessary for and even constitutive of the labor of resurrection. Barfield and her organization SOSAD's secular resurrections therefore represent a significant move forward in democratic necromancy.

6

Seeding Restorative Kinship

Clementine Barfield and SOSAD's Otherworldly Democratic Horticulture

In the summer of 1986, two weeks after her sixteen-year-old son Derick was killed and her fifteen-year-old son Roger gravely injured in an act of teen violence, Clementine Barfield organized a meeting for Detroit families affected by violence against children and teens. The resulting organization, called at first "Mothers of the Slain" and then "The Group with No Name" before members settled on the name "Save Our Sons and Daughters" (SOSAD), was founded by Barfield and others the following year. SOSAD members were resolute at the outset, stating, "At our first meeting held January 4, 1987, at the Church of the New Covenant, Mrs. Barfield, together with other parents of slain children, Marsha Edwards, Yvonne Givens, Luvenia Hilson, Beverly Raines, Vera Rucker, Anita Totten, Lula Winbush, and 87 concerned citizens decided that we had to go beyond mourning and begin working together to create positive alternatives for our young people."[1] Barfield recalls that many members of the press also attended that first meeting, and thus local ministers realized that youth antiviolence work had national implications and would get media attention. They told Barfield, "Okay, you can sit down now, and we'll make you Rosa Parks." When she told them that she couldn't sit down, she had one dead son and another had been shot in the head, her own pastor replied, "You're stupid. You think you women can make a difference?"[2] But make a difference they did.

The organization would not only have an impact on the national conversation about youth violence but would become, in the words of youth violence expert and at the time assistant dean of Harvard's School of Public Health Deborah Prothrow-Stith, "a model of community-based organizing for the rest of the country."[3] Chapters of SOSAD were started in Birmingham, Alabama; Flint, Michigan; Fresno, California; Louisville, Kentucky, St. Louis, Missouri; and Washington, DC, and the organization received

The Labors of Resurrection. Shatema Threadcraft, Oxford University Press. © Oxford University Press (2025).
DOI: 10.1093/9780197758618.003.0007

requests for help from groups in "Atlanta, Columbus, Los Angeles, Milwaukee, Omaha, and San Francisco." The largest and most successful chapter was founded in Philadelphia. That chapter is connected to our own moment, as it was among the first groups to respond to the death of Trayvon Martin, working with his mother to bring attention to his killing in 2012.[4]

SOSAD was a precursor to contemporary healing justice work and an important stop on the road to today's abolition feminism. But the organization also presented an expansive challenge to both the composition of the Black public sphere and received understandings of "the public" as a whole, and therefore to the bounds of US democracy: SOSAD also not only critiqued the War on Drugs, as Melynda Price has noted, but elaborated and put into practice an alternative to that war—a resourced, participatory democratic peace.[5] Barfield would write, "We recognize the insidious war that is being waged against children all over the world. Our mission of peace in Detroit is linked to a vision of world peace. This vision goes beyond individual effort and desire. Together we can stop the shooting, maiming, and killing of our children."[6] And as Erroll Henderson has noted, the organization saw key institutions of the US state—the police, schools, and institutions of public health—as premature-death-making institutions. It countered the impact of those institutions by inviting all community members to participate with it in creating life-giving and life-affirming alternative institutions for children in Black communities, including the now popular urban gardening programs, which the organization innovated.[7] As Barfield understood it, in a community beset by drug wars and the War on Drugs, peace could only be brought about via the collective occupation and transformation of Black urban space, and transformation through both social and topographical cultivation, tilling, and sewing. "Beyond mourning the death of my son, I started planting seeds," she said, "seeds for peace."[8]

SOSAD, like contemporary abolition feminists, critiqued the tendency of community members to cede their capacities for care and safety provision to police and the state, and they enacted their alternative vision of care and safety provision via explicit communion with their dead. That is, the peace that SOSAD sought was not only for the living; the dead, too, would reap the benefits of this collectively provisioned peace. And, more than that, the peace could not come about *without* the dead; they were a part of this transformational occupation. Life worlds could only be revived amid the death worlds of drug wars and the War on Drugs via mass communal participation that included the participation of the dead. Life world revivification required the labor of resurrection—that is, resurrecting, communing with, and continuing to care for the dead in speech and in deed via practices of what Rebecca Louise Carter has named "restorative kinship" and by ensuring the dead's representation and participation within the emerging transformed public space. SOSAD organized around the idea of democratically constructed life worlds (within which the dead could dwell, participate, and be nurtured) that would provide "our children (both the living and the dead) with an opportunity to develop as human beings."[9]

Cultivating the Private, Expanding the Public

Clementine Barfield resolved to grieve in public, and in her efforts to organize the parents of slain children, she encouraged other grieving parents to do the same. There was so much grief, so many grieving parents. Detroit became the homicide capital of the United States in 1974, earning the nickname "Murder City" in that year, and by 1985 it had the highest rate murder rate among large cities, twice that of Chicago.[10] Forty-three children sixteen and younger were shot and killed the year Derick died, and 365 kids sixteen and younger were shot but survived.[11]

Barfield would lead an extraordinary organization. Her capacity to do so was remarkable, but perhaps not wholly surprising. Her story before this defining tragedy included strong familial bonds and a history of community-oriented action and was thus very much in keeping with what SOSAD became. Barfield was the thirteenth of fifteen children, raised in a family of farmers in the Mississippi Delta. Four of her siblings died of natural causes before she was born. After her mother's health failed, she accompanied her to Detroit to join siblings who had migrated there. By the time her children were shot she was the former first lady of a church, a leader in the New Covenant Baptist Church where the first SOSAD meetings were held, a union steward, had served on the AFSCME Political Action Committee, and was an active member of her children's parent-teacher organization.[12]

Of her early organizing efforts, Barfield recalls, "I started hunting down other mothers whose children had been killed. I called funeral homes and asked if they got a certain child's body. Sometimes I wouldn't even have a name, just a corner where the body was found."[13] Barfield's early efforts evolved into a project of marshaling the community's collective resources toward what had long been conceived of as private burdens, collective work to support their own and their wider community's emotional health and well-being, which paid dividends in their considerable public sphere work. The results were impressive:

> Once we started getting funding, we hired counselors and trained them and then let them counsel with people. It's not as though people just knew how to work with survivors of homicide victims. Because working with grief was something that in our communities had always been very private. People kept it in the closet as though it was something dirty or ugly. But we brought it out in the open. Put a face on it. And we taught people how to work with us and how to help us. Some were psychiatrists, counselors, and the like and we focused on healing. Because it wasn't just about any one of our individual grief. It was about all of us, collectively. And individually we might try to heal our broken selves alone but together we were a force, a force to be reckoned with.[14]

Barfield and others began a weekly bereavement support group that remained a part of the Detroit chapter's work. All were encouraged to join the group's public work, but the support group was limited to parents who had lost children. Parents could get through this, together. Inviting parents to the group, Sue Meagher wrote: "Children aren't supposed to die. But they do. With their death the family has lost someone important in their lives, and they very naturally grieve. The process can be startling, beliefs are challenged, emotions can be out of control and physical energy is depleted. The intensity and longevity of these feelings can be overwhelming. Family members and counselors share their thoughts and feelings at SOSAD EVERY MONDAY NIGHT AT 7 p.m. It is an opportunity to share coping strategies, to learn that our problems are not unique to us alone and to help others as well as to be helped. Please come and share. We all need each other."[15]

The organization's grief support programming later expanded to include a family support group, a bereaved persons and those who care for them group, a male grief support group, a child counseling group, and a survivors of violence support group.[16] SOSAD also ran a twenty-four-hour crisis hotline and organized a crisis response team that went into schools, churches, and door-to-door in neighborhoods after children were slain. The organization held an expansive view of violence survivors and thus of those among community members who needed support. Describing SOSAD's "crisis response" to a firebombing that killed three children and their babysitter,

SOSAD member Rosemary Hagerman-McGhee wrote, "Many people do not know that when a tragic homicide occurs, all the residents in a neighborhood are affected. Feelings of vulnerability and fear escalate to both children and adults. The Crisis Response team talked to residents in their homes and on the street and informed them of the free follow-up Grief Counseling Services at the SOSAD OFFICE. SOSAD is prepared to bring a Crisis Response team to any neighborhood which has suffered a violent killing. We will also train block clubs and neighborhood groups in Crisis Response. Call 362-5200."[17] The group also understood perpetrators of violence as among the population of survivors, and provided mental health services for "children who hurt."

This aspect of the organization's work was a precursor to contemporary healing justice work, which facilitates survivor- and community-led intervention to interrupt generational trauma and systemic oppression and promote emotional, physical, spiritual, psychic, and environmental well-being. SOSAD's work was a trauma-informed, care- and emotions-attentive effort to instantiate a fuller vision of abolition democracy, that is, a democracy wherein all have the economic, social, and political, but also the emotional and caring resources to live as equal members. Their work, as we shall see, also included important elements of Morrisonian democracy, that is, care for, dialogue with, and impassioned representation of the dead.

The organization's collective creation and maintenance of space to mourn themselves and to attend to individual and communal mourning, mental health, and well-being—this collective attention to the private lives of community members—was novel. But SOSAD also held novel ideas about public space and "the public." The sheer range of people and the amount of public space they organized—from teachers and students to police officers and the incarcerated, from the spots where children were slain to City Hall and every physical and sonic space in between—defies belief. Perhaps no organization in history has held and actualized a more expansive view of the public. As Barfield noted, SOSAD organized at funerals, but also at schools, in churches, and on buses; it organized the street and prisons; it organized funeral directors, teachers, students, administrators, bus drivers, inmates, and police officers.[18] The organization thereby expanded the social roles and social spaces of democracy, constantly emphasizing the need for mass participation to transform communities.

Barfield was explicit about her belief that it was the community's ceding of public space that allowed violence to proliferate within it: "Instead of hiding behind barred doors and windows, we can and must march out of our homes and our churches and begin walking the streets in large and small groups, making clear to everyone, young and old, that we are reclaiming our communities, looking out for each other, and saving our sons and daughters." Her belief in the power of the people was ironclad. "Today in Detroit," she said, "the gun has become what the auto industry used to be: the symbol of power. We must replace the destructive power of the gun with the positive power which can be found in each and every one of us."[19] Not only did she pen a piece entitled "Anti-Drug War Will Be Won at the Grassroots"—a piece implicitly critical of policing-centered solutions to the problem—Barfield would also tell the *Washington Post*, "Not saying that we as mothers can solve the problem, but we the people can solve the problem, because it is going to take everybody's involvement to change things."[20] And SOSAD evinced a remarkable—indeed, at times downright unbelievable—commitment to broad communal participation, to dialogue, to petitioning regarding the norms by which we live and govern ourselves, hallmarks of democracy. This is perhaps best demonstrated in a piece called "What to Do about Problem Houses," featured in their November 8, 1988, newsletter:

> ***Meet with other concerned neighbors. If you are bothered, others are too.
>
> ***Send a delegation to the house to meet the occupants and discuss the matter. Hear their side of the story. Assume things can be worked out.
>
> ***Contact the landlord if it is a rental house. He/she may not know the seriousness of the problem.
>
> ***Petition the landlord if he/she won't take action. Public pressure works!
>
> ***Call the police regularly. As many neighbors as possible should do this. Anyone carrying on illegal activities does not want the hassle.
>
> ***Write letters to the house. "Dear Drug Dealer, We're watching you and we don't like what we see." Be creative.
>
> ***Develop a neighborhood code of conduct on how we will treat each other. Present it for signing by all neighbors including those in the problem house.
>
> ***Get support from outside the block. Bring the issue to other neighborhood support groups.
>
> REMEMBER: IF YOU DEFINE THE SPIRIT OF YOUR BLOCK, THE DRUG DEALERS WILL BE THE ONES WHO DON'T BELONG.

(The guidelines were developed by Block Captains in the Sherman Park Area of Milwaukee. They meet regularly to help each other).[21]

Barfield believed in the power of planting—in the need, as she stated in founding SOSAD, to plant seeds for peace, in the power of community members planting themselves, in the need for community members to stand tall like trees—and she would often return to this theme. She made a connection, for example, between planting and the community's collective occupation of public space as a violence prevention strategy. Adults, concerned community members, could become like trees. "We have to physically plant ourselves at the scene of every shooting or homicide in our neighborhood. WE MUST MAKE HOPE VISIBLE. Our children need to see with their own eyes that in the midst of devastation people are standing up together and struggling for a better world."[22]

But it was not enough for adult community members to plant themselves. Children must be planted too. The organization often represented the children they cared for—both the living and the dead—as trees and the conditions they worked to change as the soil in which the children/trees were growing. "Planting a tree," Barfield would write, "symbolizes our recognition of the need of children to be rooted in caring, nurturing communities."[23] Yet tree planting was not merely a metaphor, no weighty symbolic gesture for the organization; it was central to their work, as evidenced by HARVEST, SOSAD's urban gardening program. As well, members also took the call to change the environment in which their children were planted quite literally, especially Joanne Wilson, who wrote several columns for the newsletter with such titles as "Let's Add Earthwork to Homework," "Be Environmentally-Friendly," "Earth Watch in the City," and "Recycle Michigan." The newsletter also printed the Global Educational Associates' "Earth Covenant: A Citizens' Treaty for Common Ecological Security." Barfield herself, evincing an awareness of the slow environmental violence that also threatened the city's children, would write, "We are killing each other today through violence and also in more subtle ways, like poisoning our atmosphere and environment so that breathing becomes more difficult every day. We cry loudly when a child or someone's shot to death, but we turn our heads as poison fills our lungs and contaminates the food we eat. . . . SOSAD is determined not to allow this victimization to continue. Together with the Detroit Area Greens and other local organizations, we are urging schools, churches, and individuals to plant a Tree of Life to celebrate Earth Day 1990."[24]

Barfield's call to occupy public space was realized, in part, in the organization's "public information" approach to violence.[25] In keeping with the arboreal theme, SOSAD distributed leaflets to community members with information on gun violence alongside testimonials from kids about why they wanted guns. They also distributed a monthly newsletter, with columns by Barfield and the legendary organizer James Boggs, to four thousand people, and letters to the editor attest to the newsletter's national circulation. SOSAD ran a speakers' bureau and hosted a weekly talk show on WDTR 90.9.[26] Barfield testified before Congress and appeared on the *Oprah Winfrey Show*, *Phil Donahue Show*, and *20/20*.[27] SOSAD partnered with universities on gun violence research and ran peace-training workshops for college students from around the nation. SOSAD's CEASE FIRE program lobbied for the elimination of handguns, but it never did all its work behind closed doors. It cultivated an expansive public presence, with members holding weekly vigils for the dead at City Hall and going door to door in Detroit's Black communities to talk about the dangers of gun violence.

Like contemporary prison abolitionists, SOSAD did not fail to see prisons as part of public space nor its occupants as members of "the public." They held that the incarcerated must not be overlooked as community members available to provide much-needed care and affirmation for children. As a result of this view, SOSAD opened Child of the Month Clubs in several Michigan prisons. Incarcerated SOSAD members raised funds for children in need and hosted visits to the prison, not to scare the kids straight—Barfield would say that they learned early on that they "could not scare children," who "weren't afraid of death"—but so that the incarcerated could participate in nurturing and affirming children, and that children could maintain their connections with their incarcerated fathers and mothers.[28] The parents contributed portions of their wages to support the children of incarcerated parents.

SOSAD saw children as part of the public as well and organized them in the work to save their own lives. SOSAD encouraged, facilitated, and made space for teen volunteers to speak on the problem of violence in schools and in churches, and to contribute to their newsletter (through the Kids' Corner and Teen Speakout columns), and through their work with children the organization's adult members gained a better understanding of the pervasiveness of communal violence. SOSAD member Allen Martin reported on the visit of the crisis response team in the neighborhood where three young children died in a firebombing: "I told them how sorry I was for all the killings and violence in their area, how much we need them and how important each of their lives is to me and the community. For at least an hour these children, ranging in age from toddlers to 21-year-olds, listened and shared their feelings about violence with me. Almost everyone raised a hand when I asked how many knew someone who had been killed and how many knew someone who carried a gun. They cried out, 'We are only children, and we deserve to live!'"[29]

Price notes that the organization's efforts helped raise awareness among teachers and other authority figures regarding the sheer amount of violence and death children were witnessing and why they felt the need to have weapons and use violence to protect themselves.[30] But this approach to organizing was not uncontroversial; it was not always welcomed. "Part of the struggle of SOSAD's work was the level of concern among adults who were either oblivious to or underestimated the impact of youth violence on the city's children," Price writes. "Ms. Barfield frequently received pushback from teachers and principals when she visited schools, but she and other SOSAD members worked hard to do presentations to children. Often school administrators SOSAD encountered were unaware of the intensity of the problem the group was trying to fix.... In one visit, school officials chided children who responded yes to the question of whether they had known someone who had been killed. To illuminate for the school administrators the truths the children were telling, Ms. Barfield asked the children to talk about their experiences. She recalled, 'These children got up and started reciting like a poem—reciting who they knew that had been killed.' What's more, 'A lot of children had witnessed those deaths.'"[31]

Barfield credits SOSAD's HARVEST Program with kick-starting the urban gardening movement.[32] It did that and so much more. The program is symbolic of SOSAD's overall philosophy. The organization conceived of children as analogous to plants in meaningful ways, and their understanding was a significant rebuke of the reigning liberal individualist orthodoxy evident in the War on Drugs. See Figure 6.1. The program was a verdant manifestation of the topographical and resource-based changes the organization hoped to make in communities threatened with the barrenness that pervasive gun violence wrought. Children needed to be planted in caring, nurturing communities, as Barfield said, and not in the soil in which they found themselves, a toxic mixture of drugs, undereducation, deindustrialization, and unemployment.[33] The children could not be expected to

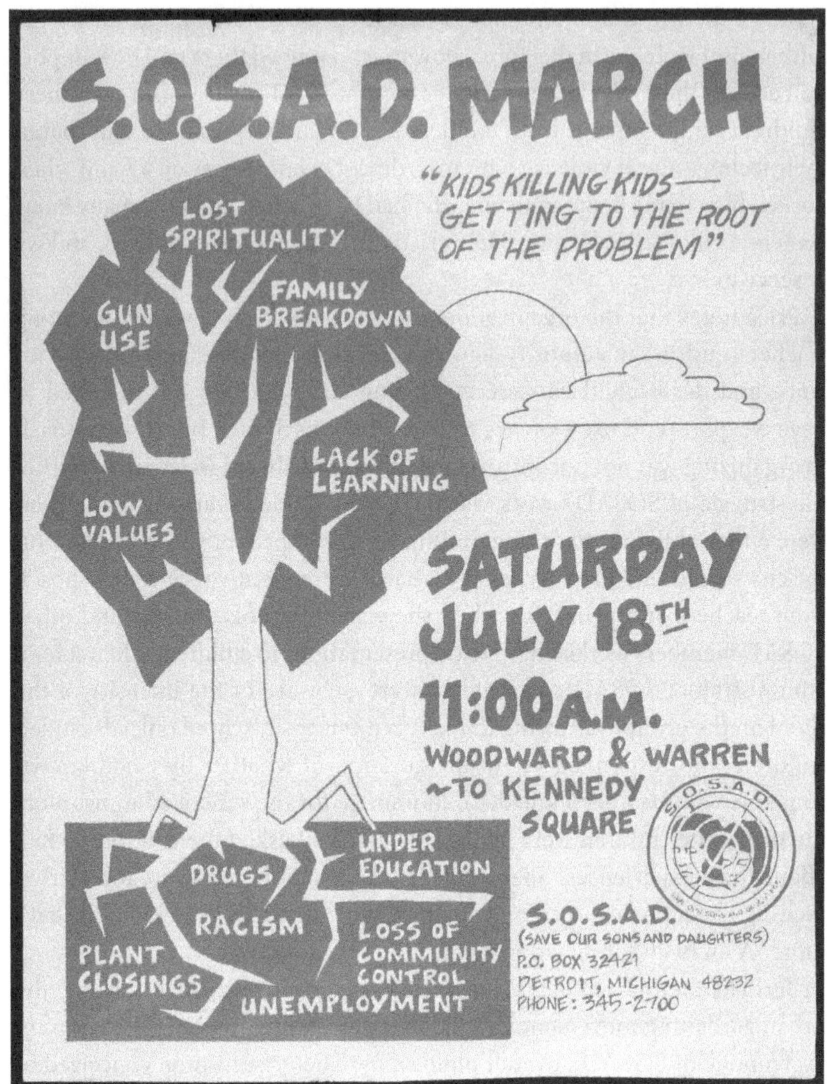

Figure 6.1 SOSAD Tree Leaflet.

change—nor brutally punished for failing to change—until the soil in which they found themselves was changed.

In efforts analogous to their painstaking emotional health work, SOSAD demonstrated its commitment to cultivation, to transformation, to changing the soil themselves through work and will, by mobilizing community resources and untapped individual and community potential to create life worlds where children could be rooted, grow, and flourish amid "devastation," violence, and death.

Barfield remarked that she realized that the only time Detroit-area kids saw dirt was at funerals, "where they saw dirt shoveled onto the graves of their friend or family member."[34] The organization endeavored to change that through the Urban Farm Trainee Program, which gave participants "the skill of growing their own food" and an opportunity to "learn that the Earth represents Life."[35] Marsha Jones-Wright, the HARVEST '88 Coordinator, stated the near- and long-term goals and itinerary of the program, as well as the group's request for broader community involvement, as follows: "Our goals are to create jobs and teach young people skills they can carry with them for the rest of their lives. This can be extremely beneficial to our families as well as our youth, due to the present economic state of our country. Harvest '88 will help to develop Self-Esteem and give our youth a sense of accomplishment. . . . We need everyone who reads this to support and work on this project because saving our youth is saving our future."[36] Two months later, echoing the broader group's planting metaphor, she wrote, "Everything starts with a seed. Some offer hope, some despair, some promise a future and some even in the midst of the noise and haste, greatness. Harvest '88 is a project whose purpose is to sow a vision for greatness in the youth of Detroit."[37]

Barfield was clear about how the Harvest Program fit within the organization's efforts to nurture the community's children. It was, for example, integral to the Arms Around the Children campaign, which brought their emotional health efforts and their physical environmental efforts together and involved "a pledge and a commitment to all the wonderful children in Detroit that we are embracing them with love and security." The campaign held a "Stop the Violence" concert, youth rally, and "giant hug" as its main event in the summer of 1989, but it also provided "work and activities" for children all summer, including the farming and gardening programs. "Kids need to see things live and grow in order to counteract the death and violence they see around them," Barfield wrote in an effort to recruit volunteers for the program. "Detroiters who have lived and farmed in the South can offer this valuable skill to neighborhood youth. My 78-year-old father is teaching this skill to his grandkids and the kids in his neighborhood. You can teach the children in your neighborhood basic skills, like carpentry, sewing, cooking, knitting, mechanics, car repair. Our children need all the advantages they can get in life. They need to connect with the strengths and the hope that still exist in our people. Share with them your hope and your strengths. Help to preserve our future which is our youth. PUT YOUR ARMS AROUND THE CHILDREN! VOLUNTEER!"[38]

The SOSAD newsletter printed kids' testimonials regarding their appreciation for the community, skills, and recognition they received in the gardening program:

> "What I enjoy most about HARVEST '88 is that there are people who care about you. There were speakers who taught us how to plant. We were in the newspapers, on the news and on TV." —Anthony Blackman, 13.
>
> "Everyone knows everyone and can relate to their problems. Even sometimes when we don't have enough money to get paid, we still are willing to work. We really work hard. I will never ever forget this summer." —Rhonda L. Chism, 14.
>
> "The people of Harvest '88 make me laugh. Sometimes they make me upset, but I still get along with them." —Latanya Graham, 12.
>
> "The thing I enjoy most is that I meet new people and it is a great learning experience. I think that it will be a good reference for other jobs." —Stephanie Holloway, 12.[39]

The program also proved a transformative experience for adult participants. Patrice Brown, a nineteen-year-old student at Central State University who ran writing workshops for the Urban Farming Trainees, said, "Harvest '88 has been one of the most rewarding experiences of my short lifetime. . . . With the right guidance and support I see great things from this group of young people. I see potential poets, evangelists, educators, computer specialists, journalists, public speakers, and counselors. To all my students and new friends, I wish continued success and that you remain inspired by each other's friendship. This program has introduced several beautiful young people to me. Each one of these students has taught me a little more about myself and how to relate to others."[40] The program allowed children to spend creative time around caring adults, giving them the opportunity for employment wherein they could develop a progressive skill set in a nurturing environment. They themselves were tended as they planted.

Yet the gardening program was not only about nurturing young life; it was also an opportunity for children to learn how to commune with their dead. Tree planting was something that adults could do to let children see that adults valued and honored their dead and for children to learn to do the same. In her monthly column, Barfield stated, "One way to show how much we care is by planting trees in memory of the lives that have been lost to violence."[41] Tree planting, as an act of reverence and remembrance, would have been particularly meaningful for SOSAD and its children, given the symbolic connections the organization often drew between children and trees. Returning to the Earth Day event at Belle Isle, we see that Barfield, in her call for parents to join her, presents tree planting as world-making work and as *an act of care for both the living and the dead*, inviting all to plant a "Tree of Life": "Sunday, April 22, we will be planting a tree in Belle Isle to memorialize the 6000 Detroiters who have been killed in the last decade and to affirm our commitment to protect the Earth and improve the quality of life in the decade before us. Come and bring your children. Take home a tree to plant and to remind them of the nurturing that all living things need to grow."[42]

If children were trees, then tree planting was always an act of care for the living and the dead. By memorializing and tending to the dead in this way, out of a concurrent concern for and with the participation of the living, transforming the physical and emotional environment that they insisted that living children needed to thrive while also building children's emotional and productive capacities through tree planting and through caring for their dead, providing the children with space and opportunity to spend constructive, creative time in reverent community, a community that, through the trees, expressly included those children passed on, SOSAD built a new life world via communal participation amid the death world. This life world was expressly connected to the dead; those gone too soon were present and represented. In this, we see the participatory creation of life worlds wherein both dead and living children could be rooted and grow. The living children could only flourish with and among their dead by learning to and helping to tend them, even as they themselves were tended. I cannot sum up their work better than Price, who says of it: "Through their relationships with their children, both dead and living, they crafted public roles to solve a complex problem at its roots. In this sense, their analysis was more complex and astute than the analysis that informed any government program." For those children here on earth, Price says, "They understood that solving the problem of violence against and among Black children meant surrounding them with love, building healthy self-esteem, and finding meaningful work for teenagers on the cusp of adulthood."[43] Their solutions for these children were indeed more complex and astute than contemporaneous government programs, and they deserve recognition and praise. But so does their work with and for the children passed on. It is their ongoing relationship to their dead children and their labors of resurrection to which I now turn.

Representing the Dead/Resurrecting the Dead

Tree planting was but one way the organization kept the dead present, cared for, and represented. SOSAD also did this in weekly vigils for the dead at City Hall. In one of the group's first public actions, in July 1987, SOSAD was joined by twenty-five hundred Detroiters to "march down Woodward Avenue carrying home-made wooden crosses with the names of slain children" in an action designed "to create an overwhelming awareness in the community" that, as SOSAD put it, "our kids are killing each other." The marchers distributed "tens of thousands" of leaflets recommending "actions that everyone can take to make a difference."[44]

The organization also engaged in the direct political representation of the dead through its Court Watchers program. The Court Watchers ensured that their dead would not be misrepresented by attending the trials of those charged with killing what SOSAD called "our young people." They took this action because defendants, in their words, usually had "a large group present to intimidate the family," and if the victim's family was not supported, "the defense attorney and witnesses feel free to lie about the victim."[45] Barfield related an incident that made the necessity of this representational work abundantly clear. Speaking of her experience at the trial of the young man accused of killing her son, she said:

> The day of sentencing, which was the latter part of October, the judge allowed me three minutes to say what it was I felt like saying about the court proceedings and about the trial. I told him then that I was trying to form a support group among the parents and how important it was that he not send a message to the community that it's ok for a child to be killed and (the killer) not get any time for it. But he interrupted me and my 3-minute speech by saying, "Well, Mrs. Barfield, your boys were out looking for trouble." And that just devastated me. We were treated as though we were the criminals. The whole guilt process was laid on my son Roger, not on the criminal. It was as though my son that was killed was totally unimportant.[46]

This representational work was necessary, then, as police, prosecutors, and courts often blamed children for their own deaths.

Yet it is important to note that this representational work was not the totality of SOSAD's justice work. It is worth pausing to dwell on this. SOSAD wanted perpetrators to be held accountable, they wanted the criminal justice system to recognize their children as human beings and therefore to punish those who hurt them. But justice was not only or even primarily about holding perpetrators accountable. Police and the courts—that is, punishment—could not bring justice. Justice could only come about through collective communal care and tending for and to the dead as well as the living, even in the most infertile conditions. Justice could only come through changing those conditions. Justice came about through the collective work of building a better world, a life world, by parenting the living and the dead in public space, even as they organized privacy to care-fully attend to survivor grief. Justice for their deceased children, for the parents of deceased children, for living children, was to be found through building life worlds in which the dead could dwell. SOSAD's Harvest Program, Arms Around the Children Campaign, and its Earth Day Tree of Life Event—not the Court Watchers program—best represent their understanding of the requirements of justice.

As well, Price points out that SOSAD did more than represent the dead—its members resurrected them, and this resurrection was central to the organization's transformative political work. She calls attention to participants' ongoing resurrective labor, their "repeated resurrection of their children in narrative," and the ways in which "the work of the mothers like Barfield continues to breathe life into their children long after their deaths." In Barfield, Price says, we see "constant tending to the life, death and imagined future of her son."[47]

SOSAD's work was a secular and expressly political manifestation of what Rebecca Louise Carter has named "restorative kinship," wherein death changes the nature of the maternal relationship but by no means ends it. Carter examines the communal mourning and grief support practices of a group for mothers who have lost sons to violence at Liberty Street Baptist Church in the Central City neighborhood in New Orleans. "The religious work of women at Liberty Street suggests a kind of *restorative* kinship," Carter argues, "one that asserts the value of those who have been lost by restoring their position within the family and community in this world and the next."[48] The women are encouraged to celebrate and mark the birthdays and death anniversaries of their loved ones. It is a practice for both the living and the dead.

For the mourning women, it ensures that they will not be alone during extremely difficult times.[49] But the grief support group's practices also signify what Carter sees as the "expanded forms of kinship" that have developed in Black communities forced to grapple with pervasive premature death.[50] The women needed their relationships with one another, but they also needed their ongoing relationships with their dead to heal what group member Danielle referred to as their "kin pain," the ache they felt after losing a relative. Carter refers to the work the women do as a form of what Patricia Hill Collins calls "motherwork," saying:

> What was most remarkable, however, was the ways that mothering activities extended to the *deceased*, as the women addressed their kin pain by claiming and caring for their children and grandchildren long after their deaths. The marking of birth and death anniversaries provided an important structure for this, testing the perceived limits of human existence and giving women the space to assert continuous connectivity and thus value in the face of its denial or destruction. Particularly where social and physical death seemed to overlap in nonnegotiable conclusion, these boundless practices of motherwork formed the foundation of restorative kinship in the Crescent City.[51]

The women's practices were not unique to them and have been observed in other Black communities in the United States. Carter references Klass, Silverman, and Nickman's work on "continuing bonds," wherein Black Protestants, in particular, develop ongoing links to their deceased "through the prominence of a church funeral after death, the gathering of the family and community during mourning, a belief in the afterlife and the consideration of death as a transition rather than a final stopping point." The women of Liberty Street demonstrate their continuing bonds by gathering family and community, and explicitly including the deceased among those gathered. Carter quotes the psychologist Ronald K. Barrett, whose work on Black mourning practices has demonstrated that unlike within the European/Western worldview where when a person dies, that is the end, "In the traditional black cultural experience, you are born, you die and then you continue to exist in other realms."[52] Carter says that Cheryl Mattingly observed this in her own research during a birthday party in a graveyard that a mother hosted for her deceased six-year-old daughter:

> Belinda's mother Andrena organizes the event, and as invited children run and play in the grass around the tombstone, she shares a view of life and death as continuous. In reference to Belinda, Andrena declares that "she's still havin' her birthday. Her life is going on in heaven forever." Mattingly frames this party/funeral as an event that "played upon and resisted the usual convention of space and time . . . it remade a blank impersonal space, or even a mournful space, into an underworld playground, one where children (above the ground) could safely play with their dead." The research thus reveals the literal and symbolic collapsing that such practices allow as the usual demarcations for the beginnings and ends of life blur, allowing relatedness to extend across social, physical, and metaphysical realms.
>
> Restorative kinship practices at Liberty Street, especially the repeated marking of birthdays and death anniversaries, provided an important scaffolding for these same processes as the place of the deceased in earthly and now eternal realms was confirmed. This is the renegotiation of subjectivity in the space of death, where the deceased Black subject, as Biehl, Cood, and Kleinmann might theorize, is "at once a product and agent of history; the site of experience, memory, storytelling, and aesthetic judgment; an agent of knowing as much as of action; and the conflicted site for moral acts and gestures amid impossibly immoral societies and institutions."[53]

This "scaffolding" is, as always, just the beginning:

> The confirmation of eternal dwelling, however, was just the first step. For it was through these relations, in heaven and on earth, that the work of the Lord proceeded. This belief was framed in several ways, but it referred most frequently to the work the women continued to perform to fulfill the religious and social mission of the church and the connection they felt with their deceased loved ones who watched over them from heaven with pride. Danielle spoke about this with certainty, describing how Rock looked down on her from heaven with pride for all the organizing work she was doing. "He telling me, 'look at my mama,'" she said. "And I mean, I got joy in this here. . . . It's not a time I leave group that I don't look up and say . . . 'My son.' And in my spirit, I can hear him say, 'Mama, do the work

> of the Lord.' You know?" The encouragement meant a lot; it enabled the women to persist in their efforts, knowing that while their work was challenging, the effort was being praised from on high. The women spoke also of the work the deceased were doing in heaven. As Mrs. Adams shared with the group on the anniversary of Marcus's death, laughing and crying all at once, "I think about my son up there with the Lord. He's up there doing the work. And I'm doing the work down here. . . . So I . . . you know . . . I cry. When I think about him, I cry, I cry. . . . I thank God that we will see him and God one day."[54]

SOSAD members engaged in similar practices. Indeed, one of them, Ms. Drew-Williams, engaged in the exact same practice. She hosted a party every year, "complete with sheet cake," for her son who was killed on his birthday. The *New York Times* referred to this as "a coping strategy," completely failing to perceive the party as a vital part of an ongoing set of relationships for the mothers.[55] SOSAD mother Carolyn Adams wrote, in a piece for the newsletter entitled "Happy Birthday, James," "Your birthday is coming, and I have decided not to be down. I am going to celebrate your life. We will try not to cloud the day with sadness because you are not here with us. *We know you are with us in spirit.* David and I want your new little brother, Anthony, to celebrate your birthday too. We have decided to have him christened on that day. Love from Mom, David, and Anthony." The piece concludes by noting "James would have been 17 on March 25. He died on Father's Day 1990."[56]

But the continuing relationship would go beyond the practice of marking significant days. "Part of the work for Ms. Barfield," Price writes, "is the constant retelling of her child's life and death. These episodes of remembrance of a child whose death reshaped the course of her life are not limited to memorializing the dates of his birth or his death."[57] Barfield's ongoing relationship with her son is evident in a speech she gave at Penn State University entitled "Beyond Mourning the Death of My Son," in which she shared about her son's aspiration for the ministry. "Through her words," Price notes, "the listener can see the verdant future that Barfield saw, *and could still see*, for her son."[58] In Price's account of Barfield's tireless resurrective labor, we see the unending work of remembrance, but also, as she says, imagination and I would add constant dialogue with her son as she continued to piece together a vision of the future—his future—for herself and others with his ongoing input. Derick is indeed "the site of experience, memory, storytelling and aesthetic judgment, an agent of knowing" and through her ongoing dialogic process he becomes not only the product of history but "an agent of history," an agent of action and certainly "the conflicted site for moral acts and gestures amid impossibly immoral societies and institutions."[59]

SOSAD's restorative kinship practice was secular—indeed, expressly political—in that Barfield did not present a vision of Derick as passed on to another realm, as looking down on her from heaven, doing his heavenly work and watching her good works, but as here on earth, restored to his rightful relationships here on earth, as part of an ongoing dialogue with her, out of time, at once youthful and fully grown, and ever ready to do his own good works here. Nor did she present herself as doing the Lord's work: she explicitly worked for the Black community of Detroit. Barfield was the former first lady of a church, and the group held its first meetings in a church; it is not the case that the Liberty City support group's interpretation of events was unavailable to Barfield, as an active member of her church, and to other members of SOSAD. It was simply a path they chose not to take.

Carter also speaks of restorative kinship as an assertion of value within a system that has denied such value. Restorative kinship puts the lost relatives in right relations, returns them to their relationships. Premature death is often the marker of a social system that has devalued the now tragically shortened life of the deceased, and the restored kinship relationship revalues that life "by restoring their position within the family and community in this world and the next."[60] Barfield repeatedly speaks of wanting to show the courts and everyone else that Derick's life had value—but, for her, perhaps the most vital part of the restoration of that relationship is the political, and indeed *participatory* democratic creation of the social environment appropriate to a life thusly valued.[61] Barfield's kinship practice is also more archival and excavative. In her constant retelling of his story, her "constant tending to the life, death and imagined future" in order to, as Price says, "breathe life" into her son for her audience, for the publics she engages around the nation, she returns to her past moments with him, reliving past conversations to construct a vision of his future, and thus continuing their mother-son relationship.[62] In constantly tending his life, death, and imagined future, in constantly tending the story of his life, she continued to care for him. Her restorative kinship efforts were not only critical, in that Barfield took the evidence she had regarding the life Derick wanted, his character, his "spirit"—which will always be with us—and her knowledge of her family history, but interpreted that evidence, and used her expertise alongside the community participation she mobilized to bring about a better world for him. Her efforts were also dialogic, a two-way process, in which she engaged in ongoing conversations with him about the world he needed to thrive. Here, Barfield's aforementioned mobilization of communal participation is key, as her restorative dialogue with Derick was an important part of the much larger dialogue in which she was engaged. Her newspaper columns demonstrate her constructing and engaging a public that she invites to join in both the discursive and material transformative work to change conditions, but her narration of events demonstrates that Derick is very much a part of that public. She remained in dialogue with Derick about what he needed throughout her work just as much as she engaged in dialogue with community members about the work. She brought him back repeatedly to ensure that the conditions that killed him would not remain obscured, and therefore as part of her work to change the world. And Barfield's labors of resurrection, her constant work to bring Derick back to us in speech and action, her continuing dialogue with him within a broad participatory act of communal transformation, indeed saved the lives of other children.

As grieving parents, Barfield and SOSAD members did not continue their relationships with their deceased children for themselves alone. They did so for world-making purposes, as a necessary part of their transformative work here on earth. Price expresses this point well:

> The repeated resurrection of their children in the narrative for change is not simply a longing for the past when their children were alive. More than that, Black mothers of murdered children also bring their children with them into the present to make clear, as Hartman says, the "skewed life chances, limited access to health and education, premature death, incarceration and impoverishment: that characterize the lives of young Black people . . . the work they are doing . . . articulating . . . their children's unmet future is also about working to create a life for all Black children that is free of the violence and subjection that took the lives of their children."[63]

If Derick did not return and stay with her and the other children—with us—Barfield could not have conceived her vital work, and thus she would not have had the vision. Without this restored kinship, moreover, she would not have had the strength to do the work, and the conditions that ended Derick's life and threatened the lives of other children may well have remained.

SOSAD: A Vital Bridge between Abolition and Morrisonian Democracy

It is instructive to think of Barfield's thought and practice alongside fellow democrats W. E. B. Du Bois, Mamie Till-Bradley, Mariame Kaba, and Toni Morrison. Du Bois was concerned that all members of a democracy have the social, political, and economic capital to participate as equals. SOSAD not only expanded the capacities of concern to include members' emotional and caring capacities, but also conceived of community members themselves as important resources. Barfield's organization held that people had untapped capacities within themselves, including capacities to care, that, when exercised collectively, could transform communities, creating life worlds within death worlds. And unlike Du Bois, their vision of democracy included dialogue and communion with the dead.

Barfield's work was a part of the repertoire of resurrection, of democratic necromancy. SOSAD's work differed significantly from Till-Bradley's redemptive-suffering-inflected martyrdom and reincarnation for democratic work. Unlike Till-Bradley, SOSAD members did not assert that their children had died for a reason or that their deaths were anything other than tragic. They at times participated in narratives of youth innocence, but they did not assert that the children were blameless. Indeed, serious rifts arose in the organization when some sought to work on behalf of children who participated in the drug trade and who perpetuated violence.[64]

SOSAD's work was an important stop on the road to contemporary abolition feminism, which seeks the abolition of police and the prison industrial complex, and which critiques surveillance, policing, and incarceration as solutions to society's social problems and instead sees the latter as death-making institutions.[65] SOSAD sought to build a world safe for children via a somewhat improvised participatory democracy. SOSAD sought to build a better world for children not only via their lobbying efforts but also by calling a public into being around youth violence and working with that engaged public to discuss problems and make decisions about how to change the way in which they all lived—decisions that they would then implement themselves, collectively, as they engaged that public in weekly deliberative exchange regarding community members' emotional health and well-being, via campaigns of public information, in newsletters, complete with letters to the editor, in leaflets, radio programming, in churches, schools, and prisons regarding youth violence. The organization critiqued the tendency to alienate community capacities for safety provision to the police and the state and enacted their alternative vision via explicit communion with their dead. The call for community members to create nurturing life worlds for children through the collective provision of care, in opposition to what abolitionists have called the death worlds of surveillance, policing, and incarceration, anticipated much of contemporary abolitionist work. SOSAD practiced a pragmatic, semi-abolitionist maternalism that was sensitive to its members' status as marginalized maternal figures, as Price notes that at the time the predominant understanding of Black women among the wider public was either as welfare queens or as crack fiends. They were pragmatic, in that they worked with police, as they worked with inhabitants of other social roles. They also worked to have perpetrators held accountable within the criminal legal system. But they were never naïve about who the police were and where they, as Black parents, stood with them. A piece in the newsletter stated, "Every time we talk to the mother of a child who has been killed, we hear the same story about police indifference." It told the story of Mrs. Matthews and her son David. "David," she said,

> was killed in the next block at 7:10 a.m. according to the police report. A man knocked on my door and told me. I thought I would be called by the police, but I had to make the initial call. Around 2 p.m. two police officers came back and stayed a few minutes. Later I was called by a Sgt. Bradley. I started calling every morning at 9 a.m. The third morning they told me they had had 7 new cases since David's. I kept calling to ask when there was going to be a hearing. But they never told me. It kind of makes you feel bitter, but you know you can't afford to be because you need their help. Later I found out they had released the man who killed David.

Mrs. Matthews would go on to call SOSAD.[66]

More important, they did not believe that policing and punishment were the solution to the problems they faced and offered explicit critiques of the limits of policing and enacted their own solutions. Their urban gardening program was an implicit critique of the War on Drugs, but they also offered explicit ones. SOSAD printed a piece entitled "The Winnable War" that argued the point: "Police actions can temporarily close down a drug house. But in order to prevent drug dealers and buyers from returning, the community needs to show that it is willing to pick up where the police leave off. Drug dealers must believe that they are fighting not just the police but also the entire community." What's more, SOSAD not only organized in prisons, as contemporary PIC abolitionists do, but also called for something akin to what contemporary abolitionists refer to as "community accountability," which conceives of violence as a communal and not an individual problem and wherein community members work together to decrease violence and its harms. They understood community members, and not simply individual family members, as among those harmed by violence—as evidenced in their proto-healing justice emotional health and well-being work—and those same community members as those who must be accountable for the violence. Barfield put it this way: "It is no accident that we are losing a generation . . . we sit back and cry for help, always thinking that someone else is going to save us. *But there is no one to save us but us. We can't expect to solve our problems until we recognize that we are the problem, and we are also the solution!*"[67] Violence was a collective problem to be solved collectively. She would also write: "We must organize to rebuild our communities. Everyone can do something to make a difference. We can march against the crack houses on our block. We can develop treatment programs like Narcotics Anonymous to help wean our neighbors and families from their addictions. We can transform vacant lots into community gardens and children's parks where neighbors can work and play together. We can work towards creating small businesses in our neighborhoods to provide jobs and role models for our young people. We can organize block parties and festivals to celebrate the positive achievements of our youth."

Perhaps the strongest case for Barfield and SOSAD's place as pragmatic maternalist precursors to abolition feminism is the similarity in Barfield's vision and that of the abolitionist Mariame Kaba. Both women argue that we must not alienate our capacities for harm reduction, and thereby our capacities for world building, to others, notably the police. In fact, there is a striking similarity between Barfield's and Kaba's accounts of what reduces harm, what keeps community members safe, and what justice demands. Separated by four decades, with Barfield operating at the opening of the War on Drugs and Kaba at what is hopefully the close of it, SOSAD and contemporary abolition feminists came to the same conclusion: peace and justice require that we do not alienate our capacities to reduce harm and leave that work to others—to state violence workers, to social workers—but instead we reduce harm via resources (and we ourselves are among those resources, as are both the vaunted and the dishonored in our communities), via appealing to and engaging the demos in a project of collective care and tending.

Communities cannot create the good, the life worlds, without one another. The bad is created around us when we alienate our responsibilities for collective care and safety provision. The care-filled democratically resourced peace requires all of us—bus drivers, funeral directors, preachers, teachers, children, police, the incarcerated, the living, and the dead—to bring it about. Their work was an implicit, and at times explicit, critique of the individualizing logic of crime control, the War on Drugs, and carceral state responses to violence. Their program for a democratically resourced peace (wherein the people, both living and dead, are the most important of those resources) and the participatory provision of life worlds were their rebuke.

Their necromancy inspired, sustained, and propelled the work they did. They created life worlds in which they could continue to parent their deceased children. If their children could not reside in the worlds they created, as grieving mothers they may have had little incentive to create them. The children were present, and, like the living children, they were also cared for. They had to be nurtured and kept, had to be represented in the new world created. Without keeping them there, those worlds would surely fail. And the resurrective labor was democratic. It included representing the dead within the democracy, in courts, at City Hall, on the streets but also in SOSAD's socially and physically transformative gardens, engaging the demos in deliberation regarding how best to tend, collectively, the gardens created of, for, and by the living and the dead, and then working with that engaged demos to change the conditions under which they all lived in order to create life worlds amid death and destruction.

The labors of resurrection they undertook is democratic work because it is about giving voice to those killed by structurally unjust conditions so that the injustice that killed them might be ended for the living. The dead, then, must not simply haunt us, but remain a part of the political community, be given a voice within it, so that the injustice can be addressed and remedied. It is not that the dead must be avenged; it is that their perspective, their lives, provide information about what is wrong and must be made right for the democratic community to thrive. Without their voices, the constant recounting and accounting of their lives and deaths and the conditions that shaped them, the polity cannot know enough to correct itself. SOSAD's labors were a democratic service because they undertook them for the purpose of informing the polity about the consequences of its choices and the necessity and urgency of change. And this is but one important way in which the democratic labors of resurrection seed new life worlds.[68]

SOSAD's labors show us that necropolitical orders require this resurrective labor *and* that this labor creates unique publics that facilitate a different kind of democratic activity. As we will see, their work contained vital elements of a Morrisonian democracy, wherein care for the living and the dead is central. Without bringing their dead into the present with them, without continuing their bonds with them, continuing to parent them in narrative and in deed, SOSAD's mothers may not have had the strength and inspiration to move forward, and they could not bring the conditions that produced their children's deaths to the fore for community members and transform them. The work they did to help living children connect with their dead, tree planting for example, helped to transform the conditions that produced those deaths. This is what death labor, or necromancy can do in a democracy. This understanding and practice of death labor teaches us, these labors of resurrection teach us something about what can constitute justice and thriving in democratic space. Again, these practices create unique publics that facilitate a different kind of democratic activity, democratic activity that includes the dead. The practices hold space for confronting loss collectively, in community, for healing, but they also allow the parents of the dead-too-soon to continue parenting their deceased children as a constitutive part of that healing, as they, through their tears and with those same deceased children, effect physical, emotional, and political transformation and innovate new forms of political practice necessary to confront death worlds, which included recalling those so often left for dead, perhaps most incredibly the incarcerated, into the work of nurturing children *and* having living children recall the dead, plant the dead, tend the dead, as the mothers grieved, recalled, planted, and parented.

7

Revivifying Ephemeral Publics

Margaret Prescod and the Black Coalition Fighting Back Serial Killers

Beginning in the 1970s, serial killers and serial murders targeted and terrorized Black women in cities around the country, including Atlanta, Boston, Detroit, Los Angeles, Newark, Oakland, Pensacola, Pittsburgh, San Diego, Seattle, and Washington, D.C.[1] The lack of police response to these violent deaths spawned coast-to-coast Black feminist mobilization. In Los Angeles, the case of the man who would come to be called the "Southside Slayer" broke when two survivors came forward with a description of the murderer and his car. (A third survivor was unable to come forward because she was in a coma.) The Los Angeles Police Department called a press conference on September 24, 1985, telling reporters the man who had attacked the three "prostitutes" was most likely the same man who had killed ten other prostitutes by stabbing and strangulation since September two years earlier. Christine Pelesik writes of what happened after the press conference: "On October 2, 1985 . . . Margaret Prescod and eleven other female activists picketed outside of LAPD's downtown headquarters. It would become the first of many weekly vigils. Standing next to a macabre prop—a plywood coffin draped with flowers—Prescod, a Barbados-born community activist, accused the police of not caring about the murdered women because they were mostly poor, black, drug-addicted sex workers. 'There seems to be selective protection to different groups and classes of our community,' Prescod bellowed. 'They are not giving this case the same kind of attention they did the Night Stalker.'"[2] Six years and a continent away from Barbara Smith in Boston, yet still embedded in a similar context of pervasive risk of violence and death for Black women, Prescod and others initiated the first action of the group that would become the Black Coalition Fighting Back Serial Murders and began their labors of resurrection. See Figure 7.1.

The protesters' indictment was difficult to contest, as the LAPD had assigned a hundred and fifty officers to the contemporaneous Night Stalker

The Labors of Resurrection. Shatema Threadcraft, Oxford University Press. © Oxford University Press (2025).
DOI: 10.1093/9780197758618.003.0008

Figure 7.1 Rosemary Kaul, Margaret Prescod of Black Coalition Fighting Back Serial Murders handing out flyers about the Southside Slayer on Rodeo Drive in Beverly Hills, California, 1986.

and Hillside Strangler cases, while the detail on the Southside Slayer murders expanded from thirteen to fifty only after the women launched their protest campaign. This belated task force was called the "Prostitute Killer Task Force" until the Coalition convinced the LAPD to change its name to the "Southside Slayer Task Force" and to refrain from referring to the killings themselves as "prostitute slayings." Activist Rachel West of the US Prostitutes Collective (US PROS) argued, "From the start, the police, the media, elected officials and civic leaders were slow to respond to the murders, giving the impression that the deaths of the women were not important enough to cause much of a stir." Other serial murders, she said, such as the Night Stalker and Hillside Strangler killings, "received far greater attention and were treated as a general crisis."[3]

The women's protest efforts were not well received. A broad swath of LA's male leadership—including police chief Daryl Gates, LAPD spokesman Commander William Booth, task force head Lieutenant John Zorn, and southern California Southern Christian Leadership Conference head Reverend Mark Ridley-Thomas—either openly mocked the women or provided a clearly pejorative "no comment" when questioned regarding the women's work.[4] The soon-to-be infamous Gates called the women "asinine" and told the *Los Angeles Times*: "They're insensitive to the men who are working the case. Those dummies should be applauding them instead of casting negative light on the investigation." These men are clowns, and it is always worth pausing to ridicule a cast of men on the wrong side of history. Alas, far more compelling than these sexist, dismissive Scooby-Doo villain-esque men, both white and Black, in formal and informal leadership positions, within the state and civil society—more interesting, too, than a notoriously racist and misogynist police chief's being upset at a Black feminist organization critical of his work—and more interesting than the all-too-common institutional racist sexism on display with the task force, was how the Coalition came to be, how Prescod herself came to sex worker necromancy, her contributions to our understanding of the causes of Black femicide, as well as the truant democratic innovations the group put into practice to aid the dead and living women for whom they labored.

Prescod, as it turns out, had developed an understanding of the police as a Black femicidal institution before she ever indicted the LAPD for its neglect. The organization she cofounded nearly a decade earlier, Black Women for Wages for Housework, and another affiliated organization with which she worked, US PROS, centered sex workers in their praxis, carefully attended to the workers' relations with the police, and, ultimately, helped Prescod to see the resonances between the oppression of sex workers and Black women as well as a connection between policing and violence against Black women. Her critique of the police would lead her to expand Smith's initial diagnosis of the drivers of Black femicide to include the devaluation of women's work and its attendant resource deprivation, policing, and whorephobia. For the Coalition, crime control policies like broken windows policing and any policies designed to "clean up the street" ended up authorizing any and all "cleaning up" of "street women" and, eventually, simply all Black women on the street.[5] Prescod and the Coalition would bring into being a revivifying political formation to counter these deadly policies. Because of this revival work, the Coalition is not only part of the story of abolition feminism; its efforts are an important instance within Black women's democratic necromancy and among their impressive repertoire of resurrection.

Prescod's Long Journey to Grim Sleep on the Southside

It is something of a happy accident that Prescod found herself in Los Angeles at the time of the murders—a (gendered) coincidence, in fact, as she had recently relocated from New York City because of her husband's job. As it happened, Prescod's extraordinary political biography meant that she was uniquely positioned to understand the set of forces at play in these Black femicidal murders, and particularly the role of the state, via police and policing, in producing violence against Black women and their disproportionate death. In 1976, Prescod cofounded Black Women for Wages for Housework (BWfWfH) with Wilmette Brown. She was a longtime spokesperson for the US Prostitutes Collective, which began as the New York Prostitutes Collective, founded in the 1980s by "a group of Black Women who worked in different aspects of the sex industry and their supporters," and she had done sex worker organizing "on and off" for ten years before the killings began, including work aimed at ending police harassment against sex workers.[6]

Prescod would recall two incidents that helped to crystallize the significance of sex work in her understanding of Black women's oppression. The first involved US sailors as part of the imperial-military sex trade, which she witnessed as a girl in Barbados. A *Wall Street Journal* profile of her work noted: "She still remembers the way old women there would doll up their granddaughters whenever a shipload of US sailors dropped anchor. The memory has convinced her that women become prostitutes because they need money—not because they are naturally attracted to a life of selling sex."[7] She moved to New York as a teenager, earned a degree from Long Island University, did graduate work at Columbia, and taught in Ocean Hill–Brownsville in Brooklyn before moving on to do adult literacy work with the City University of New York.[8] The *Wall Street Journal* detailed the proximate event that led her to sex worker organizing: "Mrs. Prescod, who came to this country as a teen-ager, says she long wanted to help immigrant women like herself, but she didn't get interested in prostitutes until 1978, when she was teaching remedial reading at Queens College in New York City. Some of her students lost their scholarships in a welfare-fraud scandal, and Mrs. Prescod formed a group to fight for new funds. But the students had already taken other action: 'Right in my very own organization, under my nose, half the women were becoming hookers to stay in school,' she says. 'It became clear that if I was going to do the kind of organizing that I was committed to doing, I was going to have to deal with prostitution.'"[9]

By that point, Prescod was already organizing, if a bit aimlessly. In the late 1960s and early 1970s, she searched for a cause to call her own. She told the *Los Angeles Times* that she had "a little bout with black separatism, cultural nationalism, discovered being African." She attended feminist study groups and even a Barbados study group. Finally, she found the cause she had been searching for in the Wages for Housework Campaign. When Prescod and her friend Brown encountered Wages for Housework's literature, they were impressed enough to borrow money to attend a Wages for Housework conference in London. Upon their return, they founded International Black Women for Wages for Housework. "That was it for me," Prescod recalled, laughing. "I left the Barbados group and told the men how I felt about making the fishcakes while they sat around and talked about all they were going to do back in the West Indies."[10]

The International Wages for Housework Campaign had been founded in 1972 by Selma James, Silvia Federici, and Maria Rose Della Costa. The campaign organized "to get recognition and compensation by government for the unwaged work women do in the home, on the land and in the community, to be paid by dismantling the military industrial complex." The group held that through their work in the home, on the land, in the community, and in churches, schools, and community groups, women produced and reproduced the workforce. They provided most of the world's health care and did not receive a wage for it. "In making the case that women's contribution is the basic ingredient to all industry and all profit," the group said, "we establish our entitlement to benefits, higher wages, social services, childcare, grants, unpolluted land, information, technology. Welfare and child benefits are not charities but wages we are owed."[11]

Black Women for Wages for Housework centered the concerns of Black and other women of color within the Wages for Housework campaign. From the outset they understood the violent, sexist, racist economic order that deprived women of the resources they needed and were owed as global in scope. They advanced an internationalist, Black feminist argument for reparations, demanding back pay for Black women's triple shifts under plantation slavery forward. "From Soweto to New York, London to Nicaragua, Bhopal to Trinidad—Black/Third World Women, internationally the majority of the majority of the world's people, carry the burden of the world's work and get the least wealth in return. We are a network of Black/Third World Women claiming reparations for our unwaged work, including slavery, imperialism, and neocolonialism," one statement explained. "Our work," BWfWfH proclaimed, "is to ensure that the issues and concerns of Black/Third World Women are a priority in shaping the work of the Wages for Housework campaign: to see to it that challenging racism and challenging sexism, which reinforce each other, are prioritized equally. . . . Our campaigning on welfare, immigration controls, police illegality, health, rape and domestic violence, nuclear power/weapons and ecological devastation integrate Black/Third World, women's and green issues."[12] Thus, from its outset, the group was critical of, among many other things, police power.

Prescod would remind her audience that housework was usually left out of accounts of slavery, "whether it was in the slave master's house or in the hovels where most slaves lived."[13] In Prescod's analysis, and in contrast to a racially unmarked gendered analysis of household labor, the mammy reproduced everyone, including her white mistress: "What did the work of the mammy involve? It involved reproducing everyone, and by that I mean not just bearing children but raising them, looking after the men, other women, yourself, making sure everyone was fit for the next day. And reproducing not only her own children, her man and herself, but also reproducing the master and his family, his children, his wife. The mammy was responsible for keeping everyone going." But the group not only challenged standard accounts of the period of enslavement but, as we shall see, they also challenged received understandings of the term "housework."[14]

Wages Due Lesbians, another of the autonomous organizations associated with the Wages for Housework campaign and a group of which BWfWfH cofounder Wilmette Brown was also a member, was founded in 1975 by lesbian women "of different races, nationalities, backgrounds, ages and dis/abilities." The group campaigned for housework wages for lesbian women, who did "unwaged work . . . in common with other women" and carried "the additional physical and emotional housework of surviving in a hostile and prejudiced society." The group explained: "We organize as lesbian women to prevent money and resources going to 'normal' women only—reinforcing the power of the family against all women."[15]

The US Prostitutes Collective, or US PROS, with whom Prescod also organized, was, with the English Collective of Prostitutes, part of the International Prostitutes Collective. US PROS organized with Black Women for Wages for Housework and advocated for the abolition of laws around sex work, for "human, legal and civil rights" for sex workers, and for "higher benefits, student grants, wages and other resources so that no woman is forced by poverty into sex with anyone." The organization aligned with the broader Wages for Housework movement, seeing the campaign's work as ultimately benefiting all women, including sex workers. "By attacking the sexism which dooms most women to poverty and a 24-hour workday," US

PROS wrote, "wages for housework strengthens us against the prostitution laws and lays the basis for prostitutes and non-prostitute women to act together. We oppose police/government control of prostitution—we, not the state, must control our bodies and our money."[16]

Collectively, Black Women for Wages for Housework, Wages Due Lesbians, and the US Prostitutes Collective brought something unique to the Wages for Housework campaign: they expanded the organization's analysis of the power and problems of "the home" to the plantation, the doctor's office, the jail cell, the child welfare office and the streets, with Brown, in particular, advancing an analysis of racialized heteronormativity as a form of labor discipline that women of color in particular were violently punished and often criminalized for transgressing. Beth Capper and Arlen Austin argue that these groups "re-visioned" the fight, conceiving of the struggle for wages for housework as a fight against "heterosexual work discipline" that kept women in low and unwaged work. They explain: "BWfWfH and WDL impressed that 'the home' disciplines the sexualities and labors of even those seemingly excluded from its domain. Both groups emphasized that heteronormativity, as a modality of a work-discipline, especially targeted women of color (and) lesbians who were refused by, or who refused, the regulatory ideals of (white) femininity associated with the housewife, and who faced criminalization, sexual violence, forced sterilization, welfare austerity, and the loss of child custody for their transgressions."[17]

Black Women for Wages for Housework placed women on welfare and sex workers at the center of its organizing and analysis. In bringing these women "from margin to center," they were, indeed, able to challenge and expand significantly the standard definition of "housework." Prescod asked, "What makes the work of a housewife with two children in the suburbs respectable and that of a woman on welfare degrading?" In her analysis, only residential segregation, municipal neglect, and poverty separated their labors: "Some women maybe live out in the suburbs and have a house with a little white fence around and all that stuff. And the Black woman is in another neighborhood where she has to do some other kinds of housework: it's a lot of work fighting rats and roaches and that kind of thing; worrying about your kids being mugged, you being mugged, and maybe it's your kid who's doing the mugging because he doesn't have any money—and you sure don't have any to give him." Here Prescod calls attention to, as Capper and Austin note, Black women doing the "housework of managing everyday racism and racial violence."[18] Prescod continued, "But in both situations, you're doing housework" and, therefore, both women, white and Black, should demand compensation.[19]

A poster for a June 19 BWfWfH rally to "Fight Against Welfare Cuts [and] Demand Wages for Housework for All Women from the Government" stated the group's position on welfare succinctly: "Welfare is the first money we women have won directly from the government for the work we do in our homes. It is not much and it hardly pays for all our work. But it is a start and it is our money. The attack on welfare women is an attack on all women. To keep us in line. To keep us all working for nothing. To convince us that housework is not work, that we should not be paid for it, that we should do it for 'love.' But love doesn't pay our bills." The Black Women for Wages for Housework "Birth Announcement" details the group's work organizing in welfare offices and lists topics to be addressed at its June 1976 public meeting, which included presentations on the forced sterilization of welfare mothers and cuts to welfare as part of "a broader crisis in New York City."[20] Yet because the campaign also centered Black sex workers in addition to women on welfare in their analysis, Prescod was able to discern a direct connection between policing and heterosexual labor discipline, between austerity-driven feminine deprivation and desperation and policing, as well as to the role of policing in the phenomenon of gender-related violence and Black femicide.

Black Women for Wages for Housework developed a sophisticated analysis of sex work as a vitally important form of housework, sex work's disciplinary role within gendered racial capitalism, and the relationship between policing in general and the punitive regulation of street-based sex work in particular in Black women's disproportionate experience of gender-related violence. For the organization, sex workers were simply houseworkers unbound. It was dangerous, criminalized, yet paid housework that many women were forced into because other housework they performed was unpaid. "Prostitution is not a game, it is WORK—the work of servicing men sexually to get the means to live. It is the work of being at the disposal of men's sexual needs and their fantasies of what a woman is supposed to look like, supposed to do, supposed to be. . . . We are forced to sell our sexual services on the streets, in hotels and massage parlours, or in our apartments—to take on the *second* job of prostitution—because we are not paid for the *first* job we all do as women, housework, the job of producing and taking care of everybody so that we all can work and make profits for the Man."[21]

The "crime" of sex work was that sex workers rejected pervasive "heterosexual work discipline" by refusing to do the work men expected women to do for free, refusing to be poor. For their crimes against patriarchy, for their efforts at liberation, they were expelled from the home as courts took their children away. Their plight kept other women in line, performing low-waged and unwaged but "respectable" work: "To turn back the rising tide of our refusal to be penniless, the Man makes sure that part of the job of being a prostitute is to be used as a sign to other women of where the bottom is—to be labeled a whore, and an unfit mother, a Negress (which they used to call us), a loose woman. So, part of the work of being a prostitute is to be made an example of what it costs *us* to refuse the poverty the *Man* forces us to live in, to be a whip against other women to make sure that they strive always to be 'respectable' though poor."[22] And just as they questioned the hierarchical and invidious distinctions made between the labors of the suburban housewife and those of the urban single mother on public assistance, Black Women for Wages for Housework critiqued the hypocritical, divisive, and demobilizing moral superiority attributed to some forms of "women's work" at play in the criminalization of sex work. These moral distinctions normalized and facilitated violence against sex workers and by extension—given the racist, sexist structure of the formal economy, where Black women were often the last hired and the first fired and therefore always suspected of sex work whenever they appeared on the street, and the racist enforcement of prostitution laws—violence against Black women.

Black Women for Wages for Housework saw violence against women—what they called "terrorism"—as the most extreme form of the heterosexual labor discipline that functioned to keep women in unwaged and low wage work – both physical and emotional labor - and they came to understand police as both significant perpetrators of *and* implicit authorizers of this violence.[23] In the group's analysis, unlike that of their "dominance" feminist contemporaries with whom they would later organize in Take Back the Night Campaigns, police carried out this terror alongside individual men. BWfWfH immediately clocked the ever greater investment in policing as a ticking time bomb of gender-based violence against Black women, with prostitution laws marking sex workers as appropriate objects of violence, the vigorous enforcement of prostitution laws as normalizing violence against sex workers, the racist enforcement of prostitution laws as producing the prostitute as Black, and thus the legitimization and normalization of police violence against sex workers as escalating all forms of violence against Black women. Anne Fischer writes, "Members of the WfH-affiliated U.S. Prostitutes Collective (U.S. PROS) argued that because broken windows policing was geared toward clearing 'disorderly' people off city streets, these police practices directly contributed to the murder of sex workers and sexually profiled women. 'Raids against prostitute women are a go-ahead to violent men,' they said in a statement. 'After all they too are removing "bad women" from the streets.'"[24] The group drew attention not only to the role of the state, via the racist enforcement of prostitution laws, but also to the formal economy, via discriminatory hiring practices—even within sex work, that is brothel versus street-based work—in producing the prostitute as Black. The structural forces that left women, and Black women in particular, with few economic options other than sex work meant that *all* Black women were *always* suspected of sex work—that is, Black women were "sexually profiled," and therefore always subject to police harassment and violence in and removal (either temporarily through arrest or permanently via death) from public space.[25] Furthermore, "[w]ho among us, as Black women, is above prostitution?" BWfWfH suggestively asked. None of us, they held and in the eyes of others, none of us, it would seem. But that difficult truth brought into focus the scope of the problem *and* its solution. "Racism—our being forced as Black women always to have the least money, the least possibility of getting a job, the least access to school, the worst housing, and the first 'opportunity' to be fired, fined, or jailed—already means that all Black women are *suspected* of being or *expected* to be prostitutes anyway! In a sweep arrest—when women who are just walking down the street can be arrested as prostitutes—who gets swept up first? It's always open season on Black women."[26] As this analysis made clear, with the policing of prostitution came the gendered racial profiling of Black women, and therefore increased harassment, violence, and removal in economically depressed areas. Only resources—money, secure housing—combined with fewer police and less policing, prevented violence against Black women.

The group did not only draw attention to the fact that the normalization of violence against sex workers led to an increase in the violence Black women experienced from the police; they also drew attention to what its targets might recognize as the disturbing familiarity of said violence. The group highlighted similarities in the violence sex workers were subject to and the violence Black women confronted daily in their communities. The violence both groups of women experienced were, in fact, one and the same. "An attack against prostitutes is an attack on all women," BWfWfH wrote.

"The struggles of prostitute women against police harassment on the streets, against beatings, against fines and jails, against being declared 'unfit mothers' in the courts and having our children taken away, against being treated like animals and outcasts, against pimps, racketeers, and businesses that profit from our misery, and, what is key to all of these attacks, against not having any money to call our own, are struggles that we as Black women are all forced to make." Police were given leave to enact the same forms of violence against Black women that they enacted against sex workers simply because they were there. Police harassed, beat, fined, and jailed Black women just as they harassed, beat, fined, and jailed sex workers, and the police could hardly be distinguished from the cast of men exploiting and harming resourceless women. Black women and sex workers faced the same terror, the same gendered violence, be it from men or the Man: "The terrorism that is practiced by the Man and by individual men against prostitute women is a terror we all know, a terror in the Black community that always falls first and heaviest on Black women. Whether it is the terror of being beaten in the bedroom or in a parked car, on the street or in the jail, or the terror of not being able to find a decent place to live where the police don't feel free to break down the door, it is terror rooted in our having to be at everyone's disposal because we don't have the money to be able to say NO, to be able to *choose* where and how we want to live and whom we want to sleep with."[27]

The observations above only strengthened the group's argument that whether they engaged in sex work or not, no Black women were above prostitution and that the common factors in this pervasive violence was women's lack of resources because they were not paid fairly for the work they did and the police. Police, pimps, and racketeers are authorized to beat prostitutes just as they are given leave to beat you, they explained. Your position in the economy means that you are always suspected of prostitution, so police, pimps, and racketeers will always have an excuse for their violence against you. Look closely and see that you are already subject to the same violence that threatens sex workers. Police, they would eventually argue, are not only a drain on the resources that are owed to you as women, they are also a major violent threat to prostitutes and to all Black women. They are a force in your immiseration and a source of violence against you that you are forced to subsidize. For BWfWfH, no woman could be free if she was not paid fairly for *all* of the labor she performed and the Black woman could not be free, could not live a life free from violence, if the prostitute (a woman rendered Black by the economy and policing) was not free of the police. Black women could never be free in a context where prostitution was criminalized, that criminalization was violently enforced against sexually profiled women on the street as police ignored and added to the myriad forms of violence in under-resourced women's lives and the resources that should have gone to women for their necessary work went to the police, thereby subsidizing excessive violence against Black women.

The Coalition

Prescod founded the Black Coalition Fighting Back Serial Murders in 1986. The organization was active until the mid-1990s and became active again in August 2008, when the "Grim Sleeper," as one killer would be dubbed after taking a thirteen-year hiatus, became active again.[28] The murders around which the Coalition organized were, in fact, the work of multiple serial killers operating in South Los Angeles at the time, serial killers of what activists estimate to have been at least two hundred Black women.[29] The Black Coalition was composed of members of BWfWfH, WDL, and US PROS and would build its analysis of the conditions that produced this serial Black femicidal violence on the dimly lit streets of South LA on the foundation of analysis advanced by these organizations. The Coalition would also bring this analysis into the Take Back the Night Movement, with which it organized, analysis that helped it, according to Fischer, expand the idea of *from whom* the night needed to be taken back. As well, the organization would bring the Black female necromantic tradition into both the Wages for Housework and TBTN campaigns.

Take Back the Night was a march-based movement, wherein women reclaimed the streets during dark hours. The organization's historical account states that "In 1972, women at the University of Southern Florida donned witches' brooms and black capes, marching through campus to demand resources and safety for women. In 1973, San Francisco citizens protested violent 'snuff' pornography films. In 1975, Philadelphia residents rallied after microbiologist Susan Alexander Speeth was stabbed to death on the sidewalk after work. In 1976, a Tribunal Council of Women from 40+ countries met in Belgium to advocate for the safety of women on the street."[30] Fischer argues that the Black Coalition brought a critique of state power and how it increased violence against women into TBTN organizing and that the BCFBSM's critique of the racialized criminalization of sex work and of policing diverged sharply from the groups of women organizing to take back the night who felt that the police could and should play a role in protecting women from individual men.[31] "Antiviolence feminists like Prescod . . . exposed and challenged the state's powerful role as a generator of violence against women, especially through the selective, racist enforcement of prostitution laws. And second, they argued that the discriminatory police power to harass, arrest and abuse left Black women profoundly vulnerable to nonstate harm."[32]

Indeed, when the Black Coalition began organizing with TBTN, Prescod would bring the BWfWfH's understanding of the racialized gendered disciplinary power of policing, US PROS's abolitionist stance toward prostitution laws, and WDL and BWfWfH's expansive understanding of the category of housework to bear on TBTN's understanding of male danger on the streets. Police, at best, did nothing to help women, and at their worst were part of what hurt them. Prostitution laws were effectively state pronouncements on good and bad women—a clear signal of which women could be subject to harm and who should presumably be exempt from it, who belonged to the community and who stood apart from it and were therefore legitimate objects of violence. Prescod would also draw attention to racist divisions in sex-working labor wherein Black women were more likely to be involved in street-level sex work as opposed to the call girl work that white women were more likely to engage in and the fact that police, tasked as they were with cleaning up the street, only enforced the laws against Black women on the street. Thus, the economy and the state worked in tandem to produce the prostitute as Black. Non sex-working Black women on the street were then subject to sexual profiling and thus to harassment and violence from police and, because prostitution laws operated as a social signal, other men as well. What's more budgeting that prioritized policing over that which really kept women safe—resources—most certainly exposed women to greater harm, not least of which by leaving them few noncriminalized survival options.

On March 29, 1985, a little less than seven months before the LAPD would call their press conference to announce the serial murders, Prescod would participate in a panel, "Women and Prostitution: Up Against the Law," with Philadelphia Assistant District Attorney Pamela Cushing. The panel took place at the University of Pennsylvania Law School and was sponsored by Penn's Women's Law Group and Women in Dialogue. Kissette Bundy, who covered the piece for the *Philadelphia Tribune*, would open the piece echoing Prescod's earlier critique of the invidious moral hierarchy attributed to different aspects of women's work saying, "It's called selling. Something we have all done at some time to convince employers we are worth the paycheck we receive. Margaret Prescod agrees, but sees no difference between selling your brains, your hands, or the area called the 'private parts.'" Cushing would present a carceral feminist argument for the necessity of prostitution laws and therefore makes an excellent foil for highlighting where Prescod was in her analysis of the role of policing in violence against women at the time of the murders, of budgeting priorities that privileged policing, as well as her views on what was necessary for women's safety and well-being, though the latter is not hard to surmise, given her organizing work in the previous decade. Cushing would argue, "Prostitution is something we want to keep illegal. We do not want to say that men can control our bodies. Keeping the laws the way they are is helping women."

Prescod appeared as the spokesperson for the International Network of Prostitutes' Collective, which advocated for the abolition of prostitution laws, and vehemently disagreed with Cushing's understanding of both the problem and its solutions. Bundy would quote Prescod as saying, "What is needed—there must be changes as how women are viewed in this society. If you really want to get to the root of prostitution, you get to the economic dependency." Of the INPC Prescod would say, "Our long range goal is to provide solutions that are economically viable. So that no woman or child has to turn to prostitution." Bundy would continue, "[Prescod] said the majority of women who are prostitutes are single mothers and would leave the life if there was something else they could do that would feed, clothe and/or provide a better education for their children." Prescod would point out that economic crisis led many to prostitution. Bundy would continue:

> Arguing that prostitution laws work against much of the ground feminists' groups have gained with a woman's right to her own body, the INPC says vice laws label prostitutes as "bad people," alienating them from the community, making them vulnerable to rape, extortion, kidnapping and industry exploitation. Likewise police sweeps, neighborhood vigilantes, and district pornography zones only push the illegality of prostitution further underground, the INPC says . . . INPC would rather see the money now spent rounding up prostitutes used instead for safe houses for juvenile runaways, retraining programs, housing, child care costs and for

> resuscitating social services subject to federal cutback. . . . Seeking "control of our working conditions," INPC lobbies for abolition of prostitution laws rather than legalization of prostitution.

The group opposed legalization and chose to advocate for the abolition of all prostitution laws because of the racist division of labor within sex work, a division that would continue to expose Black women to disproportionate police violence. Even though there were more white women in prostitution, Black women did street-based sex work while white women were call girls, and in a context in which police worked most pointedly to punish street crime and clear the streets that meant that Black women were disproportionately beaten, arrested and incarcerated.[33] Prescod would explain, "Legalization will not deter the sexist and racist aspects of the sex industry. . . . There is a hierarchy in the sex industry, the same as in society." Legalization would do nothing to change the division of sex working labor, who would be slotted into legal work and whose work would still be criminalized and subject to violence.

The BCFBSM's divergence from the mainstream of the TBTN and its persistent police antagonism was evident in that it held weekly vigils outside Los Angeles police headquarters. Their vigils would spread around the country and abroad, as the Coalition organized a multicity Take Back the Night action "with coordinated vigils, pickets and die-ins."[34] As part of that campaign, the Philadelphia chapter of Wages for Housework would announce the following vigil on July 17, 1986:

> Wages for Housework Campaign, Philadelphia in support of the BLACK COALITION FIGHTING BACK SERIAL MURDERS
>
> COME JOIN AN
> I N T E R N A T I O N A L
> VIGIL
> FOR THE 17 VICTIMS, MOSTLY BLACK
> AND PROSTITUTE WOMEN, OF THE
> "SOUTHSIDE SLAYER" (SERIAL MURDERER)
> IN LOS ANGELES, CALIFORNIA
> To protest inaction by police and federal agencies, in solving the killings
>
> To support the BLACK COALITION FIGHTING BACK SERIAL MURDERS and its demands, including the demand for involvement by federal authorities

> To bring attention to these killings as well as to the 45–90 women killed in Seattle in a 4 year period, 5 women in San Diego and 7 in Oakland, CA
> Thursday July 17, 1986
> 12 noon–1 pm
> Outside the Federal Building
> 6th & Arch Streets
> Philadelphia, PA
> Bring flowers—Dress in black or wear black ribbon

The flyer also noted simultaneous vigils taking place in Los Angeles, San Francisco, Tulsa, Oklahoma, and London, England: the TBTN Coalition would commemorate the first anniversary of the Black Coalition with a "mass" candlelight vigil. A flyer announced the event as follows:

> TAKE BACK THE NIGHT, Saturday October 25
> MARCH AND RALLY in Exposition Park co-sponsored by the Take Back the Night Coalition, the BLACK COALITION FIGHTING BACK SERIAL MURDERS and the LA City Commission on the Status of Women.
>
> - PROTEST THE MURDERS OF 17 WOMEN—MOST OF THEM BLACK—IN SOUTH-CENTRAL L.A.
> - DEMAND AN END TO ABUSES AGAINST REFUGEE, UNDOCUMENTED AND IMMIGRANT WOMEN
> - DEMONSTRATE YOUR OPPOSITION TO VIOLENCE AGAINST WOMEN

The archive shows that this vigil changed at least one mind. Gene Ford, writing in the Marxist-humanist newsletter *News & Letters*, would report that the vigil took place at "64th and Main Street, in the heart of dark and gloomy South-Central L.A., the area where 18 women have been murdered by a serial killer." Though TBTN had hoped for a mass vigil, Ford would report "At this very street corner, about 30 people, mostly women, Black and white, participated in a very exciting candlelight vigil." Perhaps the most noteworthy part of the vigil Ford reports is his own evolving understanding of violence against women on the street via analogy to racial violence:

> When she [Prescod] asked people to say what they thought I had a chance to speak out against the senseless racist murder at Howard Beach and the

> attack upon Blacks in segregated Forsyth County, Georgia, where being Black is cause enough for racists to attack. In the same sense, women should not be open to attacks by sexists because they are women and are out on the street at any time. This is an attack upon the whole Black community. I really get a feeling for what "Take Back the Night" meant at this vigil. Being a Black man at this vigil, I felt more needed to be there to show our support for Black women, who are human beings, and should be treated as such.[35]

I want to stress that although Prescod called attention to police inaction regarding the murders in her coalition work—a familiar refrain, and something with which Black people throughout the nation would agree—her writings and public statements make clear that she had developed an understanding of the police as a Black femicidal institution before she ever indicted the LAPD for its neglect. In her account, even if they wanted to (and they did not), the police could not keep Black women safe. Only resources—the resources that enable women to say no—could do that. Prescod had long been critical of austerity-based welfare cuts. She would vehemently decry the redirection of those resources to policing—a practice that she knew would leave women in desperate circumstances with less ability to say no, thereby negatively impacting their autonomy and directly endangering their lives by leaving them with few noncriminalized survival options, thus putting them on a collision course with violent police alongside an array of other violent and exploitative men. Prescod saw this resource redirection as creating the conditions for the murder of Black sex workers and, as Fischer says, other "sexually profiled" women, particularly poor and working-class Black women.[36] Of those other women so sexually profiled, West, who was a member of the Coalition, would write:

> The Black Coalition has stated again and again that they are not convinced that all the women murdered were prostitutes and that the police have offered little evidence to support that claim. When the police could not dig up a prostitution arrest record on victim 17, they immediately said, "but she was a street woman." This statement reflects the attitude of the police towards poor women generally, especially if they are black. We all know only too well that any of us at any time can be labeled a prostitute woman, if we dare step out of line in the way we speak and dress, in the hours we keep, the numbers of friends we have, or if we are "sexual outlaws" of any kind. When prostitute women are not safe, no woman is safe. Historically serial

murderers who begin with prostitute women inevitably go on to murder any women.[37]

Prescod's critique of the gendered division of labor and the racialized division of sex working labor, the police, and prostitution laws would lead her to expand Barbara Smith's initial elaboration of the causes of Black femicide to include gendered resource deprivation, policing, and whorephobia. Recall that it was Smith who connected the dots between race, sex, and femicide: "We've got to understand that violence against us as women cuts across all racial, ethnic and class lines. This doesn't mean that violence against Third World women does not have a racial as well as sexual cause. Both race and sex lead to violence against us. . . . It's true that the victims were all black and that Black people have always been targets of racist violence in this society, but they were also *all* women. Our sisters died because they were women just as surely as they died because they were black." Prescod's contribution was to point out that, yes, these Black women died because they were Black women, but also because they were made poor not only by the devaluation of women's work and Black women's work in particular, but by a sexist division of labor where much of women's labor, including the labor Black women performed to survived under racist conditions, was uncompensated. Black women made poor by racist sexism could expect no societal protection from violence, be it from men or "the Man," because of their association with sex work, in a culture where the law pronounced sex workers as bad women and appropriate targets of violence. The society explicitly and tacitly condoned police and other men's violence against sex workers and thus against Black women. What's more, violence against sex workers served a disciplinary function in patriarchal society; it kept other women in their place. It was thus a form of the violent disciplining of all women. Prescod saw these Black femicidal murders as consistent with Lagarde y de los Rios's more intersectional definition, wherein a variety of structural forces, including racism, classism, and whorephobia, intersect to endanger the lives of Black women on the street and elsewhere.

But when she stood by that coffin draped with flowers, Prescod was not only offering a huge leap forward in our understanding of the causes of Black femicide; she was also—like Smith, Ida B. Wells, Mamie Till-Bradley, and Clementine Barfield before her—insisting that the dead are indeed present in our democracy and therefore that they must be represented within it. The Black Coalition Fighting Back Serial Murders endeavored to expand the demographics of the democracy to include the truly marginal among the Black female dead: the "sexual outlaws" and the "sexually profiled," as well as those all but left for dead. They did so, in part, by working to expand the geographic spaces of critical dialogue regarding the women's death—to revive spaces that had themselves all but been left for dead—and via innovative discursive practice.

Black Femicide and Innovative, Ephemeral Democracy

Prescod's activism fits within the tradition outlined above. It sits alongside Wells's reanimation labor via the excavation of the quotidian details of lives lost, her political accountability via accounting, Till-Bradley's conjuring of the first of many reincarnations of Till via her participatory lynching-as-crucifixion scenario, Barfield's secular restorative kinship practices, and her repeated resurrection of her son in speech and in deed as she performed her supernatural democratic horticulture. It fits closely with the resurrective labors of Smith who, like Prescod, sought to expand the bounds of democratic community to include Black women killed because they were, among other things, Black women. Prescod, however, sought to include the most marginal of the Black feminine dead, sex workers and other so sexually profiled.

The methods Smith and Prescod employed to attend to the Black femicides haunting our democracy were distinct. Smith employed radical democratic enumeration while Prescod used dialogue, representation, salvage, and revivification. The publics they called into being were somewhat ad hoc—Smith's had been born of sheer frustration; she had been, after all, "steaming" before she dashed off her pamphlet. Prescod's were fleeting, "roving." They were ephemeral and, as we shall see with Toni Morrison in the next chapter, just the thing to capture—if only ever for a moment—these women "out of bounds."

Smith's 1979 pamphlet in response to the serial murder of Boston-area Black women called a new public into being, a public that claimed the dead women not just as part of a significant series the police and the media refused to acknowledge, but as a part of itself, an emerging "we" composed to the living and the dead now placed into new relationship with one another by Smith's call. By intervening to correct a lax record—by counting—Smith began her activism with the production of what Catherine D'Ignazio calls "counterdata" or data in the service of democratic dissent. "Counterdata science," D'Ignazio says, "is a citizenship practice," "an informatic form of enacting democratic dissent, prompting protest and insisting on political engagement."[38] Through counterdata science, Smith was asserting a new politics, countering hegemonic data science, and enacting "alternate imaginaries of what data science is, who does it, and who benefits."[39] Her radical enumeration, which included counting and then scratching the numbers out, was an act of care for the living and the dead, even as it called the living into new community with the dead. The new circle of living women called by Smith's words could only become part of the archive she had been forced to make for the dead by understanding themselves to have and publicly claiming an important form of commonality with the dead women, an ongoing political link with women now in another realm. Smith and the dead and living women became a new thing, a new "we" in response to Smith's call.

The Coalition's work to represent dead Black female sexual outlaws and other sexually profiled women, like Smith's, required democratic innovation. The Coalition's activism sought to expand the Black public not only demographically, but geographically. It engaged the least "public" of Black counterpublic spaces—not churches, hair salons, or barbershops, but liquor stores, vacant strip malls, and public buses—via their innovative use of what Juli Grigsby has named their "roving counterpublics," that in an impressive act of democratic revival, reclaimed all of South Los Angeles as open for democratic dialogue regarding the murders. "Roving counterpublics," she says, "move against the developed public and counterpublic to make use of space that builds from Black women's interstitial lived experiences that increases their proximity to racialized sexual violence." She continues, "The activism of the BCFB instead engages public space not traditionally considered a Black counterpublic space like those we have become familiar with, such as the barbershop, hair salon or church. In choosing locations marked by precarity, the BCFB made the statement that no place in South Central was out of bounds, too devastated, or uninhabitable."[40] The women aimed to begin critical conversations regarding the murders at liquor stores, vacant strip malls, public buses, and in stalled rush hour traffic. "Thus, by developing roving counterpublics that moved through the city with the people, coalition members reclaimed South Los Angeles as open for political dialogues."[41]

News coverage from the time constantly emphasizes how dark the places where the dead women were found, how desolate. The Coalition brought the light of publicity, brought democratic life, to these spaces. The Coalition held weekly vigils at police headquarters, their "macabre props" keeping the dead present, represented within the demos, in a move that asserted that there was no contradiction between sex work and citizenship, and through that claiming the women as part of the political community, indeed restoring them to their right political relationship with the community, after their deaths, but they also held press conferences at the sites of the women's murders, a practice which helped salvage these dimly lit spaces of sex-related death as democratic space, while humanizing the women. That is, the only way that the dead could be adequately represented, brought back into the life of the demos, kept present in our democracy, is via the revival of dead and dying space for democratic dialogue. They thus helped to bring these once profane spaces of sex-related Black death into the bounds of democracy via dialogue but also by memorializing, by practicing secular sanctification in these spaces of death, by being in political community with their dead.

They said their names and brought light to dark corners back then, and today, with the ROSESLA (Reclaiming Our Sisters Everywhere South LA) memorial project, members of the Coalition continue to "say their names," and, further, resolve to "etch them in stone"—to keep them here with us forever—in an effort to "restore dignity to victims," to validate "their humanity and the humanity of their surviving families alike," to restore the women who have now passed out of this realm to their correct political relationship with us all:

> The South LA community has been traumatized by the violent loss of so many precious lives over such a protracted period. This loss and trauma must be acknowledged. We refuse to accept the silence and indifference that often follows these murders. We say the names of these Black women and girls who are victims of serial murderers in South LA and etch them in stone. Each victim is a mother's child, a father's daughter, a sibling's sister, a friend. . . . There is no official commemoration of these devastating events. A monument is a public statement of worth. It restores dignity to the victims, validates their humanity and the humanity of their surviving families alike. It declares undeniably that these Black lives mattered. The location of the memorial will be determined in consultation with surviving family members and other community members. A number of public spaces, parks and other suitable sites in South Los Angeles are currently under consideration.[42]

Prescod is both part of the foundations of abolition feminism and a foremother of contemporary Black anti-femicide activists. Her roving, episodic "wes" more closely resemble Morrison's small hidden publics than Crenshaw's call to transform larger ones. Prescod's praxis, indeed, gestures toward something that we can see most clearly in Morrison. While all the activism within this tradition contains key elements of the Morrisonian democracy to which I now turn—Wells's concern to highlight and correct the record, to recall and write down, Till-Bradley's concern with embodiment, with the flesh, Barfield's work to care for and tend the dead, and to do so with attention to nature and the environment—Smith and Prescod's concern with femicide and with the feminine dead links them most closely to Morrison and Prescod's ephemeral publics in overlooked, forgotten, and disregarded spaces, publics created to address the concerns of the most marginal of the Black feminine dead resembles Morrison's the most closely of all the women profiled herein.

8

Toward a Truant Black Feminist Democracy

Toni Morrison and the Democratic Work of the Dead

Black women constitute 10 percent of the US female population, yet they make up 59 percent of women murdered. Indeed, though men are more likely to be killed than women, Black women are more likely to be killed than white men. But not all deaths are created equal. Men are more often killed in public—on the street, at sporting events, or in bar fights. Women, when they are killed, are usually killed in private and for reasons related to intimacy, sex, and sexuality. Catherine D'Ignazio notes that men "are not frequently violated and killed in their homes," and in contemporary America "men's bodies are not typically desecrated in brutal and sexualized ways." (Lynching is an important recent counterexample). Even when women are killed by the police, these deaths usually take place inside the home and are connected to the victims' intimate relationships, as when police killed Breonna Taylor because they were looking for her former partner.[1]

Black femicide is defined as the misogynoiristic killing of Black women because they are Black women *or* the misogynistic killing of Black women because they are women facilitated by structural racism as it intersects with a variety of other oppressive social conditions. Black femicide is a serious problem. Mortality data from thirty states shows that from 1999 to 2020, Black women aged twenty-five to forty-four were six times more likely to be murdered than their white counterparts. Most of those deaths were the result of intimate partner violence. For example, Black women account for 44.6 percent of pregnancy-related fatal intimate partner violence. Reproductive violence and obstetric racism are also factors. Pregnancy- and abortion-related deaths are forms of passive femicide, and Black women are at least three times more likely to die from pregnancy-related complications than white women.[2]

The Labors of Resurrection. Shatema Threadcraft, Oxford University Press. © Oxford University Press (2025).
DOI: 10.1093/9780197758618.003.0009

The rate of death is not only utterly sobering but also on the rise: a Black woman was killed by her intimate partner every nineteen hours in 2015, whereas one was killed every six hours in 2022.[3] The intimate partner violence Black women experience is made more deadly by a surrounding context of workplace discrimination and related resource deprivation, including housing insecurity, medical neglect, and inadequate public safety provision. Societal hierarchies are also a factor, as homophobia, transphobia, femmephobia, and stereotypes that normalize violence against women who defy gender norms—including sex workers, single mothers, and transwomen—expose Black women to disproportionate violence and premature death.

Despite this bleak picture, the most widespread activism regarding premature Black death is in response to the deaths of Black men. The pioneering legal theorist Kimberlé Crenshaw, who has been a significant voice calling attention to Black femicide and violence against Black women, laments the lack of large-scale mobilization in response to Black women's deaths. Crenshaw understands this mobilization asymmetry as being partially rooted in Black women's lack of "narrative capital," and she has called for Black women to "share their stories" of violence to redistribute this capital in Black communities and increase mobilization in response to women's deaths.[4] Yet redistributing narrative capital to Black women is a more complicated project than simply sharing stories, because women will not offer their stories in a narrative vacuum. Again, most Black women die "unspectacularly," in private and in the context of intimate relationships. At the same time, Black political leaders, most notably W. E. B. Du Bois, have written spectacular violence, and specifically lynching, into the story of who Blacks are and why they are here—that is, into the story of Black peoplehood. Therefore, those who call on Black women to share their stories of private violence must reflect not only on the difficulty of sharing these stories of violent intimacy publicly but on how likely such stories are to resonate in a spectacular death-attentive context. The difficulty is heightened by testimonial injustice, wherein Black women are assigned less credibility and therefore many are unlikely to be believed, as well as by hermeneutical injustice, that is, that our language is less equipped to communicate the experiences of the most marginal among us. We must reflect on the fact that some stories cannot yet be told, as well as on how these stories may lack resonance, given the dominant narratives of Black peoplehood. But what if these are not stories to pass on?

Toni Morrison was aware of the profound political impact of spectacular violence against Blacks. In delivering a talk titled "Alienation and the State" to the PEN Congress in 1986, Toni Morrison told her audience:

> It's interesting to me and painful to me because I know that perhaps as far as most people are concerned I am invited here and I am sitting here because I have written books and because people have read them. And I'm sure that's part of the reason. But for me the *whole* reason that I am invited here and the whole reason that I am sitting here is because some Black children got their brains shot out in the streets all over this country and had the "good fortune" to be televised. So that slowly and slowly, after years and hundreds of years of mangled lives and bodies, the state began to pay attention. Well of course it's more complicated than that. But in fact I am a read as opposed to unread writer because of those children. And I am clear on that point, I am very clear on that point because had I lived the life that the state planned for me from the beginning I know that if I had the gifts of Homer I would have lived and died in somebody's kitchen, on somebody else's land, and never written a word. That is what the state always planned for me as a black person and as a female person. And that knowledge is bone deep and it informs everything I do. Any achievement I claim has been bought and paid for by those children and the mangled lives of those who went before them and were not televised.[5]

In this way, Morrison expressed the inextricable links between her profile as a prominent Black writer and mobilizations around the spectacular public deaths of American Black children. Yet it is to her considerable insights regarding private violence to which I turn below. In this chapter, I argue that Morrison, and specifically her conceptions of transformative justice and truant democracy, provides a blueprint for how and with whom Black women should share their stories—that is, for how they should mobilize the narrative capital they already possess and build more. I make this argument, first, by examining Morrison's vision of justice, and, second, by juxtaposing the democratic visions of Du Bois and Morrison, including the ethical foundations of their envisioned democracies, the forms of violence to which they attended in the struggle for multiracial democracy, and the people—as opposed to the ephemeral collectives—they each, respectively, sought to build via storytelling.

Crenshaw seeks to transform large-scale movements in response to violence against women. But the women are not owed large-scale movements; they are owed justice. Morrison's model of storytelling offers them that. Morrison does not see justice as being brought about by mass movements, and her stories do not seek to bring about such movements. Contemporary Black femicide activists might consider her work as a model for a different form of collective, one that is more inclusive *because of* its scale and instability. Frankly, her work on justice and democracy may well be read as an endorsement of what many of them have already put into practice.

Morrison reframes privacy, intimacy, anonymity, and secrecy—the central problems I put forward regarding the political complications of Black women's spectacular death deficit—as opportunities to reflect on and build complex narratives around women's violent lives, their deaths, and the dead they keep, and to build caring and healing community and enact transformative justice around those complex narratives. Morrison envisions a form of democracy practiced not by broad sections of the population but principally among those who have experienced intimate injustice, both survivors *and*—via forms of what Rebecca Louise Carter has named "restorative kinship"—those who have not survived. Morrison's answer is not simply to organize around the bodies of the dead but to talk with them and to call forth feminine publics composed of both the living and the dead in "invisible" space, in clearings, in "the ruin," publics that pointedly address the intimate injustices as well as the epistemic injustices that further shield these often private acts from our knowledge and understanding. Yet she expressly rehabilitates the domestic collective, the home—the space of much violence against women, but importantly the space that the denial of secure access to exposes Black women to even more violence, and the space which Du Bois himself considered to be something of a ruin in Black communities—and assures us that much of what we need to move forward is there.

Morrisonian truant democracies are the spaces in which her vision of intimate justice is enacted. They not only affirm the political significance of sexual and reproductive violence at the heart of Black femicide but also aim to create the conditions for sexual freedom and to enact the reparative reproductive justice that is absent from Du Bois's account of abolition democracy. Morrisonian democracies sidestep the surrounding spectacular-violence-attentive context to call much needed attention to the fact that it is also and has always been a context of sexual, reproductive, gynecological and obstetric injustice and one in which Black women's bodies have long counted for more than their words, a context of testimonial and hermeneutical injustice and profound misrecognition. In light of the above, Morrisonian democraacies attend equally to bodies and words. Squarely facing the hermeneutical injustice and misrecognition Black women face in the wider society, they are spaces of language creation; they thus mirror the project of Morrison, their champion, of "transforming inarticulate places into conversational territories."[6]

Storytelling is central to the process: survivors and those who have passed on share stories in truant, ephemeral collectives with those who have experienced or are at acute risk of experiencing similar injustices. Notably, Morrison emphasizes affirmation and recognition over persuasion, but her democracies can also be agonal spaces, and participants are never discouraged from exercising their capacities for judgment. Morrisonian democracies are spaces of storytelling, testimony, language creation, deliberation, reflection, and ultimately of collectively produced action, but also of bodily healing, of touch, of the laying on of hands. What Morrison shows us is that it is perhaps no tragedy that Black women have not had the great reckonings Crenshaw seeks, as those who have experienced intimate injustice may not need to turn to the wider population, but to themselves and their sisters alone.

In the preceding four chapters, I profiled the democratic necromancy of several women and argued that some of the most innovative contributions to our democracy have come from the kind of nonnormative women Du Bois dismissed and derided—loudmouthed, ungovernable women like Ida B. Wells; single mothers like Mamie Till-Bradley and Clementine Barfield; lesbians, sex workers, and women who have cast their lot with them like Barbara Smith and Margaret Prescod. Smith and Prescod are significant among this group as women who acted in defense of women killed *because* they had sex and *because* they were women. It is not the women so long trapped in democracy's household, then, but those marginal to it and expelled from it, though still constrained by what Prescod's co-organizer Wilmette Brown called its gendered "heterosexual work discipline," who have made some of the most key democratic contributions.[7] And they have made these contributions not by turning away from the dead, as Du Bois did, but by and while communing with them.

I see these women's democratic contributions as containing key elements of Morrisonian democracy. That is, we see Morrison's project of postfiguration, her work "to transfigure the complexity and health of Afro-American culture into a language worthy of that culture,"[8] in Wells's concern to highlight and correct the record, to recall and write down. Till-Bradley shares Morrison's concern with embodiment, with the flesh. Barfield and Morrison are united in their ongoing dialogue between the living and the dead, their work to care for and tend the living and the dead, and to do so with attention to nature and the environment. Smith and Prescod's concern with femicide and with the feminine dead links them most closely to Morrison, with Prescod's ephemeral publics brought together in overlooked, forgotten, and disregarded spaces—publics created to address the concerns of the most marginal of the Black feminine dead linked most closely of all.

Farah Jasmine Griffin and the Spaces of Morrisonian Justice

I opened the book *Intimate Justice: The Black Female Body and the Body Politic* with the stories of several women who had experienced intimate injustice. Among them was the story of Elaine Riddick, a woman who was sterilized by the North Carolina Eugenics Board after she had been raped when she was only a girl of fourteen. In the book, I ask: what does justice for Riddick (and other women) require?[9] Griffin, in her award-winning 2021 book *Read Until You Understand: The Profound Wisdom of Black Life and Literature*, suggests that, instead of looking to theorists like John Rawls, I might have found the answer to my question in Morrison's work, specifically in her 2012 novel *Home*.[10] Today, in the wake of the *Dobbs* decision and in a context in which those who assault Black women are far less likely to be held accountable for doing so, and in which the injustices Black women face so rarely inspire mass movements, I am transfixed by a statement Griffin makes regarding *Home*: "There is no movement seeking justice for Cee, just a community of women who heal her wounds, teach her how to incorporate her physical and emotional scars into the woman she has become and send her off to do some good in the world."[11] There is no movement, just a community of women who heal her and send her off to do good in the world. This is a deeply moving vision of justice to contemplate for a group of women so long ignored by the wider society. As well, in the wake of the *Dobbs* decision, in a context in which murder is the leading cause of death for all pregnant women in the United States and thus is a brutal way in which men continue to exercise their right to choose, but also in a context in which pregnant Black women are not only three times more likely to be murdered than their pregnant white and Latinx peers, they are eight times more likely to be murdered than their non-pregnant Black peers, in a context, as well, in which Black women are three times more likely to die in childbirth, I am grateful to have discerned that Morrisonian justice is not only for the living.

Griffin, in fact, gives us a great deal to think about regarding Morrisonian justice, including the relationship the thinker saw between justice and space. The notion of justice Morrison proposes is healing, Griffin says, but not fully reparative. It allows the recipient (and sometimes the perpetrator/witness) time and space to gain both self-knowledge and the capacity to go out and "do some good in the world." It is not retributive; it is, instead, transformative. It is not procedural; it is radically informal. Morrisonian justice also has spatial dimensions; it requires the cultivation of space, and Griffin identifies three significant spaces—the outdoors, the ruin, and home—that play important roles in Morrison's understanding of justice.

Morrison gave her account of "outdoors" in her first novel, *The Bluest Eye.* The term demonstrates Morrison laboring to renovate "the language of her inheritance" so that it is capable of capturing the Black American experience. Griffin gives an amazing reading of Morrison's outdoors in her 2015 Wendy Rosenthal Gellman lecture at Cornell University, "We Do Language: History, Meaning & Language in Toni Morrison's Fiction," that is worth quoting at length:

> Claudia says, "Outdoors, we knew, was the real terror of life. The threat of being outdoors surfaced frequently in those days. Every possibility of excess was curtailed with it. If somebody ate too much, he could end up outdoors. If somebody used too much coal, he could end up outdoors. People could gamble themselves outdoors, drink themselves outdoors. Sometimes mothers put their sons outdoors, and when that happened, regardless of what that son had done, all sympathy was with him. He was outdoors, and his own flesh had done it. To be put outdoors by a landlord was one thing—unfortunate, but an aspect of life over which you had no control,

since you could not control your income. But to be slack enough to put oneself outdoors, or heartless enough to put one's own kin outdoors—that was criminal." Outdoors, we knew was the real terror of life. The sentence signals that there is more to the word than the dictionary definition. The phrase "we knew" asserts a knowledge held by a particular group, the two sisters Claudia and Frieda, black residents of Medallion, black people in America. The sentence is a signal to the reader to be attentive to a deeper meaning. Outdoors is not only an inconvenience, it constitutes a terror, intense fear, or dread or that which causes it. There is also the suggestion of violence or the potential of violence. Outdoors is a condition imposed from without and from within. Those who are put outdoors require our sympathy. Those who put someone outdoors are judged. It goes against Christ's dictum in Matthew 25:31–46 that we are to provide food, clothing, and shelter to those from whom it has been denied. What he calls the least of these. To put someone outdoors is to lose honor in the eyes of the Lord. This is the only basis in the Gospels for a final judgment.

Griffin continues:

> . . . if the first paragraph defines outdoors, the second uncovers the philosophical implications of the term. "There is a difference between being put *out* and being put out*doors*. If you are put out, you go somewhere else; if you are outdoors, there is no place to go. The distinction was subtle but final. Outdoors was the end of something, an irrevocable, physical fact, defining and complementing our metaphysical condition." . . . No one in *The Bluest Eye* is more outdoors than the child, Pecola Breedlove. She is outdoors in relation to everything and everyone surrounding her. The blues sing about a condition in order to gain some control over it, to narrate it, and therefore contain it within the blues women's own narrative. It is then given to the listener like a sacred text, a tool to help build endurance, to help find the sweetness and humor in the midst of the terror. But Pecola has no blues song. She is not socialized into this alternative universe, except as its victim and its scapegoat. Her father twice puts her outdoors, first by burning up his house. When she arrives at Claudia's family's home, Claudia says, "She came with nothing. No little paper bag with the other dress, or a night gown, or two pair of whitish cotton bloomers. She just appeared with a white woman and sat down." She doesn't even have a black mother or aunt to accompany her.

Griffin notes that, in this early text, Morrison also signals the opposite of outdoors, its remedy:

> . . . Goodness, the good, is implied in this passage. It is the opposite of putting one outdoors. It is taking them in. Claudia's family, the McTears, quietly take Pecola in. She says, "Frieda and I stopped fighting each other and concentrated on our guest, trying hard to keep her from feeling outdoors." The two sisters agree, together, to take care of Pecola. They enact an ancient hospitality by treating their guest well, making her comfortable, giving her a sense of home, in this case, in order to counter the trauma of being outdoors. They make her laugh and feed her graham crackers and milk. Goodness here does not call attention to itself. It does not ask for anything in return. The young girls grow in their effort to comfort and care for Pecola.

Tragically, the girls do not ultimately succeed in their efforts to make home for Pecola: "Pecola is put out by her father and her community. When the middle-class Geraldine finds her inside of her beautiful home, she yells, get out you nasty little black bitch. Get out of my house. The language is violent, cutting, destructive, and hateful. Combined with other acts, they contribute to the child's destruction and vulnerability and prepare the way for her ultimate victimization, the act of incest, which finally destroys her."

Griffin holds that Morrison came to endorse transformative justice through a process of considering and explicitly rejecting other notions of justice. In *Song of Solomon*, for example, Griffin says that "She is especially interested in the nature of justice and its relationship to vengeance and history, retribution and repair."[12] Griffin notes that in the novel most discussions of justice take place between men, in all-male spaces—in barbershop conversations regarding the murder of Emmett Till and among the men of the Seven Days secret fraternal society, who avenge Black death with uncomfortably and precisely equal white death. Notably, the men of Seven Days enact justice outdoors, and thereby, in its enactment, their version of justice leaves the men themselves outdoors, the first of Morrison's significant spaces. To be outdoors, to be put outdoors, as Cholly Breedlove had his family put outdoors in *The Bluest Eye*, is to be in a space beyond the communal provision of care.[13]

Because the men in *Song of Solomon* see justice as vengeance, and because they are members of a dominated group as well as beings who value survival, most must forgo justice seeking. Griffin says that those who choose to enact vengeance must do so secretly, and many are eventually driven mad by this, as is the case with the North Carolina Mutual Life Insurance agent Robert Smith, whose suicide opens the novel, as well as the protagonist Milkman Dead's best friend-turned-antagonist Guitar. It should be noted that, in a bit of foreshadowing, the chaos surrounding Agent Smith's suicide allows a small crack in the concurrent ongoing intimate injustice that is unremarked and unaddressed by the men, as Milkman's mother, Ruby, becomes the first Black woman to give birth at "No Mercy" Hospital in the confusion the suicide causes.

Morrison pairs the men's often thwarted and otherwise maddening and self-destructive conception of justice with another, Griffin says, "in the figure of an elderly woman named Circe." Morrison's Circe, like her namesake, is also a witch of a kind, as she is a midwife. She is a longtime servant to the Butlers, the white family whose patriarch murdered Milkman's grandfather and stole his land. The land theft ruined Milkman's father, driving the elder Dead to seek money to the destruction of his capacity to care for others. Circe enacts her own sense of justice by withholding and redirecting the care she has so long been forced to provide, presiding over the Butler plantation as it falls into disrepair and caring for the Butlers' victim's children, Macon and Pilate, Milkman's father and aunt. She, then, enacts her vision of justice by bringing into being another of the three significant Morrisonian spaces, the ruin.

The ruin, Griffin says, is a decaying structure at the verge of being overrun by nature. Circe oversees the ruining of the Butler plantation with studied care-less-ness—carelessness with an eye toward justice—willfully failing to intervene as nature takes its course, and thereby overseeing a kind of laissez-faire retributive justice by withholding the labor of maintenance that Black women have so long been forced to provide. She directs her care instead to the bodies of the victim's children, to the descendants of those from whom the Butlers stole, in a way that helps to enact restorative justice. Griffin notes: "She takes from the Butler's wealth, made by slavery and then by stealing the land of freedmen, to *care* for the orphaned children of one of their victims. She feeds them, provides them shelter and love, hides them from harm, and sends them on their way. . . . She enacts an ethic of care that helps ensure their well-being and their ability to become self-sufficient. . . . She is a healer, but she is also a justice seeker. She helps to bring a long-term sense of justice into being. It is not justice for those who were the immediate recipients of harm, nor does it punish those who have caused the harm. But it helps to create a more just society for the progeny of both."[14] Milkman, however, is not convinced by Circe's understanding of justice. He joins the book's other male characters in dismissing and belittling the sense of justice held by the women, though masculine vengeance will prove disastrous for him as well. The contrast between the men's and the women's sense of justice is stark and Morrison's endorsement of the women's position is evident.

But Morrison's critique of masculinist understandings of justice went further than that on offer in *Song of Solomon*. She would, quite incredibly, present justice as vengeance as being founded on the male desire to dominate women in the first play she wrote, *Dreaming Emmett*. Notably, in the play she also dismisses, via pointed silence, nonviolence as an adequate response to the never-ending litany of Emmett Tills. The New York State Writers Institute at SUNY-Albany commissioned Morrison to complete *Dreaming Emmett* in commemoration of the first anniversary of the Martin Luther King Jr. holiday. The play itself has quite a story. It was only staged January 4 through February 2, 1986, at Capital Repertory Theater's Market Theater in Albany, New York, before Morrison shelved it, painstakingly collecting all existing copies of the script.[15] In the play, Morrison resurrects Till as a vengeful ghost. It is worth remarking that Till's was not the only angry ghost with whom Morrison was spending time then, as she took a break from writing her celebrated novel *Beloved* to complete the play.

Morrison's decision to write a play commemorating the celebration of the life of a man who was faithful to the principles of nonviolent resistance by bringing back to life an unwillingly martyred child bent on revenge is quite telling. It suggests that King's dream has done little to interrupt Till's nightmare, nor the repeated nightmares of the litany of Tills.[16] Indeed, the play reveals that these Tills are never far from Morrison's mind. And yet vengeance for them was not hers. In the play, she resurrects Till but does not endorse his quite understandable plan to exact revenge.

In *Dreaming Emmett*, Till has gotten no rest since his murder. He has been dreaming his death for the last forty years and has resolved to end his suffering by making a movie about his life, to exact revenge, to be given a proper burial, and, thereby, to get his death right. In Morrison's version of events, Till indeed propositioned Carole Bryant (named Princess in the play), and, even though he was only a boy of fourteen, it is meaningful that he has done so. He brings the white woman who started it all, her husband, and his brother as well as his Till's two Mississippi friends, George and Eustace, and his mother into his restless dream world so that they might star in his movie, *How I Spent My Summer Vacation.*

The November 20, 1985, draft of the play begins with arresting author's notes that set the scene and provide character descriptions:

> Author's Notes:
> In every way possible, this play should have the quality of a dream. Not dreamy, or dream-like (meaning fuzzy or floating) but the way sustained dreaming really is: sometimes the pace seems to slow down to agonizing lengths; sometimes the movement or speech is oddly rapid. . . .[17]
>
> The action takes place NOW in an abandoned cotton mill—that is to say, what an abandoned cotton mill looks like to someone who has never seen one. It should be constructed in such a way as to suggest rusted violence: pulleys, blades, platforms, loading bays, motors, teeth, ropes etc. But the ropes can be used as a child's swing or a clothesline; the bays can be slept on; the blades can be shelter. Cotton that bursts from one or two huge bales is an obviously theatrical touch of the dreaming set-maker. Exaggeration is the pose to be struck.
>
> CHARACTERS
>
> EMMETT—A mannish and manly fourteen year old black boy. He is at the age when braggadocio and vulnerability combine but don't mix. He is moody, a chameleon—capable of infectious humor and frightening violence. Small-framed, he has a good singing voice and can move from cold menace to warm charm in a flash. He is able to make us cry and to drive us to fury. His accent Northern; when he affects a Southern one it sounds false.[18]

The plot of his movie is simple and easy to understand, with one particularly confusing exception: Till's plan is to lynch the white men and the white woman responsible for his murder, to hold his friends accountable for their role in his death, to have everyone—both the living and the dead—make him a kite to play with, and then to have them all give him a proper burial.[19] Straightforward enough, with the exception of the bizarre kite detour. But the plot to do his death "right" is interrupted by a Black woman who calls bullshit on the entire thing:

EMMETT

I got this whole thing worked out. I thought about it—a lot. I had a—lifetime, understand, to think about it. See, I narrowed everything down to six things. [Coughs as for a speech] Six. Number one: lynch Major. Number two: lynch Buck. Number three: lynch Princess. Not a big lynching, mind you, because ain't nobody but me left to do it. Now if I had a crowd, or even a friend—which brings me to number four: Ask George where he was on the night of August 24, 1955, or any god dam night after they tied that cotton gin fan on my neck and dumped me in the river. I mean, like, how come those crackers still alive? . . .[20]

EMMETT

[Annoyed] Number five! Make me a kite. You, [to BUCK] and you. [To MAJOR] and you. [To PRINCESS.] . . .[21]

At the end of Act I, Emmett throws a bloated corpse to the ground and, revealing his final wish to the other members of the cast:

He pulls out a beautiful light blue suit, snap brim hat, and white wing-tipped shoes. Then he drags out what appears to be a bloated and decaying corpse and throws it down among them.]

EMMETT

Number Six! Proper burial in a proper suit by the proper murderers! Move!!

[They rush for their crumpled faces, scrambling, putting on wrong masks, confused and trying to hide. When they finally begin the dressing and shrouding, while EMMETT sings and dances to a powerful, sexy, R & B song, he is interrupted by a figure from the audience. A Black girl climbs upon the stage, screaming;]

GIRL

Stop it! Stop it! [She kicks the corpse out of their hands and continues to kick it out of sight.
I don't want to hear any more.

EMMETT

Get out of here! You can't come in here. I'm making a movie here.

GIRL

I don't like your movie.

EMMETT

I'm doing this, girl. You aint in my dream.

GIRL

Maybe *that's* the trouble with it. I'm not in it!

DARKNESS.[22]

This is a powerful moment at which to end the act. The audience is not only unsettled by Till's somewhat unsympathetic and violent behavior but also disoriented by an utterly surprising feminine intervention regarding what "the trouble with it" is.

The Black girl's disruptions continue through Act II. Her name is revealed to be Tamara Ashanti. It is suggested that this is a name that she has given herself, which, given Morrison's own project, is meaningful. Morrison's notes describe her as a "black girl in her early twenties. Glib, managerial, independent, sassy, but very loving—when she initiates it." Ashanti is critical of everyone with the exception of Emmett's Ma. She is critical as well of the sexual violence of which white men are capable, of the sexual harassment she experiences on stage at the hands of Till's murderers that goes unremarked by everyone else, of the white woman's call for white men to defend her when Princess swears that she is capable of defending herself, of the white woman's illicit desire for Black men, of Emmett's decision to call her out of her name, a "bitch," and of Emmett's lack of concern for the well-being of his mother. Emmett's Ma is the only person in the cast with whom Tamara claims a relationship ("She is my sister."):

TAMARA

. . . (to EMMETT) AND I DON'T LIKE THE WAY YOU TREAT YOUR MAMA. YOU HAVEN'T SAID TWO KIND WORDS TO HER. AND WHAT ABOUT HER BACK! YOU DREAMED THIS MESS UP WHY COULDN'T YOU DREAM UP A PILLOW SO YOUR MAMA COULD SIT COMFORTABLE-LIKE? SUPPOSED SHE'S THIRSTY AND WANTS A NICE CUP A COFFEE. WOULD YOU LIKE A NICE CUP OF COFFEE, MA'AM?

MA

LOVE ONE

TAMARA

SEE WHAT I MEAN? ASIDE FROM ME AND HER, THERE'S NOT A PERSON UP HERE WHO CARES WHETHER YOU LIVE, DIE, EAT, GO HUNGRY—

GEORGE

HEY, WAIT NOW.[23]

Tamara argues that, instead of being so blindly bent on revenge, Till should be caring for his mother, reciprocating the care and concern she and other women have shown him. She indicts the revenge plot and the supposed sexual harassment Emmett committed as childish and ultimately, quite incredibly, about her:

TAMARA

THEY KILLED HIM BECAUSE THEY COULD. AND BECAUSE SHE HAD TO BE WATCHED OVER.

PRINCESS

STAY OUT OF THIS.

TAMARA

I CAN'T DO THAT, SWEETHEART, CAUSE IT' ABOUT ME.

PRINCESS

YOU WASN'T EVEN THERE.

TAMARA

NO, BUT MY ABSENCE WAS. MY ABSENCE WAS DEFINITELY THERE.

EUSTACE (to GEORGE)

WHAT THE DEVIL IS SHE TALKING ABOUT NOW?

TAMARA

WHEN HE WANTED TO PROVE HE WAS A MAN, HE NEEDED MY ABSENCE. WHICH IS ANOTHER WAY OF SAYING HE NEEDED ME, BECAUSE, ONE THING IS SURE, IF HE HAD MADE A PASS AT ME, HE'D BE ALIVE, AND THAT'S HARD. WHAT HE WANTED WAS EASY.

GEORGE

ONE OF THESE DAYS SOMEBODY GOING TO BLOW YOUR HEAD OFF

TAMARA

THAT'S EASY TOO
[EMMETT shoots].[24]

Ashanti's bold claims reveal how incisively Morrison understood, even at this early moment in her written explorations of justice, what was missing, unbalanced, and not working about masculinist retributive justice, how easily a desire for violent vengeance could be turned on Black women. This silences George, as well it should. Later in the play, Tamara pointedly ridicules Till's understanding of power:

TAMARA

YOU DON'T WANT MUCH DO YOU. JUST "MAKE ME A KITE" AND THEN YOU KILL EVERYBODY. THAT YOUR IDEA OF POWER? MALE POWER? YOU COULDN'T EVEN LEAVE HOME. COULDN'T EVEN SPEND A SUMMER IN THE COUNTRY WITHOUT TRYING TO IMPRESS SOMEBODY ABOUT YOUR POWER. OVER A WOMAN. AND WHAT KIND OF WOMAN? YOU DIDN'T HAVE A PICTURE OF A LITTLE COLORED GIRL IN YOUR WALLET. NOBODY DARED YOU TO MAKE A PASS AT A LITTLE COLORED GIRL DID THEY? BECAUSE YOU'D LOSE THE DARE. BECAUSE SHE WOULD BREAK YOUR ARM IF YOU DID AND WOULDN'T HAVE TO CALL NOBODY TO HELP HER DO IT. OR BECAUSE SHE'D TAKE YOU UP ON IT AND SMILE AT YOU, BE SWEET AND LOVE YOU HARD AND LOND AND MAYBE YOU'D LOVE HER BACK WHICH WOULDN'T DO

BECAUSE WHERE WOULD THE POWER BE THEN? IF YOU LOVE HER BACK THAT'D BE WEAK. ONLY TWO POSSIBILITIES WITH A LITTLE BLACK GIRL. SHE BREAKS YOUR ARM—YOU LOSE. SHE LOVES YOU—YOU LOSE.

EMMETT

YOU WALKED UP HERE. YOU WERE NOT INVITED.

TAMARA

I KNOW, BUT I AM HERE.

EMMETT

I NEVER DREAMED YOU.

TAMARA

WHY NOT? [EMMETT turns away] WHY NOT?

EMMETT

I DON'T KNOW.

TAMARA

YES YOU DO.

EMMETT

YES. I DO. YOUR MOUTH.

TAMARA

YOU MEAN IF I WAS QUIET, I COULD BE IN YOUR DREAM? IF I JUST WOULDN'T SAY ANYTHING?[25]

Morrison's decision to make the King/Till story a story about Black women, her bold indictment of justice as vengeance as masculinist hubris, her argument that a violent retributive cycle erased Black women and their needs regarding justice before it ultimately harmed them too are all breathtaking. And there is so much meaningful silence. Morrison's deafening silence regarding King. The cast's silence at the intimate injustice the Black female interloper endures onstage. Till's wish to silence Ashanti. But Morrison is not silent about her belief that vengeance is not the way. And, on the one hand, Morrison places too much culpability on Till's fourteen-year-old shoulders.

He is bearing weight that is more appropriately shouldered by grown men, for whom he is made to stand in. But on the other hand, his shoulders are indeed broad enough to bear the responsibility Tamara gives him: he can better care for his mother and sisters. Perhaps therein lies the justice he seeks.

The play is compelling, but it is also unfinished. Though Morrison never returned to the play itself, she did return to her meditations on justice. *Dreaming Emmett*, then, is far from her final word on the subject. That would come twenty-seven years later with her 2012 novel *Home*, Griffin says, that in it "Morrison turns most fully to an exploration between an ethic of care and its potential for achieving a kind of *restorative*, or better still, *transformative* justice."[26] *Home* details Vietnam veteran Frank's journey to rescue his sister Cee, who has been sterilized by a eugenicist doctor in Atlanta, and take her "home" to Lotus, Georgia. Ironically, Lotus has never truly felt like home for the siblings. Necessarily neglected by exhausted, overworked parents who were also traumatized by the racial pogrom that drove them to live with their father's father and his cruel wife, the children cast about but cling to each other. Yet when they arrive back in the town after Cee's sterilization, Frank gives her to a community of women. The women shoo Frank away and begin a long process of healing (not curing) Cee's body, mind, and spirit. In the end, the change in Cee is apparent: "Cee was different. Two months surrounded by country women who loved mean had changed her." And in witnessing her transformation into a woman who has incorporated her scars into the new person she has become, Frank is also transformed. Morrison, Griffin says, reminds us that "there is nothing that can make up for the crimes against her victimized characters":

> At best, they can learn to live, how to survive, how to be healed, not cured, and how to go on and "do some good in the world." In her model, the offender is not reconciled with the victim, but the victim is cared for and embraced by the community. And witnessing this, the victims' brother, who in another instance has been an offender, must come to terms with the trauma he has caused and, rather than continue to be paralyzed by it, he must do something ethically productive, indeed good. As a result, at novel's end a victim and a victimizer are transformed.[27]

Again, Griffin argues that Morrison endorsed a notion of collectively enacted transformative justice that allowed the survivor (and some, though not all, perpetrators) to be healed (not cured), permitting the survivor the space to attain self-knowledge and, ultimately, multiply goodness. The transformation comes about via the communal—indeed, the democratic—provision of care. Transformative justice advocates have spoken about the importance of *prefiguration* in the process, that is, the importance of living as if the world were as you wanted it, and Griffin says that the novel, in Morrison's hands, "allows us to imagine what a society governed by an ethic of care, a society devoted to restoring and repairing those who have been harmed, giving them the space for transformation might look like."[28] I will return to the place of storytelling, of prefiguration, and Morrison's postfiguration—her word-work as world work, as justice work—below.

It is no accident that Morrison named the novel containing her most considered reflection on justice after her last, most precious, significant space, home. But home does not simply exist. It must be created, collectively, through everyday caring practices, including care for the body, caring dialogue, and the creation of caring, and in that way just, language. And we have no choice but to build these homes on, within, and among the "ruin." Griffin says, "Home is a space we can build together, a safe space, with out of doors, but not outdoors, a safe space with open doors and windows, that lets sun in and fresh air but is not overwhelmed by it, as is the ruin." Griffin says, "Her challenge, our challenge, is how to quote 'convert a racist house into a race-specific, yet non-racist home.' Such a structure acknowledges, recognizes, and even values the multiplicity of our difference without deeming it something negative or setting up a hierarchy. Home is imagined as a space where 'race-specific, race-free language is both possible and meaningful.' It is a space where we work to create together and for the writer, and I think for the reader as well, that work begins with language." Griffin goes on to emphasize the importance of language creation for Morrison, "In her Nobel speech, Morrison insists that word work is sublime, she says, 'because it is generative; it makes meaning that secures our difference, our human difference—the way in which we are like no other life. We die. That may be the meaning of life, but we do language. That may be the measure of our lives.'"[29]

Home, then, is a space of language creation for Morrison; the justice we may find there requires it. The work of using language as an act of care requires the creation of language within these communities. When we create language together in the right, caring way, we collectively help to bring about transformative justice, we help to create home in her ideal sense. "In Morrison's novels, one approaches the space in those instances where good, simple, and unadorned, triumphs. Where language and the people who *create* and engage in it do so, not as an act of violence, but instead as an act of caring for one another, simply because it is the right thing to do."[30]

Language creation is no passing interest for Morrison. Lawrie Balfour speaks of the author's twinned projects, first, to remake the language of her inheritance, that is, to remake English, and, second, "to transfigure the complexity and health of Afro-American culture into a language worthy of that culture," thus to remake English into a language capable of capturing the Black experience.[31] Morrison, then, is herself engaged in "word-work" as "world-work," to correct conditions named by Kristie Dotson and Miranda Fricker, wherein language itself is always better equipped to name and describe the experiences of the powerful and less-equipped to communicate the experiences of the marginalized.[32] More poetically, Balfour quotes Sharon Holland as saying that Morrison was about the work of "transforming inarticulate places into conversational territories."[33] It is not surprising, then, that language creation figures into her account of justice. Her novels reflect and refract her wider project, as she also models ideal spaces of collective language creation within them. These feminine communities of justice will be healing—healing bodies, which is often necessary in the wake of intimate injustice, and just as necessarily, healing the self and one another, healing the spirit, through talking to and talking through, through dialogue, and through collectively creating more just words and through more just words, more just worlds.

Morrison demonstrates the transformation of the ruin into home most clearly in her novel *Paradise*. On her way to her most developed, care-centered account of justice, she came to disavow even the laissez-faire version of retributive spatial justice of the kind enacted by Circe and instead endorsed the express transformation of ruined white space via the transformation of the people living and loving on, around, and among said ruins. *Paradise*'s ruin consists of a former embezzler's mansion turned convent and Native boarding school, which still showcased genocidal settler colonial hubris and avarice: "Then there is the grandeur. Only the two who are wearing ties seem to belong here and one by one each is reminded that before it was a Convent, this house was an embezzler's folly. A mansion where bisque and rose-tone marble floors segue into teak ones. Isinglass holds yesterday's light and patterns walls that were stripped and whitewashed fifty years ago. The ornate bathroom fixtures, which sickened the nuns, were replaced with good plain spigots, but the princely tubs and sinks, which could not be inexpensively removed, remain coolly corrupt. The embezzler's joy that could be demolished was, particularly in the dining room, which the nuns converted to a schoolroom, where stilled Arapaho girls once sat and learned to forget."[34] The Convent's contemporary inhabitants pay it all no mind as they go about their transformative practices of caring—and here, importantly, not for children and descendants, but for themselves and for one another—that make the place *home.*

The novels *Paradise* and *Home* both take intimate justice as their central object. The enactment of said justice is informal, but collective. The novels contain justice-enacting communities of care, small, often invisible, spontaneous feminine publics that are, in fact, as Balfour tells us, Morrisonian democracies. When these feminine publics are viewed as such, the ruin can only be understood as what remains of the unsustainable, ludicrously ornate—filled to the brim with anachronistic European pretensions in an alien land—white settler colonial democracy, and this is indeed the foundation on which we have no choice but to build Morrisonian democracies, to build our healing transformative homes. These publics have clear leaders, initiators really, like Ethel Fordham in *Home*, but they also involve the progressive transfer of skill to initiates through practice, dialogue, and reflective time and space.

Care for others within these Morrisonian democracies—care for those whom like Cee who has "nothing to do but pay them attention," and truly she had nothing to pay those who cared for her but attention—begins with ministration to broken bodies, but it also includes tending one another with words and even tending our broken and inadequate words. It involves language, dialogue, talking with, giving "a talking to"—indeed, in *Home* the women first perform the work necessary to heal Cee's body and then Ethel gives her a "talking to"—and then talking to and for one's self, at home (25):

> First the bleeding: "Spread your knees. This is going to hurt. Hush up. Hush, I said."
>
> Next the infection: "Drink this. You puke, you got to drink more, so don't."
>
> Then the repair: "Stop that. The burning is the healing. Be quiet." . . . As she healed, the women changed tactics and stopped their berating. Now they brought their embroidery and crocheting, and finally they used Ethel Fordham's house as their quilting center. . . . Surrounded by their comings and goings, listening to their talk, their songs, following their instructions,

> Cee had nothing to do but pay them the attention she had never given them before. . . . The final stage of Cee's healing had been, for her, the worst. She was to be sun-smacked, which meant spending at least one hour a day with her legs spread open to the blazing sun. Each woman agreed that that embrace would rid her of any remaining womb sickness. . . . What followed the final sun-smacking hour, when she was allowed to sit modestly in a rocking chair, was the demanding love of Ethel Fordham, which soothed and strengthened her the most. (121–125)

Mrs. Fordham's demanding love, Griffin says, was a call to self-determination, self-actualization, and to further the multiplication of goodness, as enacted by the women who had taken two months of their lives to heal her: "You young and a woman and there's serious limitation in both, but you a person too. Don't let Lenore or some trifling boyfriend and certainly no devil doctor decide who you are. That's slavery. Somewhere inside you is that free person I'm talking about. Locate her and let her do some good in the world" (126).

Cee's sterilization, like that of her real-world counterpart Elaine Riddick, is a physical assault facilitated by medical racism. It is an act of acute intimate injustice, and so again, what does justice for Riddick require? After too long a fight, Riddick received ten thousand dollars in compensation for her sterilization. That is not justice. That is certainly not enough money, and it should also make us reflect on the fact that money will never be enough. Perhaps she is healed, but she can never be cured. But as it happens, Riddick is also a tireless advocate. Among other things, she is executive director of the Rebecca Project.[35] She sees her work as a way to keep what happened to her from happening to other poor Black women and girls and other women and girls of color in this country and throughout the world. She works to ensure that criminalized women, among whom Black women are always overrepresented, are given the space to create and nurture families. She, then, is on a Morrisonian justice journey as she is out doing "goodness" in the world via her work to lessen intimate injustice. It is meaningful to me—and it should be meaningful to us all—that the justice Riddick has chosen to enact is a form of Morrisonian justice, though it should come as no surprise that Morrison, and Griffin as one of her best readers, is on to something. *Home* answers the question of what justice might look like for Riddick. And miraculously, after everyone failed her, Riddick is somehow doing her part. It is we who have yet to complete our tasks. Justice for Riddick requires that we ensure that she—and all other little Black girls, all Pecolas, everyone—is never again left outdoors, that we rebuild the ruin, that we make home.

The Space, Ethics, and Transcendent Demos of Morrisonian Democracy

In addition to her understanding of justice Morrison also presents a significant challenge to Du Bois regarding Black death and democracy. Morrison's conception of democracy has been called a "fugitive's democracy,"[36] but I argue that we should attend to Morrison's endorsement of a "truant democracy," especially as it is enacted by her favorite practitioners, wayward women. Morrison did not, as Du Bois did, seek to build a stable yet insufficiently inclusive demos, or "we." Instead, she focused on ephemeral collectives. Her democracy is concerned with addressing and repairing the intimate injustices at the heart of femicides *and* the epistemic injustices that further shield these often private acts from our view, our understanding. Like Ida B. Wells, Morrison chose radical humanization over martyrdom. Indeed, she chose to celebrate the flesh, the profane, while encouraging us to sustain and deepen our political connections to our morally transgressive feminine dead. I juxtapose Du Bois with Morrison because Morrisonian truant democracy is a feminist corrective to Du Bois's abolition democracy. It is no coincidence that her model citizens are the women he held in barely concealed contempt.

This account builds on and should be read alongside important feminist critiques of Du Bois. Most pointedly, it is an extension of Saidiya Hartman and Alys Weinbaum's account of the failures of Du Bois's radical democratic vision and of Weinbaum's analysis of how Black feminists have confronted these failures head on, providing their own feminist "propaganda of history." It is equally indebted to Deborah Gray White and Stephanie Camp's notions of truancy in their pioneering analyses of women's experiences within enslavement, in particular Camp's arguments regarding how truants "plaited" a rival geography into the terrain of captivity, creating momentary spaces for independent activity and meaning creation within a system of brutality. White's analysis reveals that women who sought to balance familial ties with the need for respite from the brutality of enslavement most often chose truancy over flight. Without this powerful insight, I would not have understood as well what Morrison proposed. Finally, this account of Morrisonian truant democracy echoes Jasmine Syedullah's work on enslaved women and their descendants' congregational abolitionist praxis, which emphasizes not only stealing away for brief moments and gathering together but also the significance of testimony, storytelling, and the transformational impact of these practices on participants. "Congregation gathers around story, song, the breath," Syedullah writes, making space "in the face of a totalizing force of antiblackness." The task, then, "is to trace black feminist protocols of abolitionist aspirations that breathed new life into the future of black life through congregations of counterdiscourses, through the physical exchange of stories, of accounts and witness that slipped the seeds of slavery's destruction past sediments of respectability and spread dissent like wildfire through captive encampments."[37] Burn, baby, burn.

While Du Bois and Morrison both engaged in reconstructive history and in democratic storytelling, Morrison's stories, the storytelling she models within them, and the communities her characters build around these stories provide a better model and method for confronting unspectacular Black female death. A survey of the two thinkers' work reveals significant differences in emphasis that culminate in distinctive, indeed divergent, democratic visions. While Du Bois was concerned with public things, Morrison occupied herself with secrecy, private deaths, and intimate injustices. Her work reflects on incest (*The Bluest Eye*, 1970), infanticide following sexual assault (*Beloved*, 1987), women killed because they have had sex (*Jazz*, 1992), women killed because they are women (*Paradise*, 1998), forced sterilization (*Home*, 2012), and more. Du Bois troubled himself a great deal with respectability politics. He took pains to call attention to the race's shining lights. Morrison, by contrast, chose to highlight and expound upon the inner lives of the disreputable, the disrespected, the forgotten. Reflecting on Morrisonian democracy, Balfour notes that Morrison "pays attention to the private or disregarded spaces of African American experience . . . often places where communities of women gather, away from the imperatives of the patriarchal order."[38]

A bit of a somatophobe, Du Bois praised the ideal, the form, the self-sacrificial Christian virtues of the Sermon on the Mount. Morrison, by contrast, reserved her praise for the profane—literally, the flesh. The good news is delivered not on mounts but in clearings. Take the sermon of Baby Suggs, holy, in *Beloved*: "Here," she said, "in this here place, we flesh; flesh that weeps, laughs; flesh that dances on bare feet in grass. Love it. Love it hard. Yonder they do not love your flesh. They despise it. . . . You got to love it. This is flesh I'm talking about here. Flesh that needs to be loved. Feet that need to rest and to dance; backs that need support; shoulders that need arms, strong arms I'm telling you. And O my people, out yonder, hear me, they do not love your neck unnoosed and straight. So love your neck; put a hand on it, grace it, stroke it and hold it up" (103–104). We know that this was a deeply held belief for Morrison, as Baby Suggs would impart this somatophilic philosophy to her granddaughter Denver, who would repeat it for us: "Slaves not supposed to have pleasurable feelings on their own; their bodies not supposed to be like that, but they have to have as many children as they can to please whoever owned them. Still, they were not supposed to have pleasure deep down. She said for me not to listen to all that. That I should always listen to my body and love it."[39] This is not a minor ethical distinction in a context in which the female body, sexuality—the flesh—is very much implicated in Black women's unspectacular deaths. Relatedly, the pillars of Morrison's democracy exceed schools, land, and political rights. They require somatophilic clearings that affirm and repair bodily autonomy, love, and care.

Morrison also presents a vision of democratic leadership that is distinct from that of Du Bois. Her leader is not the citizen-soldier of *Black Reconstruction*—though she too has survived tremendous conflict—nor is it a member of his Talented Tenth. She is most often socially marginalized, albeit a well-respected font of folk knowledge. She is a woman who has experienced intimate injustice and survived it and who remains at great risk of further intimate injustice. As a survivor—or, as in the case of *Paradise*'s Connie, one who may not have survived—her leadership is driven by a calling to help a woman in need. The leader initiates collective action, healing, and dialogue. She gives she who is in need a "talking to." Following her lead, participants register not simply their consent but their ongoing agreement through their teamwork. Among the important effects created by her actions is the space for speech, reflection, and judgment for she who needs help. The process of speaking, of collective storytelling, helps the survivor (or she who has not survived) to recover and develop a sense of self, as with Cee in *Home* and Pallas in *Paradise*. In the process, we observe the progressive development of her capacities.

Both thinkers saw a link between expansive democratic participation and racial justice. "If America is to become a government built on the broadest justice to every citizen," Du Bois held, "then every citizen must be enfranchised." He argued that participation in democratic activities, and voting central among them, brought about self and group knowledge unrealizable under other forms of government. The demos, he believed, should concern itself with the regulation of economic activity; he argued for "the careful, steady increase of public ownership of industry" so that economic activity would not threaten other significant concerns, such as learning and the creation of beauty.[40]

Morrison, like Du Bois, theorized a relationship between an expansive demos and racial justice, as well as the democratic activities essential to her vision of justice. Yet she theorized a distinctive sphere of democracy's enactment *and* concern, and with it a distinct group of democrats. Du Bois and Morrison held opposing views of the Black dead and the place of resurrection within the multiracial democracy. Again and again, Du Bois killed his Black Jesus, a stand-in for lynched—and thus spectacularly dead—Black men. But he rarely resurrected him. He explicitly de-emphasized the supernatural aspects of Christ's sacrifice to convey that no one was coming to save Blacks, that they would have to save themselves. Du Bois thus left it to the living to do the work of resurrection. He came to see the work of resurrection as building a multiracial democracy—and in the US context this required abolition democracy, where all had the educational, economic, and political resources they needed to live as equal members.

The dead of Morrison's concern, by contrast, are the unspectacularly dead, those who die in the wake of intimate injustice—sexual assault, infanticide, those who are murdered because they are women. They are killed in the ruined houses of white settler colonial democracy that we, *with their help*, must make into home. Again, Griffin argues that ruined houses and homes are significant spaces within Morrison's understanding of justice, and they are therefore important in Morrisonian democracy. They are the spaces of small-scale democratic practices aimed at repair in the wake of intimate injustice. *Home* provides the space for inchoate self-knowledge to come to full flower, the space for healing when there can be no cure, wherein collective storytelling, and the collective provision of healing care, through their very enactment, helps build within the healed the capacity to go out and "do some good in the world." And, importantly, Morrison reminds us via Baby Suggs, holy, that "not a house in the country ain't packed to the rafter with some dead Negro's grief."[41]

Here, then, we see the full temporal and transcendent dimensions of Morrisonian democracy. It is not simply, then, that Morrison's collectively enacted, transformative justice aims to make the world a better place for progeny and future generations, as Griffin correctly notes, and as we see in *Song of Solomon*, when the domestic and midwife Circe allows her thieving employers' plantation to fall into ruin by withholding the care she had been compelled to give while redirecting that care to the progeny of their victims' children, Macon and Pilate Dead. It is also the case that collectively enacted, just care makes the world a better place for our dead. It explicitly, and with their input, repairs and enables our relationships with our dead. This is a necessary form of repair, for the dead never have the luxury of a martyr's end in Morrison, and they therefore cannot and do not leave it to the living to do the democratic work that there is always left to be done. Morrison holds that "people who die bad don't stay in the ground"; remarkably, they stay on and labor alongside the living to create a better, more care-filled world. If Morrison's democracy, like Sethe's 124 in *Beloved*, is "a house peopled by the living activity of the dead" (221, 35), it is so because the ruined racist house of white democracy can only be turned into the transformative, care-filled, non-racist home wherein Morrisonian justice can be found via the inclusion of the voices and work of the dead. Morrison is thereby able to surpass even the impressively expansive boundaries of Du Bois's demos.

Morrison reveled in the supernatural. The dead are her characters' companions, and they themselves have much work to do. Morrison resurrected the dead, and her characters—the women and girls especially—were rarely troubled by it. They commune with and enact responsibilities to the dead. To take but one example, in *Song of Solomon*, the men see death as an end in itself regarding justice, as is true for the members of the vengeful secret society of the Seven Days. Morrison's character Pilate, by contrast, tends to a murdered man's bones in the name of justice, her "inheritance," and speaks solemnly of her responsibilities to the man her brother has killed to protect her.[42] She continues her relationship with her dead father, seeing and speaking to him regularly, heeding the sage advice he gives from his too-shallow grave without question. Her sister-in-law Ruth tends to her father as well, both immediately and long after his death. Yet Morrison presents her fullest account of the role of the dead in democracy in her novel *Paradise*, to which I turn below.

Morrisonian democracy is concerned primarily not with formal rights, not with the franchise, nor with the economy, but with repairing intimate injustice. There is indeed little voting, though much deliberation. It is, in fact, a space of language creation, for as Morrison, who loved and based a 1993 lecture series on *The Words to Say It*, would tell her Nobel Prize audience that the fact that "we do language" may well "be the measure of our lives." It addresses intimate injustices via small-scale, care-filled, informal practices among ephemeral collectives of wayward, wild, and often altogether invisible women, both living and dead, who come together and disperse. It is enacted, then, by the truant among the fugitive. It rests not so much upon a foundation of land, voting rights, and schools but upon homes (often ruined white homes, only truantly held), folk healing knowledge, and a willingness to listen to the concerns of the dead. It is also founded on a gloriously profane ethic, the call not only to love one's neighbor—for surely she is suffering too—but also to love one's flesh, no matter how much it is despised. Its most devoted practitioners are those of illest repute. Morrison calls all who have experienced intimate injustice and the socially marginalized who are at risk of acute intimate injustice into collective action, into storytelling, language creation, deliberation, reflection, and individual and collective judgment, as well as into the collective work of healing bodies and spirits. This process builds their individual and collective agency.

The contrasts between the two thinkers—public/intimate, formal/ informal, soldier/folk healer, reputable/wayward, spirit/flesh, living/dead—are not coincidental. Hartman and Weinbaum have drawn attention to Du Bois's failures of analysis regarding Black women in *Black Reconstruction*'s "general strike," and therefore in his democratic vision, as well as to the correctives Black feminists like Morrison offered. Hartman writes, "The material relations of sexuality and reproduction defined black women's historical experience as laborers and shaped the character of their resistance to slavery, yet this labor falls outside the heroic account of the black worker and the general strike." This, she says, has dire consequences for what Du Bois imagined for women within his abolition democracy: "Marriage and protection rather than sexual freedom and reproductive justice were the only ways conceived to redress her wrongs and remedy the 'wound dealt to [her] reputation as a human being.' The sexual violence and reproduction characteristic of enslaved women's experience fails to produce a radical politics of liberation or a philosophy of freedom."[43]

But where Du Bois failed, Weinbaum argues that Angela Davis, Darlene Clark Hine, and Toni Morrison, among others, took up his unfinished work and provided "a counternarrative" that spoke to "the continued relevance of enslaved women's protest against their reproductive and sexual exploitation." These efforts required considerable methodological innovation, for they were forced to confront an intolerably racist and sexist archive in order to prevail over received notions of evidence. Davis wrote from a jail cell with limited access to documentation, yet she asserted the fact of Black women's resistance, their insurgency, by drawing attention to slaveholders' gendered counterinsurgency practices. Her audience felt what she claimed so deeply that it is now accepted as fact. Morrison, too, helped to completely change our understanding of enslavement, employing "the creative latitude offered by fiction to enter into the battle over historical 'truth' while at the same time sidestepping some of the thorny questions historians have raised about archive and interpretation." Her *Beloved* is not simply a literary masterpiece, it is a potent rejoinder to the analytical failures of *Black Reconstruction.* Weinbaum reads *Beloved* as "an exploration of women's participation in the general strike, against sexual and reproductive bondage and as a meditation on women's withdrawal of sexual and reproductive labor and products from circulation."[44] My exploration of Morrisonian democracy, echoing Syedullah's account of truant Black feminist congregation, extends this line of inquiry by pointing out that in the end, Sethe could not and did not do her work alone. Aware of the femme-sized gap in abolition democracy, Morrison asserted a politics to confront the remainder of slavery's afterlives. And, true to *Beloved*'s major theme, it was a politics in which the dead could take part.

Democracy and the Dead

Juliet Hooker writes of the capacities Black people have been forced to cultivate—including the capacity for sacrifice—in our racially inegalitarian polity. Part of that inequity includes pervasive violence and premature death, living in what Christina Sharpe has called "the wake." I would add to Hooker's list the capacity to be in political community with the dead. Rebecca Louise Carter examines the religious work among mothers grieving children at Liberty Street Baptist Church in New Orleans, work that "suggests a kind of *restorative* kinship, one that asserts the value of those who have been lost by restoring their position within the family and community in this world and the next." Carter quotes Ronald K. Barrett, a psychologist whose research on Black mourning practices has demonstrated that in "the traditional black cultural experience, you are born, you die and then you continue to exist in other realms." This is contrasted to the European/Western worldview that sees death as the end of existence. Carter argues that restorative kinship practices involve a "renegotiation of subjectivity in the space of death" wherein the deceased is "at once a product and agent of history, the site of experience, memory, storytelling and aesthetic judgment, an agent of knowing as much as of action, and the conflicted site for moral acts and gestures amid impossibly immoral societies and institutions."[45]

Many historical and contemporary collectives have enacted aspects of Morrison's vision of democracy, including the supernatural publics composed of both the living and the dead that pioneering Black femicide theorist Barbara Smith of the Comabahee River Collective called into being with her pamphlet "Six Black Women: Why Did They Die?" Smith told a compelling and mobilizing story of serial murder via her "counterdata" practices *and* attempted to care for this transcendent collective. Hers was only one instance of the ephemeral collectives that Terrion Williamson says often come together around the otherwise unremarked deaths of Black women. While not explicitly organized around care for the dead, Tarana Burke's early (and at the time largely unknown) word and world-building work around sexual violence in Selma, Alabama, is another important example.[46] Yet Clementine Barfield of the Detroit-based anti-youth violence organization Save Our Sons and Daughters is most instructive here.

Following his death by gun violence, Barfield practiced a Morrisonian democratic form of restorative kinship with her son Derick, and in her efforts we see how the dead can take part in these democracies. Examining a speech Barfield delivered at Penn State, Melynda Price writes: "Part of the work for Ms. Barfield is the constant retelling of her child's life and death. Through her words the listener can see the verdant future that Barfield saw *and could still see* for her son."[47] In Price's telling of Barfield's tireless resurrective labor, we witness the unending labor and critical imaginative work of remembrance. Barfield's constant dialogue with Derick was informed by her recollection of his life as she continued to piece together a vision of the future—*his* future—for the children of Detroit.

With Derick's ongoing input as well as the input of others, Barfield, community members and Save Our Sons and Daughters worked to transform an urban landscape ravaged by violence, drugs, and the War on Drugs. Derick indeed remains the site of experience, memory, storytelling, and aesthetic judgment. Through his mother's ongoing dialogue with him, he becomes "an agent of history" and certainly "the conflicted site for moral acts and gestures amid impossibly immoral societies and institutions." Such practices suggest a distinct epistemology, yet it may be helpful to see Morrisonian democrats as exercising something akin to Hannah Arendt's "enlarged mentality," where one trains one's imagination to "go visiting." "Critical thinking," as Hannah Arendt says, "goes on in isolation, but by the force of imagination it makes others present and thus moves in a space that is potentially public, open to all sides." All deliberation involves imagination and interpretation, and Price emphasizes that Barfield's efforts are critical, in that she takes what she knows of Derick, his hopes and dreams and the injustices he faced, into her conversations with him and with others about him.[48]

Black Femicide and Morrisonian Democracy

If *Home* represents Morrison's most developed thinking regarding justice, *Paradise* is her most considered reflection on Black death and democracy—indeed, on Black femicide and democracy. Balfour argues that responsibility is a major theme in Morrison's democratic thought, as "Morrison's essays and fiction advance an account of democratic life that dwells on the efforts of African Americans, individually and collectively, to take responsibility for themselves," and the book, at its core, concerns Black women's responsibilities to one another, the living and the dead.[49]

Paradise presents the static lives, vibrant, revelatory afterlives, and in-betweens of the people of a deathless Black Eden—Ruby, a town created and ruled by Black men, isolated and thus free from white violence, "Her sweet colored boys unshot, unlynched, ummolested, unimprisoned."[50] It opens on the deathless men's plot to kill the perhaps already dead female inhabitants of another kind of paradise, a convent seventeen miles away. Ruby is named for the sister of the town's founding brothers. She died the right kind of death, and that death is honored in the town's name even as all other death is held at bay. The perhaps-dead women of the convent all would have "died bad" and therefore, under Morrisonian rules, cannot stay in the ground. Sarah Appleton Aguiar argues:

> As Morrison includes in *Beloved* dead characters cohabiting with the living, the possibility that all or some of the women—Mavis, Gigi, Seneca, and

> Pallas—are dead before they reach the convent is a viable one. Each has suffered tragic and potentially fatal circumstances before her arrival. Pallas has been chased and raped; maybe she has drowned. Seneca has been "hired" by a sadistic woman to indulge her sexually violent fantasies; maybe she, too, has been murdered. Gigi participated in a riot that left at least one child dead. And maybe Mavis's husband suffocated her, or she has been murdered by the daughter who dreams apologies to her.[51]

In twinned spaces—one orderly, patriarchal, oligarchic, utopian, founded by once identical twin brothers, the other disorderly, wholly feminine, borderline anarchic but also sporadically radically democratic, volatile but full of wild beauty and cultivated care—the book considers Black community comfort with the "right" kinds of gender-based violence and the "right" kinds of Black female dead, as well as the deaths left unaccounted for, ungrieved, the dead to whom we are not adequately accountable—and it works to unsettle that comfort. The feminine democratic space is a crumbling convent, a ruin of what was once an ornate embezzler's mansion and then a Catholic school for Arapaho girls, where they "learned to forget."[52] The feminine democracy is expressly enacted on the ruin of white settler colonial democracy, complete with its perverse and agnotological Christian veneer. This is indeed the setting for both experiments, in which we have no choice but to build anew, but it is made unavoidably explicit in the women's case—it is enacted in the domestic space that Morrison seeks to rehabilitate. The men's political community is fugitive. They are descendants of families who settled an Oklahoma town after fleeing Louisiana in the 1890s. The women's democracy, by contrast, is truant, as the living women come to the convent for refuge but always return to the patriarchal community just down the road.

The book reflects on gender-based violence as well as individual and community response to violence against different "kinds" of women. Consider the resolve of Haven's founding men regarding the specter of violence against women they have "claimed": "They were proud that none of their women had ever worked in a whiteman's kitchen or nursed a white child. Although field labor was harder and carried no status, they believed the rape of women who worked in white kitchens was if not a certainty a distinct possibility—neither of which they could bear to contemplate. So, they exchanged that danger for the relative safety of brutal work."[53] Contrast this to the lesser founding brother Steward's reaction to Elder Morgan's story of violence against a woman "unclaimed":

> In 1919. Taking a walk around New York City before catching his train, he saw two men arguing with a woman. From her clothes, Elder said, he guessed she was a street walking woman, and registering contempt for her trade, he felt at first a connection with the shouting men. Suddenly one of the men smashed the woman in her face with his fist. She fell. . . . Elder hit the whiteman in the jaw and kept hitting until attacked by the second man. Nobody won. All were bruised. The woman was still lying on the pavement when a small crowd began yelling for the police. Frightened, Elder ran and wore his army overcoat all the way back to Oklahoma for fear an officer would see the condition of his uniform. . . . Steward liked that story, but it unnerved him to know it was based on the defense of and prayers for a whore. He did not sympathize with the whitemen, but he could see their point, could even feel the adrenaline, imagining the fist was his own.[54]

The convent of *Paradise*, on the other hand, is a haven for all women, including women the men of Ruby have "claimed":

> For more than twenty years Lone had watched them. Back and forth, back and forth: crying women, staring women, scowling, lip-biting women or women just plain lost . . . women dragged their sorrow up and down the road between Ruby and the Convent. They were the only pedestrians. Sweetie Fleetwood had walked it, Billie Delia too. And the girl called Seneca. Another called Mavis. Arnette, too, and more than once. And not just these days. They had walked this road from the very first. Soane Morgan, for instance, and once, when she was young, Connie as well. Many of the walkers Lone had seen; others she learned about.[55]

Men never walked the road in quiet desperation, Lone notes. They drove. And though they often headed in the same direction, they never sought the truant communion and salvation that women found there.

Magali Cornier Michael outlines the democratic practices among the convent's women. "The women who find their way to the Convent for stays of varying lengths . . . are included in the community and have a voice in how they will participate in it." At the convent, the women engage in "difficult dialogic coalition work" and "the process of joining together and shrieking their stories," while also listening to the stories of the other women. These practices are transformative, endowing each with new subjectivities and new agency that is "coproduced." By speaking and listening in turn and "through the process of negotiating strategic alliances across their differences to heal themselves from the consequences of the injustice they have been made to suffer, the convent women create a nurturing, dialogic space from which their own refashioned subjectivities emerge, subjectivities that, collectively, cannot only survive a racist and sexist culture but work to resist and redress its injustice."[56]

Pallas's story best illustrates the character of this Morrisonian democracy. Billie Cato, quite revealingly, rescues a vomiting, mute Pallas from the waiting room of the clinic where she worked and takes her to the Convent, saying, "This is a place where you can stay for a while. No questions. . . . Anyway you can collect yourself there, think things through, with nothing or nobody bothering you all the time. They'll take care of you or leave you alone—whichever way you want it."[57] Pallas would, indeed, get the help she needed:

> "Who hurt you, little one?" asked Connie.
>
> Seneca sat down on the floor. She had scant hope that Pallas would say much if anything at all. But Connie was magic. She just stretched out her hand and Pallas went to her, sat on her lap, talk-crying at first, then just crying, while Connie said, "Drink a little of this," and "What pretty earrings," and "Poor little one, poor, poor little one. They hurt my poor little one."
>
> It was wine-soaked and took an hour; it was backward and punctured and incomplete, but it came out—little one's story of who had hurt her.

After Connie helps her to find her voice, the other women take her to the kitchen, where they eat and celebrate her breakthrough.[58]

Paradise dramatizes the threat "unclaimed" women represent to patriarchal society, a threat Ruby's leaders resolve must end in mass femicide. But it also highlights how the "claimed" living women and the "unclaimed" dead need one another, as Aguiar points out: "The Convent women and the women of Ruby fulfill each other's needs. The Convent women seek the living, and the women seek what they need from the dead. And what each seeks, the other unknowingly possesses: Mavis, Gigi, Seneca and Pallas seek life (or its illusions), and Soane, Annette, Sweetie and Billie Delia seek death (or its possibilities). Although the Convent women rarely actively seek out the other women, they do administer to the life affirmations of these women. For the Convent shelters Ruby's women, providing food and care and a 'haven' for their anger and fears."[59]

What does it mean for dead women to seek life or its illusions? What are death's "possibilities" for living women? Morrison provides a clue regarding the latter when she reveals how much the living women lack in their patriarchal paradise and demonstrates how often the dead women attend to those deficiencies:

> From the beginning its people were free and protected. A sleepless woman could always rise from her bed, wrap a shawl around her shoulders and sit on the steps in the moonlight. And if she felt like it she could walk out the yard and on down the road. No lamp and no fear. A hiss-crackle from the side of the road would never scare her because whatever it was that made the sound, it wasn't something creeping up on her. Nothing for ninety miles around thought she was prey. She could stroll as slowly as she liked, thinking of food preparations, war, of family things, or lift her eyes to stars and think of nothing at all. Lampless and without fear she could make her way. And if a light shone from a house up a ways and the cry of a colicky baby caught her attention, she might step over to the house and call out softly to the woman inside trying to soothe the baby. The two of them might take turns massaging the infant stomach, rocking, or trying to get a little soda water down. When the baby quieted they could sit together for a spell, gossiping, chuckling low so as not to wake anybody else. The woman could decide to go back to her own house then, refreshed and ready to sleep.[60]

What does Ruby offer its women? Freedom from white violence, and even death itself, in exchange for masculine protection and a freedom that hardly deserves the name. The suggestion here is that the only way to build a livable world, a world in which the women have real freedom, transformative justice, and care—and not the laughably truncated freedom to do feminine labor masculine protection has afforded them—is to sustain and nurture their relationships with the dead women.

In this supposed Black civic paradise, *only* via communion with the Black female dead are the living women given food that they themselves are not expected to prepare, care, emotional support, antidepressants, access to abortions, affirming prenatal and postpartum care for the mothers of children born out of wedlock, child death doula services, rest, and safe harbor for nonnormative sexual relationships, as well as the opportunity for egalitarian dialogue, deliberation, talking things through with others in an effort to find one's voice, the space to work collectively toward to solutions to problems, the space to sustain one another through decision-making, and the space for self-actualizing reflection for the town's living women.[61] The female dead are the linchpin of Morrisonian democracy. Morrison seems to insist that communion with (and necessarily within that responsibility and accountability to) the women who "died bad" is the best way forward to workable intimate and civic life for the claimed and ever living women.

And what does it mean for dead women to seek life or its illusions? The women who seek life in fact seek life keepers of the kind Williamson highlights, the living who keep their stories - their life stories and not simply tales of the violent circumstances of their deaths. The book provides guidance on how the Black female living can honor their responsibilities to the Black female dead—that is, how the Black female living can help the dead who "seek life"—as the Black female dead continue their democratic work. They do so via engagement, relationship, communion. They cannot ignore those who die of Black femicide or white violence; they must face them, be accountable to them through their life keeping, work with them. We, in turn, must keep them present if we are to move forward together. This is a lesson for both Blacks and US democracy.

Finally, if the women are already dead, what was it, really, that the patriarchal men were trying to eradicate? It could only have been this truant communion, this truant democracy. And what is Morrison trying to say to us when, after the femicide that perhaps wasn't, the women's bodies mysteriously and suggestively disappear, leaving only their testimony behind? Did the perhaps-dead women forestall the attempt at eradicating the truant democracy through this testimony? And is it significant to Morrison's democratic theory that it is testimony they do not broadcast, but simply leave—whisper, really—in the basement of this enlarged domestic space? And did they leave, or were they now forever with the ever-living women? Morrison presents a Black male utopia and then slowly unravels it via the feminine dead in favor of her own female-centered, domestic version of democratic justice for the living and the dead alike.

Unspectacular Death and the Quietly Kept Work of the Truant Black Feminist "We"

The large-scale movements Kimberlé Crenshaw desires depend on widely broadcast ethically constitutive storytelling in the service of the construction of an expansive and stable we. But large scale ethically constitutive wes are at great risk of being exclusionary in some way, presumably along familiar lines of normative gender and sexuality. Conversely, adequately gender-inclusive and sexuality-inclusive people-building narratives may never appeal to people in significant numbers to build mass loyalty of the kind enjoyed by the lynching-as-crucifixion story. As well, I am hesitant to advocate an attempt to dethrone the crucifixion story that comes at the price of Black women sharing stories of violation in large groups, a context that has proven indifferent to those stories. These are contexts in which we have not only an entrenched crucifixion story but also master narratives about gender, about Black female sexuality—for example, the narrative that women and especially Black women lie or cannot be trusted when it comes to sex and sexual assault.

But that does not mean that Black women must abandon democratic storytelling. Morrison suggests how and with whom Black women should share their stories in a racist, patriarchal world, how they may be affirmed, healed, and empowered even as they "sidestep" the masculinist mass movements around them. What, then, is the relationship between Morrisonian democracy, Du Bois's abolition democracy, and our own? Though this message is clear in her fiction, Morrison's remarks at the 1986 PEN conference, "The Writer and the State," put a fine point on her skeptical view of mass politics. Morrison titled her remarks "Alienation and the State," and in them she gave the state what Erica Edwards calls a "side eye and a sidestep." Edwards identifies Morrison's relationship to the state in this address, following Stephen Best, as a kind of "besideness." The concept of "besideness," of paying that which disrespects you no mind, is a useful way to think about Morrison's democratic practice. Its impact can be profound, especially when considered alongside Camp's truant "plaiting," where that which is beside you progressively transforms the whole. Morrisonian democracy is designed for participants to steal away, heal in loving, challenging community, and return with new and expanded capacities. It can exist undetected within an abolitionist democracy, as it existed undetected in *Paradise* and as it has within our own.[62]

Crenshaw focuses on what has never been at the expense of nourishing what has been and is. She would change the direction of large-scale masculinist movements like the Movement for Black Lives. But Morrison's democratic vision reveals the tremendous value of what Black women have long been doing and will continue to do. Morrison provides a map to and a road forward from the kinds of projects that deserve our attention, support, and resources. Like W. E. B. Du Bois before her, Morrison appreciated the link between storytelling, democracy, and justice. But unlike Du Bois, she did not craft stories for mass movements, formal politics, or to build a mass "we," and her work opens up the possibility that we may not need such movements, hard as they are to come by for Black women. The work of truant Black feminist effervescent and episodic collectives may only require quietly kept stories of the violence and death that targets Black women, told to accompany the informal (and perhaps destined to be overlooked) practices of Black feminine democracy—stories of the small and not the great dead, whispered woman to woman. The aim is not to tell Christlike stories of male martyrdom in hopes of inspiring a movement for peoplehood. Instead, one tells stories of ordinary women's grief and suffering, of their collective healing, of the ongoing democratic work of their dead. You postfigure collectives who are perpetually coming together, only to come apart and then to come together again. You describe the practices of these collectives. You model the behavior not of a great man, but of small communities of perfectly ordinary women, made extraordinary in their coming together with and for the dead. This is Morrison's good news. For Black femicide activists, I think it is possibly the best news of all.

Conclusion

There are many ways to tell a true story. And even if many of the important things I have said may seem troublingly unverifiable, I assure you that most of the above is true. I have chosen to tell a ghost story, but the story of Black femicide in the United States could, and indeed should one day, be told as a story about data and power, about how—as I observed while writing this book—statistics regarding Black female murder rates traveled from obscure activist and non-profit websites to esteemed journals, *The Lancet*, for example. I want to close, however, by thinking of the above as a story of engineering, with the ghosts tinkering and helping to reconfigure the machine.

Aimi Hamraie's book *Building Access: Universal Design and the Politics of Disability* presents the history of Universal Design which included conflicts over what they call "access knowledge," and develops the concepts of "crip technoscience" and "epistemic activism" as "analytics for understanding the ambivalent relationships between disability activism, scientific research about disabled users, and liberal political discourse in the project of creating a more accessible world." Hamraie presents "technoscience as an arena of world-building and meaning making," and they see knowledge as a form of design. They say, "If liberal citizenship demanded smooth belonging and rehabilitation, crip technoscience involved strategic friction, disorientation, and nonconformity. Activists engaged in self-taught design practices, creating their own tools, curb cuts, and ramps with repurposed materials, learning to code and hack computers and tinkering with the structure of everyday life. . . . Crip technoscience thus took shape as a politicized, world-altering practice with overt and subtle manifestations."[1]

I want to acknowledge, first, that disability justice/access communities and communities of Black women are not mutually exclusive. Black women have been a part of activism and knowledge production around disability, have been involved in disability rights and justice work, even as that work has been overlooked and dismissed by the broader field of disability studies.[2]

Black women were part of the technoscience communities referenced above and disabled citizens are a crucial part of the communities to which I refer. The inventor, nurse, physical therapist, forensic scientist, newspaperwoman, and committed misfit Bessie Blount, who created a "portable

The Labors of Resurrection. Shatema Threadcraft, Oxford University Press. © Oxford University Press (2025).
DOI: 10.1093/9780197758618.003.0010

receptacle support" system that allowed disabled veterans to eat independently (and notably, with reference to official disregard for particular knowers, makers, and, indeed, users, a system the Veterans Administration declined so she sold it well below market value to the French government), taught amputees to write with their feet and teeth - a skill she had acquired in defiance for being forbidden from writing with her left hand at Diggs Chapel, the one-room segregated school she had attended in Hickory, Virginia - and who also integrated interpretative dance, a passion of hers, into rehabilitative therapy, is one important case in point.[3] That Blount, like me, was a lefty who wore corrective lenses yet did not appear to have identified as a member of the disabled community and perhaps, more important, did not suffer systematic marginalization because of these things, but was an ally and was certainly not a validated knower herself, reminds us, as Alison Kafer has noted, of the subjective and politicized boundaries of disability.[4] As well, Fannie Lou Hamer survived childhood polio, the disease leaving her with a permanent limp, and was forcibly sterilized and suffered a brutal and further disabling physical assault in jail—the beating worsened her limp and permanently damaged her kidneys—for attempting to register to vote; the latter two events are reminders of the fact that we should be attentive, as Kafer notes, to how racism and our drive to imprison can be disabling.[5] And Kafer tells as well of how the asthmatic Bernice Johnson Reagon struggled in the literally rarefied air of some white feminist spaces.[6] The point I want to make, however, is we might think of the radical world- and meaning-makers, the curb cutters above as companions in this work, and we should think of Morrison's work as analogous in important ways to their crip technoscience. We might think of Black feminist congregation in clearings as democratic curb cuts, spaces that allow, both via word work and truantly held physical spaces, ramps to democratic participation for the marginalized. Morrisonian truant democrats should see themselves as engaged in analogous technoscience projects, as another group of democracy's misfits, who, through word work and world work, construct all of our ramps to a new, more accessible, livable world.

Hamraie attends to the built environment, how ideology is materialized in the built environment—with the stairway standing as the iconic case in point and with the 1990 Capitol Crawl protest as the iconic counterpoint. Their work showed me that it is important that we reflect on the material and ideological architecture that separates Black survivors and those who have not survived from access to all that they need. With that in mind,

Hamraie's crip pioneers, with their sledgehammers, under cover of darkness, remind me of Stephanie Camp's truants within the plantation system, who nested a rival geography within the heart of the vile thing.[7] Morrison, like these inspiring radical knowledge and world architects, changed the American episteme—Farah Jasmine Griffin demonstrates how, truly, she gave us all "outdoors"—in her clearing she gave suggestions for where, how and to whom we should testify in a world that disbelieves us and gave us new and even simply repurposed tools to interpret our experiences.[8] Perhaps most important, she modeled all of the above for us and invited us to join in that work ourselves in ephemeral congregation, often only in the dark of night, too, and by lamplight alone if necessary. She taught us to see the ruins of white democracy as on-ramps to elsewhere, complete with bridges to the beyond.

And so now, with our sisters, our sister ancestors, and allies, let us begin. Again.

Notes

Introduction

1. Williamson, "In the Life"; Fischer, *Streets Belong to Us*, 175.
2. Russell and Ellis, "Annihilation by Murder," 161.
3. Smith, "Interview with Kimberly Springer," 71–72.
4. Williamson, "Why Did They Die?" 330–331.
5. Ibid., 330.
6. Smith, "Interview with Kimberly Springer," 73.
7. Grant, "Who's Killing Us?" 145.
8. Smith, "Interview with Kimberly Springer," 72; Grant, "Who's Killing Us?" 147.
9. Smith, "Interview with Kimberly Springer," 72.
10. Williamson, "Why Did They Die?" 329.
11. Smith, "Interview with Kimberly Springer," 72.
12. Ibid.; Williamson, "Why Did They Die?" 329, Grant, "Who's Killing Us?" 149–150.
13. Williamson, "Why Did They Die?" 329–330; Grant, "Who's Killing Us?" 150.
14. D'Ignazio, *Counting Feminicide*, 83; Williamson, "Why Did They Die?" 337–338. Williamson says that the members of the Combahee River Collective "did not need evidence of a single crazed killer in order to believe that the women's deaths were connected because, for them, the notion of connection was 'a broader, but equally palpable, phenomenon.'" Ibid., 331.
15. I want to thank Marcus Lee for calling my attention to a potential point of contention here. Smith noted Morrison's evident discomfort with homosexuality, both in Smith's reading of Morrison's *Sula* as a lesbian novel and in Morrison's decision not to reference James Baldwin's queer identity in her eulogy for him. I want to acknowledge this, point out that I am claiming only that Smith's radical democratic enumeration contained elements of and resonances with Morrisonian democracy in its care and concern for the dead, and note what I see as Morrison's evolving comfort with same-sex relationships throughout the course of her own writing, as evidenced in *Paradise*. Smith, "Black Feminist Criticism."
16. Sarmiento, Acosta, Roth, and Zambrano, "Latin American Model Protocol," 14–15.
17. Williamson, "Why Did They Die?" 336.
18. Waller, Joseph, and Keyes, "Racial Inequities," 1, 9.
19. Lawn and Koenen, "Homicide." See also Kivisto, Kivisto, and Mills, "Racial Disparities."
20. Waller, Joseph, and Keyes, "Racial Inequities," 1.
21. Sarmiento, Acosta, Roth, and Zambrano, "Latin American Model Protocol"; Njoku, Evans, Nimo-Sefah, and Bailey, "Listen to the Whispers"; Centers for Disease Control and Prevention, "Working Together."
22. Hanchard, *Spectre of Race*.
23. Hooker, *Black Grief, White Grievance*.
24. Crenshaw, "#MeToo"; Fam and Biello, "#SayHerName."
25. Cone, *Cross*, 105.
26. Ibid., 3.
27. Blum, "Lynching as Crucifixion."
28. Blum writes: "In most of his stories of black Christs, Du Bois ended the narratives with the crucifixion. He refused to offer readers the solace of a resurrected black Christ. 'Jesus Christ in Georgia' concluded with Christ crying out to the black convict, 'This day thou shalt be with me in Paradise!' The story 'Pontius Pilate' ended with the black Jesus shouting, 'My God, my God! Why has Thou forsaken me!' In 'The Son of God,' Christ's mother continued to have faith in her son after his death, but her only 'Sign of Salvation' was a noosed rope. In the confines of this story, her son did not return. Only in one of Du Bois's stories, 'The Gospel According to Mary Brown,' did the crucified Christ return from the dead. Yet death once again prevailed.

According to the story's conclusion, after she encountered her resurrected son, 'softly Mary laid herself down at His feet, and died.'" Ibid., 206–207.

29. Jasmine Yarish points out that he referred to black women only twice in the entirety of *Black Reconstruction*. "Reconstructing Home," 138.
30. Du Bois, *Black Reconstruction*. For an analysis of how his issues with women, gender, and normative sexuality compromised his social scientific analysis in *The Philadelphia Negro*, see Cohen, "Deviance as Resistance."
31. Du Bois, *Philadelphia Negro*.
32. Wilmette Brown, "The Autonomy of Black Lesbian Women," quoted in Smith, "Black Feminist Criticism."
33. I acknowledge my debt to Lawrie Balfour and her elaboration of the Fugitive's Democracy in Morrison's work. Balfour, "Toni Morrison."
34. Hooker, *Black Grief, White Grievance*, 23, 43, 51.
35. See Carter, *Prayers for the People*.
36. Barrett and Heller, "Death and Dying."
37. Arendt, *Human Condition*, 7.
38. Benhabib, *Reluctant Modernism*, 130.
39. Arendt, *Human Condition*, 7.
40. Pitkin, "Justice," 338.

Chapter 1

1. Davis, "Reflections," Hartman, *Scenes of Subjection*, 85.
2. Samuels, Mehta, and Wiederkehr, "Why Black Women."
3. Feimster, *Southern Horrors*, 158.
4. Kirschke, *Art in Crisis*, 55.
5. See Mappingpoliceviolence.org.
6. Crenshaw, "#MeToo."
7. Foucault, *Society Must Be Defended*, 245.
8. Mbembe, "Necropolitics," 40.
9. Wright, "Necropolitics, Narcopolitics, and Femicide," 709.
10. Mbembe, "Necropolitics," 12, 14.
11. Wright, "Necropolitics, Narcopolitics, and Femicide," 709; Mbembe, "Necropolitics."
12. Mbembe, "Necropolitics," 12.
13. Wright, "Necropolitics, Narcopolitics, and Femicide."
14. D'Ignazio, *Counting Femicide*.
15. Wright, "Necropolitics, Narcopolitics, and Femicide."
16. Mbembe, "Necropolitics," 40.
17. Sharpe, *In the Wake*.
18. Threadcraft, "North American Necropolitics."
19. Waller, Joseph, and Keyes, "Racial Inequities," 1.
20. Threadcraft and Miller, "Black Women."
21. Waller, Joseph, and Keyes, "Racial Inequities," 9.
22. Solarte-Erlacher, "Rosalind Page."
23. Waller, Joseph, and Keyes, "Racial Inequities," 9.
24. Violence Policy Center, "When Men Murder Women."
25. The latter includes obstetric racism, which compounds a variety of problems, including that of access, within a capitalist system of health care provision, wherein said racism is particularly egregious given the state's role in suppressing a noncapitalist birthing regime that attended Black women prior to the current medical complex and gendered racially discriminatory policing within contexts that offer few alternatives for safety provision, especially secure housing. Hoberman, *Medical Racism*, 2.
26. Russell and Van de Ven, "Crimes against Women"
27. Gross, "Women Burned."
28. Radford and Russell, *Femicide*, 3.
29. D'Ignazio, *Counting Feminicide*.
30. Ibid.
31. Ibid.
32. Potterat et al., "Mortality."

33. Willis et al., "Causes of Mortality."
34. In 2013, 453 Black women fell victim to men in single-victim/single-offender homicides. Among those who knew their offenders, 56 percent were the wife, common-law wife, ex-wife, or girlfriend of the man who killed them. Covid-19 Task Force, "Intersection."
35. Richie, *Arrested Justice.*
36. Squires et al., "Missing and Murdered."
37. Lipsitz, "In an Avalanche"; Crenshaw, "Private Violence."
38. Benfer et al., "Eviction."
39. Squires et al., "Missing and Murdered," 27.
40. Potterat et al., "Mortality."
41. Butler, "Racial Roots."
42. Squires et al., "Missing and Murdered," 30; Epstein, Blake, and González, "Girlhood Interrupted"; Roberts, *Shattered Bonds.*
43. Dinno, "Homicide Rates."
44. Gamarel et al., "Stigma."
45. Saffin, "Identities under Siege"; Roberts, *Torn Apart.*
46. Davis, "Criminalization of Black Girls," 2.
47. Stanley, "Fugitive Flesh," 10.
48. Ibid., 12.
49. Spade, *Normal Life,* 9, 11.
50. Kidd, Goodman, and Robbins, "State Abortion Bans."
51. I thank Juliet Hooker for directing my attention to the broader health concerns here.
52. CDC, "Working Together"; Hoyert, "Maternal Mortality Rates," 2021, 2022; U.S. Bureau of Labor Statistics, "Civilian Occupations."
53. I want to acknowledge the significant contributions of Annie Menzel to my understanding of the mechanisms of the Black maternal mortality crisis and its status as a socially produced form of Black femicide. See Menzel, "Midwife's Bag."
54. Menzel, *Fatal Denial.*
55. Davis, "Obstetric Racism," 561–562.
56. Davis, "Reproducing While Black," 60.
57. Davis, "Obstetric Racism," 561.
58. Muigai, "Something Wasn't Clean," 86–88.
59. Menzel, *Fatal Denial,* 294.
60. Ibid., xx.
61. Mullings and Wali, *Stress and Resilience.*
62. Menzel, *Fatal Denial,* xx.
63. Mullings and Wali, *Stress and Resilience,* 163–64.
64. Geronimus et al., "Weathering," 826.
65. Menzel, *Fatal Denial,* 223.
66. Ibid., 224.
67. Ibid., xx; Lu and Halfon, "Racial and Ethnic Disparities."
68. Cheng and Horon, "Homicide"; Palladino, "Homicide and Suicide."
69. Simmons, "Why Are They So Mad?"
70. Crenshaw, "Private Violence," 1439–1441.
71. Ibid., 1455.
72. Ibid., 1440.
73. Ibid., 1455.
74. Richie, *Arrested Justice,* 7.
75. Crenshaw, "Private Violence," 1455.
76. INCITE, "Police Violence."
77. Crenshaw, "Private Violence," 1454–1455, 1418, 1453.
78. Quoted in Yang, "Breonna Taylor."
79. Crenshaw, "Private Violence," 1440.
80. Quoted in Yang, "Breonna Taylor."
81. Purvis and Blanco, "Police Sexual Violence," 1497.
82. Fricker, *Epistemic Injustice,* 1.
83. Purvis and Blanco, "Police Sexual Violence." See also Trombadore, "Police Officer Sexual Misconduct."

84. Antione, "Color of Lawlessness."
85. United Nations Human Rights Committee, "In the Shadows," 31.
86. See Sedensky and Merchant, "Hundreds of Officers."
87. Spina, "Protector Becomes a Predator."
88. Kaba and Ritchie, "S&P Analysis and Vision."
89. Ibid.
90. Richie, *Arrested Justice*, 7.
91. Saar, Epstein, Rosenthal, and Vafa, "Sexual Assault," 9–18.
92. Gatens, *Imaginary Bodies*, 24.
93. Crenshaw, "Mapping the Margins," 1251.
94. Richie, *Arrested Justice.*
95. Dotson, "Conceptualizing Epistemic Oppression," 117; Fricker, *Epistemic Injustice*, 1.
96. Richie, *Arrested Justice*, 18.
97. Ibid., 17, 4.
98. Hinton, *War on Poverty.*
99. See Mikati et al., "Disparities in Distribution."
100. Geronimus et al., "Weathering," 826.
101. Ibid.
102. Bartky, *Femininity and Domination*, 79, 71, 72.
103. Hartman, *Scenes of Subjection.*

Chapter 2

1. The report states that "The Task Force was convened on November 29, 2021, by the Department of Public Safety and Research In Action (RIA). The DPS contracted with RIA to conduct research and prepare the final report on behalf of the Task Force." Research in Action describes itself as "a Black queer female-led, multi-racial and gender-diverse social benefit corporation created to reclaim the power of research by centering community expertise and driving actionable solutions for racial justice." The report thanked "15 black women and girls across interviews and focus groups," which they convened "to learn from their lived experiences as survivors of interpersonal and systemic violence." Squires et al., "Missing and Murdered."
2. Richardson, "Office."
3. Squires et al., "Missing and Murdered," 51.
4. Ibid., 43.
5. Ibid., 44.
6. Black and Missing Foundation, "About the Foundation."
7. US Congress, "Neglected Epidemic," 2.
8. Nawaz, "Woman Who Escaped Kidnapper."
9. US Congress, "Neglected Epidemic," 2.
10. Nawaz, "Woman Who Escaped Kidnapper."
11. Lara, "SoCal Woman Shines Spotlight."
12. Our Black Girls, "About OBG" (emphasis mine).
13. Black Girl Tragic, "About."
14. D'Ignazio, *Counting Feminicide.*
15. Posey, "Black Femicides Matter."
16. Vargas, "She's Spent Years."
17. Henry, "We're Truly Not Valued."
18. Solarte-Erlacher, "Rosalind Page."
19. D'Ignazio, *Counting Femicide.*
20. Solarte-Erlacher, "Rosalind Page"; D'Ignazio, *Counting Femicide.*
21. Solarte-Erlacher, "Rosalind Page."
22. Ibid.
23. Ibid.
24. Invisible Institute, "Beneath the Surface."
25. Chicago Missing Persons, "About."
26. Canvas Rebel, "Meet Marcbelle Davis."
27. My Sister's Keeper Defense, "About."
28. Black Gun Owners Magazine, https://m.facebook.com/photo.php?fbid=221814999643529&vanity=blackownedguns&slug=a.101081708383526.

29. She Loaded Defense, "About"; see also https://instagram.com/sheloadedselfdefense/?hl=en.
30. Skip's Tactical Solutions, "Avery."
31. For example, Alecia Roberson says, "Empowered Personal Protection (EPP) was founded based on a need to provide training for women who were purchasing firearms and/or interested in firearms training an option to have a female instructor who understands that women are evolving in the second amendment culture and the nuances we face in this arena. . . . I am the Dayton Ohio Chapter Facilitator of A Girl and A Gun Women's Shooting League, a ladies-only organization established by women shooters for women pistol, rifle, and shotgun shooters!"
32. Girls Getta Grip Gun Club, "Goals for GGGGC Members."
33. On January 26, 2021, she posted a link to an event hosted by the Free Roots Project, "The Cost of Rejection: A Conversation about the Risk Women Take When Rejecting Advances." Her caption read, "Women are not safe when men approach them. Tune in to learn something! Follow @Oshundefense for self-defense and firearms training." On January 25, 2021, she posted part of a story about a woman who was unlikely to face charges after she killed her boyfriend. Her caption reads, "If someone is trying to end your life, you must defend yourself. Contact @oshundefense and learn how to shoot, how to protect your [*sic*], and what to do in the event of a shooting. Follow @oshundefense for more self-defense and firearms training." See https://www.instagram.com/oshundefense/?hl=en.
34. Third Eye Watching, "Educate Train Empower Defend," https://www.3rdeyewatching.com/aboutus.
35. Defensive Unicorns, "Defensive Unicorns Owner."
36. Reign, "Meet the Organizers."
37. The prison nation is characterized, among other things, by an ideology that holds that violations of normative behavior, which includes normative masculine *and feminine* behavior, should be punished by the state; such punishment increases the other forms of violence, including lethal intimate partner violence, that Black women experience.
38. Fischer, *Streets Belong to Us*, 200.
39. Kim, "Carceral Feminism," 222–223.
40. Crenshaw, "Private Violence," 1452–1453.
41. Kim, "Carceral Feminism," 224.
42. Davis, Dent, Meiners, and Richie, *Abolition. Feminism.*
43. INCITE, "Incite! History."
44. INCITE, "Stop Law Enforcement Violence."
45. INCITE, "Statement on Gender Violence" (emphasis in original).
46. Ibid.
47. Richie, *Arrested Justice*, 15–16.
48. Kaba and Ritchie, *Survived and Punished.*
49. Moore, *Legal Spectatorship*, 148, 149.
50. Survived and Punished, "Roots."
51. Kim, *Carceral Feminism*, 225–228.
52. Kim, "Restorative Justice," 7.
53. Spade, *Normal Life.*
54. Saffin, "Identities under Siege."
55. Spade, *Normal Life*, 17.
56. Spade, "Solidarity Not Charity," 136.
57. Reign, "Meet the Organizers."
58. Mingus, "Pods and Pod Mapping."
59. Hassan, "Our Right to Heal."
60. Just Practice, "About Just Practice."
61. Just Practice, "Transformative Justice Help Desk."
62. African American Policy Forum, "About #SayHerName."
63. Crenshaw, "Urgency of Intersectionality."
64. Crenshaw and Ritchie, "Say Her Name," 1–2.
65. Crenshaw, "#MeToo."
66. African American Policy Forum, "Our Demands."
67. Ibid.
68. African American Policy Forum, "About #SayHerName."

69. African American Policy Forum, "Policy Recommendations."
70. African American Policy Forum, "About #SayHerName."
71. African American Policy Forum, "Policy Recommendations."
72. Crenshaw, "#MeToo"; Fam and Biello, "#SayHerName."
73. Woodly, *Reckoning*; Sawyer and Gampa, "Implicit and Explicit."
74. Dotson, "Conceptualizing Epistemic Oppression"; Fricker, *Epistemic Injustice*.
75. Ross and Solinger, *Reproductive Justice*.
76. Southern Birth Justice, "Birth Justice Framework" and "Programs."
77. Birthing Project USA, "Black Infant Mortality" and "About Us."

Chapter 3

1. Hill, "Twenty-First Century Lynching"; Anderson, "Lynching Photos"; Taylor, "Trayvon Martin's Lynching"; Wilkerson in the *Guardian*, August 25, 2014; Miles, "U.S. Police Killings." Other contemporaneous article titles include "Police Killings Picked Up Where Lynching Left Off" (Donovan X. Ramsey for *NewsOne*, August 29, 2014), "Police Killings Surpass the Worst Years of Lynching, Capital Punishment and a Movement Responds" (Jerome Karabel, *Huffington Post*, November 4, 2015), and "Sixty Years after Emmett Till's Murder, Black Lives Still Matter" (Errin Whack, *NBC News*, August 28, 2015). Also see Magan, "Speaking in St. Paul."
2. Phillonese Floyed quoted in Morgan and Cowan, "George Floyd's Brother"; Smith-Abass, "Lynching of George Floyd."
3. Pelton, "America Is on Fire"; Crusto, "Black Lives Matter"; Urban Assembly Unison School, "Lynching of George Floyd." See also Schwarz, "Police Killings"; Deegan-McCree, "Floyd and Arbery Killings"; Fountain, "Modern-Day Lynching"; and Davis, "What Is a Lynching?"
4. Wood, *Lynching and Spectacle*, 183.
5. Giddings, *Sword among Lions*, 7.
6. Alexander, "The Crisis," 3.
7. Modernist Journals Project, introduction to *The Crisis*, https://modjourn.org/journal/crisis/; Alexander, "The Crisis," 4; Schuyler, "Forty Years," 58. Shawn Alexander quotes founder of the Southern Poverty Law Center and NAACP chairman Julian Bond's father, Horace Mann Bond, as saying, "Through *The Crisis* Du Bois helped shape my inner world to a degree impossible to imagine in the world of contemporary children and the flood of various mass media to which they are exposed." Alexander, "The Crisis," 4–5. Langston Hughes echoed Bond's sentiments, saying, "So many thousands of my generation were uplifted and inspired by the written and spoken words of Dr. W. E. B. Du Bois that for me to say that I was so inspired would hardly be unusual. My earliest memories of written words are those of Du Bois and the Bible." Quoted in ibid., 5.
8. Du Bois, *Dusk of Dawn*, 226; Alexander, "The Crisis," 4–5; Schuyler, "Forty Years."
9. Kirschke and Sinitiere, "Print Propagandist," 37.
10. Glaude, *Exodus*, 53–54.
11. Ibid., 56.
12. Gorup, "Strange Fruit," 819.
13. Ibid., 821.
14. Mathews, "Southern Rite," 20; Patterson, *Rituals of Blood*, 173, 175.
15. Patterson, *Rituals of Blood*, 175.
16. Ibid., 73.
17. Smith, *Stories of Peoplehood*, 73, 45.
18. Cone, *Cross*, 105, 3.
19. Ibid., 9.
20. Brooks, "Chicago Defender."
21. Cone, *Cross*, 101.
22. Alexander, "The Crisis," 5–6.
23. Wood, *Lynching and Spectacle*, 183; Michaeli, *The Defender*, 26; Goldsby, *Spectacular Secret*, 67.
24. Zangrando, *NAACP Crusade*, 21.
25. See Du Bois, "Jesus Christ in Georgia," "Pontius Pilate," "Gospel," "Second Coming," and "Son of God."

26. Blum, "Lynching as Crucifixion," 191, 198.
27. Du Bois, "Gospel," 43.
28. Blum, "Lynching as Crucifixion," 191, 201.
29. Ibid., 191.
30. Ibid., 203.
31. Du Bois, "Son of God."
32. Du Bois, "Pontius Pilate," 53–54.
33. Blum, "Lynching as Crucifixion," 204.
34. Kuhl, "Resurrecting Black Manhood," 171–172, Blum, "Lynching as Crucifixion," 204–205.
35. Smith, *Stories of Peoplehood*, 9, 45, 58, 69.
36. Ibid., 32, 36, 34.
37. Cone, *Cross*, 105; West, *Prophesy Deliverance*, 35; Pinn, *Why, Lord?*
38. Smith, *Stories of Peoplehood*, 64–65, 97–98.
39. Blum, "Lynching as Crucifixion," 198.
40. Smith, *Stories of Peoplehood*, 101–102.
41. This popular imagination is consistent with the empirics. Again, Crystal Feimster writes that of the four thousand plus Blacks lynched between 1880 and 1930, fewer than two hundred were women (*Southern Horrors*, 158). And today, Sam Singyangwe of Mapping Police Violence reports that only about 1 in 20 Blacks killed by police are women. Sinyangwe told Melissa Harris-Perry of MSNBC that of the 304 Black Americans killed by police in 2014, 12 were women, or about 4 percent of police murder victims. See Harris-Perry, "Transcript." Many of these women, again, are killed because of their connections to male partners and relatives and because of intimacy. And, relatedly, when they are killed by police, they are rarely killed in public.
42. "One might say that she articulates an idea of 'fugitive democracy' that is critically similar to and different from Sheldon Wolin's 1996 essay by that name. Morrison, like Wolin, recognizes the danger to collective life when survival requires the continual erection and reinforcement of boundaries. Her account of freedom is derived from "the political potentialities of ordinary citizens" and rejects the gladiatorial image of state power conjured by Hobbes and decried by Wolin. Morrison's work is also avowedly democratic, insofar as it pursues "that egalitarianism which places us all (readers, the novel's population, the narrator's voice) on the same footing. And her essays and fiction return repeatedly to a conception of collective life that resonates deeply with Wolin's fugitive democracy. . . . Such moments play a pivotal role in Morrison's fiction. In *Beloved*, for example, former slaves respond to Baby Suggs, an 'unchurched preacher,' when she calls a free community into being and enjoins her neighbors to love the flesh their white masters exploited and despised. . . . Morrison's writing is replete with such instances, when diverse individuals come together to oppose the ongoing power of slavery and its legacies. Her words illustrate what it means to think of democracy 'as something other than a form of government.'" Balfour, "Toni Morrison," 543–544.
43. Du Bois, *Black Reconstruction*.
44. Du Bois, *Philadelphia Negro*, 364–365. See also Cohen, "Deviance as Resistance."

Chapter 4

1. Hartman, "Venus in Two Acts."
2. Kuhl, "Countable Bodies," 134; Hooker, *Black Grief, White Grievance*, 161, 169.
3. Hooker, *Black Grief, White Grievance*, 161.
4. Goldsby, *Spectacular Secret*, 64; Giddings, *Sword among Lions*, 160–163, 207; Raiford, "Ida B. Wells," 299.
5. She discerned the will of God. She saw God on the side of the oppressed. She exposed the oppressive nature of society, and she confronted evil. She sought to create a community of faith partnership, justice, and unity. Townes, "Ida B. Wells."
6. Goldsby, *Spectacular Secret*, 64, 69.
7. Giddings, *Sword among Lions*, 207.
8. Ibid., 26; Wells, *Crusade for Justice*, 29, 22; Goldsby, *Spectacular Secret*, 63; Giddings, *Sword among Lions*, 228–229.
9. Giddings, "Making Ida B. Wells."
10. Goldsby, *Spectacular Secret*, 66.

11. Giddings, *Sword among Lions*, 160–163.
12. Penn, *Afro American Press*, 133; Giddings, *Sword among Lions*, 141.
13. Giddings, *Sword among Lions*, 189, 228.
14. Bacon, "History of *Freedom's Journal*," 2–3; Cornish and Russwurm, "To Our Patrons."
15. Squires, "Rethinking."
16. Goldsby, *Spectacular Secret*, 64; Robinson, "Thread-Bare Lie."
17. Wells, *Autobiography*, 136.
18. White, "Saddle-Colored Sapphira," 317.
19. Ibid., 321.
20. Ibid., 322–323.
21. Ibid., 322, 326.
22. Wells, *Crusade for Justice*, 189–190.
23. Giddings, "Making Ida B. Wells."
24. Wells, *Crusade for Justice*, 80.
25. Ibid., 91.
26. Ibid., 92–93.
27. Ibid., 91–92.
28. Ibid., 92.
29. Ibid., 92–93.
30. Ibid., 54.
31. Ibid.
32. Ibid., 93.
33. Wells, "She Pleads," 216.
34. Wells, *Crusade for Justice*, 93.
35. Ibid., 94.
36. Ibid., 94–95.
37. Ibid., 80.
38. Giddings, *Sword among Lions*, 194–195.
39. Rushdy, *End of American Lynching*, 67.
40. Ibid., 68.
41. Wells, "She Pleads," 215.
42. Goldsby, *Spectacular Secret*, 251.
43. Raiford, "Ida B. Wells," 315, 317.
44. Ibid., 317–318.
45. Ibid., 315.
46. Ibid., 318.
47. Ibid.
48. Penn, *Afro-American Press*, 186.
49. Lucey, "Fighting Editor"; Penn, *Afro-American Press*, 183.
50. Goldsby, *Spectacular Secret*, 67.
51. Pumphrey, "Finding Asylum," 75–76. Though Mitchell may have opened Wells's eyes regarding the need to say their names, he was not as instrumental in helping her to move past Victorianism. "As a product of one of the city's best African American schools and member of some of its most celebrated social organizations, Mitchell cultivated a middle-class politics of respectability and approach to racial uplift that came along with accompanying gender norms." Ibid., 76.
52. It is worth noting that while we follow her in saying their names, Wells would inspire in others a commitment to "say their names" in her own time. Memphians, inspired to migrate by the lynching, Wells's call to leave, and her reporting of Moss's last words to go West, would name three streets in Guthrie, Oklahoma, Moss, Stewart, and McDowell, after three men of the Curve lynching.
53. Wells, "East Saint Louis Massacre," 461.
54. Ibid.
55. Hooker, *Black Grief, White Grievance*, 160–161.
56. Goldsby, *Spectacular Secret*, 63; Hooker, *Black Grief, White Grievance*, 166.
57. Williamson, "Why Did They Die?" 338.
58. Ibid.

Chapter 5

1. Metress, "No Justice, No Peace," 89–90.
2. Ibid., 90.
3. Alexander, "Can You Be BLACK," 88.
4. Mobley and Benson, *Death of Innocence*, 14–17.
5. Ibid., 168.
6. Colin, "Mother's Tears."
7. Bradley, "Mamie Bradley's Untold Story," March 8, 1956.
8. Cone, *Cross*, 105, 3, 97.
9. "*Eyes on the Prize*," interview clip.
10. Dawan, "Photos."
11. Quoted in Feldstein, *Motherhood*, 108.
12. "Nation Shocked, Vow Action in Lynching of Chicago Youth," *Chicago Defender*, September 10, 1955; Feldstein, *Motherhood*.
13. Metress, "No Justice, No Peace," 88.
14. Skelton, "Ode to Mississippi," in Metress, "No Justice, No Peace," 90.
15. Alexander, "Can You Be BLACK," 88.
16. Ibid., 93, 79.
17. Ibid., 80.
18. Ibid., 79.
19. Ibid., 81.
20. Ibid., 78.
21. Edwards, *Charisma*, 18.
22. Ibid., 16–17; Taylor, "Afterword."
23. Steele, "Black and Middle Class."
24. Quoted in Alexander, "Can You Be BLACK," 89–90 (emphasis mine).
25. Ibid., 85.
26. Quoted in ibid., 88.
27. Metress says in "No Justice, No Peace" that the image of Till as "sacrificial Christ figure remains strong today." As evidence, he points to Michael Eric Dyson referring to Till's "sainted sacrifice" and of his mother, "who without her knowledge or consent was called upon to sacrifice her only-begotten son." Till-Bradley may not have chosen the role—and others may have downplayed her part in the drama, as notoriously sexist NAACP LDF lawyer Robert Ming did—but once she understood the role to have been divinely chosen for her, she stepped into it as perhaps no other could have done.

Chapter 6

1. "Preserve Our Future Which Is Our Youth," SOSAD correspondence, undated.
2. Barfield, "Beyond Mourning."
3. "Force for Change," *Chicago Tribune*, October 24, 1993.
4. Barfield, "Beyond Mourning"; Price, "What Would Mama Do?" 17–18.
5. Price, "What Would Mama Do?" 21.
6. Barfield, "Global Pain and Global Change," SOSAD Newsletter 17 (October 9, 1988), SOSAD Archive.
7. Henderson, "Revolutionary Lessons."
8. Citizen Manual Detroit, "Youth Murders in Detroit."
9. SOSAD Pledge, quoted in Price, "What Would Mama Do?" 8.
10. Chicago Tribune, "Murders Torment Detroit."
11. Barfield, "Beyond Mourning."
12. Price, "What Would Mama Do?" 4; Price "Afterlife of Black Motherhood," 4, 23.
13. Wilkerson, "Detroit Crime Feeds on Itself and Youth," *New York Times*, April 29, 1987, cited in Price, "What Would Mama Do?" 6.
14. Barfield, "Beyond Mourning."
15. Meager, "Bereavement Support Group," SOSAD Newsletter 18 (November 8, 1988), SOSAD Archive.
16. The support groups were advertised in the organization's monthly newsletter. See SOSAD Newsletter 9–10 (Fall 1991) and 6 (Spring 1992), SOSAD Archive.

17. Hagerman-McGhee, "SOSAD'S CRISIS RESPONSE TEAM," SOSAD Newsletter 6 (Spring 1992), SOSAD Archive.
18. See SOSAD Correspondence, "Letter to Funeral Directors," February 5, 1988; "Letter to Ministers," February 27, 1991; "Letter to Bereaved Parents," February 13, 1990; "Letter to Principal," January 25, 1989; "Letter to Chief William Hart, Detroit Police Department," January 4, 1989; "Letter to Parents," January 25, 1989; "Letter to City Council," January 17, 1989; "Letter to Dr. Arthur Jefferson, Superintendent Detroit Public Schools," December 8, 1988, all in SOSAD Archive. Also see Price, "What Would Mama Do?"
19. SOSAD Newsletter 4, no. 3 (March 10, 1990).
20. Barfield, "Anti-Drug War Will Be Won at the Grassroots," SOSAD Newsletter 28 (October 6, 1989); Naughton, "Murder City."
21. Jones, "Moving Forward with Harvest '88," SOSAD Newsletter (November 8, 1988), SOSAD Archive.
22. SOSAD Newsletter, February 1992, SOSAD Archive.
23. Barfield, "Movement Growing to End War at Home," SOSAD Newsletter 6 (Spring 1992), SOSAD Archive.
24. Barfield, "The Ultimate Love," SOSAD Newsletter 4, no. 4 (April 10, 1990), SOSAD Archive.
25. See Northrop and Hamrick, "Weapons," 4.
26. SOSAD Newsletter 17 (October 9, 1988), SOSAD Archive.
27. SOSAD Newsletter 15 (August 11, 1988) and 17 (October 9, 1988), SOSAD Archive.
28. Barfield, "Beyond Mourning"; Price, "What Would Mama Do?" 11.
29. SOSAD Newsletter 6 (Spring 1992), SOSAD Archive.
30. Price, "Afterlife of Black Motherhood," 12.
31. Barfield, "Beyond Mourning," quoted in Price, "Afterlife of Black Motherhood," 12.
32. Barfield, "Beyond Mourning."
33. SOSAD Newsletter 6 (Spring 1992), SOSAD Archive.
34. Price, "Afterlife of Black Motherhood," 14; Barfield, "Beyond Mourning."
35. "Preserve Our Future Which Is Our Youth," SOSAD Correspondence, SOSAD Archive.
36. SOSAD Newsletter 11 (April 11, 1988), SOSAD Archive.
37. SOSAD Newsletter, June 17, 1988, SOSAD Archive.
38. SOSAD Newsletter 24 (May 9, 1989), SOSAD Archive.
39. SOSAD Newsletter, August 11, 1988, SOSAD Archive.
40. Barfield would report incarcerated members having similar transformative experiences through their Child of the Month Program. Barfield, "Beyond Mourning."
41. SOSAD Newsletter 6 (Spring 1992), SOSAD Archive.
42. SOSAD Newsletter 4, no. 4 (April 10, 1990), SOSAD Archive.
43. Price, "Afterlife of Black Motherhood," 23.
44. "Preserve Our Future Which Is Our Youth."
45. "We Need Court Watchers," SOSAD Newsletter 4 (August 18, 1987), SOSAD Archive.
46. Naughton, "Murder City."
47. Price, "Afterlife of Black Motherhood," 18, 25, 2.
48. Carter, *Prayers for the People*, 189.
49. Ibid., 185.
50. Ibid., 188.
51. Ibid., 190.
52. Ibid., 193.
53. Ibid., 191.
54. Ibid., 194.
55. Wilgoren, "Detroit Mothers Mourn."
56. Adams, "Happy Birthday, James," SOSAD Newsletter 5, no. 3 (March 4, 1991), SOSAD Archive (emphasis mine).
57. Price, "Afterlife of Black Motherhood," 1. Price notes: "In the SOSAD archives and other documentation, there is always a retelling of how the child died, but also who the child was." Ibid., 23.
58. Ibid., 26–28 (emphasis mine).
59. Price, "Afterlife of Black Motherhood," 32.
60. Carter, *Prayers for the People*, 189.
61. Barfield, "Beyond Mourning"; Naughton, "Murder City."

62. Price, "Afterlife of Black Motherhood," 20.
63. Ibid., 19, 32.
64. Price, "What Would Mama Do?" 16.
65. Gilmore, *Golden Gulag.*
66. "It Kind of Makes You Feel Bitter," SOSAD Newsletter 5 (October 10, 1987), SOSAD Archive.
67. Barfield, "THE MARCH GOES ON!" SOSAD Newsletter 4 (August 18, 1987), SOSAD Archive.
68. I thank Deva Woodly for clarifying this final point for me.

Chapter 7

1. Fischer, *Streets Belong to Us*, 175; Russell and Ellis, "Annihilation by Murder," 161. Terrion Williamson notes: "In fact, since the early 1970s there have been at least fifty distinct serial murder cases throughout the United States in which black women have been the sole or primary targets. The number of victims in each case ranges from three to more than 20 and in larger cities like Los Angeles, Chicago and Detroit, there has been overlap among active serial killers across time periods and within particular geographic locations." In the accompanying note, Williamson explains her decision to use the term "serial murder": "usually when I refer to 'black serial murder' here, I am talking about cases in which at least three people, all or most of them black women, were killed in separate incidents by the same person. Because my approach is victim-centered, however, I do also consider cases in which a series of similar murders have been attributed to more than one perpetrator, even when those perpetrators are not themselves considered serial murderers." Williamson, "In the Life," 112.
2. Pelesik, *Grim Sleeper*, 30–31.
3. West, "U.S. PROStitutes Collective."
4. Police Chief Gates called the charges Prescod's coalition has made "asinine" and the women "dummies" for making them. LAPD spokesman Booth refused to comment on Prescod or the coalition, other than observing that "they certainly have been exercising their First Amendment rights." And Lieutenant Zorn, who headed the task force investigating the serial murders, would say about Prescod "not a word. I've got no comment." Neither did Ridley-Thomas. Asked to comment on Prescod, he said, "I respectfully choose not to comment." Hendrix, "Passionate Pursuer's Crusade."
5. Fischer, *Streets Belong to Us*, 176.
6. Williams, "Prostitutes Collective."
7. Ibid.
8. Hendrix, "Passionate Pursuer's Crusade."
9. Williams, "Prostitutes Collective."
10. Hendrix, "Passionate Pursuer's Crusade." The organization's birth announcement states: "We came together for the first time at a conference sponsored by the New York Wages for Housework Committee on Wages for Housework and Welfare, which was held in Brooklyn on April 24, 1976. We've been meeting every week since then."
11. International Wages for Housework Campaign, "The International Wages for Housework Campaign."
12. International Wages for Housework Campaign, "International Black Women for Wages for Housework."
13. Prescod-Roberts, "Black Women," 13.
14. Ibid, 14.
15. International Wages for Housework Campaign, "Wages Due Lesbians."
16. International Wages for Housework Campaign, "English Collective."
17. Capper and Austin, "Wages for Housework," 448.
18. Ibid., 452.
19. Prescod-Roberts, "Black Women," 33.
20. Black Women for Wages for Housework, "Birth Announcement."
21. Black Women for Wages for Housework, "Money for Prostitutes."
22. Ibid.
23. Fischer, *Streets Belong to Us*, 176.
24. Ibid.
25. Ibid., 184.
26. Black Women for Wages for Housework, "Money for Prostitutes."

27. Ibid.
28. Grio Staff, "Ten Black Women."
29. "Interactive Map: Serial Killers."
30. Take Back the Night, "Events."
31. Fischer, *Streets Belong to Us*, 174–175.
32. Ibid.
33. Bundy, "Anti-Prostitution Laws."
34. Fischer, *Streets Belong to Us*, 175.
35. Ford, "LA Vigil."
36. Fischer, *Streets Belong to Us*, 175.
37. West, "U.S. PROStitutes Collective," 285.
38. D'Ignazio, *Counting Feminicide*, 67.
39. Ibid., 74.
40. Grigsby, "Count Women's Lives," 16–17.
41. Ibid., 17.
42. Rose South LA, "Take Action."

Chapter 8

1. Waller, Joseph, and Keyes, "Racial Inequities," 1; Threadcraft and Miller, "Black Women"; Bonn, "White Females"; D'Ignazio, *Counting Femicide*, 28; Crenshaw, "Private Violence."
2. Waller, Joseph, and Keyes, "Racial Inequities," 9, 1; Davis, "Obstetric Racism"; Sarmiento, Acosta, Roth, and Zambrano, "Latin American Model Protocol"; Njoku, Evans, Nimo-Sefah, and Bailey, "Listen to the Whispers."
3. Solarte-Erlacher, "Rosalind Paige."
4. D'Ignazio, *Counting Femicide*; Crenshaw, "#MeToo."
5. Morrison, "Alienation and the State."
6. Holland, *Raising the Dead*, 3–4.
7. Capper and Austin, "Wages for Housework."
8. Balfour, *Imagining Freedom*, 54.
9. Threadcraft, *Intimate Justice.*
10. Griffin, *Read until You Understand*, 89.
11. Ibid.
12. Ibid.
13. Griffin, "We Do Language."
14. Griffin, *Read until You Understand*, 83–84.
15. The play is only available via the Morrison Archive at Princeton University.
16. Williams, "People Know Him," 724, 731.
17. Toni Morrison, "Dreaming Emmett," November 20, 1985, ii.
18. Ibid., iii.
19. Williams, "People Know Him," 724, 731.
20. Morrison, "Dreaming Emmett," November 20, 1985, 18.
21. Ibid., 19.
22. Ibid., I-30-31.
23. Ibid., II-10.
24. Ibid., II-23-24.
25. Ibid., II-34-35.
26. Griffin, *Read until You Understand*, 85.
27. Ibid., 86.
28. Ibid., 91.
29. Griffin, "We Do Language."
30. Ibid. (emphasis mine).
31. Balfour, *Imagining Freedom*, 54.
32. Fricker, *Epistemic Injustice*; Dotson, "Conceptualizing Epistemic Oppression."
33. Balfour, *Imagining Freedom*, 56.
34. Morrison, *Paradise*, 3–4
35. Riddick is a Depo Provera and contraceptive expert and became the Victims Coordinator for Attorney Willie Gary's Depo Provera class action lawsuit. She explicitly connects the distribution of Depo Provera to women of color in the United States and Africa today to what happened

to her. Riddick now serves as the executive director of the Rebecca Project for Justice. Their mission is as follows: "The Rebecca Project works diligently to reform intersecting health, child welfare and criminal justice policies impacting vulnerable families. Among our primary advocacy goals are expanding comprehensive family treatment services, improving conditions of confinement for incarcerated women and girls, promoting alternative sentencing for women and girls, challenging the unacceptable levels of gendered violence, and urging for policies of health and healing for families at the margins. Change in policy: (a) appropriation gains to expand family-based treatment, (b) number of bills that include sentencing alternatives to maternal incarceration, (c) improved conditions of maternal incarceration and parent-child relationship during a mother's sentence, and (d) elevated visibility on violence against vulnerable women and girls." The Rebecca Project, like Riddick, argues that the distribution of Depo Provera is unequivocally a racialized and indeed racist issue, citing UN data that indicates the drug is hardly ever used by white or affluent women in America or Europe. Riddick's bio also indicates that she is also building the Elaine Riddick Sister Sanctuary for girls at risk in Georgia—girls who are potential victims of sex trafficking, homeless, or pregnant without a place to call home. I can say, then, that Riddick is working to intervene in what President Obama once called the sexual assault to prison pipeline that many young black women in the United States are funneled through.

36. Balfour, "Toni Morrison."
37. Hartman, "Belly of the World"; Weinbaum, "Gendering the General Strike"; White, *Ar'n't I a Woman*, 74; Camp, "Closer to Freedom," 36; Syedullah, "Becoming More Ourselves," 113.
38. Balfour, "Toni Morrison," 550–551.
39. Morrison, *Beloved*, 247.
40. Du Bois, *Darkwater*, 91.
41. Morrison, *Beloved*, 60.
42. Morrison, *Song of Solomon*, 97.
43. Hartman, "Belly of the World," 166–167.
44. Weinbaum, "Gendering the General Strike," 447, 453, 458.
45. Carter, *Prayers for the People*, 191.
46. D'Ignazio, *Counting Femicide*, 35; Williamson, "Why Did They Die?" 336; Burke, *Unbound*, 224, 236.
47. Price, "What Would Mama Do?" 22.
48. Carter, *Prayers for the People*, 191; Arendt, *Kant's Political Philosophy*, 43.
49. Balfour, "Toni Morrison," 542.
50. Morrison, *Paradise*, 101.
51. Aguiar, "Passing on Death," 514.
52. Morrison, *Home*, 4.
53. Morrison, *Paradise*, 99
54. *Ibid*, 94–95
55. *Ibid*, 270.
56. Michael, "Re-Imagining Agency," 655–656, 654, 645, 643.
57. Morrison, *Paradise*, 175–176.
58. *Ibid*, 173–179.
59. Aguiar, "Passing on Death," 515.
60. Morrison, *Paradise*, 8–9.
61. *Ibid*, 102, 113–114, 144, 145.
62. Edwards, "The Blood."

Conclusion

1. Hamraie, *Building Access*, 5, 16–17.
2. Schalk, *Black Disability Politics*, 5–6.
3. Virginia Changemakers, "Bessie Blount Griffin"; Baker, "Bessie Blount Griffin"; Kelly, "Bessie Blount Griffin."
4. Kafer, *Feminist, Queer, Crip*, 6, 9.
5. Barber, "Fannie Lou Hamer's Disability," 153, 168.
6. Kafer, *Feminist, Queer, Crip*, 152.
7. Camp, *Closer to Freedom*, 36.
8. Griffin, "We Do Language."

Works Cited

African American Policy Forum. "About #SayHerName: Fill the Void. Lift Your Voice. Say Her Name." #SayHerName. https://www.aapf.org/sayhername.

African American Policy Forum. "Our Demands." #SayHerName. https://www.aapf.org/our-demands.

African American Policy Forum. "Policy Recommendations." #SayHerName. https://www.aapf.org/our-demands.

Aguiar, Sarah Appleton. "'Passing on' Death: Stealing Life in Toni Morrison's *Paradise*." *African American Review* 38, no. 3 (2004): 513–519.

Alexander, Elizabeth. "'Can You Be BLACK and Look at This?': Reading the Rodney King Video(s)." *Public Culture* 7, no. 1 (1994): 77–94.

Alexander, Shawn Lee. "*The Crisis: A Record of the Darker Races*; An Introduction." In *Protest and Propaganda: W. E. B. Du Bois, The Crisis, and American History*, edited by Amy Helene Kirschke and Phillip Luke Sinitiere, 1–15. Columbia: University of Missouri Press, 2014.

Anderson, William C. "From Lynching Photos to Michael Brown's Body: Commodifying Black Death." *Truthout*, January 16, 2015.

Antoine, Chagmion. "The Color of Lawlessness: Sexual Abuse by Police, Nationwide." *Women's Media Center*, May 4, 2016.

Arendt, Hannah. *The Human Condition*. Chicago: University of Chicago Press, 1958.

Arendt, Hannah. *Lectures on Kant's Political Philosophy*. Edited by Ronald Beiner. Chicago: University of Chicago Press, 1989.

Bacon, Jacqueline. "The History of Freedom's Journal: A Study in Empowerment and Community." *Journal of African American History* 88, no. 1 (2003): 1–20.

Baker, Benjamin. "Bessie Blount Griffin." Blackpast, September 21, 2018. https://www.blackpast.org/african-american-history/bessie-blount-griffin-1914-2009/.

Balfour, Lawrie. "Toni Morrison and the Fugitive's Democracy." In *African American Political Thought: A Collected History*, edited by Melvin L. Rogers and Jack Turner, 541–562. Chicago: University of Chicago Press, 2020.

Balfour, Lawrie. *Toni Morrison: Imagining Freedom*. Oxford: Oxford University Press, 2023.

Barber, Rebekah. "How Fannie Lou Hamer's Disability Informed Her Fight for Voting Rights." The 19th, July 19, 2023. Https://19thnews.org/2023/07/fannie-lou-hamer-disability-voting-rights-activism/.

Barfield, Clementine. "Beyond Mourning the Death of My Son." Address to Penn State Forum, Nittany Lion, February 28, 2008. WPSU Public Media, https://radio.wpsu.org/medicine-and-health/2008-02-28/penn-state-forum-clementine-barfield-president-of-save-our-sons-and-daughters.

Barrett, Ronald K., and Karen S. Heller. "Death and Dying in the Black Experience." *Journal of Palliative Medicine* 5, no. 5 (2002): 793–799.

Bartky, Sandra Lee. *Femininity and Domination: Studies in the Phenomenology of Oppression*. New York: Routledge, 1990.

Benfer, Emily A., David Vlahov, Marissa Y. Long, Evan Walker-Wells, J. L. Pottenger Jr., Gregg Gosalves, and Danya E. Keene. "Eviction, Health Inequity, and the Spread of COVID-19: Housing Policy as a Primary Pandemic Mitigation Strategy." *Journal of Urban Health* 98, no. 1 (February 2021): 1–12.

Benhabib, Seyla. *The Reluctant Modernism of Hannah Arendt*. Thousand Oaks, CA: SAGE, 1996.

Birthing Project USA. "About Us." https://www.birthingprojectusa.org/, 2023.

Birthing Project USA. "Black Infant Mortality." https://www.birthingprojectusa.org/, 2023.

Black and Missing Foundation. "About the Black and Missing Foundation." https://blackandmissing.com/about, 2023.

Black Girl Tragic. "About." https://www.blackgirltragic.com/about, 2023.

Black Women for Wages for Housework. "Birth Announcement." In *Wages for Housework: New York Committee, 1972–1977; History, Theory, Documents*, edited by Silvia Federici and Arlen Austen, 116–117. Brooklyn: Atonomedia, 2017.

Black Women for Wages for Housework. "Money for Prostitutes Is Money for Black Women." New York, 1977. Gender and Sexuality Collection, Freedom Archives (online), https://freedomarchives.org/Documents/Finder/DOC46_scans/46.GenderAndSexuality.MoneyforProstitutes.Web.pdf.

Blum, Edward J. "Lynching as Crucifixion: Violence and the Sacred Imagination of W. E. B. Du Bois." In *The Souls of W. E. B Du Bois: New Essays and Reflections*, edited by Edward J. Blum and James R. Young, 188–208. Macon, GA: Mercer University Press, 2009.

Bonn, Scott A. "White Females Are Rarely Murder Victims or Perpetrators: The Reality of Gender, Race, and Homicide." Wicked Deeds (blog), *Psychology Today*, October 12, 2015.

Bradley, Mamie, as told to Ethel Payne. "Mamie Bradley's Untold Story." *Chicago Daily Defender*, February 27–29, March 1, 1956, 5–8.

Brooks, Gwendolyn. "The Chicago Defender Sends a Man to Little Rock." Fall 1957. In *The Making of African American Identity* III, 1917–1968. Toolbox Library, National Humanities Center, https://nationalhumanitiescenter.org/pds/maai3/protest/text11/brookschicagodefender.pdf.

Bundy, Kissette. "Anti-Prostitution Laws Called 'Racist' and 'Sexist.'" *Philadelphia Tribune*, March 29, 1985.

Burke, Tarana. *Unbound: My Story of Liberation and the Birth of the Me Too Movement*. New York: Flatiron, 2021.

Butler, Cheryl Nelson. "The Racial Roots of Human Trafficking." *UCLA LAW Review* 62 (2015): 1468–1469.

Camp, Stephanie M. *Closer to Freedom: Enslaved Women and Everyday Resistance in the Plantation South.* Chapel Hill: University of North Carolina Press, 2004.

Canvas Rebel. "Meet Marchelle Davis." https://canvasrebel.com/meet-marchelle-davis/.

Capper, Beth, and Arlen Austin. "'Wages for Housework Means Wages against Heterosexuality': On the Archives of Black Women for Wages for Housework and Wages Due Lesbians." *GLQ* 24, no. 4 (October 2018): 445–466.

Carter, Rebecca Louise. *Prayers for the People: Homicide and Humanity in the Crescent City.* Chicago: University of Chicago Press, 2019.

Centers for Disease Control and Prevention. "Working Together to Reduce Black Maternal Mortality." April 3, 2023. https://www.cdc.gov/healthequity/features/maternal-mortality/index.html/.

Chicago Missing Persons Project. "About." http://chicagomissingpersons.com/.

Chicago Tribune. "Murders Torment Detroit." January 13, 1987. https://www.chicagotribune.com/news/ct-xpm-1987-01-13-8701040022-story.html.

Citizen Manual Detroit. "Youth Murders in Detroit: Case Study; Save Our Sons and Daughters (SOSAD)." https://citizenmanual.com/activities/case-studies/save-our-sons-and-daughters-sosad/, 1986.

Cohen, Cathy. "Deviance as Resistance: A New Research Agenda for the Study of Black Politics." *Du Bois Review: Social Science Research on Race* 1, no. 1 (2004): 27–45.

Colin, Mattie Smith. "Mother's Tears Greet Son Who Died a Martyr." *Chicago Defender*, September 10, 1955.

Cone, James H. *The Cross and The Lynching Tree.* Maryknoll, NY: Orbis, 2011.

Cornish, Samuel E., and John B. Russwurm. "To Our Patrons." *Freedom's Journal*, March 16, 1827.

Covid-19 Task Force on Domestic Violence. "The Intersection of Race and Domestic Violence." https://www.covid19taskforcedv.org/intersection-of-race-and-dv#:~:text=In%202013%2C%20453%20Black%20women,2013%20FBI's%20Supplementary%20Homicide%20Report.

Crenshaw, Kimberlé. "From #MeToo and #BlackLivesMatter to #SayHerName." Lecture, #SayHerName: A Lecture Series on Violence against Black Women, Dartmouth College, Hanover, New Hampshire, 2019.

Crenshaw, Kimberlé. "From Private Violence to Mass Incarceration: Thinking Intersectionally about Women, Race, and Social Control." *UCLA Law Review* 59, no. 6 (2012): 1418.

Crenshaw, Kimberlé. "Mapping the Margins: Intersectionality, Identity Politics, and Violence against Women of Color." *Stanford Law Review* 43, no. 6 (1991): 1241–1299.

Crenshaw, Kimberlé. "The Urgency of Intersectionality." TEDWomen, October 2016. https://www.ted.com/talks/kimberle_crenshaw_the_urgency_of_intersectionality?hasProgress=true&language=en.

Crenshaw, Kimberlé, and Andrea Ritchie, with Rachel Anspach, Rachel Gilmer, and Luke Harris. *Say Her Name: Resisting Police Brutality against Black Women.*

African American Policy Forum, July 2015. https://scholarship.law.columbia.edu/faculty_scholarship/3226.

Crusto, Mitchell F. "Black Lives Matter: Banning Police Lynchings." *Hastings Constitutional Law Quarterly* 48, no. 1 (2020): 3–71.

Davis, Angela. "Reflections on Black Women's Role in the Community of Slaves." *The Black Scholar* 3, no. 4 (December 1971). Available from University of Alabama Libraries Special Collections, https://digitalcollections.libraries.ua.edu/digital/collection/u0003_0001823/id/2/.

Davis, Angela Y., Gina Dent, Erica R. Meiners, and Beth E. Richie. *Abolition. Feminism. Now.* Chicago: Haymarket, 2022.

Davis, Brittany. "Criminalization of Black Girls in the Juvenile Legal System: Overview of Pathways to Confinement and Strategies for Supporting Successful Reentry." Center for Court Innovation, 2020.

Davis, Dána-Ain. "Obstetric Racism: The Racial Politics of Pregnancy, Labor, and Birthing." *Medical Anthropology* 38, no. 7 (2019): 560–573.

Davis, Dána-Ain. "Reproducing While Black: The Crisis of Black Maternal Health, Obstetric Racism and Assisted Reproductive Technology." *Reproductive Biomedicine and Society Online* 11 (November 1, 2020): 56–64.

Davis, Daron. "What Is a Lynching? Are We Still Seeing Them Today." *Fayetteville Observer*, July 11, 2021.

Dawan, Shaila. "How Photos Became Icon of Civil Rights Movement." *New York Times*, August 28, 2005.

Deegan-McCree, Michael. "Floyd and Arbery Killings Are Modern Day Lynchings." *USA Today*, June 3, 2020.

Defensive Unicorns. "Defensive Unicorns Owner." https://defensiveunicornsllc.com.

D'Ignazio, Catherine. *Counting Feminicide: Data Feminism in Action*. Cambridge: MIT Press, 2024.

Dinno, Alexis. "Homicide Rates of Transgender Individuals in the United States: 2010–2014." *American Journal of Public Health* 107, no. 9 (2017): 1441–1447.

Dotson, Kristie. "Conceptualizing Epistemic Oppression." *Social Epistemology* 28, no. 2 (2014): 115–138.

Du Bois, W. E. B. *Black Reconstruction in America, 1860–80*. New York: Free Press, 1998.

Du Bois, W. E. B. *Darkwater: Voices from within the Veil*. Mineola, NY: Dover, 1999.

Du Bois, W. E. B. *Dusk of Dawn: An Essay toward an Autobiography of a Race Concept*. 1940. Reprint, New York: Oxford University Press, 2014.

Du Bois, W. E. B. "The Gospel According to Mary Brown." *The Crisis* 19, no. 2 (December 1919): 41–43.

Du Bois, W. E. B. "Jesus Christ in Georgia: A Story." *The Crisis* 3, no. 2 (December 1911): 70–74.

Du Bois, W. E. B. *The Philadelphia Negro: A Social Study*. La Vergne, TN: Lighting Source, 2007.

Du Bois, W. E. B. "Pontius Pilate." *The Crisis* 21, no. 2 (December 1920): 53–54.

Du Bois, W. E. B. "The Second Coming." *The Crisis* 15, no. 2 (December 1917): 59–60.

Du Bois, W. E. B. "The Son of God." *The Crisis* 40, no. 12 (1933): 276–277.

Du Bois, W. E. B., ed. *The Crisis: Record of the Darker Races*. New York: NAACP, November 1910–December 1922. 23 vols. Accessed via the Modernist Journals Project (searchable database), Brown and Tulsa Universities, ongoing. https://modjourn.org/journal/crisis/.

Edwards, Erica. *Charisma and the Fictions of Black Leadership*. Minneapolis: University of Minnesota Press, 2012.

Epstein, Rebecca, Jamilia J. Blake, and Thalia González. "Girlhood Interrupted: The Erasure of Black Girls' Childhood." Center on Poverty and Equality, Georgetown Law. https://genderjusticeandopportunity.georgetown.edu/wp-content/uploads/2020/06/girlhood-interrupted.pdf., 2017.

"*Eyes on the Prize*: Interview with Charles Coles Diggs Jr." November 6, 1985. American Archive of Public Broadcasting. http://americanarchive.org/catalog/cpb-aacip-151-p843r0qr6v.

Fam, Alli, and Peter Biello. "#SayHerName: Lecture Series at Dartmouth Focuses on Intersectionality." *New Hampshire Public Radio*, August 7, 2019.

Feimster, Crystal N. *Southern Horrors: Women and the Politics of Rape and Lynching*. Cambridge, MA: Harvard University Press, 2011.

Feldstein, Ruth. *Motherhood in Black and White: Race and Sex in American Liberalism, 1930–1965*. Ithaca, NY: Cornell University Press, 2000.

Fischer, Anne Gray. *The Streets Belong to Us: Sex, Race, and Police Power from Segregation to Gentrification*. Chapel Hill: University of North Carolina Press, 2022.

Ford, Gene. "LA Vigil for Black Women." *News & Letters* 32, no. 2 (February 13, 1987). https://www.marxists.org/history/etol/newspape/news-and-letters/1980s/1987-02-13.pdf.

Foucault, Michel. *Society Must Be Defended: Lectures at the Collège de France, 1975–1976*. New York: Picador, 2003.

Fountain, John W. "A Modern-Day Lynching in Minneapolis." *Chicago Sun-Times*, June 5, 2020.

Fricker, Miranda. *Epistemic Injustice: Power and the Ethics of Knowing*. New York: Oxford University Press, 2009.

Gamarel, Kristi E., Laura Jadwin-Cakmak, Wesly M. King, Ashley Lacombe-Duncan, Racquelle Trammell, Lilianna A. Reyes, Cierra Burnks, Bré Rivera, Emily Arnold, and Gary W. Harper. "Stigma Experienced by Transgender Women of Color in Their Dating and Romantic Relationships: Implications for Gender-Based Violence Prevention Programs." *Journal of Interpersonal Violence* 37, no. 9–10 (May 2022): NP8161–NP8189.

Gatens, Moira. *Imaginary Bodies: Ethics, Power and Corporality*, New York: Routledge, 1995.

Geronimus, Arline T., Margaret Hicken, Danya Keene, and John Bound. "'Weathering' and Age Patterns of Allostatic Load Scores." *American Journal of Public Health* 96, no. 5: 826–833.

Giddings, Paula. *Ida: A Sword among Lions; Ida B. Wells and the Campaign against Lynching*. New York: Amistad, 2008.

Giddings, Paula. "Making Ida B. Wells." *Making: WEBZ Chicago*. Podcast. December 8, 2022.

Gilmore, Ruth Wilson. *Golden Gulag: Prisons, Surplus, Crisis, and Opposition in Globalizing California*. Oakland: University of California Press, 2007.

Girls Getta Grip Gun Club. "Goals for GGGGC Members." https://girlsgettagrip.com, 2023.

Glaude, Eddie. *Exodus! Religion, Race, and Nation in Early-Nineteenth-Century Black America*. Chicago: University of Chicago Press, 2000.

Goldsby, Jacqueline. *A Spectacular Secret: Lynching in American Life and Literature*. Chicago: University of Chicago Press, 2006.

Gorup, Michael. "The Strange Fruit of the Tree of Liberty: Lynch Law and Popular Sovereignty in the United States." *Perspectives on Politics* 18, no. 3 (2000): 819–834.

Grant, Jaime. "Who's Killing Us?" In *Femicide: The Politics of Woman Killing*, edited by Jill Radford and Diana E. H. Russell, 145–160. New York: Twayne, 1992.

Griffin, Farah Jasmine. *Read until You Understand: The Profound Wisdom of Black Life and Literature*. New York: W. W. Norton, 2021.

Griffin, Farah Jasmine. "'We Do Language': History, Meaning, and Language in Toni Morrison's Fiction." *Wendy Rosenthal Gellman Lecture on Modern Literature*, Cornell University, March 5, 2015. Video. https://www.cornell.edu/video/farah-jasmine-griffin-history-meaning-language-toni-morrison-novels.

Grigsby, Juli. "Count Women's Lives: Roving Counterpublics and Black Women's Activism in South Central Los Angeles." Unpublished manuscript.

Grio Staff. "Ten Black Women You Should Know." *The Grio*, October 20, 2009. Https://thegrio.com/2009/10/20/in-every-social-movement-in/.

Gross, Kali Nicole. "The Historical Truth about Women Burned at the Stake in America? Most Were Black." *Washington Post*, February 25, 2022, https://www.washingtonpost.com/opinions/2022/02/25/black-women-history-burned-at-stake/.

Hamraie, Aimi. *Building Access: Universal Design and the Politics of Disability*. Minneapolis: University of Minnesota Press, 2017.

Hanchard, Michael G. *The Spectre of Race: How Discrimination Haunts Western Democracy*. Princeton, NJ: Princeton University Press, 2018.

Harris-Perry, Melissa. "Melissa Harris-Perry, Transcript 05/13/2015," MSNBC, May 3, 2015. http://www.msnbc.com/transcripts/melissa-harris-perry/2015-05-03.

Hartman, Saidiya. "The Belly of the World: A Note on Black Women's Labors." *Souls* 18, no. 1 (2016): 166–173.

Hartman, Saidiya. *Scenes of Subjection: Terror, Slavery, and Self-Making in Nineteenth-Century America*. New York: Oxford University Press, 1997.

Hartman, Saidiya. "Venus in Two Acts." *Small Axe* 12, no. 2 (2008): 1–14.

Hassan, Shira. "Our Right to Heal: Liberatory Harm Reduction," *Yes Magazine*, January 19, 2023. https://www.yesmagazine.org/health-happiness/2023/01/19/harm-reduction.

Henderson, Errol, "From Save Our Sons and Daughters (SOSAD) to #BlackLivesMatter: Revolutionary Lessons from Black Women in the Urban Peace and Justice Movement."

2019 National Conference of Black Political Scientists (NCOBPS) Annual Meeting, November 27, 2018. Available https://ssrn.com/abstract=3291057.

Hendrix, Kathleen. "Passionate Pursuer's Crusade against the South Side Slayer: Margaret Prescod Trying to Raise Community Awareness on the Streets of South-Central L.A. . . . and Beverly Hills." *Los Angeles Times*, October 16, 1986.

Henry, Daja E. "'We're Truly Not Valued': In New Orleans, Black Mothers Are Increasingly the Victims of Gun Violence." The 19th, July 17, 2023. https://19thnews.org/2023/07/new-orleans-black-mothers-gun-violence-victims/.

Hill, Karlos K. "Twenty-First-Century Lynching?" Cambridge Blog, Cambridge University Press, February 29, 2016.

Hinton, Elizabeth. *From the War on Poverty to the War on Crime: The Making of Mass Incarceration in America*. Cambridge, MA: Harvard University Press, 2016.

Hoberman, John. *Black and Blue: The Origins and Consequences of Medical Racism*. Oakland: University of California Press, 2012.

Holland, Sharon Patricia. *Raising the Dead: Readings of Death and (Black) Subjectivity*. Durham, NC: Duke University Press, 2000.

Hooker, Juliet. *Black Grief, White Grievance: The Politics of Loss*. Princeton, NJ: Princeton University Press, 2023.

Hoyert, Donna L. "Maternal Mortality Rates in the United States, 2021." National Center for Health Statistics, Centers for Disease Control and Prevention, March 2023. https://www.cdc.gov/nchs/data/hestat/maternal-mortality/2021/maternal-mortality-rates-2021.pdf.

Hoyert, Donna L. "Maternal Mortality Rates in the United States, 2022." National Center for Health Statistics, Centers for Disease Control and Prevention, May 2024. https://www.cdc.gov/nchs/data/hestat/maternal-mortality/2022/maternal-mortality-rates-2022.pdf.

INCITE! "Incite! History." https://incite-national.org/history, 2023.

INCITE! "Police Violence and Domestic Violence." https://incite-national.org/wp-content/uploads/2018/08/toolkitrev-domesticviolence.pdf, 2023.

INCITE! "Statement on Gender Violence and the Prison Industrial Complex, 2001." https://incite-national.org/incite-critical-resistance-statement/.

INCITE! "Stop Law Enforcement Violence." https://incite-national.org/stop-law-enforcement-violence/, 2023.

"Interactive Map: Serial Killers in South L.A." *Los Angeles Times*, August 3, 2010.

International Wages for Housework Campaign. "English Collective of Prostitutes and US PROStitutes Collective." Pamphlet, London, n.d. Women Against Imperialism Collection, Freedom Archives (online). https://freedomarchives.org/Documents/Finder/DOC500_scans/500.020.Wages.for.Housework.pdf.

International Wages for Housework Campaign. "International Black Women for Wages for Housework." Pamphlet, London, n.d. Women Against Imperialism Collection, Freedom Archives (online). https://freedomarchives.org/Documents/Finder/DOC500_scans/500.020.Wages.for.Housework.pdf.

International Wages for Housework Campaign. "The International Wages for Housework Campaign." Pamphlet, London, n.d. Women Against Imperialism Collection, Freedom

Archives (online). https://freedomarchives.org/Documents/Finder/DOC500_scans/500.020.Wages.for.Housework.pdf.

International Wages for Housework Campaign. "Wages Due Lesbians." Pamphlet, London, n.d. Women Against Imperialism Collection, Freedom Archives (online). https://freedomarchives.org/Documents/Finder/DOC500_scans/500.020.Wages.for.Housework.pdf.

Invisible Institute. "Beneath the Surface." https://invisible.institute/beneath-the-surface, 2023.

Just Practice. "About Just Practice." https://just-practice.org/about-just-practice/, 2023.

Just Practice. "Welcome to the Transformative Justice Help Desk." https://just-practice.org/the-help-desk, 2023.

Kaba, Mariame, and Andrea Ritchie. "S&P Analysis and Vision." Survived and Punished. https://survivedandpunished.org/analysis/, 2023.

Kaba, Mariame, and Andrea Ritchie. "Survived and Punished." https://survivedandpunished.org, 2023.

Kafer, Alison. *Feminist, Queer, Crip*. Bloomington: Indiana University Press, 2013.

Kelly, Kate. "Bessie Blount Griffin, Physical Therapist and Inventor." *America Comes Alive!* https://americacomesalive.com/bessie-blount-griffin-physical-therapist-and-inventor/, 2024.

Kidd, Camille, Shaina Goodman, and Katherine Gallagher Robbins. "State Abortion Bans Threaten Nearly Seven Million Black Women, Exacerbate the Existing Black Maternal Mortality Crisis." Issue brief, National Partnership for Women and Families, May 2024. https://nationalpartnership.org/report/state-abortion-bans-threaten-black-women/.

Kim, Mimi E. "From Carceral Feminism to Transformative Justice: Women-of-Color Feminism and Alternatives to Incarceration." *Journal of Ethnic and Cultural Diversity in Social Work* 27, no. 3 (2018): 219–233.

Kim, Mimi E. "Non-Law Enforcement Restorative Justice Addressing Domestic and Sexual Violence: Evaluation Results from the CHAT Project Pilot." 2022. https://chatproject.org/wp-content/uploads/2022/09/CHAT-Pilot-Evaluation-FULL-REPORT-August-2022.pdf.

Kirschke, Amy Helene. *Art in Crisis: W. E. B. Du Bois and the Struggle for African American Identity and Memory*. Bloomington: Indiana University Press, 2007.

Kirschke, Amy Helene, and Phillip Luke Sinitiere. "Du Bois as Print Propagandist." In *Protest and Propaganda: W. E. B. Du Bois, The Crisis, and American History*, edited by Amy Helene Kirschke and Phillip Luke Sinitiere, 28–48. Columbia: University of Missouri Press, 2014.

Kivisto, Aaron J., Samantha Kivisto, and Lisa S Mills. "Racial Disparities in Pregnancy-Associated Intimate Partner Homicide." *Journal of Interpersonal Violence* 37, no. 13–14 (2022): NP10938–NP10961.NP10938–9.

Kuhl, Michelle. "Countable Bodies, Uncountable Crimes: Sexual Assault and the Anti-lynching Movement." In *Interconnections: Gender and Race in American History*, edited by Carol Faulkner and Alison M. Parker, 133–160. Rochester, NY: Rochester University Press, 2012.

Kuhl, Michelle. "Resurrecting Black Manhood." In *The Souls of W. E. B. Du Bois: New Essays and Reflections*, edited by Edward J. Blum and Jason R. Young, 160–187. Macon, GA: Mercer University Press, 2009.

Lara, Jovana. "SoCal Woman Shines Spotlight on Cases Involving Missing, Murdered Women of Color." ABC7 (Los Angeles), October 2, 2021. https://abc7.com/missing-women-murdered-of-color-gabby-petito-media-coverage/11071274/.

Lawn, R. B., and K. C. Koenen. "Homicide Is a Leading Cause of Death for Pregnant Women in US." *British Medical Journal* 379 (October 19, 2022): o2499.

Lipsitz, George. "'In an Avalanche Every Snowflake Pleads Not Guilty': The Collateral Consequences of Mass Incarceration and Impediments to Women's Fair Housing." *UCLA Law Review* 59 (2012): 1746, 1770.

Lu, Michael C., and Neal Halfon. "Racial and Ethnic Disparities in Birth Outcomes: A Life-Course Perspective." *Maternal and Child Health Journal* 7, no. 1 (2003): 13–30.

Lucey, Donna M. "The 'Fighting Editor' of the Richmond Planet: Crusading Journalist John Mitchell Jr. Took on the Lynchers." *Humanities* 31, no. 4 (July/August 2010). https://www.neh.gov/article/fighting-editor-richmond-planet.

Magan, Christopher. "Speaking in St. Paul, NAACP Leader Compares Recent Police Killings to Lynchings." *Twincities.com*, July 10, 2016. https://www.twincities.com/2016/07/10/naacp-leader-compares-recent-police-killings-to-lynchings/.

Mathews, Donald G. "The Southern Rite of Human Sacrifice." *Black History Bulletin* 65/66 (2002): 20–47.

Mbembe, Achille. "Necropolitics." *Public Culture* 15, no. 1 (2003): 11–40.

Menzel, Annie. *Fatal Denial: Racism and the Political Life of Black Infant Mortality*. Oakland: University of California Press, 2024.

Menzel, Annie. "The Midwife's Bag, or, the Objects of Black Infant Mortality Prevention." *Signs: Journal of Women in Culture and Society* 46, no. 2 (2021): 283–309.

Metress, Christopher. "'No Justice, No Peace': The Figure of Emmett Till in African American Literature." *Multi-Ethnic Literatures and the Idea of Social Justice* 28, no. 1 (Spring 2003): 87–103.

Michael, Magali Cornier. "Re-Imagining Agency: Toni Morrison's Paradise." *African American Review* 36, no. 4 (Winter 2002): 643–666.

Michaeli, Ethan. *The Defender: How the Legendary Black Newspaper* Changed America. Boston: Houghton Mifflin Harcourt, 2016.

Mikati, Ihab, Adam F. Benson, Thomas J. Luben, Jason D. Sacks, and Jennifer Richmond-Bryant. "Disparities in Distribution of Particulate Matter Emission Sources by Race and Poverty Status." *American Journal of Public Health* 108 (April 2018): 480–485.

Miles, Tom. "U.S. Police Killings Reminisce of Lynching, U.N. Group Says." *Reuters*, September 23, 2016.

Mingus, Mia. "Pods and Pod Mapping Worksheet." Bay Area Transformative Justice Collective, June 2016. https://batjc.wordpress.com/resources/pods-and-pod-mapping-worksheet/.

Mobley, Mamie, and Christopher Benson. *The Death of Innocence: The Story of the Hate Crime That Changed America.* New York: Random House, 2003.

Moore, Kelli. *Legal Spectatorship: Slavery and the Visual Culture of Domestic Violence.* Durham, NC: Duke University Press, 2022.

Morgan, David, and Richard Cowan. "George Floyd's Brother Decries 'a Modern-Day Lynching' in Testimony to Congress." *Reuters*, June 10, 2020. https://www.reuters.com/article/us-minneapolis-police-protests/george-floyds-brother-decries-a-modern-day-lynching-in-testimony-to-congress-idUSKBN23H1NB.

Morrison, Toni. "Alienation and the State: Conference Paper." The Writer and the State, Forty-Eighth PEN International Annual Congress, January 14, 1986. Audio file. https://archive.pen.org/featured-collection/the-imagination-of-the-state/.

Morrison, Toni. *Beloved.* New York: Vintage Classics, 2004.

Morrison, Toni. *The Bluest Eye.* New York: Vintage, 2007.

Morrison, Toni. "Dreaming Emmett." C1491, box 283, Toni Morrison Papers, Manuscripts Division, Department of Special Collections, Firestone Library (hsvm), Princeton University.

Morrison, Toni. *Home.* New York: Vintage, 2013.

Morrison, Toni. *Jazz.* New York: Vintage, 2004.

Morrison, Toni. *Paradise.* New York: Vintage, 2014.

Morrison, Toni. Song of Solomon. New York: Vintage, 2004.

Muigai, Wangui. "'Something Wasn't Clean': Black Midwifery, Birth, and Postwar Medical Education in *All My Babies.*" *Bulletin of the History of Medicine* 93, no. 1 (Spring 2019): 82–113.

Mullings, Leith, and Alaka Wali. *Stress and Resilience: The Social Context of Reproduction in Central Harlem.* Norwell, MA: Kluwer Academic/Plenum, 2001.

My Sister's Keeper. "About." https://www.mskdefense.com/, 2023.

Naughton, Jim. "In Murder City, the Mothers' Crusade: Their Own Children Are Dead, but These Women Are Determined to Save the Rest." *Washington Post*, June 21, 1987. https://www.washingtonpost.com/archive/lifestyle/1987/06/22/in-murder-city-the-mothers-crusade/4e647249-8bd4-45e6-a36f-6cab31c22b40/.

Nawaz, Aman. "Woman Who Escaped Kidnapper Highlights Often Ignored Plight of Missing Black Women." *PBS NewsHour*, October 25, 2022.

Njoku, A., M. Evans, L. Nimo-Sefah, and J. Bailey. "Listen to the Whispers before They Become Screams: Addressing Black Maternal Morbidity and Mortality in the United States." *Healthcare* 11, no. 3 (February 3, 2023): 438.

Northrop, Daphne, and Kim Hamrick. "Weapons and Minority Youth Violence." Background paper prepared for the Forum on Youth Violence in Minority Communities: Setting the Agenda for Prevention. Atlanta, Georgia, December 10–12, 1990, The Centers for Disease Control and Prevention and Minority Health Professions Foundation with the Morehouse School of Medicine.

Our Black Girls. "About OBG." https://ourblackgirls.com/about-our-black-girls/, 2023.

Palladino, Christie Lancaster, Vijay Singh, Jacquelyn Campbell, Heather Flynn, and Katherine Gold. "Homicide and Suicide during the Perinatal Period: Findings from the National Violent Death Reporting System." *Obstetrics and Gynecology* 118, no. 5 (November 2011): 1056–1063.

Patterson, Orlando. *Rituals of Blood: The Consequences of Slavery in Two American Centuries.* New York: Basic, 1999.

Pelesik, Christine. *The Grim Sleeper: The Lost Women of South Central.* Berkeley, CA: Counterpoint, 2017.

Pelton, M. Lee. "A Message from the President: America Is on Fire." *Emerson Today*, June 1, 2020.

Penn, Irvine Garland. *The Afro-American Press and Its Editors.* New York: Wiley, 1891.

Pinn, Anthony B. *Why, Lord? Suffering and Evil in Black Theology.* London: Continuum, 1999.

Pitkin, Hanna Fenichel. "Justice: On Relating Private and Public." *Political Theory* 9, no. 3 (1981): 327–352.

Posey, Brianne M. "Black Femicides Matter: Conceptualizing the Killings of Black Girls and Women as Structural and Cultural Violence." *Homicide Studies* 28, no. 3 (November 2023): 313–340.

Potterat, John J., Devon D. Brewer, Stephen Q. Muth, Richard B. Rothenberg, Donald E. Woodhouse, John B. Muth, Heather K. Stites, and Stuart Brody. "Mortality in a Long-Term Open Cohort of Prostitute Women." *American Journal of Epidemiology* 159, no. 8 (April 2004): 778–785.

Prescod-Roberts, Margaret. *Black Women: Bringing It All Back Home.* Bristol: Falling Wall, 1980.

Price, Melynda. "The Afterlife of Black Motherhood: Clementine Barfield and Anti-Violence Organizing among Black Mothers of Murdered Children in Detroit." Unpublished essay.

Pumphrey, Shelby. "Finding Asylum: Race, Gender, and Confinement in Virginia, 1885–1930." PhD diss., Michigan State University, 2020.

Purvis, Dara E., and Melissa Blanco. "Police Sexual Violence: Police Brutality, #MeToo, and Masculinities." *California Law Review* 108, no. 5: 1496–1497.

Radford, Jill, and Diana Russell, eds. *Femicide: The Politics of Woman Killing.* New York: Twayne, 1992.

Raiford, Leigh. "Ida B. Wells and the Shadow Archive." In *Pictures and Progress: Early Photography and the Making of African American Identity*, edited by Maurice O. Wallace and Shawn Michelle Smith, 299–320. Durham, NC: Duke University Press, 2012.

Reign, Eva. "Meet the Organizers Offering Self-Defense Tools and Training to the Trans Community." *Them*, January 11, 2021.

Richardson, Ruth. "Office of Missing and Murdered Black Women and Girls Legislation Passes Off the House Floor." *Legislative News and Views*, February 20, 2023. https://www.house.mn.gov/members/profile/news/15519/36507.

Richie, Beth. *Arrested Justice: Black Women, Violence, and America's Prison Nation.* New York: New York University Press, 2012.

Roberson, Alecia. Empowered Personal Protection. https://www.empoweredpersonalprotection.com/about-1.

Roberts, Dorothy. *Shattered Bonds: The Color of Child Welfare.* New York: Basic Books, 2002.

Roberts, Dorothy. *Torn Apart: How the Child Welfare System Destroys Black Families—and How Abolition Can Build a Better World.* New York: Hachette, 2022.

Robinson, Stacy. "Exposing the 'Thread-Bare Lie': How Ida B. Wells Used Investigative Journalism to Uncover the Truth about Lynching." *Chicago Stories: Ida B. Wells.* WTTW Interactive. https://interactive.wttw.com/chicago-stories/ida-b-wells/exposing-the-thread-bare-lie-how-ida-b-wells-used-investigative-journalism-to-uncover-the-truth-about-lynching, 2023.

Rose South LA. "Take Action." https://rosesouthla.org/#about, 2023.

Ross, Loretta J., and Rickie Solinger. *Reproductive Justice: An Introduction.* Oakland: University of California Press, 2017.

Rushdy, Ashraf H. A. *The End of American Lynching.* New Brunswick, NJ: Rutgers University Press, 2012.

Russell, Diane E. H., and Candida Ellis. "Annihilation by Murder and the Media: The Other Atlanta Femicides." In *Femicide: The Politics of Woman Killing*, edited by Jill Radford and Diana E. H. Russell, 161–162. New York: Twayne, 1992.

Russell, Diane E. H., and Nicole Van de Ven, eds. *Crimes against Women: Proceedings of the International Tribunal.* Berkeley, CA: Russell Publications, 1976.

Saar, Malika Saada, Rebecca Epstein, Lindsay Rosenthal, and Yasmin Vafa. "The Sexual Assault to Prison Pipeline: The Girls' Story; Report." Human Rights Project for Girls, Georgetown Law Center on Poverty and Inequality, Washington, D.C.: Ms. Foundation for Women, 2015.

Saffin, Lori. "Identities under Siege: Violence against Transpersons of Color." In *Captive Genders: Trans Embodiment and the Prison Industrial Complex*, 2nd ed., edited by Eric A. Stanley and Nat Smith. 141–162. Oakland, CA: AK Press, 2015.

Samuels, Alex, Dhrumil Mehta, and Anna Wiederkehr. "Why Black Women Are Often Missing from Conversations about Police Violence." FiveThirtyEight, May 6, 2021. https://fivethirtyeight.com/features/why-black-women-are-often-missing-from conversations-about-police-violence/.

Sarmiento, Camila Bernal, Miguel Lorente Acosta, François Roth, and Margarita Zambrano. "The Latin American Model Protocol for the Investigation of Gender-Related Killings of Women (Femicide/Feminicide)." Regional Office for Central America of the United Nations High Commission for Human Rights, 2015.

Save Our Sons and Daughters (SOSAD). Save Our Sons and Daughters (Organization) Records, Box 1, Folder 1 (Activities, 1987–92) and Box 1, Newsletters (1987–92). Bentley Historical Library, University of Michigan.

Sawyer, Jeremy, and Anup Gampa, "Implicit and Explicit Racial Attitudes Changed during Black Lives Matter." *Personality and Social Psychology Bulletin* 47, no. 7 (March 2018): 1039–1059.

Schalk, Sami. *Black Disability Politics.* Durham, NC: Duke University Press, 2022.

Schuyler, George. "Forty Years of 'The Crisis.'" *The Crisis* 58, no. 3 (1951): 162–163.

Schwarz, Will. "Police Killings of Black People: The Legacy of Lynching Writ Large." *Baltimore Sun*, May 31, 2020.

Sedensky, Matt, and Nomaan Merchant, "AP: Hundreds of Officers Lose Licenses over Sex Misconduct." *Associated Press*, November 1, 2015.

Sharpe, Christina. *In the Wake: On Blackness and Being*. Durham, NC: Duke University Press, 2016.

She Loaded Defense. "About." http://sheloadeddefense.com (inactive), 2023.

Shillcock, George. "Black Girls Memorial and March Remembers Black Women and Girls Killed in Iowa and U.S." *Des Moines Register*, June 12, 2021.

Simmons, Amber. "Why Are They So Mad?: The Truth behind 'Angry' Black Women and Their Legal Invisibility as Victims of Domestic Abuse." *Harvard Blackletter Law Journal* 36 (July 22, 2020): 68.

Skip' s Tactical Solutions. "Avery." https://skipstacticalsolutions.com/about. 2020.

Smith, Barbara. "Interview with Kimberly Springer." In *Ain't Gonna Let Nobody Turn Me Around: Forty Years of Movement Building with Barbara Smith*, edited by Alethia Jones and Virginia Eubanks with Barbara Smith, 71–73. Albany: State University of New York Press, 2014.

Smith, Barbara. "Toward a Black Feminist Criticism." *The Radical Teacher* 7 (March 1978): 20–27.

Smith, Rogers. *Stories of Peoplehood: The Politics and Morals of Political Membership*. New York: Cambridge University Press, 2003.

Smith-Abass, Lyla. "The Lynching of George Floyd." SurvivorsUK. https://www.survivorsuk.org/the-lynching-of-george-floyd/, 2020.

Solarte-Erlacher, Marisol. "Rosalind Page: Black Femicides." *Resilience and Resistance Podcast*, September 15, 2022. https://www.marisolerlacher.com/podcast.

Southern Birth Justice. "Birth Justice Framework." https://southernbirthjustice.org/birth-justice., 2023.

Southern Birth Justice. "Programs." https://southernbirthjustice.org/programs-1, 2023.

Spade, Dean. *Normal Life: Administrative Violence, Critical Trans Politics, and the Limits of Law*. Durham, NC: Duke University Press, 2015.

Spade, Dean. "Solidarity Not Charity: Mutual Aid for Mobilization and Survival." *Social Text* 142, no. 38 (2022): 131–151.

Spina, Matthew. "When a Protector Becomes a Predator." *Buffalo News*, November 22, 2015.

Squires, Catherine. "Rethinking the Black Public Sphere: An Alternative Vocabulary for Multiple Public Spheres." *Communication Theory* 12, no. 4 (November 2002): 446–468.

Squires, Catherine, Brittany Lewis, Laruen Martin, Ariana Kopycinski, and Ayize James. "Missing and Murdered African American Women Task Force, Final Report, December 2022." Minnesota Department of Public Safety Office of Justice Programs.

Stanley, Eric A. "Fugitive Flesh: Gender Self-Determination, Queer Abolition, and Trans Resistance." In *Captive Genders: Trans Embodiment and the Prison Industrial Complex*, 2nd ed., edited by Eric A. Stanley and Nat Smith, 7–17. Oakland, CA: AK Press, 2015.

Steele, Shelby. "On Being Black and Middle Class." *Commentary*, January 1988.

Survived and Punished. "Roots." https://survivedandpunished.org/about2, 2023.

Syedullah, Jasmine. "Becoming More Ourselves: Four Emergent Strategies of Black Feminist Congregational Abolition." *Palimpsest* 11, no. 1 (2022): 108–140.

Take Back the Night. "Events through the Decades: 1970s." https://takebackthenight.org/history/, 2023.

Taylor, Diana. "Afterword: War Play." *PMLA* 124, no. 3 (2010): 1888.

Taylor, Keeanga-Yamahtta. "How Trayvon Martin's Lynching Galvanized a Movement." *Truthout*, March 3, 2016.

Third Eye Watching. "Educate Train Empower Defend." https://www.3rdeyewatching.com/aboutus.

Threadcraft, Shatema. *Intimate Justice: The Black Female Body and the Body Politic.* New York: Oxford University Press, 2016.

Threadcraft, Shatema. "North American Necropolitics and Gender: On #BlackLivesMatter and Black Femicide." *South Atlantic Quarterly* 116, no. 3 (July 2017): 553–579.

Threadcraft, Shatema, and Lisa L. Miller. 2017. "Black Women, Victimization, and the Limitations of the Liberal State." *Theoretical Criminology* 21, no. 4: 478–493.

Townes, Emilie. "Ida B. Wells: An Afro-American Prophet." *The Christian Century*, March 15, 1989.

Trombadore, Cara E. "Police Officer Sexual Misconduct: An Urgent Call to Action in a Context Disproportionately Threatening Women of Color." *Harvard Journal of Racial and Ethnic Justice* 32 (2016): 156–157.

United Nations Human Rights Committee. "In the Shadows of the War on Terror: Persistent Police Brutality and Abuse in the United States." May 2006. https://www.prearesourcecenter.org/sites/default/files/library/intheshadowsofthewaronterror.pdf.

Urban Assembly Unison School. "Public Statement on the Lynching of George Floyd." https://www.uaunisonschool.org/statement-the-lynching-of-george-fl, accessed October 13, 2023

U.S. Bureau of Labor Statistics. "Civilian Occupations with High Fatal Work Injury Rates, 2023." https://www.bls.gov/charts/census-of-fatal-occupational-injuries/civilian-occupations-with-high-fatal-work-injury-rates.htm.

U.S. Congress. House. Committee on Oversight and Reform. "The Neglected Epidemic of Missing BIPOC Women and Girls: Hearing before the Subcommittee on Civil Rights and Civil Liberties of the Committee on Oversight and Reform." 117th Cong., 2nd Sess., March 3, 2022. No. 117-69. https://www.govinfo.gov/content/pkg/CHRG-117hhrg47067/html/CHRG-117hhrg47067.htm.

Vargas, Theresa. "She's Spent Years Tracking the Killings of Black Women and Girls: Now, She's Planning a D.C. March." *Washington Post*, January 1, 2022.

Violence Policy Center. "When Men Murder Women." https://vpc.org/when-men-murder-women/, 2021.

Virginia Changemakers. "Bessie Blount Griffin." Virginia Changemakers, https://edu.lva.virginia.gov/changemakers/items/show/169, 2024.

Waller, Bernadine Y., Victoria A. Joseph, and Katherine M. Keyes. "Racial Inequities in Homicide Rates and Homicide Methods among Black and White Women Aged 25–44 Years in the USA, 1999–2020: A Cross-Sectional Time Series Study." *Lancet*, February 8, 2024, 1.

Weinbaum, Alys. "Gendering the General Strike: W. E. B. Du Bois's Black Reconstruction and Black Feminism's 'Propaganda of History.'" *South Atlantic Quarterly* 112, no. 3 (Summer 2013): 438–463.

Wells, Ida B. Crusade for Justice: The Autobiography of Ida B. Wells. 1970. Reprint, Chicago: University of Chicago Press, 2020.

Wells, Ida B. "The East Saint Louis Massacre: The Greatest Outrage of the Century." In *The Light of Truth: Writings of an Anti-Lynching Crusader*, edited by Mia Bay. New York: Penguin, 456–495, 2014.

Wells, Ida B. "She Pleads for Her Own Race: Miss Ida B. Wells Talks about Her Anti-Lynching Crusade." In *The Light of Truth: Writings of an Anti-Lynching Crusader*, edited by Mia Bay, 216. New York: Penguin, 2014.

West, Cornel. *Prophesy Deliverance! An Afro-American Revolutionary Christianity*. Louisville, KY: Westminster John Knox Press, 2002.

West, Rachel. "US PROStitutes Collective." *Sex Work: Writings by Women in the Sex Industry*, edited by Frederique Delacoste and Priscilla Alexander, 279–289. Pittsburgh: Cleis Press, 1987.

White, Deborah. *Ar'n't I a Woman? Female Slaves on the Plain*. New York: W. W. Norton, 1985.

White, Lisa A. "The 'Saddle-Colored Sapphira' versus the 'Slimy Rattlesnake': The Rhetorical Melee of Ida B. Wells and Edward Carmack on the Subject of Lynching." *Tennessee Historical Quarterly* 62, no. 4 (Winter 2003): 310–331.

Wilgoren, Jodi. "Detroit Mothers Mourn another Year of Loss." *New York Times*, January 1, 2003. https://www.nytimes.com/2003/01/01/us/detroit-mothers-mourn-another-year-of-loss.html.

Williams, Mary. "To These Women, That Which Is Illegal Isn't Always Immoral: Prostitutes Collective Strives to Organize Streetwalkers to Fight for Their Rights." *Wall Street Journal*, March 28, 1984.

Williams, Rhaisa. "People Know Him by Name: Time, Justice, and Memory in Toni Morrison's Dreaming Emmett." *College Literature* 47, no. 4: 721–751.

Williamson, Terrion L. "In the Life: Black Women and Serial Murder." *Social Text* 33, no. 1: 95–114, 2015.

Williamson, Terrion L. "Why Did They Die? On Combahee and the Serialization of Black Death." *Souls* 19, no. 3: 328–341, 2017.

Willis, Brian, Emily Perttu, Meghan Fitzgerald, Heather Thompson, Swarna Weerasignha, and Wendy Macias-Konstantopoulos. "Causes of Mortality among Female Sex Workers: Results of a Multi-Country Study." *Lancet* 52, no. 101658 (October 2022).

Wood, Amy Louise. *Lynching and Spectacle: Witnessing Racial Violence in America, 1890–1940*. Chapel Hill: University of North Carolina Press, 2011.

Woodly, Deva. *Reckoning: Black Lives Matter and the Democratic Necessity of Social Movements.* New York: Oxford University Press, 2021.

Wright, Melissa W. "Necropolitics, Narcopolitics, and Femicide: Gendered Violence on the Mexico-U.S. Border." *Signs* 36, no. 3 (2011): 707–731.

Yang, John. "What Breonna Taylor's Killing Says about Police Treatment of Black Women." *PBS News Hour*, June 16, 2020.

Yarish, Jasmine. "Reconstructing Home: Abolition Democracy, the City, and Black Feminist Political Thought Revisited." PhD diss., University of California, Santa Barbara, 2019.

Zangrando, Robert L. *The NAACP Crusade against Lynching, 1909–1950.* Philadelphia: Temple University Press, 1980.

Index

For the benefit of digital users, indexed terms that span two pages (e.g., 52–53) may, on occasion, appear on only one of those pages.

Figures are indicated by an italic *f*.